LINEAR ALGEBRA

Linear Algebra

RICHARD E. JOHNSON

University of New Hampshire

PRINDLE, WEBER & SCHMIDT, INCORPORATED

Boston, Massachusetts London Sydney

Library of Congress Catalog Card Number: 67-11932
Printed in the United States of America

SECOND PRINTING: AUGUST, 1968
THIRD PRINTING: JANUARY, 1970

Preface

Linear algebra is an essential tool of the pure mathematician on the one hand and of the physicist and the theoretical economist on the other. This wide applicability of the subject makes its early mastery by the science student imperative. Like most branches of algebra, linear algebra also offers a convenient language for conveying complex ideas in a simple form. In linear algebra, it is the language of vectors, linear transformations, and matrices.

This book is intended for use in an introductory course on linear algebra. Principally, it is a study of finite-dimensional vector spaces and their associated algebras of linear transformations and matrices. No attempt has been made to show any applications of linear algebra other than to geometry. At every stage in the development of the subject matter, the direct, intuitive approach has been used whenever possible. We believe this approach will give the student the necessary background to appreciate in a later course a more sophisticated development using modules and their duals. The direct approach also has the advantage of being constructive and in this way allows a wide use of examples to illustrate new results and their proofs.

The first chapter has a two-fold purpose; to discuss the theory of finite-dimensional vector spaces and to develop examples of such spaces. Matrices are introduced in Chapter Two as arrays of numbers associated with systems of linear equations. Then, in Chapter Three, matrices are used to represent linear transformations of vector spaces. Determinants are developed in Chapter Four to allow us to compute inverses of matrices and solutions of systems of linear equations. The minimal polynomial of a linear transformation is described in Chapter Five and is used to find simple matrix representations of the transformation. Chapter Six discusses the splitting of a vector space into a direct sum of invariant subspaces relative to a linear transformation. The one-dimensional invariant subspaces yield the characteristic values of the transformation. The general theory of this splitting is described in Chapter Eight. Isometries and symmetric linear transformations of Euclidean spaces are analyzed in Chapter Seven.

The book contains enough material for a three- or four-hour semester course. A possible outline for a three-hour semester course is as follows: Chapter One, 8 days; Chapter Two, 4 days; Chapter Three, 6 days; Chapter Four, 5 days; Chapter Five, 4 days; Chapter Six, 6 days; Chapter Seven, 6 days. Chapter Eight can be omitted without any harm to the course. On the other hand, it makes good reading for the superior student and can be used in this way.

Richard E. Johnson

Contents

LINEAR ALGEBRA

Chapter One

Vector Spaces

1. FIELDS

Among the common number systems of mathematics are:

$\mathbb{Z}$, the system of integers,
$\mathbb{Q}$, the system of rational numbers,
$\mathbb{R}$, the system of real numbers,
$\mathbb{C}$, the system of complex numbers.

These are increasingly larger sets of numbers,

$$\mathbb{Z} \subset \mathbb{Q} \subset \mathbb{R} \subset \mathbb{C}.$$

Each of these systems is closed under the operations of addition and multiplication, which have the following properties:

1.1 $$a + b = b + a, \quad ab = ba \quad \textit{(Commutative laws)},$$

1.2 $$a + (b + c) = (a + b) + c, \quad a(bc) = (ab)c \quad \textit{(Associative laws)},$$

1.3 $$(a + b)c = ac + bc, \quad c(a + b) = ca + cb \quad \textit{(Distributive law)}.$$

There exist numbers 0 and 1 with the following special property:

1.4 $$0 + a = a + 0 = a, \quad 1 \cdot a = a \cdot 1 = a \quad \textit{(Identity elements)}.$$

Thus 0 is called the additive identity element and 1 the multiplicative identity element. Each number a has an opposite $-a$, called the negative of a, having the following property:

1.5 $$a + (-a) = (-a) + a = 0 \quad \textit{(Additive inverse)}.$$

The five properties above hold for all elements a, b, c in any one of the systems $\mathbb{Z}$, $\mathbb{Q}$, $\mathbb{R}$, or $\mathbb{C}$. The systems $\mathbb{Q}$, $\mathbb{R}$, and $\mathbb{C}$ also have the following additional property: each nonzero number a has a reciprocal $1/a$ such that

1.6 $$a \cdot \frac{1}{a} = \frac{1}{a} \cdot a = 1 \quad (\textit{Multiplicative inverse}).$$

We are now in a position to make the following definition.

1.7. DEFINITION OF A FIELD. An algebraic system composed of a set of elements F and operations of addition and multiplication in F is called a field if and only if the operations have properties 1.1 through 1.6.

Thus, according to this definition, the systems of rational numbers, real numbers, and complex numbers are examples of fields.

There exist fields of quite a different nature from $\mathbb{Q}$, $\mathbb{R}$, and $\mathbb{C}$. For example, for each prime number p there is a unique field having exactly p elements. This field is called the field of *integers modulo p* and is denoted by $\mathbb{Z}_p$,

$$\mathbb{Z}_p = \{0, 1, 2, \ldots, p-1\}.$$

Addition and multiplication in $\mathbb{Z}_p$ are defined to be the same as addition and multiplication in $\mathbb{Z}$, reduced modulo p. That is, to find $a + b$ and $a \cdot b$ for $a, b \in \mathbb{Z}_p$, we first compute them in $\mathbb{Z}$ and then subtract multiples of p from $a + b$ and $a \cdot b$ until we find a remainder in $\mathbb{Z}_p$. For example, in $\mathbb{Z}$ we have $3 + 4 = 7$; therefore, $3 + 4 = 7 - 5 = 2$ in $\mathbb{Z}_5$, and $3 + 4 = 7 - 7 = 0$ in $\mathbb{Z}_7$. Similarly, $3 \cdot 4 = 12$ in $\mathbb{Z}$; therefore $3 \cdot 4 = 12 - 10 = 2$ in $\mathbb{Z}_5$, and $3 \cdot 4 = 12 - 7 = 5$ in $\mathbb{Z}_7$. It is not hard to show that $\mathbb{Z}_p$ with operations of addition and multiplication so defined is a field.

Since each of the fields $\mathbb{Z}_p$, p a prime, is finite, we can give complete addition and multiplication tables for it. For example, the field $\mathbb{Z}_2 = \{0, 1\}$ has the simple tables:

+	0	1
0	0	1
1	1	0

·	0	1
0	0	0
1	0	1

The field $\mathbb{Z}_3 = \{0, 1, 2\}$ has the following addition and multiplication tables:

+	0	1	2
0	0	1	2
1	1	2	0
2	2	0	1

·	0	1	2
0	0	0	0
1	0	1	2
2	0	2	1

Rational numbers and real numbers are ordered in the sense that for any two such numbers, one is greater than or equal to the other. Relative to this relation of "greater than or equal to," $\mathbb{Q}$ and $\mathbb{R}$ are ordered fields as defined below.

1.8. DEFINITION OF AN ORDERED FIELD. A field F is called an ordered field if and only if it has a relation $\geq$ with the following properties:

(1) $a \geq a$ for all $a \in F$ (*Reflexive*).
(2) If $a \geq b$ and $b \geq a$, then $a = b$ (*Antisymmetric*).
(3) If $a \geq b$ and $b \geq c$, then $a \geq c$ (*Transitive*).
(4) For all $a, b \in F$, either $a \geq b$ or $b \geq a$.
(5) If $a \geq b$, then $a + c \geq b + c$ for all $c \in F$.
(6) If $a \geq b$, then $ac \geq bc$ for all $c \geq 0$.

The other order relations $>$, $\leq$, and $<$ are defined as usual. Thus, $a > b$ if and only if $a \geq b$ and $a \neq b$; $a \leq b$ if and only if $b \geq a$; and $a < b$ if and only if $b > a$. The relation $>$ (and, similarly, $<$) has the following properties:

1.9 If $a > b$ and $b > c$, then $a > c$ (*Transitive*).

1.10 If $a > b$, then $a + c > b + c$ for all $c \in F$.

1.11 If $a > b$, then $ac > bc$ for all $c > 0$.

Proof of 1.9: If $a > b$ and $b > c$, then $a \geq b$ and $b \geq c$ so that $a \geq c$ by 1.8(3). We claim $a > c$; for if $a = c$, then $c \geq b$, $b \geq c$, and $b = c$ by 1.8(2), contrary to the assumption that $b > c$.

Proof of 1.10: If $a > b$, then $a + c \geq b + c$ for all $c \in F$. If $a + c = b + c$, then $a = b$ by the additive cancellation law, contrary to the fact that $a > b$. Hence $a + c > b + c$.

Proof of 1.11: If $a > b$ and $c > 0$, then $ac \geq bc$ by 1.8(6). If $ac = bc$, then $a = b$ by the multiplicative cancellation law (since $c \neq 0$). This is contrary to the fact that $a > b$. Hence $ac > bc$.

If we let F be an ordered field and

$$F^+ = \{a \in F \mid a > 0\}, \qquad F^- = \{a \in F \mid a < 0\},$$

then we easily prove the following:

1.12 F^+ is closed under addition and multiplication.

1.13 $F^- = \{-a \mid a \in F^+\}$.

By our remarks above, every ordered field F is partitioned into three nonoverlapping subsets: F^+, the set of *positive elements;* F^-, the set of *negative elements;* and $\{0\}$:

$$F = F^+ \cup F^- \cup \{0\}.$$

Since $(-a)^2 = a^2$ for every nonzero $a \in F$ and either a or $-a$ is in F^+, we have, by 1.12, that

1.14 $$a^2 > 0 \qquad \text{for all nonzero } a \in F.$$

In particular, $1 > 0$ since $1^2 = 1$. In turn, $1 + 1 = 2 > 0$, $1 + 2 = 3 > 0$, and so on, by the closure of F^+ under addition.

A field such as $\mathbb{Z}_p$ is not ordered. For if $\mathbb{Z}_p$ were ordered, then $1 > 0$, $2 > 0$, and so on, up to $(p - 1) + 1 > 0$, contrary to the fact that $(p - 1) + 1 = 0$.

The field $\mathbb{C}$ of complex numbers is also not ordered. Thus it contains an element i such that $i^2 = -1$, and if it were ordered, then both -1 and 1 would be in $\mathbb{C}^+$ by 1.14. However, then $0 = (-1) + 1 \in \mathbb{C}^+$ by 1.12, contrary to the fact that $0 \notin \mathbb{C}^+$.

If F is an ordered field and $A \subset F$, $A \neq \emptyset$, the empty set, then an element b of F is called an *upper bound* of set A if and only if $x \leq b$ for all $x \in A$. Similarly, $c \in F$ is called a *lower bound* of set A if and only if $c \leq x$ for all $x \in A$. If b is an upper bound of A, whereas no element of F smaller than b is an upper bound of A, then b is called a *least upper bound* (l.u.b.) of set A. By definition, if a set has a l.u.b., then the l.u.b. is unique. However, a set need not have a l.u.b. The *greatest lower bound* (g.l.b.) of a set is defined similarly.

An ordered field F is called *complete* if and only if every subset of F which has an upper bound has a l.u.b. It is easily demonstrated that every subset of a complete field which has a lower bound has a g.l.b. It may be proved that the field $\mathbb{R}$ of real numbers is uniquely characterized by the following statement.

1.15. The field $\mathbb{R}$ is a complete ordered field.

This characterization of $\mathbb{R}$ allows us to show, for example, that every $a \in \mathbb{R}^+$ has a unique nth root $\sqrt[n]{a} \in \mathbb{R}^+$ for every integer $n > 1$. Thus it can be shown that

$$\sqrt[n]{a} = \text{l.u.b. } \{x \in \mathbb{R}^+ \mid x^n \leq a\}.$$

The field $\mathbb{C}$ of complex numbers is given by

$$\mathbb{C} = \{a + bi \mid a, b \in \mathbb{R}\}, \qquad \text{where} \quad i^2 = -1.$$

An interesting property of $\mathbb{R}$ is that it can be used as a set of coordinates for the points on a line L. When this is done in the usual way, each point on L is assigned a unique real number as its coordinate, and each real number is the coordinate of a unique point on L. Furthermore, the order in $\mathbb{R}$ is preserved on L; i.e., if point B is between points A and C on L, then the coordinate of B is between the coordinates of A and C. An arrowhead is placed on L to indicate the direction of increasing coordinates, as shown in Fig. 1.1.

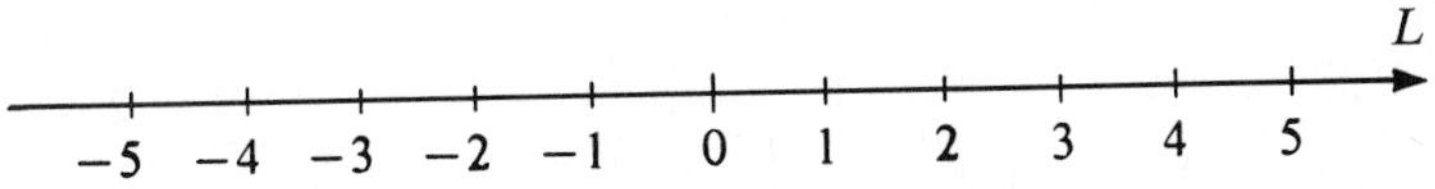

Figure 1.1

We shall call a line L having $\mathbb{R}$ as a coordinate system a *coordinate line* or a *coordinate axis*. The point on L with coordinate 0 is called the *origin*.

The numbers are assigned in a regular way on a coordinate line so that distances may be easily computed as follows.

1.16. DISTANCE FORMULA ON A LINE. If points A and B on a coordinate line have respective coordinates a and b, then the distance $d(A, B)$ between A and B is given by

$$d(A, B) = |b - a|.$$

At times it is convenient to use directed distances on a coordinate line L. If points A and B on L have respective coordinates a and b, then the *directed distance* from A to B is defined to be $b - a$. Thus, by definition, the directed distance from A to B is simply $d(A, B)$ if the direction from A to B is the direction of L, zero if $A = B$, and $-d(A, B)$ if the direction from A to B is opposite to the direction of L.

The set of all ordered pairs of real numbers is denoted by $\mathbb{R}^2$. Thus, we have

$$\mathbb{R}^2 = \{(a, b) \mid a, b \in \mathbb{R}\}.$$

We can use $\mathbb{R}^2$ as a set of coordinates for the points in a plane. This is usually done as shown in Fig. 1.2. Thus, two perpendicular coordinate axes are chosen in the plane so that they intersect at their origins. One of the coordinate axes is labeled the *x-axis* and the other the *y-axis*. Each point P has unique coordinates (a, b) in $\mathbb{R}^2$, where the coordinate of the foot of the perpendicular drawn from P to the x-axis is a and from P to the y-axis is b. Also, each ordered pair (a, b) in $\mathbb{R}^2$ are the coordinates of a unique point in the plane chosen in the obvious way. If point P has coordinate (a, b) in $\mathbb{R}^2$, then we call a the *x-coordinate* and b the *y-coordinate* of P. We shall call a plane having $\mathbb{R}^2$ as a set of coordinates in the manner described above a *rectangular coordinate plane* or a *Cartesian plane*.

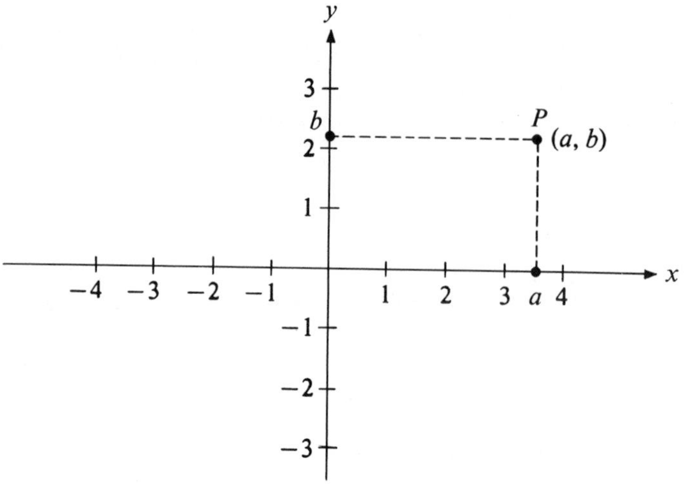

Figure 1.2

If the x-axis and the y-axis in a Cartesian plane have the same scale, then we can find the distance between any two points in the plane as follows.

1.17. DISTANCE FORMULA IN A PLANE. If points A and B in a coordinate plane have respective coordinates (a_1, a_2) and (b_1, b_2), then the distance $d(A, B)$ between A and B is given by

$$d(A, B) = \sqrt{(a_1 - b_1)^2 + (a_2 - b_2)^2}.$$

We shall not give the proof of 1.17. It follows readily from the Pythagorean Theorem and 1.16.

The set of all ordered triplets of real numbers is denoted by $\mathbb{R}^3$. Thus, we have

$$\mathbb{R}^3 = \{(a, b, c) \mid a, b, c \in \mathbb{R}\}.$$

We can use $\mathbb{R}^3$ as a set of coordinates for the points in space. This is usually accomplished by selecting three mutually perpendicular coordinate axes intersecting at their origins. Let us label these axes the x-axis, the y-axis, and the z-axis. Each point P in space has unique coordinates (a, b, c) in $\mathbb{R}^3$, where the coordinate of the foot of the perpendicular drawn from P to the x-axis is a, from P to the y-axis is b, and from P to the z-axis is c (Fig. 1.3). Also, each ordered triplet (a, b, c) in $\mathbb{R}^3$ are the coordinates of a unique point in space. If P has coordinates (a, b, c), then we call a the *x-coordinate*, b the *y-coordinate*, and c the *z-coordinate* of P. We shall call space *Cartesian three-space* if coordinates are assigned to the points of space in the manner described above.

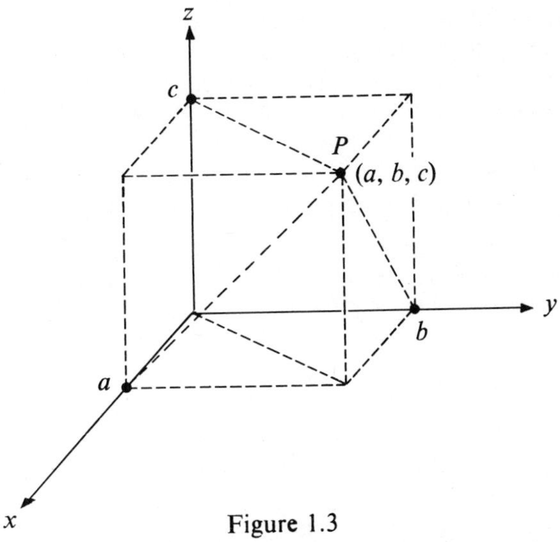

Figure 1.3

If the coordinate axes in a Cartesian three-space have the same scale, then the distance between two points can be found as follows.

1.18. DISTANCE FORMULA IN SPACE. If points A and B in coordinate three-space have respective coordinates (a_1, a_2, a_3) and (b_1, b_2, b_3), then the distance $d(A, B)$ between A and B is given by

$$d(A, B) = \sqrt{(a_1 - b_1)^2 + (a_2 - b_2)^2 + (a_3 - b_3)^2}.$$

The proof of 1.18 follows easily from the Pythagorean Theorem and 1.17.

2. VECTOR SPACES

A vector is an element of a vector space. In turn, a vector space is a set of objects, called vectors, that is closed under operations of addition and scalar multiplication and which satisfies certain algebraic laws. A precise definition of a vector space is given below.

It is worthwhile to study vector spaces for the reason that many of the algebraic systems encountered in applications of mathematics are in essence vector spaces. By studying general vector spaces, without regard to the nature of the elements, we can develop the properties common to all vector spaces.

1.19. DEFINITION OF A VECTOR SPACE. A vector space consists of a set V, an operation of addition in V, and an operation of scalar multiplication of V by a field F. Addition in V has the following properties:

(1) $\mathbf{x} + \mathbf{y} = \mathbf{y} + \mathbf{x}$ for all $\mathbf{x}, \mathbf{y} \in V$ (*Commutative law*).

(2) $\mathbf{x} + (\mathbf{y} + \mathbf{z}) = (\mathbf{x} + \mathbf{y}) + \mathbf{z}$ for all $\mathbf{x}, \mathbf{y}, \mathbf{z} \in V$ (*Associative law*).
(3) There exists an element $\mathbf{0}$ in V such that
$\mathbf{0} + \mathbf{x} = \mathbf{x} + \mathbf{0} = \mathbf{x}$ for all $\mathbf{x} \in V$ (*Identity element*).
(4) Associated with each $\mathbf{x}$ in V is an element $-\mathbf{x}$ in V such that
$\mathbf{x} + (-\mathbf{x}) = (-\mathbf{x}) + \mathbf{x} = \mathbf{0}$ for all $\mathbf{x} \in V$ (*Inverse elements*).

For each $a \in F$ and $\mathbf{x} \in V$, the scalar product of $\mathbf{x}$ by a is a unique element of V denoted by $a\mathbf{x}$. Scalar multiplication has the following properties:

(5) $a(\mathbf{x} + \mathbf{y}) = a\mathbf{x} + a\mathbf{y}$ for all $a \in F$, $\mathbf{x}, \mathbf{y} \in V$ (*Distributive law*).
(6) $(a + b)\mathbf{x} = a\mathbf{x} + b\mathbf{x}$ for all $a, b \in F$, $\mathbf{x} \in V$ (*Distributive law*).
(7) $(ab)\mathbf{x} = a(b\mathbf{x})$ for all $a, b \in F$, $\mathbf{x} \in V$ (*Associative law*).
(8) $1\mathbf{x} = \mathbf{x}$ for all $\mathbf{x} \in V$ (*Identity element*).

The eight properties of addition and scalar multiplication listed above are quite familiar to all of us. Thus, properties (1) through (4) are enjoyed by addition in F, and properties (5) through (8) are enjoyed by multiplication in F, if we consider set V as being F.

We shall call elements of V *vectors* and those of F *scalars*. Vectors are denoted by boldface letters to clearly distinguish them from scalars. Usually, we denote scalars by the first few letters of the alphabet and vectors by the last few. In writing symbols for vectors, you might wish to put an arrow over the symbol to indicate that it denotes a vector.

Additional properties of a vector space may be derived from the eight defining ones. For example, we might expect the following properties to hold, since corresponding ones hold in a field. Let V be a vector space, $\mathbf{x}, \mathbf{y}, \mathbf{z} \in V$, and $a \in F$.

1.20 If $\mathbf{x} + \mathbf{z} = \mathbf{y} + \mathbf{z}$ or $\mathbf{z} + \mathbf{x} = \mathbf{z} + \mathbf{y}$, then $\mathbf{x} = \mathbf{y}$ (*Cancellation law*).

1.21 $a\mathbf{x} = \mathbf{0}$ if and only if either $a = 0$ or $\mathbf{x} = \mathbf{0}$.

1.22 $$-(a\mathbf{x}) = (-a)\mathbf{x} = a(-\mathbf{x}).$$

Proof of 1.20: If $\mathbf{x} + \mathbf{z} = \mathbf{y} + \mathbf{z}$, then we have

$$
\begin{aligned}
(\mathbf{x} + \mathbf{z}) + (-\mathbf{z}) &= (\mathbf{y} + \mathbf{z}) + (-\mathbf{z}), \\
\mathbf{x} + [\mathbf{z} + (-\mathbf{z})] &= \mathbf{y} + [\mathbf{z} + (-\mathbf{z})] && \text{(Associative law)}, \\
\mathbf{x} + \mathbf{0} &= \mathbf{y} + \mathbf{0} && \text{(Inverse elements)}, \\
\mathbf{x} &= \mathbf{y} && \text{(Identity elements)}.
\end{aligned}
$$

If $\mathbf{z} + \mathbf{x} = \mathbf{z} + \mathbf{y}$, then $\mathbf{x} + \mathbf{z} = \mathbf{y} + \mathbf{z}$ by the commutative law and $\mathbf{x} = \mathbf{y}$ by the proof above.

Proof of 1.21: This property states that $a\mathbf{x} = \mathbf{0}$ if and only if a is the zero scalar or $\mathbf{x}$ is the zero vector. If $a = 0$, the zero element of F, then

$0 = 0 + 0$ and $0\mathbf{x} = (0 + 0)\mathbf{x} = 0\mathbf{x} + 0\mathbf{x}$ by 1.19(6). Since $\mathbf{0} + 0\mathbf{x} = 0\mathbf{x}$ by 1.19(3), we have

$$\mathbf{0} + 0\mathbf{x} = 0\mathbf{x} + 0\mathbf{x}, \qquad \text{and} \qquad \mathbf{0} = 0\mathbf{x}$$

by 1.20. A similar argument shows that $a\mathbf{0} = \mathbf{0}$.

Conversely, assume that $a \in F$ and $\mathbf{x} \in V$ are such that $a\mathbf{x} = \mathbf{0}$. If $a \neq 0$, then a^{-1} exists, and we have

$$\mathbf{x} = 1\mathbf{x} = (a^{-1}a)\mathbf{x} = a^{-1}(a\mathbf{x}) = a^{-1}\mathbf{0} = \mathbf{0}.$$

If $a = 0$, then $a\mathbf{x} = \mathbf{0}$ by the proof above. This proves 1.21.

Proof of 1.22: By 1.19(4), $a\mathbf{x} + [-(a\mathbf{x})] = \mathbf{0}$, whereas by 1.19(7) and 1.21, $\mathbf{0} = 0\mathbf{x} = [a + (-a)]\mathbf{x} = a\mathbf{x} + (-a)\mathbf{x}$. Therefore, we see that

$$a\mathbf{x} + [-(a\mathbf{x})] = a\mathbf{x} + (-a)\mathbf{x}, \qquad \text{and} \qquad -(a\mathbf{x}) = (-a)\mathbf{x}$$

by the cancellation law. A similar proof shows that $-(a\mathbf{x}) = a(-\mathbf{x})$. This proves 1.22.

The operation of subtraction in V is defined as follows:

$$\mathbf{x} - \mathbf{y} = \mathbf{x} + (-\mathbf{y}) \qquad \text{for all } \mathbf{x}, \mathbf{y} \in V.$$

It is easily shown that vector subtraction has properties similar to those of subtraction in F. For example, we have

$$a(\mathbf{x} - \mathbf{y}) = a\mathbf{x} - a\mathbf{y} \qquad \text{for all } \mathbf{x}, \mathbf{y} \in V,\ a \in F,$$

$$-(\mathbf{x} - \mathbf{y}) = (-\mathbf{x}) + \mathbf{y} \qquad \text{for all } \mathbf{x}, \mathbf{y} \in V.$$

Henceforth, we shall assume that the reader is familiar with these properties.

If V is a vector space over a field F and S is a nonempty subset of V which is closed under addition and scalar multiplication (that is, $\mathbf{x} + \mathbf{y}$ and $a\mathbf{x}$ are in S for all $\mathbf{x}, \mathbf{y} \in S$, $a \in F$), then S is a vector space in its own right. Thus $\mathbf{0} \in S$ since $\mathbf{0} = 0\mathbf{x}$ for any $\mathbf{x} \in S$. If $\mathbf{x} \in S$, then $-\mathbf{x} \in S$ also, since $-\mathbf{x} = -(1\mathbf{x}) = (-1)\mathbf{x}$. It is now clear that 1.19(1) through (8) hold for S as well as V. We call S a *subspace* of V.

For each $\mathbf{x} \in V$, the set of all scalar multiples of $\mathbf{x}$ is denoted by $F\mathbf{x}$. Thus, we have

$$F\mathbf{x} = \{a\mathbf{x} \mid a \in F\}.$$

Since

$$a\mathbf{x} + b\mathbf{x} = (a + b)\mathbf{x}, \qquad \text{and} \qquad b(a\mathbf{x}) = (ba)\mathbf{x},$$

the set $F\mathbf{x}$ is closed under addition and scalar multiplication and is therefore a subspace of V. The set of scalar multiples of $\mathbf{0}$ is simply $\{\mathbf{0}\}$. Thus $\{\mathbf{0}\}$ is a subspace of V; in fact, $\{\mathbf{0}\}$ is the least subspace of V in the sense that it is contained in every other subspace of V. Trivially, V is a subspace of itself according to our definition.

We call a subspace S of V *proper* if $S \neq \{\mathbf{0}\}$ and $S \neq V$. If $\mathbf{x} \in V$, $\mathbf{x} \neq \mathbf{0}$, then $F\mathbf{x}$ is a minimal nonzero subspace. For if S is a proper subspace of V

and $S \subset F\mathbf{x}$, and if $\mathbf{y} \in S$, $\mathbf{y} \neq \mathbf{0}$, then $\mathbf{y} = a\mathbf{x}$ for some nonzero $a \in F$. Hence, $(ba^{-1})\mathbf{y} = (ba^{-1})a\mathbf{x} = b\mathbf{x}$ is in S for every $b \in F$ and $F\mathbf{x} \subset S$. It follows that $S = F\mathbf{x}$. The subspace $F\mathbf{x}$ is proper unless $V = F\mathbf{x}$, a rather uninteresting possibility.

If S_1 and S_2 are subspaces of a vector space V, then so is their *intersection*,

$$S_1 \cap S_2 = \{\mathbf{x} \in V \mid \mathbf{x} \in S_1 \quad \text{and} \quad \mathbf{x} \in S_2\}.$$

For if $\mathbf{x}$ and $\mathbf{y}$ are in both S_1 and S_2, then so are $\mathbf{x} + \mathbf{y}$ and $a\mathbf{x}$ for every $a \in F$.

More generally, if $\{S_1, S_2, \ldots, S_n\}$ is any finite set of subspaces of V, then their intersection $S_1 \cap S_2 \cap \cdots \cap S_n$ also is a subspace of V. The notation

$$\bigcap_{i=1}^{n} S_i$$

is often used for this intersection. Evidently, $S_1 \cap S_2 \cap \cdots \cap S_n$ is the *largest* subspace of V contained in all the subspaces $S_1, S_2, \ldots, S_n$.

Another useful way of forming a subspace from two given subspaces S_1 and S_2 of a vector space V is to take their *sum:*

$$S_1 + S_2 = \{\mathbf{x}_1 + \mathbf{x}_2 \mid \mathbf{x}_1 \in S_1, \mathbf{x}_2 \in S_2\}.$$

To show that $S_1 + S_2$ actually is a subspace of V, let $\mathbf{x}_1 + \mathbf{x}_2, \mathbf{y}_1 + \mathbf{y}_2 \in S_1 + S_2$, where $\mathbf{x}_i, \mathbf{y}_i \in S_i$, and $a \in F$. Then we have

$$(\mathbf{x}_1 + \mathbf{x}_2) + (\mathbf{y}_1 + \mathbf{y}_2) = (\mathbf{x}_1 + \mathbf{y}_1) + (\mathbf{x}_2 + \mathbf{y}_2) \in S_1 + S_2,$$

$$a(\mathbf{x}_1 + \mathbf{x}_2) = a\mathbf{x}_1 + a\mathbf{x}_2 \in S_1 + S_2.$$

Thus, $S_1 + S_2$ is a subspace of V because it is closed under addition and scalar multiplication.

We can similarly form the sum of n subspaces $S_1, S_2, \ldots, S_n$ of V:

$$S_1 + S_2 + \cdots + S_n = \{\mathbf{x}_1 + \mathbf{x}_2 + \cdots + \mathbf{x}_n \mid \mathbf{x}_i \in S_i\}.$$

The sigma notation

$$\sum_{i=1}^{n} S_i$$

is often used for this sum. Since $\mathbf{0} \in S_i$ for each i, $\mathbf{x}_1 + \mathbf{0} + \mathbf{0} + \cdots + \mathbf{0} = \mathbf{x}_1 \in S_1 + S_2 + \cdots + S_n$ for each $\mathbf{x}_1 \in S_1$. That is, $S_1 \subset S_1 + S_2 + \cdots + S_n$. Similarly, we see that

$$S_j \subset \sum_{i=1}^{n} S_i \qquad \text{for} \quad j = 1, 2, \ldots, n.$$

It should be clear that $S_1 + S_2 + \cdots + S_n$ is the *least* subspace of V containing all the subspaces $S_1, S_2, \ldots, S_n$.

If $\mathbf{x}, \mathbf{y} \in V$, then either $F\mathbf{x} \cap F\mathbf{y} = \{\mathbf{0}\}$ or $F\mathbf{x} = F\mathbf{y}$. On the other hand,

$$F\mathbf{x} + F\mathbf{y} = \{a\mathbf{x} + b\mathbf{y} \mid a, b \in F\}.$$

More generally, for any $\mathbf{x}_1, \mathbf{x}_2, \ldots, \mathbf{x}_n \in V$, we have

$$\sum_{i=1}^{n} F\mathbf{x}_i = \left\{\sum_{i=1}^{n} a_i\mathbf{x}_i \mid a_i \in F\right\}.$$

We call $S = \sum_{i=1}^{n} F\mathbf{x}_i$ the subspace of V *spanned* by the vectors $\mathbf{x}_1, \mathbf{x}_2, \ldots,$ $\mathbf{x}_n$. Each vector of S is said to be a *linear combination* of the n vectors $\mathbf{x}_1,$ $\mathbf{x}_2, \ldots, \mathbf{x}_n$.

EXERCISES

In the following exercises, V is assumed to be a vector space over a field F.

1. Prove that $a\mathbf{0} = \mathbf{0}$ for all $a \in F$ (part of 1.21).
2. Prove that $-(a\mathbf{x}) = a(-\mathbf{x})$ for all $a \in F$ and $\mathbf{x} \in V$ (part of 1.22).
3. State and prove a cancellation law for scalar multiplication.
4. Prove that $a(\mathbf{x} - \mathbf{y}) = a\mathbf{x} - a\mathbf{y}$ for all $\mathbf{x}, \mathbf{y} \in V$, $a \in F$.
5. Prove that $-(\mathbf{x} - \mathbf{y}) = (-\mathbf{x}) + \mathbf{y}$ for all $\mathbf{x}, \mathbf{y} \in V$.
6. If S_1, S_2, and S_3 are proper subspaces of V such that $S_1 \cap (S_2 + S_3) = \{\mathbf{0}\}$ and $S_2 \cap S_3 = \{\mathbf{0}\}$, then prove that $S_2 \cap (S_1 + S_3) = \{\mathbf{0}\}$.
7. Let $\mathbf{x}_1$, $\mathbf{x}_2$, and $\mathbf{x}_3$ be nonzero vectors which generate a vector space V. If $\mathbf{y} \in V$, $\mathbf{y} \neq \mathbf{0}$, prove that $\mathbf{y}$ together with some two of the vectors $\mathbf{x}_1, \mathbf{x}_2, \mathbf{x}_3$ generate V.
8. Generalize Exercise 7 from 3 to n vectors.
9. If S_1 and S_2 are subspaces of V such that $S_1 \supset S_2$, then prove that $S_1 \cap (S_2 + S) = S_2 + (S_1 \cap S)$ for every subspace S of V. (This is called the *modular law*.)

3. GEOMETRIC VECTORS

For many centuries physicists have used directed line segments to represent forces, velocities, accelerations, and other entities having both magnitude and direction. We shall describe in this section the space of geometric vectors, or directed line segments, used by physicists.

Consider a Euclidean plane made up of points and lines satisfying the postulates of Euclidean geometry. Every ordered pair (A, B) of points determines a *segment* with endpoints A and B and a *direction* from the *initial point* A to the *terminal point* B. We call such a directed segment a *vector* in the plane and denote it by

$$\mathbf{AB}.$$

The set of all vectors in a Euclidean plane is denoted by

$$\mathrm{E}_2.$$

It will be convenient to have a coordinate system in the plane so that each vector **AB** has a length denoted by

$$|\mathbf{AB}|$$

and defined to be $d(A, B)$, the distance between points A and B.

We shall consider the vectors in E_2 to be *free vectors;* i.e., two vectors **AB** and **CD** will be considered to be equal,

$$\mathbf{AB} = \mathbf{CD},$$

if and only if either $|\mathbf{AB}| = |\mathbf{CD}| = 0$ (that is, $A = B$ and $C = D$) or $|\mathbf{AB}| = |\mathbf{CD}| \neq 0$ and **AB, CD** are parallel and directed in the same way (Fig. 1.4). Thus, the position of each vector in the plane is immaterial; only

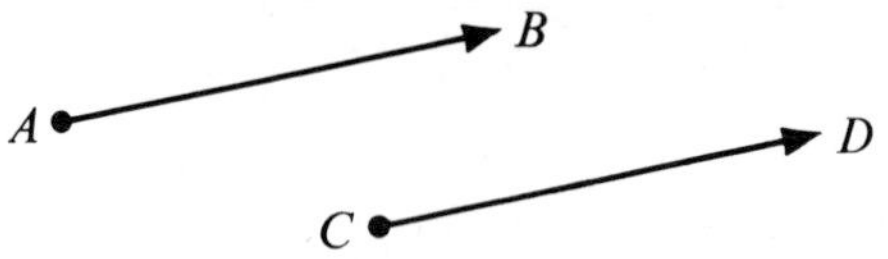

Figure 1.4

its length and direction are important. If we wish, we can assume that all vectors have the same initial point.

The sum of two vectors **AB** and **BC** is defined to be **AC**,

$$\mathbf{AB} + \mathbf{BC} = \mathbf{AC},$$

as shown in Fig. 1.5. If the two vectors **AB** and **AD** have the same initial point, then their sum is **AC**,

$$\mathbf{AB} + \mathbf{AD} = \mathbf{AC},$$

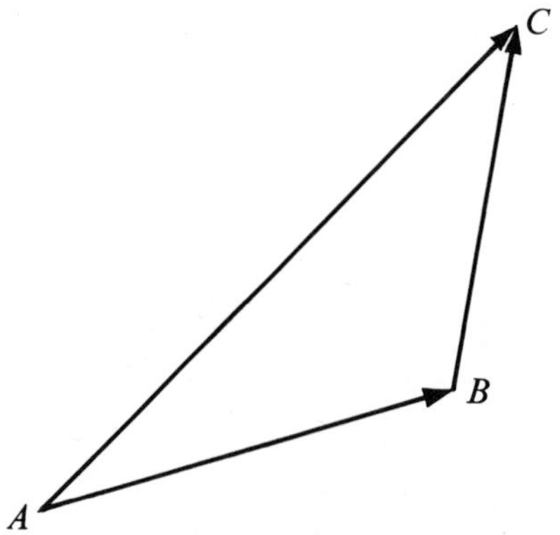

Figure 1.5

where **AC** is the diagonal of the parallelogram having **AB** and **AD** as two of its sides (Fig. 1.6). This is true because **AD** = **BC**.

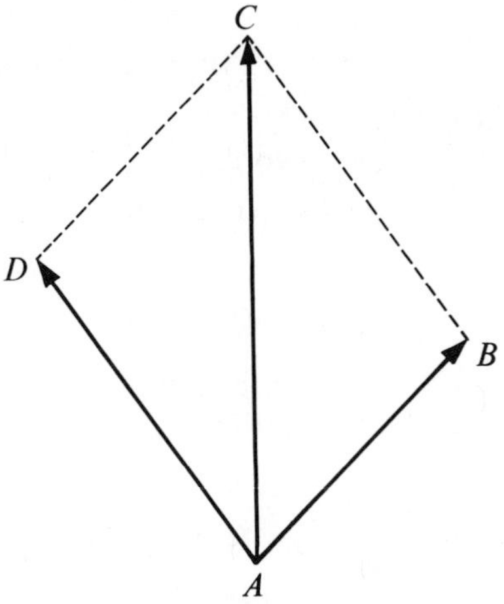

Figure 1.6

If the points A, B, and C are collinear, then there is no parallelogram associated with the sum **AB** + **BC**. This case is illustrated in Fig. 1.7.

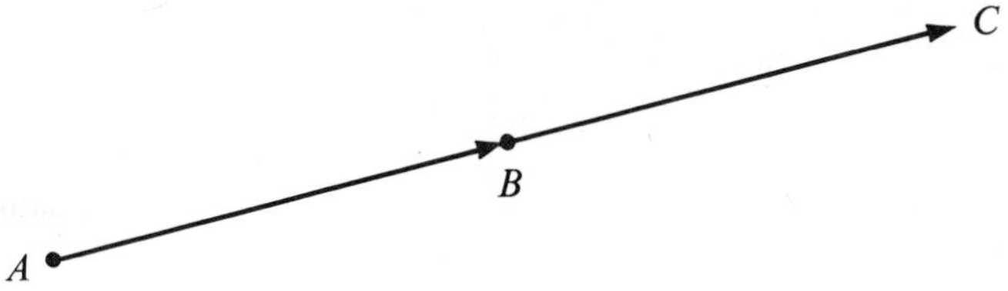

Figure 1.7

It can be easily demonstrated that vector addition is both commutative and associative.

A vector having the same initial and terminal point is called the *zero vector* and is denoted by **0**. Thus, we have

$$\mathbf{0} = \mathbf{AA}$$

for every point A in the plane. The vector **0** is not considered to have any particular direction. We see that

$$\mathbf{AB} + \mathbf{0} = \mathbf{0} + \mathbf{AB} = \mathbf{AB} \qquad \text{for all } \mathbf{AB} \in \mathrm{E}_2.$$

That is, **0** is the *additive identity element* of E_2.

Each vector **AB** has an opposite **BA**, and

$$\mathbf{AB} + \mathbf{BA} = \mathbf{BA} + \mathbf{AB} = \mathbf{0}.$$

We call **BA** the *negative* of **AB** and denote it by $-\mathbf{AB}$:

$$\mathbf{BA} = -\mathbf{AB}.$$

Thus, we have

$$\mathbf{AB} + (-\mathbf{AB}) = (-\mathbf{AB}) + \mathbf{AB} = \mathbf{0} \qquad \text{for all } \mathbf{AB} \in \mathrm{E}_2.$$

This proves the *additive inverse* property.

The difference of two vectors is given by

$$\mathbf{AB} - \mathbf{AC} = \mathbf{CB},$$

since we have

$$\mathbf{AB} = \mathbf{AC} + \mathbf{CB}.$$

Thus, $\mathbf{AB} + \mathbf{AC}$ and $\mathbf{AB} - \mathbf{AC}$ are the two diagonals of the parallelogram having **AB** and **AC** as adjacent sides (Fig. 1.8).

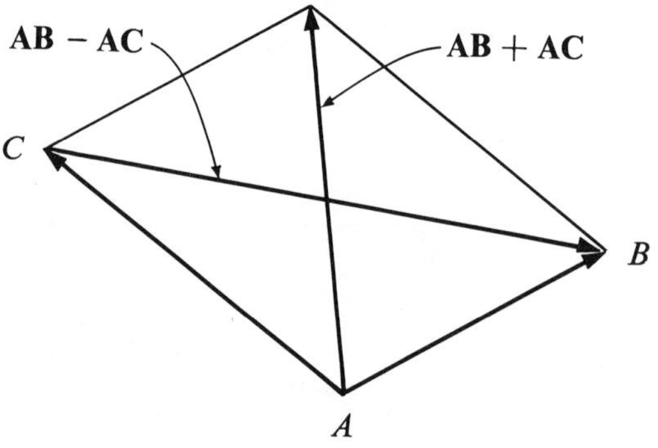

Figure 1.8

The results above may be summarized by saying that geometric vector addition in E_2 has properties 1.19(1) through (4) of addition in a vector space. However, we cannot as yet say that E_2 is a vector space, because an operation of scalar multiplication has not been defined.

We define scalar multiplication in E_2 as follows. For each vector **AB** and each $r \in \mathbb{R}$, define

$$r\mathbf{AB}$$

to be the vector whose length is $|r|\,|\mathbf{AB}|$ and whose direction is (1) the same as that of **AB** if $r > 0$, and (2) opposite to that of **AB** if $r < 0$. Also define

$$0\mathbf{AB} = \mathbf{0}.$$

In other words, if A, B, and C are collinear points, then we have

$$r\mathbf{AB} = \mathbf{AC}, \qquad \text{where } |\mathbf{AC}| = |r|\,|\mathbf{AB}|,$$

where **AB** and **AC** have the same direction if $r > 0$, and opposite directions if $r < 0$.

If **AB**, **BC** $\in E_2$ and $r \in \mathbb{R}$, then select points B' and C' so that (Fig. 1.9)

$$\mathbf{AB'} = r\mathbf{AB}, \qquad \mathbf{AC'} = r\mathbf{AC}.$$

Triangles ABC and $AB'C'$ are similar by results of Euclidean geometry, so

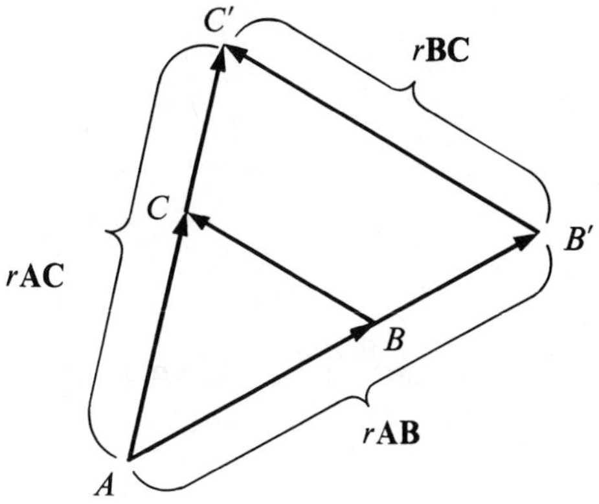

Figure 1.9

that side $B'C'$ is parallel to BC and has length $|r|$ times the length of BC. Therefore, we see that

$$\mathbf{B'C'} = r\mathbf{BC},$$

and

$$\mathbf{AB'} + \mathbf{B'C'} = r\mathbf{AB} + r\mathbf{BC} = \mathbf{AC'} = r\mathbf{AC} = r(\mathbf{AB} + \mathbf{BC}).$$

Thus we have proved that

$$r(\mathbf{AB} + \mathbf{BC}) = r\mathbf{AB} + r\mathbf{BC} \qquad \text{for all } \mathbf{AB}, \mathbf{BC} \in E_2,\ r \in \mathbb{R}.$$

If r and s are positive numbers, then the following two properties are easily shown to hold:

$$(r + s)\mathbf{AB} = r\mathbf{AB} + s\mathbf{AB} \qquad \text{for all } \mathbf{AB} \in E_2,\ r, s \in \mathbb{R}.$$

$$(rs)\mathbf{AB} = r(s\mathbf{AB}) \qquad \text{for all } \mathbf{AB} \in E_2,\ r, s \in \mathbb{R}.$$

It is also evident that

$$1\mathbf{AB} = \mathbf{AB} \qquad \text{for all } \mathbf{AB} \in E_2.$$

It now follows that scalar multiplication in E_2 has properties 1.19(5) through (8). Since we have already observed that properties 1.19(1) through (4) hold for E_2, we have the following result.

1.23. THEOREM. E_2 is a vector space.

The fact that E_2 is a vector space may be used to solve geometric problems, as the following examples illustrate.

EXAMPLE 1: Prove that the diagonals of a parallelogram bisect each other.

Solution: Let $ABCD$ be a parallelogram and let E be the midpoint of

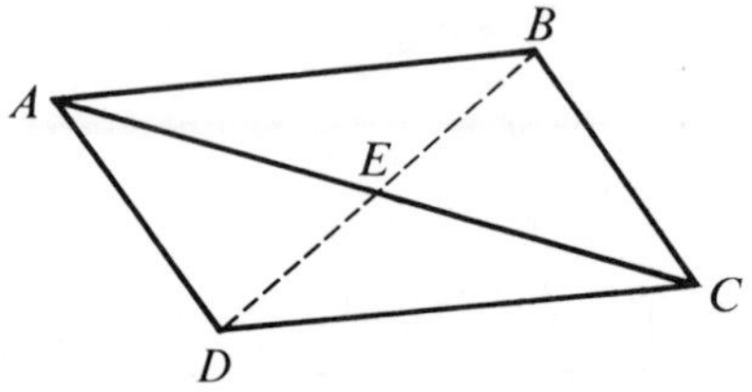

Figure 1.10

diagonal AC (Fig. 1.10). Since the opposite sides of $ABCD$ are parallel and equal, we have

$$\mathbf{AB} = \mathbf{DC}.$$

Now $\mathbf{AB} = \mathbf{AE} + \mathbf{EB}$, $\mathbf{DC} = \mathbf{DE} + \mathbf{EC}$, and $\mathbf{AE} = \mathbf{EC}$. Hence, we have

$$\mathbf{AE} + \mathbf{EB} = \mathbf{AE} + \mathbf{DE}, \qquad \text{and} \qquad \mathbf{EB} = \mathbf{DE}$$

by the cancellation law. Therefore, B, E, and D are collinear, and E is the midpoint of $\mathbf{DB}$. Thus the diagonals bisect each other.

EXAMPLE 2: Prove that the quadrilateral formed by joining the midpoints of the sides of a quadrilateral in order is a parallelogram.

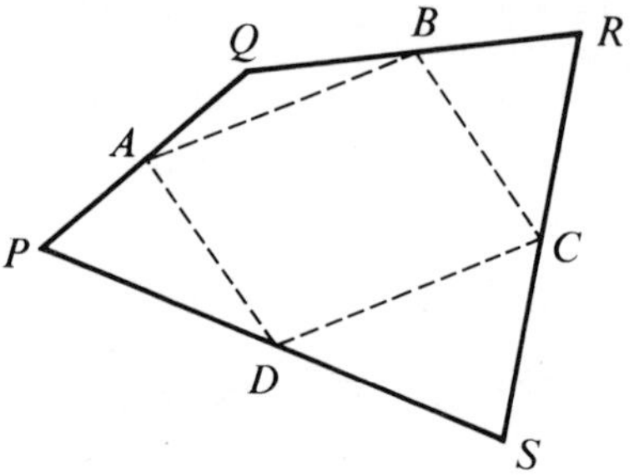

Figure 1.11

Solution: Looking at Fig. 1.11, we see that

$$\mathbf{AQ} = \tfrac{1}{2}\mathbf{PQ}, \qquad \mathbf{QB} = \tfrac{1}{2}\mathbf{QR},$$

and therefore

$$\mathbf{AB} = \mathbf{AQ} + \mathbf{QB} = \tfrac{1}{2}\mathbf{PQ} + \tfrac{1}{2}\mathbf{QR}$$
$$= \tfrac{1}{2}(\mathbf{PQ} + \mathbf{QR}) = \tfrac{1}{2}\mathbf{PR}.$$

Similarly, we have

$$\mathbf{DS} = \tfrac{1}{2}\mathbf{PS}, \qquad \mathbf{SC} = \tfrac{1}{2}\mathbf{SR},$$

and

$$\mathbf{DC} = \tfrac{1}{2}(\mathbf{PS} + \mathbf{SR}) = \tfrac{1}{2}\mathbf{PR}.$$

Consequently, we find that

$$\mathbf{AB} = \mathbf{DC},$$

and $ABCD$ is a parallelogram.

Everything we did above in a Euclidean plane can also be done in Euclidean three-space. If we denote the set of all vectors in space by

$$\mathrm{E}_3,$$

then we obtain the following result, as above.

1.24. THEOREM. E_3 is a vector space.

It is easily verified that Example 2 holds even if the points P, Q, R, and S are not coplanar (i.e., not in a plane). The proof is the same, with each vector now taken to be in E_3 rather than E_2. Algebraic properties of E_2 and E_3 are the same; that is, they are the properties of any vector space. However, we shall distinguish between these vector spaces after we introduce the dimension of a vector space.

If $\mathbf{x}$ is a nonzero vector in either E_2 or E_3, then the subspace $\mathbb{R}\mathbf{x}$ is a *line;* that is, $\mathbb{R}\mathbf{x}$ is the set of all vectors along a line L of the plane or space (Fig. 1.12). Recalling that the vectors of E_2 and E_3 are free, we see that $\mathbb{R}\mathbf{x}$ actually consists of L and all lines parallel to L.

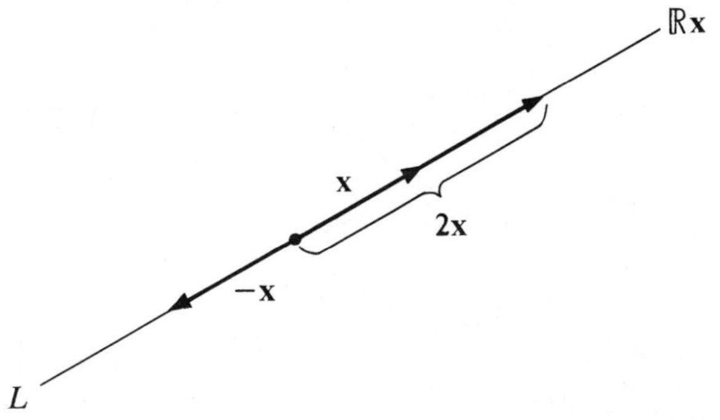

Figure 1.12

If $\mathbf{x}$ and $\mathbf{y}$ are nonzero and nonparallel vectors of E_2 or E_3, then $\mathbb{R}\mathbf{x}$ and $\mathbb{R}\mathbf{y}$ are as shown in Fig. 1.13. Since $\mathbf{x}$ and $\mathbf{y}$ are free vectors, we can select them to have the same initial point. That is, lines K and L of Fig. 1.13 intersect in one point. This shows geometrically that $\mathbb{R}\mathbf{x} \cap \mathbb{R}\mathbf{y} = \{\mathbf{0}\}$. Lines K and

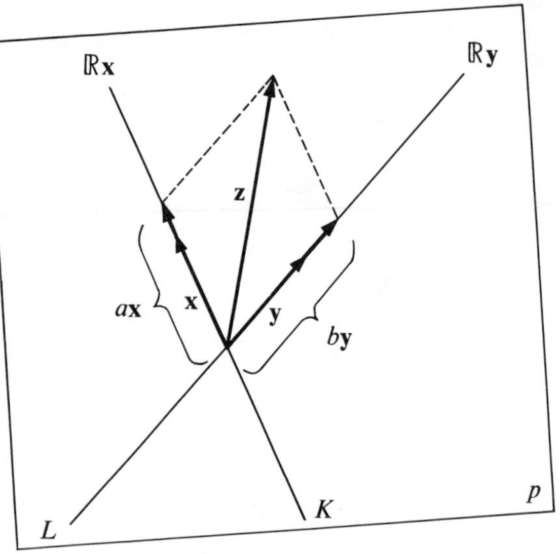

Figure 1.13

L determine a plane p. Each vector $\mathbf{z}$ in p is the diagonal of a parallelogram having two sides on K and L, as shown in Fig. 1.13, and therefore we have

$$\mathbf{z} = a\mathbf{x} + b\mathbf{y} \qquad \text{for some } a, b \in \mathbb{R}.$$

Conversely, each vector of the form $a\mathbf{x} + b\mathbf{y}$ for some $a, b \in \mathbb{R}$ is in plane p. Therefore, the subspace

$$\mathbb{R}\mathbf{x} + \mathbb{R}\mathbf{y}$$

consists of all vectors in plane p. If $\mathbf{x}, \mathbf{y} \in E_2$, then p must be the whole space; that is, $\mathbb{R}\mathbf{x} + \mathbb{R}\mathbf{y} = E_2$. If $\mathbf{x}, \mathbf{y} \in E_3$, then $\mathbb{R}\mathbf{x} + \mathbb{R}\mathbf{y}$ is a proper subspace of E_3.

EXERCISES

1. Prove vectorially that if the diagonals of a quadrilateral in a plane bisect each other, then the quadrilateral is a parallelogram.
2. If **AD** is the median drawn from A in a triangle ABC, then prove that **AD** is the arithmetic average of **AB** and **AC** [that is, $\mathbf{AD} = \frac{1}{2}(\mathbf{AB} + \mathbf{AC})$].

3. Prove vectorially that the segments joining the midpoints of opposite sides of any quadrilateral in space bisect each other.
4. Prove vectorially that the midpoints of two opposite sides of a quadrilateral in space together with the midpoints of the two diagonals are either collinear or the vertices of a parallelogram.
5. If $ABCD$ is a parallelogram in a plane and P is the midpoint of side BC, then prove vectorially that the segments AP and BD meet in a point of trisection of both.
6. Exercise 5 may be generalized by assuming that P is chosen on side BC so that $\mathbf{BP} = a\mathbf{BC}$, where $0 < a \leq 1$. Show vectorially that the point of intersection of AP and BD divides both segments in the same ratio, and find this ratio.

4. VECTOR n-TUPLES

Let F be a field and n be a positive integer. An ordered set

$$(a_1, a_2, \ldots, a_n), \qquad a_i \in F,$$

is called an *n-tuple* over F. The elements $a_1, a_2, \ldots, a_n$ are called the *coordinates* of the n-tuple. Two n-tuples are equal if and only if they have the same coordinates:

$$(a_1, a_2, \ldots, a_n) = (b_1, b_2, \ldots, b_n) \qquad \text{if and only if}$$
$$a_1 = b_1, a_2 = b_2, \ldots, a_n = b_n.$$

We shall denote the set of all n-tuples over F by

$$F^n.$$

An operation of addition may be defined in F^n coordinatewise as follows:

$$(a_1, a_2, \ldots, a_n) + (b_1, b_2, \ldots, b_n) = (a_1 + b_1, a_2 + b_2, \ldots, a_n + b_n).$$

By direct computation, we easily verify that properties 1.19(1) through (4) hold. Thus if $\mathbf{x} = (a_1, a_2, \ldots, a_n)$, $\mathbf{y} = (b_1, b_2, \ldots, b_n)$, and $\mathbf{z} = (c_1, c_2, \ldots, c_n)$, then we see that

$$\mathbf{x} + (\mathbf{y} + \mathbf{z}) = (\mathbf{x} + \mathbf{y}) + \mathbf{z}$$
$$= (a_1 + b_1 + c_1, a_2 + b_2 + c_2, \ldots, a_n + b_n + c_n),$$
$$\mathbf{x} + \mathbf{y} = \mathbf{y} + \mathbf{x} = (a_1 + b_1, a_2 + b_2, \ldots, a_n + b_n)$$
$$= (b_1 + a_1, b_2 + a_2, \ldots, b_n + a_n).$$

Also, if

$$\mathbf{0} = (0, 0, \ldots, 0),$$

then we have

$$\mathbf{x} + \mathbf{0} = \mathbf{0} + \mathbf{x} = \mathbf{x},$$

and if

$$-\mathbf{x} = (-a_1, -a_2, \ldots, -a_n),$$

then we have

$$\mathbf{x} + (-\mathbf{x}) = (-\mathbf{x}) + \mathbf{x} = (0, 0, \ldots, 0) = \mathbf{0}.$$

Scalar multiplication may be defined in F^n coordinatewise as follows:

$$r(a_1, a_2, \ldots, a_n) = (ra_1, ra_2, \ldots, ra_n).$$

We readily verify that properties 1.19(5) through (8) hold for scalar multiplication in F^n. Hence, we conclude the following.

1.25. THEOREM. *F^n is a vector space for each field F and every positive integer n.*

The vectors of F^n which have $n - 1$ coordinates 0 and the other coordinate 1 are of special significance. If δ_{ij} denotes the *Kronecker delta*, so that

$$\delta_{ij} = 0 \quad \text{if} \quad i \neq j, \qquad \delta_{ii} = 1,$$

then

$$\mathbf{u}_i = (\delta_{i1}, \delta_{i2}, \ldots, \delta_{in})$$

is the vector in F^n having 1 in the ith coordinate and zeros elsewhere. For each $a \in F$, $a\mathbf{u}_i$ has a in the ith coordinate and zeros elsewhere. Hence, we have

$$(a_1, a_2, \ldots, a_n) = \sum_{i=1}^{n} a_i\mathbf{u}_i.$$

Thus, every vector $(a_1, a_2, \ldots, a_n) \in F^n$ is a linear combination of the vectors $\mathbf{u}_1, \mathbf{u}_2, \ldots, \mathbf{u}_n$; that is, we have

1.26 $$F\mathbf{u}_1 + F\mathbf{u}_2 + \cdots + F\mathbf{u}_n = F^n.$$

In other words, the vectors $\mathbf{u}_1, \mathbf{u}_2, \ldots, \mathbf{u}_n$ span F^n.

It is more difficult to decide if vectors other than the $\mathbf{u}_i$'s span F^n, as the following examples show.

EXAMPLE 1: Do the vectors

$$\mathbf{x}_1 = (-1, 2, 0), \qquad \mathbf{x}_2 = (3, 1, -1), \qquad \mathbf{x}_3 = (1, 0, -1)$$

span $\mathbb{R}^3$?

Solution: Let S be the subspace of $\mathbb{R}^3$ spanned by $\mathbf{x}_1$, $\mathbf{x}_2$, and $\mathbf{x}_3$:

$$S = \mathbb{R}\mathbf{x}_1 + \mathbb{R}\mathbf{x}_2 + \mathbb{R}\mathbf{x}_3.$$

If we can show that $\mathbf{u}_1, \mathbf{u}_2, \mathbf{u}_3 \in S$, then it will follow that $\mathbb{R}\mathbf{u}_1 + \mathbb{R}\mathbf{u}_2 + \mathbb{R}\mathbf{u}_3 \subset S$ and $S = \mathbb{R}^3$ by 1.26. A possible way of doing this is as follows. Let

$$\mathbf{y}_1 = 3\mathbf{x}_1 + \mathbf{x}_2 = (0, 7, -1),$$
$$\mathbf{y}_2 = \mathbf{x}_1 + \mathbf{x}_3 = (0, 2, -1).$$

Then $\mathbf{y}_1, \mathbf{y}_2 \in S$, and hence $\mathbf{y}_3 \in S$, where

$$\mathbf{y}_3 = 2\mathbf{y}_1 - 7\mathbf{y}_2 = (0, 0, 5).$$

Therefore $\mathbf{u}_3 = \frac{1}{5}\mathbf{y}_3 \in S$. In turn, $\mathbf{y}_2 + \mathbf{u}_3 = (0, 2, 0) \in S$ and $\frac{1}{2}(\mathbf{y}_2 + \mathbf{u}_3) = \mathbf{u}_2 \in S$. Finally, $-\mathbf{x}_1 + 2\mathbf{u}_2 = \mathbf{u}_1 \in S$. We conclude that $S = \mathbb{R}^3$.

EXAMPLE 2: Do the vectors

$$\mathbf{x}_1 = (2, -2, 3), \qquad \mathbf{x}_2 = (3, -1, -5), \qquad \mathbf{x}_3 = (-1, -5, 27)$$

span $\mathbb{R}^3$?

Solution: Proceeding as in Example 1, we have

$$\mathbf{y}_1 = 3\mathbf{x}_1 - 2\mathbf{x}_2 = (0, -4, 19),$$
$$\mathbf{y}_2 = \mathbf{x}_1 + 2\mathbf{x}_3 = (0, -12, 57),$$

and hence $\mathbf{y}_1, \mathbf{y}_2 \in S = \mathbb{R}\mathbf{x}_1 + \mathbb{R}\mathbf{x}_2 + \mathbb{R}\mathbf{x}_3$. Unfortunately, $3\mathbf{y}_1 = \mathbf{y}_2$, so that we cannot conclude that $\mathbf{u}_3 \in S$ as we did in Example 1. We suspect that $\mathbf{u}_3 \notin S$. For if $\mathbf{u}_3 \in S$, then

$$a\mathbf{x}_1 + b\mathbf{x}_2 + c\mathbf{x}_3 = \mathbf{u}_3 \qquad \text{for some } a, b, c \in \mathbb{R}.$$

That is, we have

$$(2a, -2a, 3a) + (3b, -b, -5b) + (-c, -5c, 27c) = (0, 0, 1)$$

and

$$(1) \qquad \begin{cases} 2a + 3b - c = 0, \\ -2a - b - 5c = 0, \\ 3a - 5b + 27c = 1. \end{cases}$$

Adding the first two equations of (1), we get

$$2b - 6c = 0, \qquad \text{or} \qquad b = 3c.$$

Adding -3 times the first equation of (1) to 2 times the third equation, we get

$$-19b + 57c = 2, \qquad \text{or} \qquad b = 3c - \tfrac{2}{19}.$$

Since b cannot be both $3c$ and $3c - \frac{2}{19}$, evidently system (1) has no solution. Therefore $\mathbf{u}_3 \notin S$, as we suspected. Consequently, the vectors $\mathbf{x}_1$, $\mathbf{x}_2$, and $\mathbf{x}_3$ do not span $\mathbb{R}^3$.

EXERCISES

In each of Exercises 1 through 4, tell whether the vectors $\mathbf{x}_1$, $\mathbf{x}_2$, and $\mathbf{x}_3$ span $\mathbb{R}^3$.

1. $\mathbf{x}_1 = (1, 0, 0)$, $\mathbf{x}_2 = (1, 1, 0)$, $\mathbf{x}_3 = (1, 1, 1)$.
2. $\mathbf{x}_1 = (1, 0, -1)$, $\mathbf{x}_2 = (-1, 1, 0)$, $\mathbf{x}_3 = (1, 1, -2)$.
3. $\mathbf{x}_1 = (0, 1, 2)$, $\mathbf{x}_2 = (2, 0, 1)$, $\mathbf{x}_3 = (1, 2, 0)$.
4. $\mathbf{x}_1 = (1, 0, 0)$, $\mathbf{x}_2 = (0, 1, 0)$, $\mathbf{x}_3 = (1, -1, 0)$.
5. Find two proper subspaces S_1 and S_2 of $\mathbb{R}^3$ such that $S_1 \cap S_2 = \{\mathbf{0}\}$ and $S_1 + S_2 = \mathbb{R}^3$. Do the same for $\mathbb{R}^4$.
6. Let $\mathbf{v}_1 = a_{11}\mathbf{u}_1$, $\mathbf{v}_2 = a_{21}\mathbf{u}_1 + a_{22}\mathbf{u}_2, \ldots, \mathbf{v}_n = a_{n1}\mathbf{u}_1 + a_{n2}\mathbf{u}_2 + \cdots + a_{nn}\mathbf{u}_n$ for some $a_{ij} \in \mathbb{R}$, with $a_{11} \neq 0$, $a_{22} \neq 0, \ldots, a_{nn} \neq 0$. Prove that the vectors $\mathbf{v}_1, \mathbf{v}_2, \ldots, \mathbf{v}_n$ span $\mathbb{R}^n$.

5. INDEPENDENCE

Let V be a vector space over a field F. Two subspaces S_1 and S_2 of V are said to be independent if they are proper subspaces such that $S_1 \cap S_2 = \{\mathbf{0}\}$. More generally, we make the following definition.

1.27. DEFINITION OF INDEPENDENCE. A set $\{S_1, S_2, \ldots, S_n\}$ of subspaces of a vector space V is called independent iff

(1) $$\text{all } S_i \neq \{\mathbf{0}\}$$

and

(2) $$S_i \cap (S_1 + \cdots + S_{i-1} + S_{i+1} + \cdots + S_n) = \{\mathbf{0}\}, \qquad i = 1, 2, \ldots, n.$$

A nonindependent set of subspaces is called a *dependent* set. Thus, if $\{T_1, T_2, \ldots, T_n\}$ is a dependent set, either some $T_i = \{\mathbf{0}\}$ or $T_i \cap (T_1 + \cdots + T_{i-1} + T_{i+1} + \cdots + T_n) \neq \{\mathbf{0}\}$ for some i.

One way of establishing that a set of subspaces is independent is as follows.

1.28. THEOREM. Let $\{S_1, S_2, \ldots, S_n\}$ be a set of nonzero subspaces of a vector space V and let $S = S_1 + S_2 + \cdots + S_n$. Then $\{S_1, S_2, \ldots, S_n\}$ is independent if and only if every $\mathbf{x} \in S$ has a unique representation of the form

$$\mathbf{x} = \mathbf{x}_1 + \mathbf{x}_2 + \cdots + \mathbf{x}_n \qquad \text{for some } \mathbf{x}_i \in S_i.$$

Proof: If some $\mathbf{x} \in S$ has two different representations, say

$$\mathbf{x} = \mathbf{x}_1 + \mathbf{x}_2 + \cdots + \mathbf{x}_n = \mathbf{y}_1 + \mathbf{y}_2 + \cdots + \mathbf{y}_n,$$

where $\mathbf{x}_i, \mathbf{y}_i \in S_i$ and some $\mathbf{x}_i \neq \mathbf{y}_i$, say for simplicity $\mathbf{x}_1 \neq \mathbf{y}_1$, then

$$\mathbf{x}_1 - \mathbf{y}_1 = (\mathbf{y}_2 - \mathbf{x}_2) + (\mathbf{y}_3 - \mathbf{x}_3) + \cdots + (\mathbf{y}_n - \mathbf{x}_n).$$

Now $\mathbf{x}_1 - \mathbf{y}_1 \in S_1$, whereas $(\mathbf{y}_2 - \mathbf{x}_2) + (\mathbf{y}_3 - \mathbf{x}_3) + \cdots + (\mathbf{y}_n - \mathbf{x}_n) \in S_2 + S_3 + \cdots + S_n$. Thus $\mathbf{x}_1 - \mathbf{y}_1 \in S_1 \cap (S_2 + S_3 + \cdots + S_n)$ and, since $\mathbf{x}_1 - \mathbf{y}_1 \neq \mathbf{0}$, $S_1 \cap (S_2 + S_3 + \cdots + S_n) \neq \{\mathbf{0}\}$. We conclude that the set $\{S_1, S_2, \ldots, S_n\}$ is dependent.

Conversely, if $S_1 \cap (S_2 + S_3 + \cdots + S_n) \neq \{\mathbf{0}\}$, then we see that

$$\mathbf{x}_1 = \mathbf{x}_2 + \mathbf{x}_3 + \cdots + \mathbf{x}_n \neq \mathbf{0}$$

for some $\mathbf{x}_i \in S_i$. Therefore,

$$\mathbf{0} = (-\mathbf{x}_1) + \mathbf{x}_2 + \cdots + \mathbf{x}_n, \qquad \text{and} \qquad \mathbf{0} = \mathbf{0} + \mathbf{0} + \cdots + \mathbf{0}$$

are two different representations of the vector $\mathbf{0}$ as a sum of elements from the S_i. A similar argument can be made if

$$S_i \cap (S_1 + \cdots + S_{i-1} + S_{i+1} + \cdots + S_n) \neq \{\mathbf{0}\}$$

for $i \neq 1$. This proves 1.28.

EXAMPLE 1: Let $S_1 = \mathbb{R}(1, -1, 2) + \mathbb{R}(2, 1, 3)$ and let $S_2 = \mathbb{R}(1, 0, -1)$ be subspaces of $\mathbb{R}^3$. Is $\{S_1, S_2\}$ independent?

Solution: Since $S_1 \neq \{\mathbf{0}\}$ and $S_2 \neq \{\mathbf{0}\}$, we need only find out if $S_1 \cap S_2 = \{\mathbf{0}\}$. We can accomplish this by looking for $a, b, c \in \mathbb{R}$ such that

$$a(1, -1, 2) + b(2, 1, 3) = c(1, 0, -1).$$

Looking at each coordinate, we see that a, b, and c must be solutions of the system of equations

$$\begin{cases} a + 2b = c, \\ -a + b = 0, \\ 2a + 3b = -c. \end{cases}$$

From the second equation, we find that $a = b$. Hence, we have $3b = c$ from the first equation and $5b = -c$ from the third. Adding, we get $8b = 0$, and therefore $b = 0$, $a = 0$, and $c = 0$. We conclude that $S_1 \cap S_2 = \{\mathbf{0}\}$ and hence that $\{S_1, S_2\}$ is independent.

EXAMPLE 2: Let $S_1 = \mathbb{R}(2, -1, 0)$, $S_2 = \mathbb{R}(3, 1, -1)$, and

$$S_3 = \mathbb{R}(1, -8, 3).$$

Is $\{S_1, S_2, S_3\}$ independent in $\mathbb{R}^3$?

Solution: To find out if $S_1 \cap (S_2 + S_3) = \{\mathbf{0}\}$, we solve the equation

$$a(2, -1, 0) = b(3, 1, -1) + c(1, -8, 3),$$

or the equivalent system of equations

$$\begin{cases} 2a = 3b + c, \\ -a = b - 8c, \\ 0 = -b + 3c. \end{cases}$$

We easily show that $a = 5c$ and $b = 3c$ is a solution for any c. Therefore, $S_1 \cap (S_2 + S_3) \neq \{\mathbf{0}\}$, and the set $\{S_1, S_2, S_3\}$ is dependent.

EXERCISES

In Exercises 1 through 6, which of the sets of subspaces of $\mathbb{R}^3$ are independent?

1. $\{S_1, S_2\}$, where $S_1 = \mathbb{R}(1, 0, 0)$ and $S_2 = \mathbb{R}(1, 1, 0)$.
2. $\{S_1, S_2\}$, where $S_1 = \mathbb{R}(1, -1, 0)$ and $S_2 = \mathbb{R}(2, 1, 1) + \mathbb{R}(1, 2, 1)$.
3. $\{S_1, S_2\}$, where $S_1 = \mathbb{R}(1, 0, 1) + \mathbb{R}(-1, 1, 0)$ and $S_2 = \mathbb{R}(1, 0, 0) + \mathbb{R}(0, 1, -1)$.
4. $\{S_1, S_2, S_3\}$, where $S_1 = \mathbb{R}(1, 0, 1)$, $S_2 = \mathbb{R}(0, 1, 0)$, and $S_3 = \mathbb{R}(0, 1, 1)$.
5. $\{S_1, S_2, S_3\}$, where $S_1 = \mathbb{R}(2, 1, 2)$, $S_2 = \mathbb{R}(-1, 5, 3)$, and $S_3 = \mathbb{R}(7, -2, 3)$.
6. $\{S_1, S_2, S_3\}$, where $S_1 = \mathbb{R}(1, -1, 5)$, $S_2 = \mathbb{R}(3, 4, -7)$, and $S_3 = \mathbb{R}(1, 2, 5)$.
7. If $\{S_1, S_2, \ldots, S_n\}$ is independent, then prove that every subset of
$$\{S_1, S_2, \ldots, S_n\}$$
is also independent.
8. If some subset of $\{S_1, S_2, \ldots, S_n\}$ is dependent, then prove that $\{S_1, S_2, \ldots, S_n\}$ is also dependent.
9. If the vector space V is spanned by the n vectors $\mathbf{x}_1, \mathbf{x}_2, \ldots, \mathbf{x}_n$ and if $\{\mathbb{R}\mathbf{x}_1, \mathbb{R}\mathbf{x}_2, \ldots, \mathbb{R}\mathbf{x}_n\}$ is a dependent set, then prove that V is spanned by some $n - 1$ of the vectors $\mathbf{x}_1, \mathbf{x}_2, \ldots, \mathbf{x}_n$.
10. If $\{S_1, S_2, \ldots, S_n\}$ is independent and S is a subspace of V such that $S \neq \{\mathbf{0}\}$ and $S \cap (S_1 + S_2 + \cdots + S_n) = \{\mathbf{0}\}$, then prove that $\{S, S_1, S_2, \ldots, S_n\}$ is independent.

6. BASES

Let V be a vector space over a field F. If $\mathbf{x}_1, \mathbf{x}_2, \ldots, \mathbf{x}_n$ are vectors of V for which the set of subspaces $\{F\mathbf{x}_1, F\mathbf{x}_2, \ldots, F\mathbf{x}_n\}$ is independent, then we call the vectors $\mathbf{x}_1, \mathbf{x}_2, \ldots, \mathbf{x}_n$ *linearly independent* (abbreviated l.i.). Of course, if $\{F\mathbf{x}_1, F\mathbf{x}_2, \ldots, F\mathbf{x}_n\}$ is dependent, then we call the vectors $\mathbf{x}_1, \mathbf{x}_2, \ldots, \mathbf{x}_n$ *linearly dependent* (abbreviated l.d.). We leave the proof of the following theorem to the reader, since it is an easy consequence of 1.28.

1.29. THEOREM. The vectors $\mathbf{x}_1, \mathbf{x}_2, \ldots, \mathbf{x}_n$ of V are l.i. if and only if the only solution of the equation

(1)
$$\sum_{i=1}^{n} a_i\mathbf{x}_i = \mathbf{0}$$

is $a_1 = 0, a_2 = 0, \ldots, a_n = 0$.

Let us now make the following definition.

1.30. DEFINITION OF A BASIS. A set $\{\mathbf{x}_1, \mathbf{x}_2, \ldots, \mathbf{x}_n\}$ of vectors of a vector space V is called a *basis* of V if and only if the vectors $\mathbf{x}_1, \mathbf{x}_2, \ldots, \mathbf{x}_n$ are l.i. and span V.

Using 1.28, we see that $\{\mathbf{x}_1, \mathbf{x}_2, \ldots, \mathbf{x}_n\}$ is a basis of V if and only if every vector $\mathbf{y}$ of V has a unique representation of the form

$$\mathbf{y} = a_1\mathbf{x}_1 + a_2\mathbf{x}_2 + \cdots + a_n\mathbf{x}_n$$

for some $a_i \in F$.

EXAMPLE 1: If **AB** and **AC** are any two nonzero, nonparallel vectors of E_2, then $\{\mathbf{AB}, \mathbf{AC}\}$ is a basis of E_2. Thus **AB** and **AC** are independent (why?), and any other vector **AD** of E_2 has the unique form

$$\mathbf{AD} = a\mathbf{AB} + b\mathbf{AC}$$

for some $a, b \in \mathbb{R}$, as indicated in Fig. 1.14.

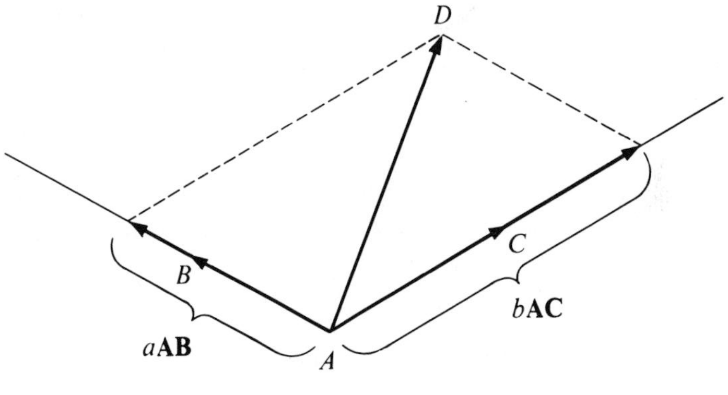

Figure 1.14

EXAMPLE 2: Are $\mathbf{x}_1 = (2, -1, 0)$, $\mathbf{x}_2 = (1, -1, 1)$, and $\mathbf{x}_3 = (0, 2, 3)$ elements of a basis of $\mathbb{R}^3$?

Solution: We see that $\mathbf{x}_1 - 2\mathbf{x}_2 = (0, 1, -2)$ and hence that $2(\mathbf{x}_1 - 2\mathbf{x}_2) - \mathbf{x}_3 = (0, 0, -7)$ and $3(\mathbf{x}_1 - 2\mathbf{x}_2) + 2\mathbf{x}_3 = (0, 7, 0)$. Also, $\mathbf{x}_1 + \frac{1}{7}(0, 7, 0) = (2, 0, 0)$. Thus the vectors $\mathbf{u}_1 = (1, 0, 0)$, $\mathbf{u}_2 = (0, 1, 0)$, and $\mathbf{u}_3 = (0, 0, 1)$ are in the space spanned by $\mathbf{x}_1$, $\mathbf{x}_2$, and $\mathbf{x}_3$. It follows that $\mathbf{x}_1$, $\mathbf{x}_2$, and $\mathbf{x}_3$ span $\mathbb{R}^3$. To test to see if $\mathbf{x}_1$, $\mathbf{x}_2$, and $\mathbf{x}_3$ are l.i., we solve the equation

$$a(2, -1, 0) + b(1, -1, 1) + c(0, 2, 3) = (0, 0, 0)$$

for $a, b, c \in \mathbb{R}$. This equation is equivalent to the system

$$\begin{cases} 2a + b = 0, \\ -a - b + 2c = 0, \\ b + 3c = 0. \end{cases}$$

Thus, we have $b = -2a$ from the first equation, $-a - (-2a) + 2c = 0$, or $a = -2c$, from the second equation, and $-2a + 3c = 0$, or $a = \frac{3}{2}c$, from the third equation. Clearly, the only solution is $a = b = c = 0$. Therefore, $\mathbf{x}_1, \mathbf{x}_2, \mathbf{x}_3$ are l.i. by 1.29, and $\{\mathbf{x}_1, \mathbf{x}_2, \mathbf{x}_3\}$ is a basis of $\mathbb{R}^3$.

As we shall presently show, it is only necessary to do half the work of Example 2 to prove that a set of three vectors is a basis of $\mathbb{R}^3$. That is, we need only show either that the three vectors are l.i. or that they span $\mathbb{R}^3$. More generally, we shall show that any n linearly independent vectors span F^n and that any n vectors which span F^n are linearly independent.

EXAMPLE 3: Prove that the three medians of a triangle meet at a point P. Show that P is a point of trisection of each median. Point P is called the *centroid* of the triangle.

Solution: In triangle ABC of Fig. 1.15, D is the midpoint of side BC,

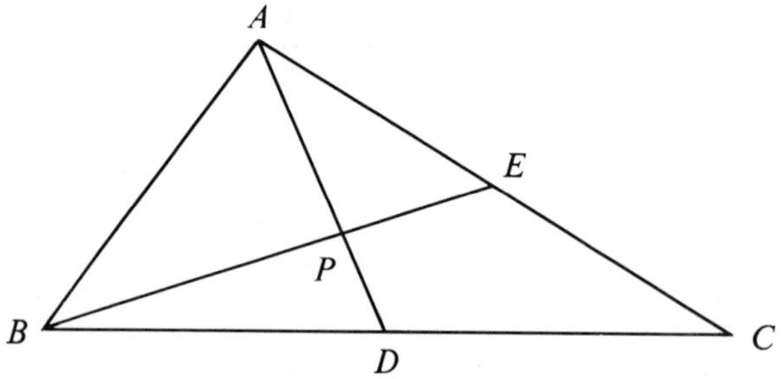

Figure 1.15

E the midpoint of AC, and P the point of intersection of AD and BE. Therefore, in E_2 we have

$$\mathbf{AD} = \mathbf{AB} + \mathbf{BD} = \mathbf{AB} + \tfrac{1}{2}\mathbf{BC} = \mathbf{AB} + \tfrac{1}{2}(\mathbf{AC} - \mathbf{AB}),$$

and

$$\mathbf{AD} = \tfrac{1}{2}(\mathbf{AB} + \mathbf{AC}).$$

Similarly, we have

$$\mathbf{BE} = \tfrac{1}{2}(\mathbf{BA} + \mathbf{BC}).$$

Since P is on **AD** and **BE**, we find that

$$\mathbf{AP} = r\mathbf{AD}, \qquad \mathbf{BP} = s\mathbf{BE} \qquad \text{for some } r, s \in \mathbb{R}.$$

Now

$$\mathbf{BP} = \mathbf{BA} + \mathbf{AP} = \mathbf{BA} + \frac{r}{2}(\mathbf{AB} + \mathbf{AC})$$

$$= \mathbf{BA} + \frac{r}{2}(\mathbf{AB} + \mathbf{AB} + \mathbf{BC}),$$

and therefore we have

(1) $$\mathbf{BP} = (1 - r)\mathbf{BA} + \frac{r}{2}\mathbf{BC}.$$

However, **BP** is also given by $\mathbf{BP} = s\mathbf{BE}$ or

(2) $$\mathbf{BP} = \frac{s}{2}\mathbf{BA} + \frac{s}{2}\mathbf{BC}.$$

Since **BA** and **BC** are l.i., we have from (1) and (2) that

$$1 - r = \frac{s}{2}, \qquad \frac{r}{2} = \frac{s}{2}.$$

Hence, we see that

$$r = s = \tfrac{2}{3}.$$

This proves that P is the point of trisection of both AD and BE away from each vertex. Since AD and BE are any two of the medians of the triangle, it follows that all three medians meet at the point of trisection of each median away from the vertex.

EXERCISES

In each of the following exercises, show that the set of vectors is l.i., and tell whether it is a basis of the given vector space.

1. $\{(1, 1), (1, -1)\}$ in $\mathbb{R}^2$.
2. $\{(2, -3)\}$ in $\mathbb{R}^2$.
3. $\{(1, 0, 0), (1, 1, 0)\}$ in $\mathbb{R}^3$.
4. $\{(2, 0, 1), (1, 2, 0), (0, 1, 0)\}$ in $\mathbb{R}^3$.
5. $\{(1, 0, 0, 0), (0, 1, 1, 1)\}$ in $\mathbb{R}^4$.
6. $\{(1, 1, 0, 0), (0, 1, 1, 0), (0, 0, 1, 1), (1, 0, 1, 0)\}$ in $\mathbb{R}^4$.
7. $\{(0, 0, 1, 1, 1), (0, 1, 1, 1, 1)\}$ in $\mathbb{R}^5$.
8. $\{\mathbf{u}_1, \mathbf{u}_1 + 2\mathbf{u}_2, \mathbf{u}_1 + 2\mathbf{u}_2 + 3\mathbf{u}_3, \ldots, \mathbf{u}_1 + 2\mathbf{u}_2 + 3\mathbf{u}_3 + \cdots + n\mathbf{u}_n\}$ in $\mathbb{R}^n$, where the $\mathbf{u}_i$'s are as defined on page 20.

7. DIMENSION

Before defining what is meant by the dimension of a vector space, let us prove the following replacement properties.

1.31. REPLACEMENT PROPERTY OF A BASIS. Let $\{\mathbf{x}_1, \mathbf{x}_2, \ldots, \mathbf{x}_n\}$ be a basis of a vector space V over a field F and let $\mathbf{y}$ be any nonzero vector of V. If we have

(1) $$\mathbf{y} = \sum_{i=1}^{n} a_i\mathbf{x}_i, \qquad a_i \in F,$$

then $a_i \neq 0$ for some i, and if $a_k \neq 0$, then

$$\{\mathbf{x}_1, \ldots, \mathbf{x}_{k-1}, \mathbf{y}, \mathbf{x}_{k+1}, \ldots, \mathbf{x}_n\}$$

is also a basis of V.

Proof: We can solve (1) for $\mathbf{x}_k$, obtaining

$$\mathbf{x}_k = -\frac{1}{a_k}(a_1\mathbf{x}_1 + \cdots + a_{k-1}\mathbf{x}_{k-1} + a_{k+1}\mathbf{x}_{k+1} + \cdots + a_n\mathbf{x}_n - \mathbf{y}).$$

Since $\mathbf{x}_k$ is a linear combination of the other $\mathbf{x}_i$'s and $\mathbf{y}$, every $\mathbf{x}_j$ is a linear combination of the other $\mathbf{x}_i$'s and $\mathbf{y}$. Consequently, we see that

$$V = F\mathbf{x}_1 + \cdots + F\mathbf{x}_{k-1} + F\mathbf{y} + F\mathbf{x}_{k+1} + \cdots + F\mathbf{x}_n.$$

Therefore, we need only show that $\mathbf{x}_1, \ldots, \mathbf{x}_{k-1}, \mathbf{y}, \mathbf{x}_{k+1}, \ldots, \mathbf{x}_n$ are l.i. to prove 1.31. If

(2) $$\sum_{i=1}^{k-1} b_i\mathbf{x}_i + b\mathbf{y} + \sum_{i=k+1}^{n} b_i\mathbf{x}_i = \mathbf{0}$$

for some $b, b_i \in F$ and $b = 0$, then all $b_i = 0$ since $\mathbf{x}_1, \ldots, \mathbf{x}_{k-1}, \mathbf{x}_{k+1}, \ldots, \mathbf{x}_n$ are l.i. If $b \neq 0$, then we can solve (2) for $\mathbf{y}$, obtaining

(3) $$\mathbf{y} = -\frac{1}{b}\left(\sum_{i=1}^{k-1} b_i\mathbf{x}_i + \sum_{i=k+1}^{n} b_i\mathbf{x}_i\right).$$

Now (1) and (3) should be the same, since the representation of $\mathbf{y}$ as a linear combination of $\mathbf{x}_1, \mathbf{x}_2, \ldots, \mathbf{x}_n$ is unique by 1.28. Clearly, (1) and (3) are not the same, for $a_k \neq 0$ in (1), whereas the coefficient of $\mathbf{x}_k$ is 0 in (3). This contradiction shows that $b = 0$, and hence all $b_i = 0$ in (2). Thus $\mathbf{x}_1, \ldots, \mathbf{x}_{k-1}, \mathbf{y}, \mathbf{x}_{k+1}, \ldots, \mathbf{x}_n$ are l.i., and 1.31 is proved.

We can extend the replacement property to several vectors as follows.

1.32. EXTENDED REPLACEMENT PROPERTY OF A BASIS. Let $\{\mathbf{x}_1, \mathbf{x}_2, \ldots, \mathbf{x}_n\}$ be a basis of a vector space V over a field F and let $\mathbf{y}_1, \mathbf{y}_2, \ldots, \mathbf{y}_k$ be any k l.i. vectors of V. Then necessarily $k \leq n$, and V has a basis made up of the k y_i's and $n - k$ of the x_i's.

Proof: If $k = 1$, then 1.32 is simply 1.31. Assume that $1 \leq m < k$ and that there is a basis of V of the form $\{\mathbf{y}_1, \ldots, \mathbf{y}_m, \mathbf{z}_1, \ldots, \mathbf{z}_{n-m}\}$, where $\{\mathbf{z}_1, \ldots, \mathbf{z}_{n-m}\} \subset \{\mathbf{x}_1, \ldots, \mathbf{x}_n\}$. Now $\mathbf{y}_{m+1}$ is a linear combination of this basis,

$$\mathbf{y}_{m+1} = \sum_{i=1}^{m} a_i\mathbf{y}_i + \sum_{i=1}^{n-m} b_i\mathbf{z}_i,$$

with some $a_i \neq 0$ or $b_i \neq 0$. We cannot have all $b_i = 0$, for then some

$a_i \neq 0$ and $F\mathbf{y}_{m+1} \cap (F\mathbf{y}_1 + \cdots + F\mathbf{y}_m) \neq \{\mathbf{0}\}$ contrary to the fact that $\mathbf{y}_1, \ldots, \mathbf{y}_{m+1}$ are l.i. Therefore, by 1.31 we can replace some $\mathbf{z}_i$ by $\mathbf{y}_{m+1}$ to obtain a new basis of V of the form $\{\mathbf{y}_1, \ldots, \mathbf{y}_{m+1}, \mathbf{w}_1, \ldots, \mathbf{w}_{n-m-1}\}$, where $\{\mathbf{w}_1, \ldots, \mathbf{w}_{n-m-1}\} \subset \{\mathbf{x}_1, \ldots, \mathbf{x}_n\}$. Continuing this process of inserting one more $\mathbf{y}_i$ in a basis of V, we eventually find a basis with n elements, k of which are $\mathbf{y}_1, \mathbf{y}_2, \ldots, \mathbf{y}_k$. Consequently, $k \leq n$, and 1.32 is proved.

There are many bases of a vector space V. However, if $\{\mathbf{u}_1, \mathbf{u}_2, \ldots, \mathbf{u}_r\}$ and $\{\mathbf{v}_1, \mathbf{v}_2, \ldots, \mathbf{v}_s\}$ are two bases of V, then by letting the $\mathbf{u}_i$'s be $\mathbf{x}$'s and the $\mathbf{v}_i$'s be $\mathbf{y}$'s in 1.32, we have that $s \leq r$. Interchanging the roles of the $\mathbf{u}_i$'s and $\mathbf{v}_i$'s, we have $r \leq s$. Therefore, we have $r = s$. That is, the number of vectors in a basis of V is an *invariant* of V; in other words, if one basis of V has r elements, then all bases of V have r elements.

1.33. DEFINITION OF DIMENSION. If a vector space V over a field F has n elements in a basis, then n is called the *dimension* of V, and we write

$$\dim V = n.$$

There are vector spaces having an infinite number of elements in a basis, but we shall not consider such spaces in this book.

In view of the extended replacement property, every set of n l.i. vectors of an n-dimensional vector space V is a basis. Also, every set having more than n vectors is dependent. By 1.32, any set of l.i. vectors of V can be extended to a basis of V. The subspace $\{\mathbf{0}\}$ of every vector space is said to have dimension 0.

The vector space E_2 has a basis consisting of two vectors by Example 1, page 25. Therefore, $\dim E_2 = 2$. If $\mathbf{x}_1$, $\mathbf{x}_2$, and $\mathbf{x}_3$ are any three noncoplanar vectors of E_3, then they are l.i. and span E_3. Thus, any $\mathbf{x} \in E_3$ is a linear combination,

$$\mathbf{x} = a\mathbf{x}_1 + b\mathbf{x}_2 + c\mathbf{x}_3,$$

of $\mathbf{x}_1$, $\mathbf{x}_2$, and $\mathbf{x}_3$, as the reader may show. It follows that $\dim E_3 = 3$, as expected.

The vectors $\mathbf{u}_1, \mathbf{u}_2, \ldots, \mathbf{u}_n$ of F^n defined on page 20 are linearly independent and span F^n. Hence, $\{\mathbf{u}_1, \mathbf{u}_2, \ldots, \mathbf{u}_n\}$ is a basis of F^n, and we conclude that

$$\dim F^n = n$$

for each field F and every positive integer n.

EXAMPLE 1: Extend the set $\{(1, -1, 1), (4, 3, -3)\}$ to a basis of $\mathbb{R}^3$.
Solution: The vectors $(1, -1, 1)$ and $(4, 3, -3)$ are l.i., since

$$\mathbb{R}(1, -1, 1) \cap \mathbb{R}(4, 3, -3) = \{\mathbf{0}\}.$$

Therefore, these two vectors together with one more vector form a basis of $\mathbb{R}^3$. We may select this third vector more or less at random, checking only to be sure it is not in $\mathbb{R}(1, -1, 1) + \mathbb{R}(4, 3, -3)$. In particular, we can use at least one of the $\mathbf{u}_i$'s in view of 1.32 and the fact that $\{\mathbf{u}_1, \mathbf{u}_2, \mathbf{u}_3\}$ is a basis of $\mathbb{R}^3$. We cannot use $\mathbf{u}_1 = (1, 0, 0)$, since $\mathbf{u}_1 \in \mathbb{R}(1, -1, 1) + \mathbb{R}(4, 3, -3)$,

$$\mathbf{u}_1 = \tfrac{3}{7}(1, -1, 1) + \tfrac{1}{7}(4, 3, -3).$$

Now $(1, -1, 1), (4, 3, -3), (0, 1, 0)$ are l.i., because

$$a(1, -1, 1) + b(4, 3, -3) + c(0, 1, 0) = (0, 0, 0)$$

if and only if

$$\begin{cases} a + 4b = 0, \\ -a + 3b + c = 0, \\ a - 3b = 0, \end{cases}$$

or $a = b = c = 0$. Therefore, $\{(1, -1, 1), (4, 3, -3), (0, 1, 0)\}$ is a basis of $\mathbb{R}^3$. It may easily be shown that $\{(1, -1, 1), (4, 3, -3), (0, 0, 1)\}$ is also a basis of $\mathbb{R}^3$.

EXAMPLE 2: If $\mathbf{x}_1 = (1, 0, 0, 0)$, $\mathbf{x}_2 = (1, 1, 0, 0)$, $\mathbf{x}_3 = (1, 1, 1, 0)$, $\mathbf{x}_4 = (1, 1, 1, 1)$, then is $\{\mathbf{x}_1, \mathbf{x}_2, \mathbf{x}_3, \mathbf{x}_4\}$ a basis of $\mathbb{R}^4$?

Solution: The only solution of the equation

$$a\mathbf{x}_1 + b\mathbf{x}_2 + c\mathbf{x}_3 + d\mathbf{x}_4 = (0, 0, 0, 0)$$

is easily shown to be $a = b = c = d = 0$. Hence, $\mathbf{x}_1, \mathbf{x}_2, \mathbf{x}_3, \mathbf{x}_4$ are l.i. by 1.29. Since $\dim \mathbb{R}^4 = 4$, every set of four l.i. vectors is a basis. Hence, $\{\mathbf{x}_1, \mathbf{x}_2, \mathbf{x}_3, \mathbf{x}_4\}$ is a basis of $\mathbb{R}^4$.

EXAMPLE 3: Prove that the vectors joining each vertex of a tetrahedron to the centroid of the opposite face meet at a point P. Does P divide each of these vectors in the same ratio? If so, what is the ratio? Point P is called the *centroid* of the tetrahedron. (See Example 3, page 26, for a similar problem.)

Solution: Let $ABCD$ be a tetrahedron (Fig. 1.16), E the centroid of face BCD, F the centroid of face ABD, and P the point of intersection of AE and CF. Then, in E_3 we have

$$\mathbf{CE} = \tfrac{2}{3}\mathbf{CH} = \tfrac{1}{3}(\mathbf{CB} + \mathbf{CD})$$

by Example 3, page 26, and similarly

$$\mathbf{AF} = \tfrac{1}{3}(\mathbf{AB} + \mathbf{AD}).$$

Now we find that

$$\begin{aligned} \mathbf{AE} &= \mathbf{AC} + \mathbf{CE} = \mathbf{AC} + \tfrac{1}{3}(\mathbf{CB} + \mathbf{CD}) \\ &= \mathbf{AC} + \tfrac{1}{3}(\mathbf{CA} + \mathbf{AB} + \mathbf{CA} + \mathbf{AD}) \\ &= \tfrac{1}{3}(\mathbf{AB} + \mathbf{AC} + \mathbf{AD}), \end{aligned}$$

and similarly

$$\mathbf{CF} = \tfrac{1}{3}(\mathbf{CA} + \mathbf{CB} + \mathbf{CD}).$$

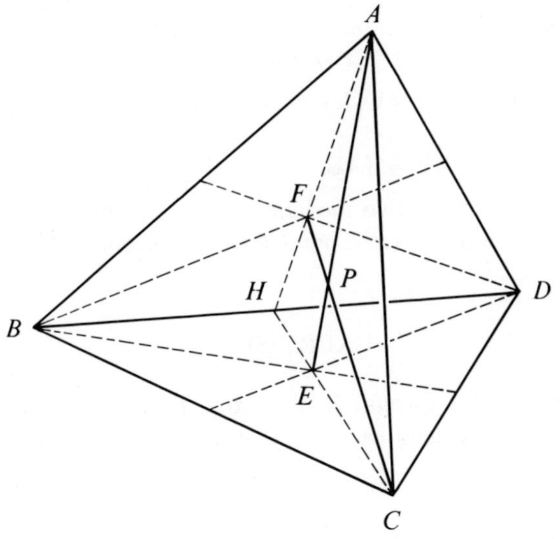

Figure 1.16

Since point P is on AE and CF, we have

$$\mathbf{AP} = r\mathbf{AE}, \qquad \mathbf{CP} = s\mathbf{CF} \qquad \text{for some } r, s \in \mathbb{R}.$$

Hence, we see that

$$\text{(1)} \qquad \mathbf{AP} = \frac{r}{3}\mathbf{AB} + \frac{r}{3}\mathbf{AC} + \frac{r}{3}\mathbf{AD}.$$

Also, we have

$$\begin{aligned}\mathbf{AP} &= \mathbf{AC} + \mathbf{CP}\\ &= \mathbf{AC} + \frac{s}{3}(\mathbf{CA} + \mathbf{CB} + \mathbf{CD})\\ &= \mathbf{AC} + \frac{s}{3}(\mathbf{CA} + \mathbf{CA} + \mathbf{AB} + \mathbf{CA} + \mathbf{AD}),\end{aligned}$$

and

$$\text{(2)} \qquad \mathbf{AP} = \frac{s}{3}\mathbf{AB} + (1 - s)\mathbf{AC} + \frac{s}{3}\mathbf{AD}.$$

The vectors **AB**, **AC**, and **AD** are noncoplanar and therefore form a basis of E_3. Consequently, the two representations of **AP** in (1) and (2) above must coincide; that is,

$$\frac{r}{3} = \frac{s}{3}, \qquad \frac{r}{3} = 1 - s, \qquad \frac{r}{3} = \frac{s}{3}.$$

Hence, we have

$$r = s = \tfrac{3}{4}.$$

This shows that the point P divides each of the segments AE and CF in the same ratio of 3/4:

$$\mathbf{AP} = \tfrac{3}{4}\mathbf{AE}, \qquad \mathbf{CP} = \tfrac{3}{4}\mathbf{CF}.$$

Since AE and CF were any two medians of the tetrahedron, it follows that all four medians meet at the same point P three-fourths of the distance from the vertex to the face.

EXERCISES

In each of Exercises 1 through 8, show that the set of vectors is linearly independent and then extend each set, if necessary, to a basis of the given vector space.

1. $\{(1, 1), (4, -4)\}$ in $\mathbb{R}^2$.
2. $\{(1, 2, 3), (2, 3, 1)\}$ in $\mathbb{R}^3$.
3. $\{(-1, 5, -5), (0, 5, -5), (0, 0, -5)\}$ in $\mathbb{R}^3$.
4. $\{(1, -1, 1, -1), (-1, 1, 1, -1)\}$ in $\mathbb{R}^4$.
5. $\{(1, 0, 0, 0), (1, 0, 1, 0), (1, 0, 0, 1), (1, 1, 1, 1)\}$ in $\mathbb{R}^4$.
6. $\{(1, 1, 0, 0), (1, -1, 0, 0), (1, 0, 1, 0)\}$ in $\mathbb{R}^4$.
7. $\{(1, 0, 0, 0, 1), (0, 1, 0, 1, 0), (0, 0, 1, 0, 0)\}$ in $\mathbb{R}^5$.
8. $\{(1, 0, 1, 0, 1), (0, 1, 0, 1, 0), (1, 0, 0, 1, 0)\}$ in $\mathbb{R}^5$.
9. Describe a one-dimensional vector space.
10. Let V be an n-dimensional space and let S be a subspace, $S \neq \{\mathbf{0}\}$. Prove that $\dim S = k \leq n$, with $\dim S = n$ if and only if $S = V$.
11. Let V be an n-dimensional vector space. Prove that for every subspace S of V there exists a subspace S' such that $S \cap S' = \{\mathbf{0}\}$ and $S + S' = V$. (We call S' a *complement* of S.) Show that S' is not unique if S is a proper subspace.
12. We call $\{\mathbf{x}_1, \mathbf{x}_2, \ldots, \mathbf{x}_k\}$ a set of *generators* of a vector space V if the vectors $\mathbf{x}_1, \mathbf{x}_2, \ldots, \mathbf{x}_k$ span V. Prove that some subset of a set of generators of V is actually a basis of V.

In each of Exercises 13 through 15, show that the set of vectors is a set of generators of the given vector space. Find a subset of the set which is a basis.

13. $\{(1, -1), (-3, 3), (2, 1)\}$ in $\mathbb{R}^2$.
14. $\{(1, 1, 0), (-1, 0, 1), (0, 1, 1), (1, 1, 1)\}$ in $\mathbb{R}^3$.
15. $\{(1, -1, 1, -1), (-1, 1, -1, 1), (2, -1, 2, -1), (-3, 1, -3, 1),$ $(1, 1, -2, -2), (2, 2, -1, -1), (1, -2, -2, 1)\}$ in $\mathbb{R}^4$.
16. If S and T are subspaces of an n-dimensional vector space V, then prove that

$$\dim (S + T) = \dim S + \dim T - \dim (S \cap T).$$

[*Hint:* If $S \cap T \neq \{\mathbf{0}\}$, extend a basis $\{\mathbf{x}_1, \ldots, \mathbf{x}_k\}$ of $S \cap T$ to a basis $\{\mathbf{x}_1, \ldots, \mathbf{x}_k, \mathbf{y}_1, \ldots, \mathbf{y}_m\}$ of S and a basis $\{\mathbf{x}_1, \ldots, \mathbf{x}_k, \mathbf{z}_1, \ldots, \mathbf{z}_t\}$ of T. Show that $\{\mathbf{x}_1, \ldots, \mathbf{x}_k, \mathbf{y}_1, \ldots, \mathbf{y}_m, \mathbf{z}_1, \ldots, \mathbf{z}_t\}$ is a basis of $S + T$. Modify the argument slightly if $S \cap T = \{\mathbf{0}\}$.]

8. ISOMORPHISMS

If A and B are two sets, then the notation

$$A \xrightarrow{f} B$$

will be used to show that f is a *mapping* of set A into set B. Thus, corresponding to each $a \in A$ is a unique element of B, denoted by $f(a)$. In the language of functions, f is a function whose domain is A and whose range is B. The *image* of f is denoted by $\operatorname{im} f$ and defined by

$$\operatorname{im} f = \{f(a) \mid a \in A\}.$$

A mapping $A \xrightarrow{f} B$ is called a 1–1 *mapping* if distinct elements of A are mapped into distinct elements of B; that is, if whenever $x \neq y$ in A, then $f(x) \neq f(y)$ in B.

1.34. DEFINITION OF AN ISOMORPHISM. If V and W are vector spaces over the same field F and $V \xrightarrow{f} W$ is a 1–1 mapping such that $\operatorname{im} f = W$, then f is called an isomorphism iff

(1) $$f(\mathbf{x} + \mathbf{y}) = f(\mathbf{x}) + f(\mathbf{y}) \qquad \text{for all } \mathbf{x}, \mathbf{y} \in V,$$

and

(2) $$f(a\mathbf{x}) = af(\mathbf{x}) \qquad \text{for all } \mathbf{x} \in V,\ a \in F.$$

In words, $V \xrightarrow{f} W$ is an isomorphism iff f is a 1–1 mapping, $\operatorname{im} f = W$, and f preserves addition and scalar multiplication.

If $V \xrightarrow{f} W$ is an isomorphism, then, by 1.34(1), we have

$$f(\mathbf{x}) = f(\mathbf{x} + \mathbf{0}) = f(\mathbf{x}) + f(\mathbf{0}) \qquad \text{for all } \mathbf{x} \in V,$$

and by 1.34(2), letting $a = -1$, we have

$$f(-\mathbf{x}) = -f(\mathbf{x}) \qquad \text{for all } \mathbf{x} \in V.$$

Hence, $f(\mathbf{0})$ is the zero vector of W and $f(-\mathbf{x})$ is the negative of $f(\mathbf{x})$ in W.

We can easily extend 1.34(1) to more than two summands. For example, $f(\mathbf{x} + \mathbf{y} + \mathbf{z}) = f(\mathbf{x} + \mathbf{y}) + f(\mathbf{z}) = f(\mathbf{x}) + f(\mathbf{y}) + f(\mathbf{z})$. By induction, we see that

$$f\left(\sum_{i=1}^{n} \mathbf{x}_i\right) = \sum_{i=1}^{n} f(\mathbf{x}_i)$$

for all $\mathbf{x}_1, \mathbf{x}_2, \ldots, \mathbf{x}_n \in V$. On combining this result with 1.34(2), we obtain

1.35
$$f\left(\sum_{i=1}^{n} a_i\mathbf{x}_i\right) = \sum_{i=1}^{n} a_i f(\mathbf{x}_i)$$

for all $a_i \in F$, $\mathbf{x}_i \in V$.

Two vector spaces V and W are called *isomorphic* if there exists an isomorphism $V \xrightarrow{f} W$ (or $W \xrightarrow{g} V$).

1.36. THEOREM. Two finite-dimensional vector spaces V and W over the same field F are isomorphic iff $\dim V = \dim W$.

Proof: Let $V \xrightarrow{f} W$ be an isomorphism and let $\{\mathbf{x}_1, \mathbf{x}_2, \ldots, \mathbf{x}_n\}$ be a basis of V. Since $\operatorname{im} f = W$, each vector in W has the form $f(\mathbf{y})$ for some $\mathbf{y} \in V$. If we have

$$\mathbf{y} = \sum_{i=1}^{n} a_i\mathbf{x}_i,$$

then

$$f(\mathbf{y}) = \sum_{i=1}^{n} a_i f(\mathbf{x}_i)$$

by 1.35. Therefore, $\{f(\mathbf{x}_1), f(\mathbf{x}_2), \ldots, f(\mathbf{x}_n)\}$ is a set of generators of W. Is it an independent set? To answer this question, suppose that

$$\sum_{i=1}^{n} b_i f(\mathbf{x}_i) = \mathbf{0}.$$

Then, we see that

$$f\left(\sum_{i=1}^{n} b_i\mathbf{x}_i\right) = f(\mathbf{0}), \qquad \text{and} \qquad \sum_{i=1}^{n} b_i\mathbf{x}_i = \mathbf{0},$$

since f is a 1–1 mapping. The vectors $\mathbf{x}_1, \mathbf{x}_2, \ldots, \mathbf{x}_n$ are l.i., and therefore $b_1 = 0, b_2 = 0, \ldots, b_n = 0$ by 1.29. In turn, this proves that the vectors $f(\mathbf{x}_1)$, $f(\mathbf{x}_2), \ldots, f(\mathbf{x}_n)$ are l.i. Consequently, $\{f(\mathbf{x}_1), f(\mathbf{x}_2), \ldots, f(\mathbf{x}_n)\}$ is a basis of W and $\dim V = \dim W$.

Conversely, assume that $\dim V = \dim W = n$, and let $\{\mathbf{u}_1, \mathbf{u}_2, \ldots, \mathbf{u}_n\}$ and $\{\mathbf{v}_1, \mathbf{v}_2, \ldots, \mathbf{v}_n\}$ be bases of V and W, respectively. Define the mapping $V \xrightarrow{f} W$ by

$$f\left(\sum_{i=1}^{n} a_i\mathbf{u}_i\right) = \sum_{i=1}^{n} a_i\mathbf{v}_i \qquad \text{for all } a_i \in F.$$

Thus, by definition, $\operatorname{im} f = W$. If $\mathbf{x}, \mathbf{y} \in V$, then

$$\mathbf{x} = \sum_{i=1}^{n} b_i\mathbf{u}_i, \qquad \mathbf{y} = \sum_{i=1}^{n} c_i\mathbf{u}_i$$

for some $b_i, c_i \in F$. Therefore, we have

$$\mathbf{x} + \mathbf{y} = \sum_{i=1}^{n} (b_i + c_i)\mathbf{u}_i,$$

and

$$f(\mathbf{x} + \mathbf{y}) = \sum_{i=1}^{n} (b_i + c_i)\mathbf{v}_i$$

$$= \sum_{i=1}^{n} b_i\mathbf{v}_i + \sum_{i=1}^{n} c_i\mathbf{v}_i$$

$$= f(\mathbf{x}) + f(\mathbf{y}).$$

Similarly, for every $a \in F$, we have

$$a\mathbf{x} = \sum_{i=1}^{n} ab_i\mathbf{u}_i,$$

and

$$f(a\mathbf{x}) = \sum_{i=1}^{n} ab_i\mathbf{v}_i$$

$$= a\sum_{i=1}^{n} b_i\mathbf{v}_i$$

$$= af(\mathbf{x}).$$

This proves that f preserves addition and scalar multiplication. Whenever $\mathbf{x} \neq \mathbf{y}$, then $b_i \neq c_i$ for some i in the above representations of $\mathbf{x}$ and $\mathbf{y}$, and hence $f(\mathbf{x}) \neq f(\mathbf{y})$. Therefore, f is an isomorphism and 1.36 is proved.

Isomorphic vector spaces are algebraically identical. That is, those properties involving only addition and scalar multiplication are exactly the same in two isomorphic vector spaces. Therefore, two vector spaces having the same dimension are algebraically identical, according to 1.36. In other words, if $\dim V = \dim W$, then the only way we can distinguish between V and W is by the nature of their elements, not by any mathematical means.

In particular, if V is an n-dimensional vector space over a field F, then V is isomorphic to F^n, since F^n is also an n-dimensional vector space over F. If $\{\mathbf{x}_1, \mathbf{x}_2, \ldots, \mathbf{x}_n\}$ is any basis of V and $\{\mathbf{u}_1, \mathbf{u}_2, \ldots, \mathbf{u}_n\}$ is the basis of F^n defined on p. 20, then the mapping $V \xrightarrow{f} F^n$ defined by

$$f\left(\sum_{i=1}^{n} a_i\mathbf{x}_i\right) = \sum_{i=1}^{n} a_i\mathbf{u}_i = (a_1, a_2, \ldots, a_n)$$

is an isomorphism according to the proof of 1.36.

The vector spaces E_2 and $\mathbb{R}^2$ have the same dimension 2 and are over the same field $\mathbb{R}$. Therefore, E_2 and $\mathbb{R}^2$ are isomorphic. Similarly, E_3 and $\mathbb{R}^3$ are isomorphic.

The isomorphism between E_2 and $\mathbb{R}^2$ may be realized as follows. First, select a rectangular coordinate system in the plane. Then the endpoints of each vector have coordinates which uniquely determine the vector. A vector, such as **OC** in Fig. 1.17, which has its initial point at the origin is called a

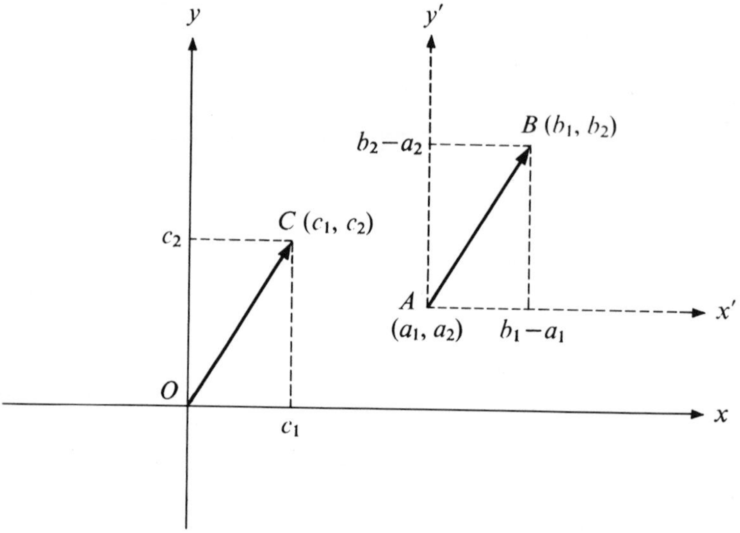

Figure 1.17

position vector. Any other vector **AB** may be compared to a position vector by selecting new x'- and y'-axes having the same direction as the x- and y-axes, respectively, and having A as the new origin (Fig. 1.17). If A, B, and C have respective coordinates (a_1, a_2), (b_1, b_2), and (c_1, c_2), then clearly **AB** = **OC** if and only if $c_1 = b_1 - a_1$ and $c_2 = b_2 - a_2$. In terms of elements of E_2 and $\mathbb{R}^2$,

$$\mathbf{AB} = \mathbf{OC} \quad \text{if and only if} \quad (c_1, c_2) = (b_1 - a_1, b_2 - a_2).$$

Given a vector **AB** whose initial point and terminal point have coordinates (a_1, a_2) and (b_1, b_2), respectively, we shall call the ordered pair of numbers $(b_1 - a_1, b_2 - a_2)$ the *components* of **AB**. The components of a position vector **OC** are simply the coordinates of its endpoint C. It is clear from our discussion above that two vectors of E_2 are equal if and only if they have the same components.

We now have a natural way to map E_2 into $\mathbb{R}^2$;

$$E_2 \xrightarrow{f} \mathbb{R}^2, \quad \text{where } f(\mathbf{x}) = (c_1, c_2), \text{ the components of } \mathbf{x}.$$

If $f(\mathbf{x}) = (a_1, a_2)$ and $f(\mathbf{y}) = (b_1, b_2)$, then we have

$$f(\mathbf{x} + \mathbf{y}) = (a_1 + b_1, a_2 + b_2),$$

because opposite sides of the quadrilateral $OACB$ in Fig. 1.18 have the same

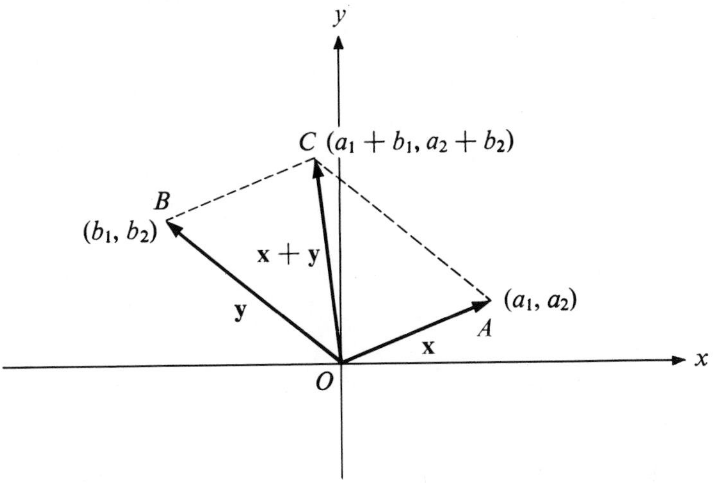

Figure 1.18

components and hence are equal. Since $(a_1 + b_1, a_2 + b_2) = (a_1, a_2) + (b_1, b_2)$ in the vector space $\mathbb{R}^2$, we have proved that

(1) $$f(\mathbf{x} + \mathbf{y}) = (a_1, a_2) + (b_1, b_2) = f(\mathbf{x}) + f(\mathbf{y}).$$

If vector $\mathbf{x}$ has components (a_1, a_2), then vector $r\mathbf{x}$ has components (ra_1, ra_2) for each $r \in \mathbb{R}$. Thus, in Fig. 1.19 we have

$$d(O, A) = \sqrt{a_1^2 + a_2^2}, \qquad d(O, B) = \sqrt{r^2a_1^2 + r^2a_2^2} = |r|\, d(O, A),$$

and the directions of **OA** and **OB** are the same if $r > 0$ and opposite if $r < 0$. Since $(ra_1, ra_2) = r(a_1, a_2)$ in $\mathbb{R}^2$, we have

(2) $$f(r\mathbf{x}) = r(a_1, a_2) = rf(\mathbf{x}).$$

Now (1) and (2) are the two properties of an isomorphism (1.34). Since f is a 1–1 mapping and $\operatorname{im} f = \mathbb{R}^2$, f is actually an isomorphism.

The above arguments for realizing the isomorphism between E_2 and $\mathbb{R}^2$ can be carried over intact to E_3 and $\mathbb{R}^3$. Thus we select a rectangular coordinate system in space, so that each vector **AB** has coordinates (a_1, a_2, a_3) and (b_1, b_2, b_3) for its initial point A and terminal point B, respectively. If we call $(b_1 - a_1, b_2 - a_2, b_3 - a_3)$ the *components* of **AB**, then two vectors of E_3

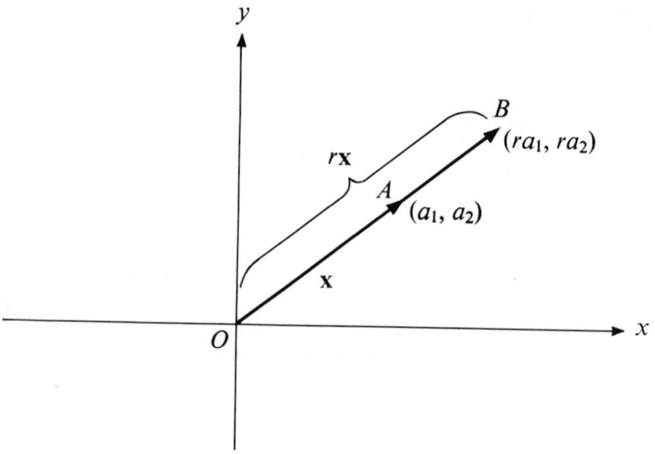

Figure 1.19

are equal if and only if they have the same components. The mapping f defined by

$$E_3 \xrightarrow{f} \mathbb{R}^3, \qquad f(\mathbf{x}) = (c_1, c_2, c_3), \text{ the components of } \mathbf{x},$$

is shown to be an isomorphism in exactly the same way as it was shown above for E_2 and $\mathbb{R}^2$.

The mapping $E_2 \xrightarrow{f} \mathbb{R}^2$ carries the vectors $\mathbf{i}$ and $\mathbf{j}$ of Fig. 1.20 into $\mathbf{u}_1 = (1, 0)$ and $\mathbf{u}_2 = (0, 1)$, respectively, of $\mathbb{R}^2$,

$$f(\mathbf{i}) = \mathbf{u}_1, \qquad f(\mathbf{j}) = \mathbf{u}_2.$$

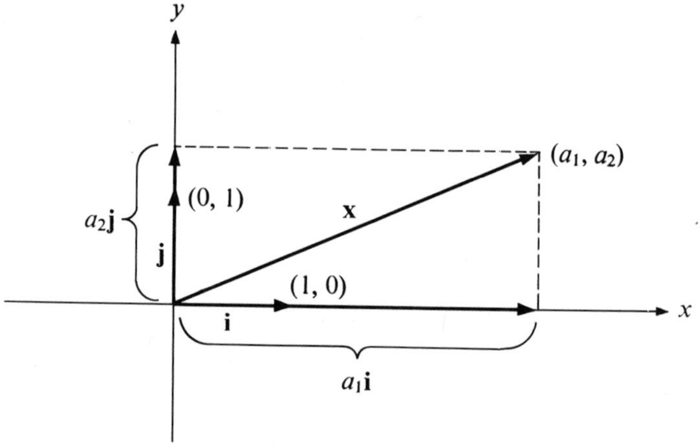

Figure 1.20

For each $\mathbf{x} \in E_2$ with components (a_1, a_2), we have

$$\mathbf{x} = a_1\mathbf{i} + a_2\mathbf{j}, \qquad f(\mathbf{x}) = a_1\mathbf{u}_1 + a_2\mathbf{u}_2,$$

as shown in Fig. 1.20. That is, the isomorphism f carries the basis $\{\mathbf{i}, \mathbf{j}\}$ of E_2 into the basis $\{\mathbf{u}_1, \mathbf{u}_2\}$ of $\mathbb{R}^2$.

Similarly, the mapping $E_3 \xrightarrow{f} \mathbb{R}^3$ carries the vectors $\mathbf{i}$, $\mathbf{j}$, and $\mathbf{k}$ of Fig. 1.21 into the vectors

$$\mathbf{u}_1 = (1, 0, 0), \qquad \mathbf{u}_2 = (0, 1, 0), \qquad \mathbf{u}_3 = (0, 0, 1)$$

of $\mathbb{R}^3$:

$$f(\mathbf{i}) = \mathbf{u}_1, \qquad f(\mathbf{j}) = \mathbf{u}_2, \qquad f(\mathbf{k}) = \mathbf{u}_3.$$

If $\mathbf{x} \in V_3$ has components (a_1, a_2, a_3), then we see that

$$\mathbf{x} = a_1\mathbf{i} + a_2\mathbf{j} + a_3\mathbf{k}, \qquad f(\mathbf{x}) = a_1\mathbf{u}_1 + a_2\mathbf{u}_2 + a_3\mathbf{u}_3,$$

as shown in Fig. 1.21.

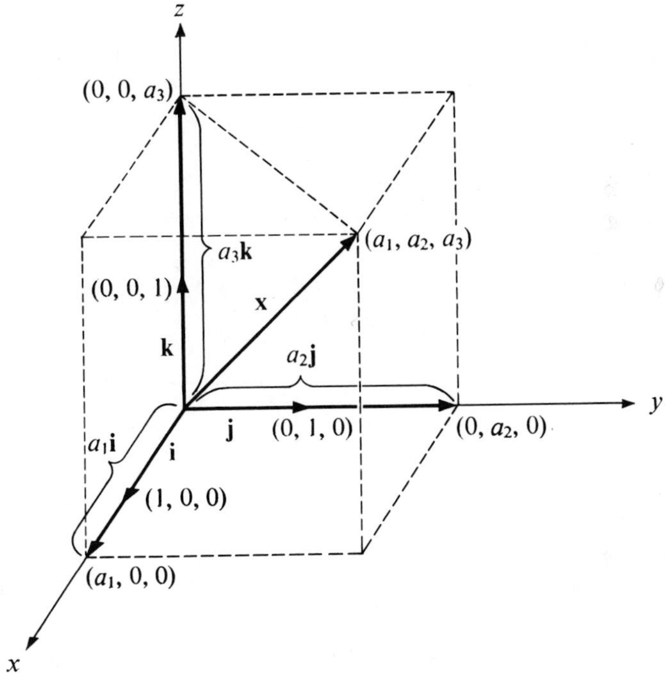

Figure 1.21

EXAMPLE 1: If A and B have respective coordinates $(-1, 3)$ and $(4, -5)$, then express the vector $\mathbf{AB} \in E_2$ in terms of the basis $\{\mathbf{i}, \mathbf{j}\}$.

Solution: Vector $\mathbf{AB}$ has components $(4 - (-1), -5 - 3)$, or $(5, -8)$. Since $(5, -8) = 5\mathbf{u}_1 - 8\mathbf{u}_2$ in $\mathbb{R}^2$, we must have

$$\mathbf{AB} = 5\mathbf{i} - 8\mathbf{j}.$$

EXAMPLE 2: If A and B have respective coordinates $(3, 0, -4)$ and $(7, -7, 5)$, then express the vector $\mathbf{AB} \in E_3$ in terms of the basis $\{\mathbf{i}, \mathbf{j}, \mathbf{k}\}$.

Solution: Vector $\mathbf{AB}$ has components $(7 - 3, -7 - 0, 5 - (-4))$, or $(4, -7, 9)$. Since $(4, -7, 9) = 4\mathbf{u}_1 - 7\mathbf{u}_2 + 9\mathbf{u}_3$ in $\mathbb{R}^3$, we have

$$\mathbf{AB} = 4\mathbf{i} - 7\mathbf{j} + 9\mathbf{k}.$$

EXAMPLE 3: Prove that the three segments joining the midpoints of opposite sides of a tetrahedron have a point in common which bisects each segment.

Solution: Let us select a coordinate system relative to the tetrahedron as shown in Fig. 1.22. Then we have in E_3

$$\mathbf{OA} = a_1\mathbf{i} + a_2\mathbf{j} + a_3\mathbf{k}, \qquad \mathbf{AB} = -a_1\mathbf{i} + (b - a_2)\mathbf{j} - a_3\mathbf{k},$$
$$\mathbf{OC} = c_1\mathbf{i} + c_2\mathbf{j}, \qquad \mathbf{CB} = -c_1\mathbf{i} + (b - c_2)\mathbf{j}.$$

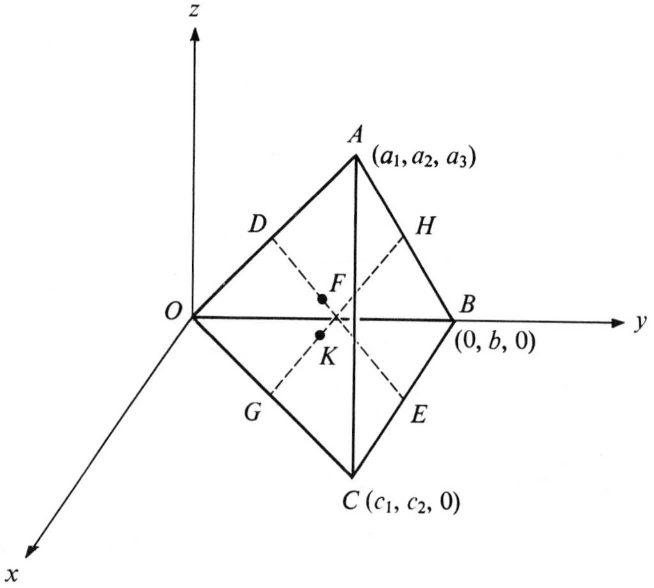

Figure 1.22

Hence, if D is the midpoint of OA and E the midpoint of BC, then we have

$$\mathbf{OD} = \tfrac{1}{2}(a_1\mathbf{i} + a_2\mathbf{j} + a_3\mathbf{k}), \qquad \mathbf{CE} = \tfrac{1}{2}[-c_1\mathbf{i} + (b - c_2)\mathbf{j}],$$
$$\mathbf{DE} = \mathbf{OE} - \mathbf{OD} = \mathbf{OC} + \mathbf{CE} - \mathbf{OD}$$
$$= \tfrac{1}{2}[(c_1 - a_1)\mathbf{i} + (b + c_2 - a_2)\mathbf{j} - a_3\mathbf{k}].$$

If F is the midpoint of DE, then we have

$$\mathbf{OF} = \mathbf{OD} + \mathbf{DF} = \mathbf{OD} + \tfrac{1}{2}\mathbf{DE}$$
$$= \tfrac{1}{4}[(a_1 + c_1)\mathbf{i} + (a_2 + b + c_2)\mathbf{j} + a_3\mathbf{k}].$$

Next, let G be the midpoint of OC and H the midpoint of AB. It may be shown as above that

$$GH = \tfrac{1}{2}[(a_1 - c_1)\mathbf{i} + (a_2 + b - c_2)\mathbf{j} + a_3\mathbf{k}].$$

Therefore, if K is the midpoint of GH, then we see that

$$\begin{aligned}\mathbf{OK} &= \mathbf{OG} + \mathbf{GK} = \tfrac{1}{2}(\mathbf{OC} + \mathbf{GH}) \\ &= \tfrac{1}{4}[(a_1 + c_1)\mathbf{i} + (a_2 + b + c_2)\mathbf{j} + a_3\mathbf{k}].\end{aligned}$$

Since $\mathbf{OF} = \mathbf{OK}$, necessarily $F = K$, and the segments DE and GH intersect at their midpoints. Since DE and GH are any two of the segments joining midpoints of opposite sides, this proves that all three segments meet in a common point of bisection.

EXERCISES

In each of Exercises 1 through 6, express the vector **AB** in terms of the basis $\{\mathbf{i}, \mathbf{j}\}$ or $\{\mathbf{i}, \mathbf{j}, \mathbf{k}\}$, whichever is applicable.

1. $A = (3, -7)$, $B = (0, 5)$ [that is, A has coordinates $(3, -7)$ and B has coordinates $(0, 5)$].
2. $A = (4, -1, 2)$, $B = (7, -3, -3)$.
3. $A = (0, -1)$, $B = (-1, 0)$.
4. $A = (3, -9, -3)$, $B = (4, 2, -8)$.
5. $A = (7, 7, -7)$, $B = (3, -4, 5)$.
6. $A = (1, 9)$, $B = (-7, 3)$.
7. If a triangle has two medians of the same length, then show that the triangle is isosceles. Is the converse also true?
8. If the vector $\mathbf{x} = 2\mathbf{i} - \mathbf{j} + \mathbf{k} \in E_3$ has initial point $(-7, 3, -5)$, then find $a \in \mathbb{R}$ so that the terminal point of the vector $a\mathbf{x}$ lies in the xy-plane. Find $b \in \mathbb{R}$ so that the terminal point of $b\mathbf{x}$ lies in the xz-plane. Find $c \in \mathbb{R}$ so that the terminal point of $c\mathbf{x}$ lies in the yz-plane.
9. If points A and B have respective coordinates (a_1, a_2, a_3) and (b_1, b_2, b_3), then find the coordinates of the point P on the segment AB such that $d(A, P)/d(A, B) = r$, where $0 < r < 1$.
10. Does the line through the two points with coordinates $(2, -1, -3)$ and $(-6, 3, 9)$ pass through the origin?
11. Find conditions under which the line passing through the two points with coordinates (a_1, a_2, a_3) and (b_1, b_2, b_3) also passes through the origin.
12. Prove that an isomorphism $V \xrightarrow{f} W$ maps each subspace of V into a subspace of W. If S is a subspace of W and $T = \{\mathbf{x} \in V \mid f(\mathbf{x}) \in S\}$, then prove that T is a subspace of V.

9. INNER PRODUCTS

Two nonzero vectors **x** and **y** in either E_2 or E_3 have a well-defined least angle θ between them, as indicated in Fig. 1.23. We always have

$$0 \leq \theta \leq \pi,$$

with $\theta = 0$ if $\mathbf{y} = a\mathbf{x}$ for some $a > 0$, and $\theta = \pi$ if $\mathbf{y} = a\mathbf{x}$ for some $a < 0$.

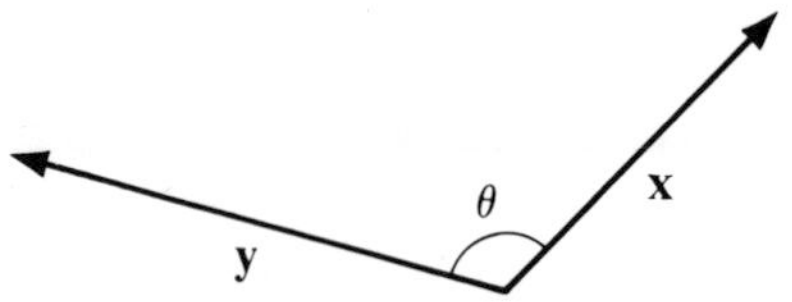

Figure 1.23

A useful operation in either E_2 or E_3 is the *dot product* defined below. If $\mathbf{x}, \mathbf{y} \in E_2$ (or E_3), then the dot product of **x** and **y** is a scalar denoted by $\mathbf{x}\cdot\mathbf{y}$ and defined by

1.37 $$\mathbf{x}\cdot\mathbf{y} = |\mathbf{x}|\,|\mathbf{y}| \cos\theta,$$

where θ is the angle between **x** and **y**. We recall that $|\mathbf{x}|$ denotes the length of vector **x**. The angle θ may be taken to be any angle if $\mathbf{x} = \mathbf{0}$ or $\mathbf{y} = \mathbf{0}$, in which case we have, by 1.37,

$$\mathbf{x}\cdot\mathbf{y} = 0 \quad \text{if} \quad \mathbf{x} = \mathbf{0} \quad \text{or} \quad \mathbf{y} = \mathbf{0}.$$

EXAMPLE 1: If vectors **AB** and **AC** are as given in Fig. 1.24, then find $\mathbf{AB}\cdot\mathbf{AC}$.

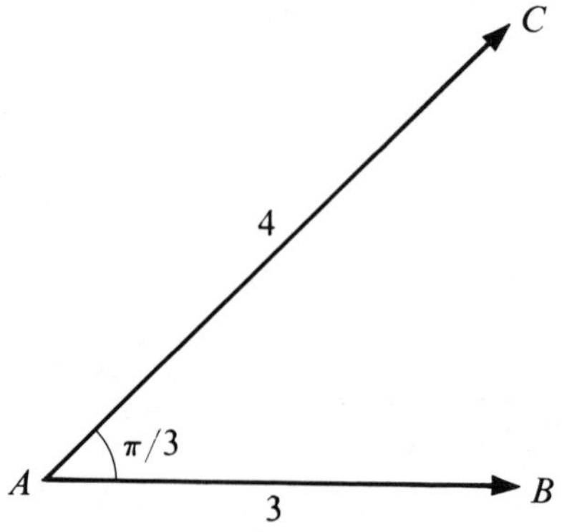

Figure 1.24

Solution: By 3.1, we have

$$\mathbf{AB}\cdot\mathbf{AC} = |\mathbf{AB}|\,|\mathbf{AC}|\cos \pi/3$$
$$= 3\cdot 4\cdot \tfrac{1}{2}, \text{ or } 6.$$

There is only one angle θ between 0 and π for which $\cos\theta = 0$, namely the right angle $\theta = \pi/2$. This fact allows us to state the following result.

1.38. THEOREM. Two nonzero vectors $\mathbf{x}$ and $\mathbf{y}$ in E_2 or E_3 are perpendicular iff $\mathbf{x}\cdot\mathbf{y} = 0$.

An operation such as the dot product, which associates with each pair of vectors $(\mathbf{x}, \mathbf{y})$ a unique scalar $\mathbf{x}\cdot\mathbf{y}$, is called an *inner product* if it has the following properties.

1.39. DEFINITION OF AN INNER PRODUCT. Let V be a vector space over an ordered field F. An operation which associates with each pair of vectors $(\mathbf{x}, \mathbf{y})$ of a vector space V a unique scalar $\mathbf{x}\cdot\mathbf{y}$ is called an inner product iff it has the following properties. For all $\mathbf{x}, \mathbf{y}, \mathbf{z} \in V$, $a \in F$:

(1) $\mathbf{x}\cdot(\mathbf{y}+\mathbf{z}) = \mathbf{x}\cdot\mathbf{y} + \mathbf{x}\cdot\mathbf{z}, \qquad (\mathbf{y}+\mathbf{z})\cdot\mathbf{x} = \mathbf{y}\cdot\mathbf{x} + \mathbf{z}\cdot\mathbf{x}.$

(2) $(a\mathbf{x})\cdot\mathbf{y} = \mathbf{x}\cdot(a\mathbf{y}) = a(\mathbf{x}\cdot\mathbf{y}).$

(3) $\mathbf{x}\cdot\mathbf{y} = \mathbf{y}\cdot\mathbf{x}.$

(4) $\mathbf{x}\cdot\mathbf{x} \geq 0, \quad$ with $\quad \mathbf{x}\cdot\mathbf{x} = 0 \quad$ iff $\quad \mathbf{x} = \mathbf{0}.$

A vector space having an inner product is called an *inner-product space.*

If we let $\mathbf{y} = \mathbf{z} = \mathbf{0}$ in (1) above and use the fact that $0 + \mathbf{x}\cdot\mathbf{0} = \mathbf{x}\cdot\mathbf{0}$, then we get

$$0 + \mathbf{x}\cdot\mathbf{0} = \mathbf{x}\cdot\mathbf{0} = \mathbf{x}\cdot(\mathbf{0}+\mathbf{0}) = \mathbf{x}\cdot\mathbf{0} + \mathbf{x}\cdot\mathbf{0}.$$

Hence, using the cancellation law in F, we get $0 = \mathbf{x}\cdot\mathbf{0}$. We state this property thus:

$$\mathbf{x}\cdot\mathbf{0} = \mathbf{0}\cdot\mathbf{x} = 0 \qquad \text{for all } \mathbf{x} \in V.$$

Using 1.39(1) and (2), we easily show that for all $a_1, a_2, \ldots, a_m, b_1, b_2, \ldots, b_n \in F$, and $\mathbf{x}_1, \mathbf{x}_2, \ldots, \mathbf{x}_m, \mathbf{y}_1, \mathbf{y}_2, \ldots, \mathbf{y}_n \in V$, an inner product space over F,

1.40
$$\left(\sum_{i=1}^{m} a_i\mathbf{x}_i\right)\cdot\left(\sum_{j=1}^{n} b_j\mathbf{y}_j\right) = \sum_{i=1}^{m}\sum_{j=1}^{n} a_ib_j(\mathbf{x}_i\cdot\mathbf{y}_j).$$

We shall presently show that the dot products in E_2 and E_3 defined by 1.37 make them into inner-product spaces. In the meantime, let us give another example of an inner-product space.

Let F be an ordered field (such as $\mathbb{R}$) and n be a positive integer. We define a dot product in F^n as follows:

1.41 $$(a_1, a_2, \ldots, a_n)\cdot(b_1, b_2, \ldots, b_n) = a_1b_1 + a_2b_2 + \cdots + a_nb_n.$$

Thus, the dot product of two vectors of F^n is a scalar in F. If $\mathbf{x}, \mathbf{y}, \mathbf{z} \in F^n$ are given by

$$\mathbf{x} = (a_1, a_2, \ldots, a_n), \qquad \mathbf{y} = (b_1, b_2, \ldots, b_n), \qquad \mathbf{z} = (c_1, c_2, \ldots, c_n),$$

then we have

$$\begin{aligned}(\mathbf{x} + \mathbf{y})\cdot\mathbf{z} &= (a_1 + b_1, a_2 + b_2, \ldots, a_n + b_n)\cdot(c_1, c_2, \ldots, c_n)\\ &= (a_1 + b_1)c_1 + (a_2 + b_2)c_2 + \cdots + (a_n + b_n)c_n\\ &= (a_1c_1 + a_2c_2 + \cdots + a_nc_n) + (b_1c_1 + b_2c_2 + \cdots + b_nc_n)\\ &= \mathbf{x}\cdot\mathbf{z} + \mathbf{y}\cdot\mathbf{z}.\end{aligned}$$

Clearly, we have

$$\mathbf{x}\cdot\mathbf{y} = \mathbf{y}\cdot\mathbf{x} = a_1b_1 + a_2b_2 + \cdots + a_nb_n.$$

Hence, we also see that $\mathbf{z}\cdot(\mathbf{x} + \mathbf{y}) = (\mathbf{x} + \mathbf{y})\cdot\mathbf{z} = \mathbf{x}\cdot\mathbf{z} + \mathbf{y}\cdot\mathbf{z} = \mathbf{z}\cdot\mathbf{x} + \mathbf{z}\cdot\mathbf{y}$. If $a \in F$, then we have

$$\begin{aligned}(a\mathbf{x})\cdot\mathbf{y} &= (aa_1, aa_2, \ldots, aa_n)\cdot(b_1, b_2, \ldots, b_n)\\ &= (aa_1)b_1 + (aa_2)b_2 + \cdots + (aa_n)b_n\\ &= a(a_1b_1 + a_2b_2 + \cdots + a_nb_n)\\ &= a(\mathbf{x}\cdot\mathbf{y}).\end{aligned}$$

A similar proof shows that $\mathbf{x}\cdot(a\mathbf{y}) = a(\mathbf{x}\cdot\mathbf{y})$. Finally, we have

$$\mathbf{x}\cdot\mathbf{x} = a_1^2 + a_2^2 + \cdots + a_n^2 \geq 0$$

by 1.14, with $\mathbf{x}\cdot\mathbf{x} = 0$ iff $\mathbf{x} = 0$. Therefore, we have proved the following result.

1.42. THEOREM. If F is an ordered field, then the vector space F^n with inner product defined by 1.41 is an inner-product space.

A real inner-product space V, that is, a vector space V over the real field $\mathbb{R}$, is often called a *Euclidean space*. We note that in E_2 and E_3, we have

$$\mathbf{x}\cdot\mathbf{x} = |\mathbf{x}|\,|\mathbf{x}| \cos 0 = |\mathbf{x}|^2.$$

This leads us to make the following definition.

1.43. DEFINITION OF LENGTH. The length of each vector $\mathbf{x}$ in a Euclidean space V is denoted by $|\mathbf{x}|$ and defined by

$$|\mathbf{x}| = \sqrt{\mathbf{x}\cdot\mathbf{x}}.$$

By 1.39(4),

$$|\mathbf{x}| = 0 \quad \text{if and only if} \quad \mathbf{x} = \mathbf{0}.$$

By 1.39(2),

$$(a\mathbf{x})\cdot(a\mathbf{x}) = a[\mathbf{x}\cdot(a\mathbf{x})] = a[a(\mathbf{x}\cdot\mathbf{x})] = a^2(\mathbf{x}\cdot\mathbf{x}),$$

and therefore we have

1.44 $$|a\mathbf{x}| = |a|\,|\mathbf{x}| \qquad \text{for all } \mathbf{x} \in V,\ a \in \mathbb{R}.$$

We recall that $\sqrt{a^2} = |a|$, the absolute value of a.

A vector of length 1 is called a *unit vector* or a *normal vector*. Some scalar multiple of every nonzero vector is a unit vector:

$$\text{if} \quad |\mathbf{x}| = b \neq 0, \qquad \text{then} \quad \left|\frac{1}{b}\mathbf{x}\right| = 1$$

by 1.44. The vectors **i**, **j**, and **k** of E_3 are examples of unit vectors.

According to 1.43, the length of a vector in $\mathbb{R}^n$ is given by

$$|(a_1, a_2, \ldots, a_n)| = \sqrt{a_1^2 + a_2^2 + \cdots + a_n^2}.$$

Thus, it is clear that each of the vectors $\mathbf{u}_1, \mathbf{u}_2, \ldots, \mathbf{u}_n$ defined on page 20 is a unit vector. Another unit vector is

$$\left(\frac{e_1}{\sqrt{n}}, \frac{e_2}{\sqrt{n}}, \ldots, \frac{e_n}{\sqrt{n}}\right),$$

where each e_i is either 1 or -1.

A useful property of a Euclidean space is as follows.

1.45. CAUCHY'S INEQUALITY. If V is a Euclidean space, then

$$|\mathbf{x}\cdot\mathbf{y}| \leq |\mathbf{x}|\,|\mathbf{y}| \qquad \text{for all } \mathbf{x}, \mathbf{y} \in V.$$

Proof: We observe that $|\mathbf{x}\cdot\mathbf{y}|$ denotes the absolute value of the scalar $\mathbf{x}\cdot\mathbf{y}$, whereas $|\mathbf{x}|$ and $|\mathbf{y}|$ denote lengths of vectors. If $\mathbf{x} = \mathbf{0}$, then $\mathbf{x}\cdot\mathbf{y} = 0$, and Cauchy's inequality is true $(0 \leq 0)$. So let us assume that $\mathbf{x} \neq \mathbf{0}$. For convenience, let

$$a = \mathbf{x}\cdot\mathbf{x}, \qquad b = \mathbf{x}\cdot\mathbf{y}, \qquad \text{and} \qquad \mathbf{z} = a\mathbf{y} - b\mathbf{x}.$$

Then, by 1.40, we have

$$\begin{aligned}\mathbf{z}\cdot\mathbf{z} &= (a\mathbf{y})\cdot(a\mathbf{y}) - 2(a\mathbf{y})\cdot(b\mathbf{x}) + (b\mathbf{x})\cdot(b\mathbf{x})\\ &= a^2(\mathbf{y}\cdot\mathbf{y}) - 2ab^2 + b^2a\\ &= a[a(\mathbf{y}\cdot\mathbf{y}) - b^2].\end{aligned}$$

Since $\mathbf{z}\cdot\mathbf{z} \geq 0$ and $a > 0$, we have $a(\mathbf{y}\cdot\mathbf{y}) - b^2 \geq 0$ and $b^2 \leq a(\mathbf{y}\cdot\mathbf{y})$, that is,

$$(\mathbf{x}\cdot\mathbf{y})^2 \leq (\mathbf{x}\cdot\mathbf{x})(\mathbf{y}\cdot\mathbf{y}).$$

Taking square roots, we obtain Cauchy's inequality.

We recall that the mappings

$$E_2 \xrightarrow{f} \mathbb{R}^2, f(\mathbf{x}) = (c_1, c_2), \text{ the components of } \mathbf{x},$$

$$E_3 \xrightarrow{f} \mathbb{R}^3, f(\mathbf{x}) = (c_1, c_2, c_3), \text{ the components of } \mathbf{x},$$

are isomorphisms. Let us show that each f preserves dot products, that is, that

1.46 $$\mathbf{x}\cdot\mathbf{y} = f(\mathbf{x})\cdot f(\mathbf{y}) \qquad \text{for all } \mathbf{x}, \mathbf{y} \in E_2 \text{ (or } E_3).$$

The proof of 1.46 for E_2 given below extends almost verbatim to E_3.

Proof of 1.46: If either $\mathbf{x} = \mathbf{0}$ or $\mathbf{y} = \mathbf{0}$, then $\mathbf{x}\cdot\mathbf{y} = f(\mathbf{x})\cdot f(\mathbf{y}) = 0$. If $\mathbf{x} \neq \mathbf{0}$ and $\mathbf{y} \neq \mathbf{0}$, then let $\mathbf{x}$ and $\mathbf{y}$ be position vectors (Fig. 1.25), θ the angle

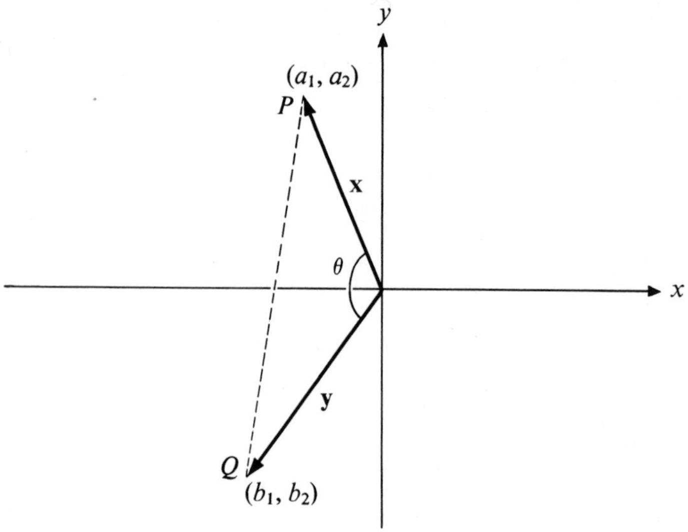

Figure 1.25

between them, and P and Q be the terminal points of $\mathbf{x}$ and $\mathbf{y}$, respectively. By the law of cosines, the distance between P and Q is given by

$$[d(P, Q)]^2 = |\mathbf{x}|^2 + |\mathbf{y}|^2 - 2|\mathbf{x}|\,|\mathbf{y}| \cos\theta.$$

Hence, in view of the definition of the dot product in E_2, we have

$$[d(P, Q)]^2 = |\mathbf{x}|^2 + |\mathbf{y}|^2 - 2(\mathbf{x}\cdot\mathbf{y}).$$

Using the distance formula, we have

$$(a_1 - b_1)^2 + (a_2 - b_2)^2 = (a_1^2 + a_2^2) + (b_1^2 + b_2^2) - 2(\mathbf{x}\cdot\mathbf{y}),$$

which reduces to

$$-2a_1b_1 - 2a_2b_2 = -2(\mathbf{x}\cdot\mathbf{y}),$$

or

$$\mathbf{x}\cdot\mathbf{y} = a_1b_1 + a_2b_2.$$

Since $f(\mathbf{x}) = (a_1, a_2)$, $f(\mathbf{y}) = (b_1, b_2)$, and $f(\mathbf{x})\cdot f(\mathbf{y}) = a_1b_1 + a_2b_2$ by 1.41, we have proved 1.46.

The isomorphism between E_2 and $\mathbb{R}^2$ and between E_3 and $\mathbb{R}^3$ preserves dot products by 1.46. Therefore, since $\mathbb{R}^2$ and $\mathbb{R}^3$ are Euclidean, the dot product in E_2 and E_3 is actually an inner product. This proves the following result.

1.47. THEOREM. The vector spaces E_2 and E_3 are Euclidean.

It is possible to define the angle between any two nonzero vectors of a Euclidean space. Looking at 1.37, which shows the relationship between vectors and their included angle in E_2 and E_3, we are led to the following definition.

1.48. DEFINITION OF ANGLE. If $\mathbf{x}$ and $\mathbf{y}$ are nonzero vectors of a Euclidean space V, then the angle between $\mathbf{x}$ and $\mathbf{y}$ is the unique angle θ such that

$$\cos\theta = \frac{\mathbf{x}\cdot\mathbf{y}}{|\mathbf{x}|\,|\mathbf{y}|}, \qquad 0 \leq \theta \leq \pi.$$

We give some examples below of the use of inner products in E_2 and E_3.

EXAMPLE 2: Under what conditions are the diagonals of a parallelogram perpendicular?

Solution: If $\mathbf{x}$ and $\mathbf{y}$ are the nonparallel sides of the parallelogram, then $\mathbf{x} + \mathbf{y}$ and $\mathbf{x} - \mathbf{y}$ are its diagonals (Fig. 1.26). By 1.38, $\mathbf{x} + \mathbf{y}$ and $\mathbf{x} - \mathbf{y}$ are perpendicular if and only if

$$(\mathbf{x} + \mathbf{y})\cdot(\mathbf{x} - \mathbf{y}) = 0.$$

Since E_2 is Euclidean, we have $\mathbf{x}\cdot\mathbf{y} = \mathbf{y}\cdot\mathbf{x}$, and

$$(\mathbf{x} + \mathbf{y})\cdot(\mathbf{x} - \mathbf{y}) = \mathbf{x}\cdot\mathbf{x} - \mathbf{y}\cdot\mathbf{y}.$$

Hence, $\mathbf{x} + \mathbf{y}$ and $\mathbf{x} - \mathbf{y}$ are perpendicular if and only if $\mathbf{x}\cdot\mathbf{x} = \mathbf{y}\cdot\mathbf{y}$, or

$$|\mathbf{x}| = |\mathbf{y}|,$$

that is, if and only if the parallelogram is equilateral. One instance of an equilateral parallelogram is a square.

EXAMPLE 3: Prove that the line joining the midpoints of opposite sides of a regular tetrahedron is perpendicular to these sides.

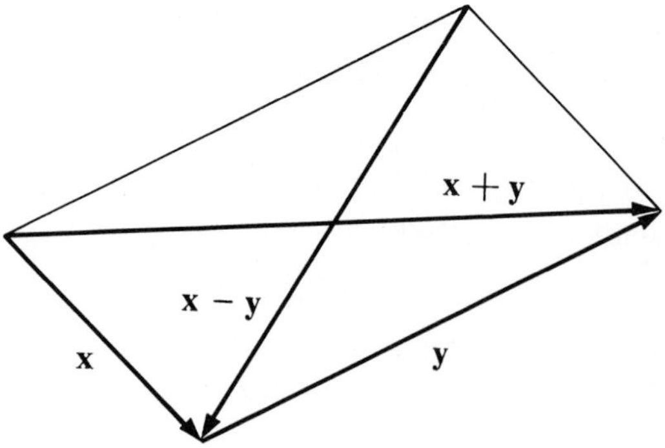

Figure 1.26

Solution: Let A, B, C, and D be the vertices of a regular tetrahedron (Fig. 1.27). Thus, by assumption, each face of the tetrahedron is an equi-

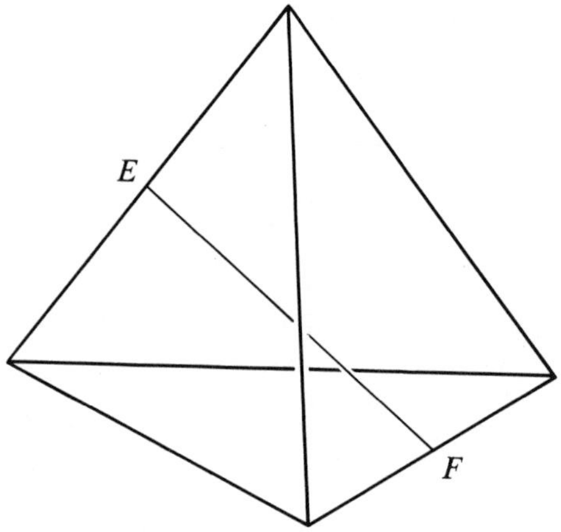

Figure 1.27

lateral triangle. Let E be the midpoint of AB and F the midpoint of CD. We wish to prove that **AB** and **EF** are perpendicular, that is, that

$$\mathbf{AB} \cdot \mathbf{EF} = 0.$$

We leave it as an exercise for you to prove that

$$\mathbf{EF} = \tfrac{1}{2}(\mathbf{AD} + \mathbf{BC})$$

in any tetrahedron. Hence, we see that

$$\mathbf{AB}\cdot\mathbf{EF} = \tfrac{1}{2}(\mathbf{AB}\cdot\mathbf{AD} + \mathbf{AB}\cdot\mathbf{BC})$$
$$= \tfrac{1}{2}(\mathbf{AB}\cdot\mathbf{AD} - \mathbf{BA}\cdot\mathbf{BC}).$$

However, since the angles between **AB** and **AD** and between **BA** and **BC** are equal, and since

$$|\mathbf{AB}| = |\mathbf{AD}| = |\mathbf{BA}| = |\mathbf{BC}|,$$

evidently

$$\mathbf{AB}\cdot\mathbf{AD} = \mathbf{BA}\cdot\mathbf{BC}.$$

Hence $\mathbf{AB}\cdot\mathbf{EF} = 0$, as we wished to show.

EXAMPLE 4: Find the angles of the triangle ABC of Fig. 1.28.

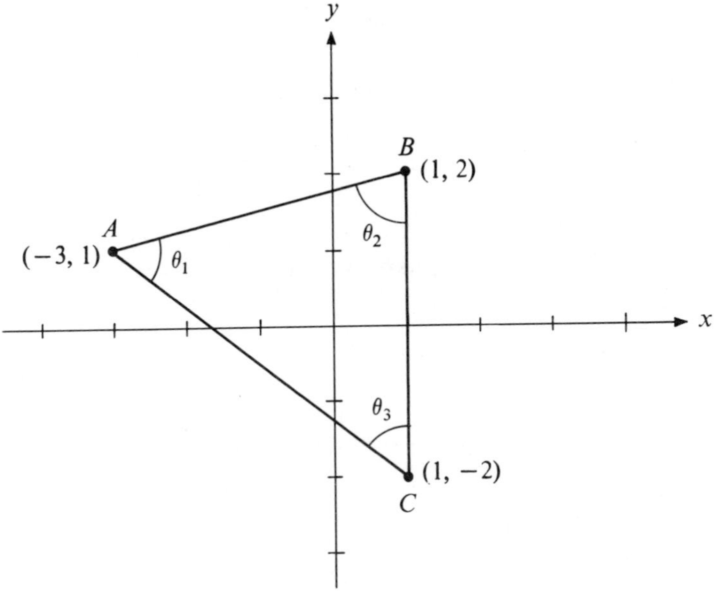

Figure 1.28

Solution: The components of **AB** are $(1 - (-3), 2 - 1)$, and the components of **AC** are $(1 - (-3), -2 - 1)$. Hence, we have

$$\mathbf{AB} = 4\mathbf{i} + \mathbf{j}, \qquad |\mathbf{AB}| = \sqrt{17}, \qquad \mathbf{AC} = 4\mathbf{i} - 3\mathbf{j}, \qquad |\mathbf{AC}| = 5,$$

and by 1.38 and 1.47,

$$\mathbf{AB}\cdot\mathbf{AC} = \sqrt{17}\cdot 5\cdot\cos\theta_1 = (4, 1)\cdot(4, -3) = 4\cdot 4 + 1\cdot(-3) = 13.$$

Therefore, we have

$$\cos\theta_1 = \frac{13}{5\sqrt{17}} = \frac{13}{85}\sqrt{17}, \qquad \text{or} \quad .6306 \text{ approx.}$$

From a table of trigonometric functions, we find that

$$\theta_1 = 50°54' \text{ approx.}$$

Similarly, we have

$$\mathbf{BA} = -4\mathbf{i} - \mathbf{j}, \qquad |\mathbf{BA}| = \sqrt{17}, \qquad \mathbf{BC} = -4\mathbf{j}, \qquad |\mathbf{BC}| = 4,$$

and

$$\mathbf{BA}\cdot\mathbf{BC} = 4\sqrt{17}\cos\theta_2 = (-4, -1)\cdot(0, -4) = 4.$$

Therefore, we see that

$$\cos\theta_2 = \frac{\sqrt{17}}{17} = .2425 \text{ approx.},$$

and

$$\theta_2 = 75°58' \text{ approx.}$$

Finally, we have

$$\mathbf{CB} = 4\mathbf{j}, \qquad \mathbf{CA} = -4\mathbf{i} + 3\mathbf{j},$$

and

$$\mathbf{CB}\cdot\mathbf{CA} = 4\cdot 5\cdot\cos\theta_3 = (0, 4)\cdot(-4, 3) = 12.$$

Hence, we obtain

$$\cos\theta_3 = .6,$$

and

$$\theta_3 = 53°8' \text{ approx.}$$

We check our work by noting that

$$\theta_1 + \theta_2 + \theta_3 = 180.$$

Of course, having found θ_1 and θ_2, we could have obtained θ_3 from the equation above.

The angles of a triangle in space can be found in exactly the same way.

EXERCISES

In each of Exercises 1 through 8, tell whether the points with given coordinates are the vertices of a right triangle.

1. (3, 0, 1), (5, −2, 2), (5, −1, 4).
2. (0, 3), (−2, −12), (−4, 11).
3. (−3, 1), (5, 4), (0, −7).

4. $(1, 1), (-1, -1), (-3, 7)$.
5. $(2, 3, 1), (1, 0, 3), (0, 2, 1)$.
6. $(1, 1, 1), (-1, 2, 2), (3, -5, 4)$.
7. $(2, 5, 1), (-1, -4, -2), (3, -6, 0)$.
8. $(2, 5, -2), (4, 5, -1), (1, 3, 0)$.

In each of Exercises 9 through 12, find a unit vector which is perpendicular to the two given vectors of E_3.

9. $\mathbf{i} - \mathbf{j}, \mathbf{i} + \mathbf{j}$.
10. $\mathbf{i} + 2\mathbf{j} - \mathbf{k}, 3\mathbf{i} - \mathbf{j}$.
11. $\mathbf{i} + \mathbf{j} + \mathbf{k}, \mathbf{i} - \mathbf{j} - \mathbf{k}$.
12. $3\mathbf{i} - \mathbf{j}, \mathbf{j} - 2\mathbf{k}$.

In each of Exercises 13 through 16, find the angles of the triangle whose vertices have the given coordinates.

13. $(5, 7), (-5, -3), (4, 6)$.
14. $(4, 2), (1, 0), (-3, -6)$.
15. $(1, 0, 0), (0, 2, 0), (0, 0, 3)$.
16. $(1, -1, 1), (-1, 1, 1), (1, 1, -1)$.
17. In a regular tetrahedron, prove vectorially that the line drawn from each vertex to the centroid of the opposite base is perpendicular to each median of that base.
18. If A, B, C, and D are the vertices of a regular tetrahedron, then prove that $\mathbf{AB} \cdot \mathbf{CD} = 0$.
19. Interpret Cauchy's inequality in the vector space $\mathbb{R}^n$.
20. Prove that the perpendiculars drawn from the vertices of a triangle to the opposite sides meet in a point.
21. Prove that the perpendicular bisectors of the sides of a triangle meet in a point.
22. Is the converse of Example 3, page 47, true? That is, if the three lines joining the midpoints of opposite sides of a tetrahedron are perpendicular to these sides, is the tetrahedron regular?

Chapter Two

Linear Equations and Matrices

1. LINEAR EQUATIONS

An equation of the form

2.1 $$a_1x_1 + a_2x_2 + \cdots + a_nx_n = b,$$

where $a_1, a_2, \ldots, a_n$ and b are in a field F and $x_1, x_2, \ldots, x_n$ are unknowns, is called a *linear equation* in n unknowns over F. The elements $a_1, a_2, \ldots, a_n$ are called the *coefficients* of the unknowns, and b is called the *constant term* of the equation. A vector $(c_1, c_2, \ldots, c_n)$ in F^n is called a *solution* of 2.1 iff

$$a_1c_1 + a_2c_2 + \cdots + a_nc_n = b$$

is a true equation. The *solution set* S of 2.1 is the set of all solutions of 2.1. Thus, S is a subset of the vector space F^n.

EXAMPLE 1: Consider the linear equation

(1) $$3x - 4y + 5z = 17$$

in three unknowns x, y, and z over the rational field $\mathbb{Q}$. The vector $(3, -2, 0)$ in $\mathbb{Q}^3$ is a solution of (1), since

$$3\cdot 3 - 4\cdot(-2) + 5\cdot 0 = 17$$

is a true equation. On the other hand, $(4, 1, 2)$ is not a solution, because

$$3\cdot 4 - 4\cdot 1 + 5\cdot 2 = 17$$

is a false equation. It is not difficult to show that

$$S = \{(a, b, \tfrac{1}{5}(17 - 3a + 4b)) \mid a, b \in \mathbb{Q}\}$$

is the solution set of (1).

Using the sigma notation, we can write 2.1 in the form

$$\sum_{i=1}^{n} a_i x_i = b.$$

This equation has solutions as long as some $a_i \neq 0$. For example, if $a_1 \neq 0$, then $(b/a_1, 0, 0, \ldots, 0) \in F^n$ is a solution.

An ordered set of linear equations over a field F is called a system of linear equations. Thus,

2.2
$$\begin{aligned} a_{11}x_1 + a_{12}x_2 + \cdots + a_{1n}x_n &= b_1, \\ a_{21}x_1 + a_{22}x_2 + \cdots + a_{2n}x_n &= b_2, \\ \cdot \quad \cdot \quad \cdot \quad \cdot \quad \cdot & \\ \cdot \quad \cdot \quad \cdot \quad \cdot \quad \cdot & \\ a_{m1}x_1 + a_{m2}x_2 + \cdots + a_{mn}x_n &= b_m, \end{aligned} \qquad , a_{ij}, b_i \in F,$$

is called a *system of m linear equations in n unknowns over F*. We have used double subscripts on the coefficients so that we might express system 2.2 in the compact form shown below.

2.3
$$\sum_{j=1}^{n} a_{ij}x_j = b_i, \qquad i = 1, 2, \ldots, m.$$

If S_i is the solution set of the ith equation

$$a_{i1}x_1 + a_{i2}x_2 + \cdots + a_{in}x_n = b_i$$

of 2.2, then

$$S = S_1 \cap S_2 \cap \cdots \cap S_m$$

is the *solution set* of system 2.2. Thus, a vector $(c_1, c_2, \ldots, c_n) \in F^n$ is a solution of 2.2 iff it is a solution of each equation of 2.2.

EXAMPLE 2: Consider the system

(1)
$$\begin{aligned} 3x - 4y + 5z &= 17, \\ -2x + \ y - \ z &= -1 \end{aligned}$$

of two linear equations in three unknowns over the rational field $\mathbb{Q}$. The triple $(3, -2, 0) \in \mathbb{Q}^3$ is not a solution of (1), since one of the equations below,

$$\begin{aligned} 3\cdot 3 - 4\cdot(-2) + 5\cdot 0 &= 17, \\ -2\cdot 3 + (-2) - 0 &= -1, \end{aligned}$$

is false. However, $(-2, -2, 3)$ is a solution because both of the equations below,

$$\begin{aligned} 3\cdot(-2) - 4\cdot(-2) + 5\cdot 3 &= 17, \\ -2\cdot(-2) + (-2) - 3 &= -1, \end{aligned}$$

are true.

Some systems of linear equations are easily solved because of the form of the system, as is illustrated below.

EXAMPLE 3: The following system of three equations in three unknowns,

$$(1)\qquad \begin{aligned} 3x - y + 5z &= -1, \\ y - 2z &= 1, \\ z &= 3, \end{aligned}$$

is said to be in echelon form. It is easily solved as follows. From the third equation of (1), we have $z = 3$. Letting $z = 3$ in the second equation, we obtain $y - 6 = 1$, or $y = 7$. Letting $z = 3$ and $y = 7$ in the first equation, we get $3x - 7 + 15 = -1$, or $x = -3$. Hence,

$$(-3, 7, 3)$$

is the only solution of system (1).

Any system of linear equations in echelon form can be solved similarly. In general, a system of linear equations is said to be in *echelon form* iff the first unknown having a nonzero coefficient in any equation does not appear (that is, has zero coefficient) in any following equation. Thus, according to this definition, the system

$$\begin{aligned} 5x_1 - 7x_2 + 3x_3 - 2x_4 &= 12, \\ x_3 + 6x_4 &= -3, \\ x_4 &= 2, \\ 0 &= 5, \end{aligned}$$

is in echelon form. Its solution set is the empty set $\varnothing$, since the last equation is false.

A common method of solving any system of linear equations is to reduce it to echelon form. A system is said to be *reduced to echelon form* if a system in echelon form is found which has the same solution set as the original system. Methods of reducing a system to echelon form are given below.

Two systems of linear equations in n unknowns over a field F are said to be *equivalent* iff their solution sets are equal. One way to obtain an equivalent system of equations from a given system is by reordering the equations, such as putting the first equation third, etc. If two equations in a system are the same, or have the same solution set, then one can be dropped from the system. Also, a true equation, such as $3 = 3$, can always be dropped from a system.

A system can be reduced to echelon form by repeated use of the following theorem.

2.4. THEOREM. The system of two equations in n unknowns over a field F,

$$\text{(1)} \qquad \begin{aligned} a_{11}x_1 + a_{12}x_2 + \cdots + a_{1n}x_n &= b_1, \\ a_{21}x_1 + a_{22}x_2 + \cdots + a_{2n}x_n &= b_2, \end{aligned}$$

in which $a_{11} \neq 0$ is equivalent to the system

$$\text{(2)} \qquad \begin{aligned} a_{11}x_1 + a_{12}x_2 + \cdots + a_{1n}x_n &= b_1, \\ a'_{22}x_2 + \cdots + a'_{2n}x_n &= b'_2, \end{aligned}$$

in which

$$a'_{2i} = a_{21}a_{1i} - a_{11}a_{2i}, \qquad i = 1, 2, \ldots, n,$$

$$b'_2 = a_{21}b_1 - a_{11}b_2.$$

Proof: The procedure used in going from (1) to (2) above is the familiar one used in elementary algebra of multiplying the first equation by a_{21}, the second equation by $-a_{11}$, and then adding equations so as to eliminate x_1. That is, system (1) has the form

$$\text{(1)} \qquad \begin{aligned} L_1 &= b_1, \\ L_2 &= b_2, \end{aligned}$$

where $L_i = a_{i1}x_1 + a_{i2}x_2 + \cdots + a_{in}x_n$, and system (2) has the form

$$\text{(2)} \qquad \begin{aligned} L_1 &= b_1, \\ a_{21}L_1 - a_{11}L_2 &= a_{21}b_1 - a_{11}b_2. \end{aligned}$$

If values are given to the unknowns $x_1, x_2, \ldots, x_n$ so that both equations of (1) are true, then $a_{21}L_1 = a_{21}b_1$, $-a_{11}L_2 = -a_{11}b_2$, and $a_{21}L_1 - a_{11}L_2 = a_{21}b_1 - a_{11}b_2$ are true equations. Thus, every solution of system (1) is also a solution of system (2).

Conversely, if values are given to the unknowns which make both equations of system (2) true, then $a_{21}L_1 = a_{21}b_1$ is also true. Hence, $a_{21}L_1 - (a_{21}L_1 - a_{11}L_2) = a_{21}b_1 - (a_{21}b_1 - a_{11}b_2)$ or $a_{11}L_2 = a_{11}b_2$ is also true, as is $a_{11}^{-1}(a_{11}L_2) = a_{11}^{-1}(a_{11}b_2)$ or $L_2 = b_2$. Thus, every solution of (2) is also a solution of (1). We conclude that systems (1) and (2) are equivalent. This proves 2.4.

We can reduce any system of linear equations to echelon form by a repeated use of 2.4 on pairs of equations of the system. In the first place, we can eliminate the first unknown (that is, x_1) from all except one of the equations. Next, we can eliminate a second unknown from all except one of the equations not containing the first unknown; and so on. This method is illustrated below with systems over the rational field $\mathbb{Q}$.

EXAMPLE 4: Reduce the system below to echelon form and then solve it.

$$\text{(1)} \qquad \begin{aligned} 2x + 3y &= 7, \\ 4x - y &= 5. \end{aligned}$$

Solution: We multiply the first equation by 2, the second by -1, and add the resulting equations to obtain the equivalent system

$$\text{(2)} \qquad \begin{aligned} 2x + 3y &= 7, \\ 7y &= 9. \end{aligned}$$

The only solution of (2) is $y = 9/7$ and $x = 11/7$. Therefore, $(11/7, 9/7)$ is the only solution of (1).

EXAMPLE 5: Reduce the system below to echelon form and then solve it.

$$\text{(1)} \qquad \begin{aligned} 3x - 5y + z &= 2, \\ 2x + y - 3z &= -4, \\ 7x - 3y - 5z &= 1. \end{aligned}$$

Solution: Letting E_1 denote the first equation, E_2 the second, and E_3 the third, let us form an equivalent system (2) from system (1) as indicated below.

$$\text{(2)} \qquad \begin{aligned} 3x - 5y + z &= 2 && (E_1), \\ -13y + 11z &= 16 && (2E_1 - 3E_2), \\ -26y + 22z &= 11 && (7E_1 - 3E_3). \end{aligned}$$

In turn, denoting the equations of system (2) by E_1', E_2', and E_3', we obtain an equivalent system (3) from system (2) as indicated below.

$$\text{(3)} \qquad \begin{aligned} 3x - 5y + z &= 2 && (E_1'), \\ -13y + 11z &= 16 && (E_2'), \\ 0 &= 21 && (2E_2' - E_3'). \end{aligned}$$

System (3) is an echelon form of system (1). Since the third equation of system (3) is false, the solution set of (3), and hence also of the given system (1), is the empty set $\varnothing$.

EXAMPLE 6: Reduce the system below to echelon form and then solve it.

$$\text{(1)} \qquad \begin{aligned} x_1 - 2x_2 + 2x_3 - x_4 &= -14, \\ 3x_1 + 2x_2 - x_3 + 2x_4 &= 17, \\ 2x_1 + 3x_2 - x_3 - x_4 &= 18, \\ -2x_1 + 5x_2 - 3x_3 - 3x_4 &= 26. \end{aligned}$$

Solution: Denoting the equations of (1) by E_1 through E_4, we obtain an equivalent system (2) as indicated below.

$$\text{(2)} \qquad \begin{aligned} x_1 - 2x_2 + 2x_3 - x_4 &= -14 && (E_1), \\ -8x_2 + 7x_3 - 5x_4 &= -59 && (3E_1 - E_2), \\ -7x_2 + 5x_3 - x_4 &= -46 && (2E_1 - E_3), \\ x_2 + x_3 - 5x_4 &= -2 && (2E_1 + E_4). \end{aligned}$$

Next, denoting the equations of (2) by E_1' through E_4', we obtain an equivalent system (3) as indicated below.

$$
(3)\qquad
\begin{aligned}
x_1 - 2x_2 + 2x_3 - x_4 &= -14 && (E_1'),\\
x_2 + x_3 - 5x_4 &= -2 && (E_4'),\\
15x_3 - 45x_4 &= -75 && (8E_4' + E_2'),\\
12x_3 - 36x_4 &= -60 && (7E_4' + E_3').
\end{aligned}
$$

The third and fourth equations of (3) are equivalent, each being equivalent to $x_3 - 3x_4 = -5$. Thus, system (3) is equivalent to the following system of three equations in four unknowns.

$$
(4)\qquad
\begin{aligned}
x_1 - 2x_2 + 2x_3 - x_4 &= -14,\\
x_2 + x_3 - 5x_4 &= -2,\\
x_3 - 3x_4 &= -5.
\end{aligned}
$$

System (4) is in echelon form and is equivalent to the given system (1).

To solve system (4), we let $x_4 = t$, any element of the field $\mathbb{Q}$. Then $x_3 = 3t - 5$ from the third equation of (4), and

$$x_2 + (3t - 5) - 5t = -2, \qquad \text{and} \qquad x_2 = 2t + 3,$$

$$x_1 - 2(2t + 3) + 2(3t - 5) - t = -14, \qquad \text{and} \qquad x_1 = -t + 2,$$

from the second and first equations of (4). Therefore,

$$\{(-t + 2, 2t + 3, 3t - 5, t) \mid t \in \mathbb{Q}\}$$

is the solution set of the given system.

EXERCISES

Solve each of the following systems of linear equations over $\mathbb{Q}$ by reducing it to echelon form (if it isn't already in echelon form).

1. $2x - 4y = 7.$

2. $\begin{aligned} x &= 2,\\ y &= 3. \end{aligned}$

3. $\begin{aligned} x + y &= 5,\\ y &= 1. \end{aligned}$

4. $\begin{aligned} 2x - y &= 4,\\ 4x - 2y &= 2. \end{aligned}$

5. $3x - 4y + 5z = 17.$

6. $\begin{aligned} 3x - 4y + 5z &= 17,\\ -2x + y - z &= -1. \end{aligned}$

7. $\begin{aligned} 2x_1 - 5x_2 &= 3,\\ x_1 - 3x_2 &= -1. \end{aligned}$

8. $\begin{aligned} x_1 + x_2 - x_3 &= 7,\\ -x_1 + 2x_2 + 3x_3 &= -2,\\ 2x_1 - x_2 - 2x_3 &= -1. \end{aligned}$

9. $$\begin{aligned} x + y + 5z &= 4,\\ 3x - z &= 7,\\ -5x + 4y + 23z &= -5. \end{aligned}$$

10. $$\begin{aligned} 3x - y + 4z &= -1,\\ x + 2y + 5z &= 4,\\ 3x - 8y - 7z &= 5. \end{aligned}$$

11. $$\begin{aligned} 2x_1 + 9x_2 + 3x_3 - x_4 &= 18,\\ 3x_1 + 13x_2 - x_3 + 2x_4 &= 5,\\ 2x_1 - 3x_3 &= -6,\\ 3x_3 - 2x_4 &= 12. \end{aligned}$$

12. $$\begin{aligned} x_1 + 3x_3 &= 1,\\ 2x_2 + x_4 &= 1,\\ 3x_3 + x_4 &= -2,\\ x_2 + 2x_3 &= 5,\\ 2x_1 - x_4 &= 1. \end{aligned}$$

2. MATRICES ASSOCIATED WITH A SYSTEM OF LINEAR EQUATIONS

Each system of m linear equations in n unknowns over a field F, such as

2.3 $$\sum_{j=1}^{n} a_{ij}x_j = b_i, \qquad i = 1, 2, \ldots, m,$$

has associated with it two rectangular arrays of elements of F,

2.5 $$A = \begin{pmatrix} a_{11} & a_{12} & \ldots & a_{1n} \\ a_{21} & a_{22} & \ldots & a_{2n} \\ & & \cdots\cdots & \\ & & \cdots\cdots & \\ a_{m1} & a_{m2} & \ldots & a_{mn} \end{pmatrix},$$

and

2.6 $$\text{aug } A = \begin{pmatrix} a_{11} & a_{12} & \ldots & a_{1n} & b_1 \\ a_{21} & a_{22} & \ldots & a_{2n} & b_2 \\ & & \cdots\cdots & & \\ & & \cdots\cdots & & \\ a_{m1} & a_{m2} & \ldots & a_{mn} & b_m \end{pmatrix}$$

We call A the *matrix of coefficients* and aug A the *augmented matrix* of system 2.3. We see that aug A is the matrix of coefficients of 2.3 augmented by the column of constant terms.

Matrix A in 2.5 is made up of m rows and n columns. The ith row of A is an n-tuple denoted by A_i,

$$A_i = (a_{i1}, a_{i2}, \ldots, a_{in}), \qquad i = 1, 2, \ldots, m,$$

and the jth column of A is an m-tuple denoted by A^j,

$$A^j = \begin{pmatrix} a_{1j} \\ a_{2j} \\ \cdot \\ \cdot \\ \cdot \\ a_{mj} \end{pmatrix}, \qquad j = 1, 2, \ldots, n.$$

EXAMPLE 1: Consider the following system of three equations in four unknowns over the rational field $\mathbb{Q}$.

$$\begin{aligned} 3x_1 + 2x_2 + 2x_3 + 2x_4 &= 27, \\ 3x_2 + 2x_3 - 8x_4 &= 20, \\ 4x_1 + x_2 \qquad\qquad + 4x_4 &= 14. \end{aligned} \tag{1}$$

The matrix of coefficients of system (1) is:

$$A = \begin{pmatrix} 3 & 2 & 2 & 2 \\ 0 & 3 & 2 & -8 \\ 4 & 1 & 0 & 4 \end{pmatrix}.$$

We call A a 3×4 matrix to indicate that it has three rows and four columns. The augmented matrix of system (1) is

$$\text{aug } A = \begin{pmatrix} 3 & 2 & 2 & 2 & 27 \\ 0 & 3 & 2 & -8 & 20 \\ 4 & 1 & 0 & 4 & 14 \end{pmatrix}.$$

We see that aug A consists of three rows and five columns and is therefore a 3×5 matrix.

The process of changing a system of linear equations into echelon form can be effected by putting its augmented matrix into echelon form. A matrix is said to be in *echelon form* if successive rows of the matrix start out with more and more zeros.

For example, the following 4×4 matrix with elements from $\mathbb{Q}$ is in echelon form.

$$B = \begin{pmatrix} 2 & 0 & -4 & 3 \\ 0 & 5 & 0 & -2 \\ 0 & 0 & 0 & 3 \\ 0 & 0 & 0 & 0 \end{pmatrix}.$$

Thus, the first row of B starts out with no zeros, the second row with one zero, the third row with three zeros, and the fourth row with four zeros.

If a matrix is the augmented matrix of a system of linear equations, then we can solve the system by changing the matrix into echelon form by use of certain operations on the rows of the matrix. One operation we shall allow is that of interchanging rows of the matrix. This corresponds to the operation of interchanging equations of the system. The other allowable operation on the rows of a matrix is that corresponding to Theorem 2.4 for systems of equations. Thus, we may replace any row by the sum of a nonzero scalar multiple of itself and a scalar multiple of another row. In symbols, we may replace the ith row A_i by $cA_i + dA_j$, where A_j is the jth row, $i \neq j$, and $c, d \in F$ with $c \neq 0$.

Let us change aug A of Example 1 into echelon form by these operations.

$$\text{aug } A = \begin{pmatrix} 3 & 2 & 2 & 2 & 27 \\ 0 & 3 & 2 & -8 & 20 \\ 4 & 1 & 0 & 4 & 14 \end{pmatrix} \quad \begin{matrix} (A_1) \\ (A_2) \\ (A_3), \end{matrix}$$

$$B = \begin{pmatrix} 3 & 2 & 2 & 2 & 27 \\ 0 & 3 & 2 & -8 & 20 \\ 0 & 5 & 8 & -4 & 66 \end{pmatrix} \quad \begin{matrix} (B_1 = A_1) \\ (B_2 = A_2) \\ (B_3 = -3A_3 + 4A_1), \end{matrix}$$

$$C = \begin{pmatrix} 3 & 2 & 2 & 2 & 27 \\ 0 & 3 & 2 & -8 & 20 \\ 0 & 0 & 14 & 28 & 98 \end{pmatrix} \quad \begin{matrix} (C_1 = B_1) \\ (C_2 = B_2) \\ (C_3 = 3B_3 - 5B_2). \end{matrix}$$

Matrix C is an echelon form of aug A.

We can use the echelon form C of aug A to solve the system of Example 1. Thus, from the third row of C, we have

$$14x_3 + 28x_4 = 98,$$

or, equivalently,

$$x_3 + 2x_4 = 7.$$

Letting $x_4 = t$, any rational number, we have

$$x_3 = 7 - 2t.$$

From the second row of C, we have

$$3x_2 + 2x_3 - 8x_4 = 20.$$

Letting $x_4 = t$ and $x_3 = 7 - 2t$, we obtain

$$3x_2 + 2(7 - 2t) - 8t = 20, \qquad \text{or} \qquad x_2 = 2 + 4t.$$

From the first row of C, we have

$$3x_1 + 2x_2 + 2x_3 + 2x_4 = 27.$$

On substituting $x_2 = 2 + 4t$, $x_3 = 7 - 2t$, and $x_4 = t$, we get

$$3x_1 + 2(2 + 4t) + 2(7 - 2t) + 2t = 27, \qquad \text{or} \qquad x_1 = 3 - 2t.$$

Therefore, the solution set of the system is

$$\{(3 - 2t, 2 + 4t, 7 - 2t, t) \mid t \in \mathbb{Q}\}.$$

EXERCISES

Find the matrix of coefficients and augmented matrix for each of the following systems of linear equations over $\mathbb{Q}$. Solve each system by reducing the augmented matrix to echelon form.

1. $$\begin{aligned} 3x - y &= 5, \\ x - 2y &= -5. \end{aligned}$$

2. $$\begin{aligned} x + 3y &= 1, \\ 3x + 9y &= 3. \end{aligned}$$

3. $$\begin{aligned} x + 2y + z &= 0, \\ 2x + 3y + z &= -1, \\ x - z &= -2. \end{aligned}$$

4. $$\begin{aligned} x_1 - x_2 - x_3 &= 1, \\ x_1 + x_3 &= -1, \\ x_2 + 2x_3 &= -2. \end{aligned}$$

5. $$\begin{aligned} x_1 + x_2 - x_3 - x_4 &= 7, \\ 2x_1 - x_2 + 3x_3 + x_4 &= 1, \\ x_1 - 5x_2 + 9x_3 - x_4 &= 3. \end{aligned}$$

6. $$\begin{aligned} 2x_1 + x_2 + x_3 + x_4 &= -3, \\ x_1 - x_2 + x_3 - x_4 &= 2, \\ 3x_1 + 2x_2 + 2x_3 + x_4 &= 3, \\ 4x_1 + x_2 - x_3 - x_4 &= -5. \end{aligned}$$

7. $$\begin{aligned} x_1 - x_2 + x_3 &= -4, \\ x_2 + x_3 - x_4 &= 5, \\ 2x_1 + x_3 - 4x_4 &= 1. \end{aligned}$$

8. $$\begin{aligned} x_1 - 2x_3 &= -5, \\ -x_2 + x_4 &= -5, \\ 2x_3 + x_4 &= 2, \\ x_1 + 2x_2 &= 1, \\ 3x_2 + 2x_3 &= 5. \end{aligned}$$

3. ROW RANK AND COLUMN RANK OF A MATRIX

An $m \times n$ matrix A over a field F has the form

$$A = \begin{pmatrix} a_{11} & a_{12} & \cdots & a_{1n} \\ a_{21} & a_{22} & \cdots & a_{2n} \\ & & \cdots\cdots & \\ & & \cdots\cdots & \\ a_{m1} & a_{m2} & \cdots & a_{mn} \end{pmatrix},$$

where $a_{ij} \in F$ is in the ith row and jth column of A. Often, we shall abbreviate the matrix above by writing

$$A = (a_{ij}).$$

The rows of A are the vector n-tuples $A_1, A_2, \ldots, A_m$, where

$$A_i = (a_{i1}, a_{i2}, \ldots, a_{in}), \qquad i = 1, 2, \ldots, m.$$

The columns of A are the vector m-tuples $A^1, A^2, \ldots, A^n$, where

$$A^j = \begin{pmatrix} a_{1j} \\ a_{2j} \\ \cdot \\ \cdot \\ \cdot \\ a_{mj} \end{pmatrix}, \qquad j = 1, 2, \ldots, n.$$

The rows $A_1, A_2, \ldots, A_m$ of an $m \times n$ matrix $A = (a_{ij})$ over a field F are elements of the vector space F^n. As such, they generate a subspace V of F^n:

$$V = FA_1 + FA_2 + \cdots + FA_m.$$

Thus, each $\mathbf{v} \in V$ has the form

$$\mathbf{v} = \sum_{i=1}^{m} c_i A_i$$

for some $c_i \in F$. We call V the *row space* of matrix A. The dimension of V is called the *row rank* of A and is denoted by $\text{rr}(A)$:

$$\text{rr}(A) = \dim V.$$

Since $\dim F^n = n$, $\text{rr}(A) \leq n$; and since V is generated by m vectors, $\text{rr}(A) \leq m$. That is, if A is an $m \times n$ matrix, then we see that

2.7 $$\text{rr}(A) \leq \min\,(m, n).$$

In a similar way, the columns $A^1, A^2, \ldots, A^n$ of an $m \times n$ matrix $A = (a_{ij})$ over a field F are elements of the vector space F'^m. We have put a prime on F'^m to indicate that the m-tuples are written as column vectors. The subspace W of F'^m generated by the column vectors of A is called the *column space* of matrix A:

$$W = FA^1 + FA^2 + \cdots + FA^n.$$

As expected, the *column rank* of A is denoted by $\text{cr}(A)$ and is defined by

$$\text{cr}(A) = \dim W.$$

Again, if A is an $m \times n$ matrix, then we have

$$\text{cr}(A) \leq \min\,(m, n).$$

If A and B are $m \times n$ matrices over a field F, and if B has the same rows as A, but possibly in a different order, then $\text{rr}(A) = \text{rr}(B)$, since A and B have the same row space. It is also true that $\text{cr}(A) = \text{cr}(B)$, although the column spaces W_1 of A and W_2 of B might be different. This is so because the column vectors of B have the same elements as the column vectors of A, although possibly written in a different order. Therefore, if a linear combination of the column vectors of A is zero, the same linear combination of the column vectors of B is zero, and vice versa. This means that the mapping

$$W_1 \xrightarrow{f} W_2, \qquad f\left(\sum_{i=1}^{n} c_i A^i\right) = \sum_{i=1}^{n} c_i B^i$$

is an isomorphism. Hence, we see that $\operatorname{cr}(A) = \operatorname{cr}(B)$.

A similar argument shows that if matrix B has the same columns as A, although possibly in a different order, then $\operatorname{cr}(A) = \operatorname{cr}(B)$ and $\operatorname{rr}(A) = \operatorname{rr}(B)$. Let us now prove the following basic theorem.

2.8. THEOREM. If $A = (a_{ij})$ is an $m \times n$ matrix over a field F, then $\operatorname{rr}(A) = \operatorname{cr}(A)$.

Proof: As usual, let $A_1, A_2, \ldots, A_m$ be the row vectors and $A^1, A^2, \ldots, A^n$ be the column vectors of A. Also, let

$$\operatorname{rr}(A) = k.$$

We might as well assume that $\{A_1, A_2, \ldots, A_k\}$ forms a basis of the row space V of A. For otherwise, we could rearrange the rows of A to obtain another $m \times n$ matrix whose first k rows do form a basis of V. We can see from our remarks above that the new matrix would have the same row and column ranks as A. Let

$$B = \begin{pmatrix} a_{11} & a_{12} & \ldots & a_{1n} \\ a_{21} & a_{22} & \ldots & a_{2n} \\ & & \ldots\ldots & \\ & & \ldots\ldots & \\ a_{k1} & a_{k2} & \ldots & a_{kn} \end{pmatrix}$$

be a $k \times n$ matrix. By assumption, we have

$$\operatorname{rr}(B) = \operatorname{rr}(A) = k.$$

If a set of column vectors of B is independent, then the corresponding set of column vectors of A is also independent. Hence, $\operatorname{cr}(B) \leq \operatorname{cr}(A)$. Actually, $\operatorname{cr}(B) = \operatorname{cr}(A)$, as we shall prove below.

Let $B^1, B^2, \ldots, B^n$ be the column vectors of B, and choose $c_j \in F$ so that

$$\sum_{j=1}^{n} c_j B^j = \mathbf{0}. \tag{1}$$

Then we have

$$\sum_{j=1}^{n} c_j a_{ij} = 0, \qquad i = 1, 2, \ldots, k.$$

Since $\{A_1, A_2, \ldots, A_k\}$ is a basis of V, there exist $d_{li} \in F$ such that

$$A_l = \sum_{i=1}^{k} d_{li} A_i, \qquad l = k+1, \ldots, m.$$

Hence, we have

$$a_{lj} = \sum_{i=1}^{k} d_{li} a_{ij}, \qquad j = 1, 2, \ldots, n, \qquad l = k+1, \ldots, m.$$

Thus, for each $l > k$, we have

$$\begin{aligned}\sum_{j=1}^{n} c_j a_{lj} &= \sum_{j=1}^{n} c_j \sum_{i=1}^{k} d_{li} a_{ij} \\ &= \sum_{i=1}^{k} d_{li} \sum_{j=1}^{n} c_j a_{ij} \\ &= \sum_{i=1}^{k} d_{li} \cdot 0 = 0.\end{aligned}$$

Therefore, we obtain

$$\sum_{j=1}^{n} c_j a_{ij} = 0, \qquad i = 1, 2, \ldots, m,$$

and we have

(2) $$\sum_{j=1}^{n} c_j A^j = \mathbf{0}.$$

We have proved that whenever (1) is true, then (2) is also true. Therefore, we see that $\text{cr}(B) \geq \text{cr}(A)$. Since we have already stated that $\text{cr}(B) \leq \text{cr}(A)$, we must have $\text{cr}(B) = \text{cr}(A)$. However, $\text{cr}(B) \leq \min(k, n) \leq k$, and therefore we have that

$$\text{cr}(A) \leq \text{rr}(A).$$

Had we started with the column vectors of A and proceeded in the same way as above, replacing columns by rows and rows by columns in our argument, we would have proved that

$$\text{rr}(A) \leq \text{cr}(A).$$

Therefore, $\text{rr}(A) = \text{cr}(A)$, and the theorem is proved.

In view of Theorem 2.8, we may make the following definition.

2.9. DEFINITION OF THE RANK OF A MATRIX. The rank of an $m \times n$ matrix A over a field F is denoted by $\text{r}(A)$ and defined to be either the row rank or the column rank of A,

$$\text{r}(A) = \text{rr}(A) = \text{cr}(A).$$

By 2.7, we find that $\text{r}(A) \leq \min(m, n)$ if A is an $m \times n$ matrix.

EXAMPLE 1: Find the rank of the following 3×4 matrix over $\mathbb{Q}$:

$$A = \begin{pmatrix} 1 & 3 & -1 & 2 \\ 4 & 1 & 0 & 1 \\ -5 & 7 & -3 & 4 \end{pmatrix}.$$

Solution: We know that $\mathrm{r}(A) \leq \min(3, 4) = 3$. If A_1, A_2, A_3 are the row vectors of A, then A_1 and A_2 are independent, since they are not scalar multiples of each other. Hence, we see that $2 \leq \mathrm{rr}(A) \leq 3$. Are the three row vectors independent? If

$$c_1A_1 + c_2A_2 + c_3A_3 = (0, 0, 0, 0),$$

then we have

$$(1) \qquad \begin{aligned} c_1 + 4c_2 - 5c_3 &= 0, \\ 3c_1 + c_2 + 7c_3 &= 0, \\ -c_1 \qquad - 3c_3 &= 0, \\ 2c_1 + c_2 + 4c_3 &= 0. \end{aligned}$$

We see that $c_1 = -3c_3$, $c_2 = 2c_3$ satisfy all equations of (1); hence, $c_1 = -3$, $c_2 = 2$, $c_3 = 1$ is a solution of (1). We conclude that $\{A_1, A_2, A_3\}$ is a dependent set. Therefore, $\mathrm{rr}(A) < 3$, and $\mathrm{rr}(A) = 2$. Hence, we find that $\mathrm{r}(A) = 2$.

If A is an $m \times n$ matrix over a field F, having rows $A_1, A_2, \ldots, A_m$ and row space V, then the following operations on the rows of A are called the *elementary row operations*.

(1) Multiply a row of A by some nonzero $c \in F$.
(2) Interchange two rows of A.
(3) Replace a row A_j of A by $cA_i + A_j$ for some $c \in F$ and $i \neq j$.

For example,

$$A = \begin{pmatrix} 3 & 1 \\ 5 & -1 \\ 6 & 2 \end{pmatrix}$$

is a 3×2 matrix over $\mathbb{Q}$ with rows A_1, A_2, A_3. The matrices

$$B = \begin{pmatrix} 3 & 1 \\ 10 & -2 \\ 6 & 2 \end{pmatrix}, \qquad C = \begin{pmatrix} 3 & 1 \\ 6 & 2 \\ 5 & -1 \end{pmatrix}, \qquad D = \begin{pmatrix} 3 & 1 \\ 5 & -1 \\ -3 & -1 \end{pmatrix}$$

are obtained from A by elementary row operations. Thus, the rows of B are $A_1, 2A_2, A_3$; of C are A_1, A_3, A_2; of D are $A_1, A_2, -3A_1 + A_3$.

If a matrix B is obtained from a matrix A by an elementary row operation, then the row space of B is the same as the row space of A. Hence, $\mathrm{r}(B) = \mathrm{r}(A)$. The proof of this fact is left to the reader. Thus, we may use the elementary row operations in determining the rank of a matrix.

The three elementary column operations of a matrix are defined similarly, and the rank of a matrix is also unchanged by these operations.

EXAMPLE 2: Find the rank of the following 4×4 matrix over $\mathbb{Q}$:

$$A = \begin{pmatrix} 2 & 1 & -1 & 3 \\ 1 & 0 & 3 & -2 \\ -3 & 1 & 0 & 5 \\ 2 & -2 & 4 & 1 \end{pmatrix}.$$

Solution: Each of the following matrices is obtained from the preceding one by an elementary row operation, starting with A:

$$(1) \begin{pmatrix} 1 & 0 & 3 & -2 \\ 2 & 1 & -1 & 3 \\ -3 & 1 & 0 & 5 \\ 2 & -2 & 4 & 1 \end{pmatrix} \begin{matrix} (A_2) \\ (A_1) \\ \\ \\ \end{matrix} \qquad (2) \begin{pmatrix} 1 & 0 & 3 & -2 \\ 0 & 1 & -7 & 7 \\ -3 & 1 & 0 & 5 \\ 2 & -2 & 4 & 1 \end{pmatrix} \begin{matrix} \\ (-2A_2 + A_1) \\ \\ \\ \end{matrix}$$

$$(3) \begin{pmatrix} 1 & 0 & 3 & -2 \\ 0 & 1 & -7 & 7 \\ 0 & 1 & 9 & -1 \\ 2 & -2 & 4 & 1 \end{pmatrix} (3A_2 + A_3) \qquad (4)\ B = \begin{pmatrix} 1 & 0 & 3 & -2 \\ 0 & 1 & -7 & 7 \\ 0 & 1 & 9 & -1 \\ 0 & -2 & -2 & 5 \end{pmatrix} (-2A_2 + A_4)$$

$$(5) \begin{pmatrix} 1 & 0 & 3 & -2 \\ 0 & 1 & -7 & 7 \\ 0 & 0 & 16 & -8 \\ 0 & -2 & -2 & 5 \end{pmatrix} (-B_2 + B_3) \qquad (6)\ C = \begin{pmatrix} 1 & 0 & 3 & -2 \\ 0 & 1 & -7 & 7 \\ 0 & 0 & 16 & -8 \\ 0 & 0 & -16 & 19 \end{pmatrix} (2B_2 + B_4)$$

$$(7)\ D = \begin{pmatrix} 1 & 0 & 3 & -2 \\ 0 & 1 & -7 & 7 \\ 0 & 0 & 16 & -8 \\ 0 & 0 & 0 & 11 \end{pmatrix} (C_3 + C_4)$$

It is clear from the echelon form of D that $\mathrm{r}(D) = 4$. Hence, we see that $\mathrm{r}(A) = 4$.

EXERCISES

Find the rank of each of the following matrices over $\mathbb{Q}$.

1. $\begin{pmatrix} 1 & -1 & 2 \\ 2 & 1 & 3 \end{pmatrix}.$

2. $\begin{pmatrix} 3 & 0 \\ 1 & 2 \\ 4 & -1 \end{pmatrix}.$

3. $\begin{pmatrix} 5 & -1 & 1 \\ 2 & 1 & -2 \\ 0 & -7 & 12 \end{pmatrix}$.

4. $\begin{pmatrix} -1 & 3 & 2 & 0 \\ 0 & 4 & 1 & -1 \\ 3 & -1 & 4 & 2 \end{pmatrix}$.

5. $\begin{pmatrix} 1 & 0 & 1 & 0 \\ 3 & 1 & -1 & 2 \\ 4 & 1 & 0 & -1 \\ 3 & 3 & -2 & 1 \end{pmatrix}$.

6. $\begin{pmatrix} -3 & 2 & 4 \\ 1 & -1 & 2 \\ -1 & 0 & 8 \\ 0 & -1 & 10 \\ -2 & 0 & 24 \end{pmatrix}$.

7. Prove that an elementary row operation on a matrix doesn't change the rank of the matrix.

4. COMPLETE SOLUTION OF A SYSTEM OF LINEAR EQUATIONS

A system of m linear equations in n unknowns over a field F,

2.3 $$\sum_{j=1}^{n} a_{ij}x_j = b_i, \qquad i = 1, 2, \ldots, m,$$

can be expressed in terms of the column vectors of its matrix of coefficients $A = (a_{ij})$ as follows. If $A^1, A^2, \ldots, A^n$ are the column vectors of A and

$$B = \begin{pmatrix} b_1 \\ b_2 \\ \cdot \\ \cdot \\ \cdot \\ b_m \end{pmatrix},$$

then the above system has the form

2.10 $$\sum_{j=1}^{n} x_jA^j = B.$$

Thus, equating the ith coordinates of the vectors on each side of 2.10, we obtain

$$\sum_{j=1}^{n} x_ja_{ij} = b_i,$$

the ith equation of the given system 2.3.

If $(c_1, c_2, \ldots, c_n) \in F^n$ is a solution of 2.3, then we see that

(1) $$B = \sum_{j=1}^{n} c_j A^j$$

by 2.10, and therefore B is in the column space of A. Conversely, if B is in the column space of A, say B is given by (1), then 2.3 has solution $(c_1, c_2, \ldots, c_n)$. That is, system 2.3 has a solution iff the column spaces of A and aug A are equal, or, iff $\text{cr}(A) = \text{cr}(\text{aug } A)$. This proves the following result.

2.11. THEOREM. If A is the matrix of coefficients of a system of linear equations over a field, then the system has a solution iff $\text{r}(A) = \text{r}(\text{aug } A)$.

If system 2.3 has two solutions, $\mathbf{u} = (c_1, c_2, \ldots, c_n)$ and $\mathbf{v} = (d_1, d_2, \ldots, d_n)$, then we find that

$$\sum_{j=1}^{n} a_{ij}c_j = \sum_{j=1}^{n} a_{ij}d_j = b_i, \qquad i = 1, 2, \ldots, m,$$

and therefore we have

$$\sum_{j=1}^{n} a_{ij}(c_j - d_j) = 0, \qquad i = 1, 2, \ldots, m.$$

That is, the vector $\mathbf{u} - \mathbf{v} = (c_1 - d_1, c_2 - d_2, \ldots, c_n - d_n)$ is a solution of the system

2.12 $$\sum_{j=1}^{n} a_{ij}x_j = 0, \qquad i = 1, 2, \ldots, m.$$

This system having zero constant terms is called a *homogeneous system of linear equations*. It is the homogeneous system associated with 2.3.

A homogeneous system 2.12 always has at least one solution, since the zero vector $(0, 0, \ldots, 0) \in F^n$ is a solution. We call $(0, 0, \ldots, 0)$ the *trivial solution* of 2.12. If we express 2.12 in the form 2.10,

$$\sum_{j=1}^{n} x_j A^j = \mathbf{0},$$

then it is clear that 2.12 has a nontrivial solution iff the column vectors of A are linearly dependent. This remark can be stated as follows.

2.13. THEOREM. Let a homogeneous system of m linear equations in n unknowns over a field F have A as its matrix of coefficients. The system has a nontrivial solution iff $\text{r}(A) < n$.

For example, if there are fewer equations than unknowns (that is, if $m < n$), then $\text{r}(A) \leq m < n$, and the system has a nontrivial solution.

Let $S \subset F^n$ be the solution set of system 2.12. If $\mathbf{u} = (c_1, c_2, \ldots, c_n)$ and $\mathbf{v} = (d_1, d_2, \ldots, d_n)$ are in S and $a \in F$, then we have

$$\sum_{j=1}^{n} a_{ij}(c_j + d_j) = \sum_{j=1}^{n} a_{ij}c_j + \sum_{j=1}^{n} a_{ij}d_j = 0, \qquad i = 1, 2, \ldots, m,$$

and

$$\sum_{j=1}^{n} a_{ij}(ac_j) = a\sum_{j=1}^{n} a_{ij}c_j = 0, \qquad i = 1, 2, \ldots, m.$$

Hence, $\mathbf{u} + \mathbf{v}$ and $a\mathbf{u}$ are also in S. This proves the following result.

2.14. THEOREM. The solution set S of the homogeneous system 2.12 is a subspace of F^n.

According to 2.13, the solution set S of the homogeneous system 2.12 is nonzero (that is, $S \neq \{0\}$) iff $\mathrm{r}(A) < n$. So let us assume that

$$\mathrm{r}(A) = k < n.$$

Also, let us assume that the unknowns $x_1, x_2, \ldots, x_n$ have been reordered, if necessary, so that the first k column vectors of A are independent and thus generate the column space of A. If $A^1, A^2, \ldots, A^n$ are the column vectors of A, then we have

$$A^j = \sum_{r=1}^{k} b_{jr}A^r, \qquad j = k + 1, \ldots, n,$$

for some $b_{jr} \in F$. Transposing A^j to the right-hand side, we can rewrite these equations as follows:

$$\sum_{r=1}^{n} b_{jr}A^r = \mathbf{0}, \qquad j = k + 1, \ldots, n,$$

where $b_{jj} = -1$ and $b_{jr} = 0$ if $r > k$ and $r \neq j$. Therefore, the vectors

$$\mathbf{v}_j = (b_{j1}, b_{j2}, \ldots, b_{jn}), \qquad j = k + 1, \ldots, n,$$

are in S. These vectors are l.i., since

$$\sum_{j=k+1}^{n} d_j\mathbf{v}_j = \left(\sum d_jb_{j1}, \sum d_jb_{j2}, \ldots, \sum d_jb_{jk}, -d_{k+1}, \ldots, -d_n\right) = \mathbf{0}$$

iff all $d_j = 0$.

If $\mathbf{u} = (c_1, c_2, \ldots, c_n)$ is any solution of system 2.12, then

$$\mathbf{v} = \mathbf{u} + \sum_{j=k+1}^{n} c_j\mathbf{v}_j$$

is also a solution, since S is a vector space. Recalling the form of the $\mathbf{v}_j$, we see that $\mathbf{v}$ has the form

$$\mathbf{v} = (d_1, d_2, \ldots, d_k, 0, \ldots, 0)$$

for some $d_i \in F$. Hence, we have

$$\sum_{j=1}^{k} d_j A^j = \mathbf{0},$$

and necessarily all $d_j = 0$, because the vectors $A^1, A^2, \ldots, A^k$ are l.i. Thus, we see that $\mathbf{v} = \mathbf{0}$, and

$$\mathbf{u} = -\sum_{j=k+1}^{n} c_j \mathbf{v}_j.$$

We conclude that

$$S = F\mathbf{v}_{k+1} + F\mathbf{v}_{k+2} + \cdots + F\mathbf{v}_n,$$

and hence that $\{\mathbf{v}_{k+1}, \mathbf{v}_{k+2}, \ldots, \mathbf{v}_n\}$ is a basis of S. In particular, we have proved the following theorem.

2.15. THEOREM. Let a homogeneous system of linear equations in n unknowns over a field F have matrix of coefficients A. The solution set S of the system is a subspace of F^n of dimension $n - \mathrm{r}(A)$.

It is now an easy matter to describe the solution set of any system of linear equations.

2.16. THEOREM. Let

$$\sum_{j=1}^{n} a_{ij} x_j = b_i, \qquad i = 1, 2, \ldots, m \tag{1}$$

be a system of linear equations over a field F and

$$\sum_{j=1}^{n} a_{ij} x_j = 0, \qquad i = 1, 2, \ldots, m \tag{2}$$

be its associated homogeneous system. If $\mathbf{u} \in F^n$ is a solution of (1) and S is the solution set of (2), then

$$\mathbf{u} + S = \{\mathbf{u} + \mathbf{w} \mid \mathbf{w} \in S\}$$

is the solution set of system (1).

Proof: If $\mathbf{v}$ is any solution of (1), then $\mathbf{v} - \mathbf{u}$ is a solution of system (2), as we saw above. Thus, $\mathbf{v} - \mathbf{u} = \mathbf{w}$ for some $\mathbf{w} \in S$, and $\mathbf{v} = \mathbf{u} + \mathbf{w} \in \mathbf{u} + S$. On the other hand, if $\mathbf{u} = (c_1, c_2, \ldots, c_n)$ and $\mathbf{w} = (d_1, d_2, \ldots, d_n) \in S$, then we have

$$\sum_{j=1}^{n} a_{ij}(c_j + d_j) = \sum_{j=1}^{n} a_{ij} c_j + \sum_{j=1}^{n} a_{ij} d_j = b_i + 0 = b_i, \qquad i = 1, 2, \ldots, n,$$

and $\mathbf{u} + \mathbf{w}$ is a solution of system (1). This proves 2.16.

EXAMPLE: Solve the following system over $\mathbb{Q}$.

$$(1)\quad \begin{aligned} 3x_1 + x_2 + 2x_3 + 4x_4 &= 1, \\ x_1 - x_2 + 3x_3 - x_4 &= 3, \\ x_1 + 7x_2 - 11x_3 + 13x_4 &= -13, \\ 11x_1 + x_2 + 12x_3 + 10x_4 &= 9. \end{aligned}$$

Solution: Let us assume that we have found the solution

$$\mathbf{u} = (2, 5, 1, -3) \in \mathbb{Q}^4$$

of the system (1) by one method or another. By 2.16, we can find the solution set of (1) by finding the solution set S of the homogeneous system

$$(2)\quad \begin{aligned} 3x_1 + x_2 + 2x_3 + 4x_4 &= 0, \\ x_1 - x_2 + 3x_3 - x_4 &= 0, \\ x_1 + 7x_2 - 11x_3 + 13x_4 &= 0, \\ 11x_1 + x_2 + 12x_3 + 10x_4 &= 0. \end{aligned}$$

The matrix of coefficients of (2) is given by

$$A = \begin{pmatrix} 3 & 1 & 2 & 4 \\ 1 & -1 & 3 & -1 \\ 1 & 7 & -11 & 13 \\ 11 & 1 & 12 & 10 \end{pmatrix}.$$

Our first task is to find $\mathrm{r}(A)$. Let us work with the columns of A so as to construct S as in the proof of 2.15. If matrix B is given by

$$B = \begin{pmatrix} 1 & 0 & 0 & 0 \\ -1 & 4 & 5 & 3 \\ 7 & -20 & -25 & -15 \\ 1 & 8 & 10 & 6 \end{pmatrix},$$

then $\mathrm{r}(B) = \mathrm{r}(A)$, since elementary column operations were used in deriving B from A as follows:

$$(3)\quad B^1 = A^2, \quad B^2 = -3A^2 + A^1, \quad B^3 = -2A^2 + A^3, \quad B^4 = -4A^2 + A^4.$$

Evidently, we have

$$(4)\qquad B^3 = \tfrac{5}{4}B^2, \qquad \text{and} \qquad B^4 = \tfrac{3}{4}B^2,$$

and hence $\mathrm{r}(B) = 2$. Now A^1 and A^2 are l.i., and A^3 and A^4 may be expressed in terms of A^1 and A^2 by using (3) and (4):

$$A^3 = \tfrac{5}{4}A^1 - \tfrac{7}{4}A^2, \qquad A^4 = \tfrac{3}{4}A^1 + \tfrac{7}{4}A^2.$$

Thus, we see that

$$\mathbf{v}_3 = (\tfrac{5}{4}, -\tfrac{7}{4}, -1, 0), \qquad \mathbf{v}_4 = (\tfrac{3}{4}, \tfrac{7}{4}, 0, -1)$$

are l.i. generators of S, according to the proof of 2.15:

$$S = \mathbb{Q}\mathbf{v}_3 + \mathbb{Q}\mathbf{v}_4.$$

Hence, we find that

$$\mathbf{u} + S$$

is the solution set of (1). That is, the solution set of the given system is

$$\{(2, 5, 1, -3) + a(\tfrac{5}{4}, -\tfrac{7}{4}, -1, 0) + b(\tfrac{3}{4}, \tfrac{7}{4}, 0, -1) \mid a, b \in \mathbb{Q}\}.$$

EXERCISES

Find the solution set of each of the following systems of linear equations over $\mathbb{Q}$ by first finding the solution set of the associated homogeneous system.

1. $3x - y = 7,$ $2x + y = 1.$
2. $x + 2y = -1,$ $3x + 6y = -3.$
3. $2x - y + 3z = 5,$ $3x + 2y - 2z = 1,$ $7x + 4z = 11.$
4. $5x + 2y - z = 0,$ $3x + 5y + 3z = 0,$ $x + 8y + 7z = 0.$
5. $x_1 - x_2 + 2x_3 + x_4 = 3,$ $2x_1 + x_2 - x_3 - x_4 = 1,$ $3x_1 + x_2 + x_3 - 3x_4 = 2,$ $3x_1 - 2x_2 + 6x_3 = 7.$
6. $x_1 + 3x_2 + x_5 = 1,$ $x_2 - x_3 + x_4 = 0,$ $x_1 + 2x_4 - x_5 = 2.$

Chapter Three

Linear Transformations and Matrices

1. LINEAR TRANSFORMATIONS

We recall that if U and V are vector spaces over the same field F, then a 1–1 mapping of U into V whose image is V and which preserves addition and scalar multiplication is called an isomorphism. In this chapter, we shall study mappings of U into V which preserve addition and multiplication. However, we shall not usually assume that the mappings are 1–1 or have image V.

If $U \xrightarrow{f} V$ is a mapping, it will be convenient most of the time, henceforth, to denote the element of V corresponding to each $\mathbf{x} \in U$ by $\mathbf{x}f$ rather than $f(\mathbf{x})$ as in Chapter 1.

3.1. DEFINITION OF A LINEAR TRANSFORMATION. Let U and V be vector spaces over the same field F. A mapping $U \xrightarrow{f} V$ is called a linear transformation (abbreviated l.t.) iff it has the following properties:

$$(1) \qquad (\mathbf{x}+\mathbf{y})f = \mathbf{x}f + \mathbf{y}f \quad \text{for all } \mathbf{x}, \mathbf{y} \in U.$$

$$(2) \qquad (a\mathbf{x})f = a(\mathbf{x}f) \quad \text{for all } \mathbf{x} \in U,\ a \in F.$$

Another common name for a l.t. is a *homomorphism*. Clearly, an isomorphism $U \xrightarrow{f} V$ is a l.t., but the converse is not true. As for isomorphisms, if $U \xrightarrow{f} V$ is a l.t., then

$$\mathbf{0}f = \mathbf{0}, \qquad (-\mathbf{x})f = -(\mathbf{x}f) \qquad \text{for all } \mathbf{x} \in U.$$

Here we have used the symbol "$\mathbf{0}$" for the zero element of both U and V. These equations follow from 3.1(2) by letting $a = 0$ and $a = -1$, respectively. By mathematical induction, we easily establish the following property of a l.t. $U \xrightarrow{f} V$:

$$3.2 \qquad \left(\sum_{i=1}^{n} a_i\mathbf{x}_i\right)f = \sum_{i=1}^{n} a_i(\mathbf{x}_i f) \qquad \text{for all } \mathbf{x}_i \in V,\ a_i \in F.$$

An example of a l.t. is the projection of E_3 into E_2, $E_3 \xrightarrow{p} E_2$ defined by

$$(a\mathbf{i} + b\mathbf{j} + c\mathbf{k})p = a\mathbf{i} + b\mathbf{j}, \qquad a, b, c \in \mathbb{R},$$

where $\{\mathbf{i}, \mathbf{j}, \mathbf{k}\}$ is the usual unit basis of E_3 and $\{\mathbf{i}, \mathbf{j}\}$ of E_2. Here we are considering E_2 to be a subspace of E_3. In particular, we have

$$\mathbf{i}p = \mathbf{i}, \qquad \mathbf{j}p = \mathbf{j}, \qquad \mathbf{k}p = \mathbf{0}.$$

To show that p is a l.t., let $\mathbf{u} = a\mathbf{i} + b\mathbf{j} + c\mathbf{k}$, $\mathbf{v} = a'\mathbf{i} + b'\mathbf{j} + c'\mathbf{k}$ be any two vectors of E_3. Then we have

$$\begin{aligned}(\mathbf{u} + \mathbf{v})p &= [(a + a')\mathbf{i} + (b + b')\mathbf{j} + (c + c')\mathbf{k}]p \\ &= (a + a')\mathbf{i} + (b + b')\mathbf{j} \\ &= (a\mathbf{i} + b\mathbf{j}) + (a'\mathbf{i} + b'\mathbf{j}) \\ &= \mathbf{u}p + \mathbf{v}p.\end{aligned}$$

Also, for every $d \in \mathbb{R}$, we have

$$\begin{aligned}(d\mathbf{u})p &= (da\mathbf{i} + db\mathbf{j} + dc\mathbf{k})p \\ &= da\mathbf{i} + db\mathbf{j} \\ &= d(a\mathbf{i} + b\mathbf{j}) \\ &= d(\mathbf{u}p).\end{aligned}$$

Hence, p has properties 3.1(1) and (2) and is therefore a l.t. Note that p is not an isomorphism, since, for example, $\mathbf{0}p = \mathbf{0}$ and $\mathbf{k}p = \mathbf{0}$, although $\mathbf{0} \neq \mathbf{k}$.

If U and V are finite-dimensional vector spaces over a field F and $U \xrightarrow{f} V$ is a l.t., then f is completely determined by what it does to a basis of U. Thus, if $\{\mathbf{u}_1, \mathbf{u}_2, \ldots, \mathbf{u}_n\}$ is a basis of U and if

$$\mathbf{u}_i f = \mathbf{v}_i, \qquad i = 1, 2, \ldots, n,$$

then for every $\mathbf{x} \in U$ there exist $a_i \in F$ such that

$$\mathbf{x} = \sum_{i=1}^{n} a_i\mathbf{u}_i.$$

Hence, by 3.2, we have

$$\mathbf{x}f = \sum_{i=1}^{n} a_i(\mathbf{u}_i f) = \sum_{i=1}^{n} a_i\mathbf{v}_i.$$

On the other hand, if we are given a basis $\{\mathbf{u}_1, \mathbf{u}_2, \ldots, \mathbf{u}_n\}$ of U and any n elements $\mathbf{v}_1, \mathbf{v}_2, \ldots, \mathbf{v}_n$, of V, then the mapping

$$\mathbf{u}_i \rightarrow \mathbf{v}_i, \qquad i = 1, 2, \ldots, n$$

of the basis of U into V can be extended in a unique way to a mapping $U \xrightarrow{f} V$ as follows:

$$\left(\sum_{i=1}^{n} a_i\mathbf{u}_i\right)f = \sum_{i=1}^{n} a_i\mathbf{v}_i.$$

We leave it as an exercise to prove that f is actually a l.t.

For example, there is a unique l.t., $E_3 \xrightarrow{f} E_3$, such that

$$\mathbf{i}f = \mathbf{j}, \qquad \mathbf{j}f = \mathbf{k}, \qquad \mathbf{k}f = \mathbf{i}.$$

Thus, for any $\mathbf{x} = a\mathbf{i} + b\mathbf{j} + c\mathbf{k} \in E_3$, we have

$$\mathbf{x}f = a\mathbf{j} + b\mathbf{k} + c\mathbf{i}.$$

Is there any nonzero vector $\mathbf{x} \in E_3$ which is mapped into itself by f? If $\mathbf{x} = a\mathbf{i} + b\mathbf{j} + c\mathbf{k}$ and $\mathbf{x}f = \mathbf{x}$, then we have

$$a\mathbf{j} + b\mathbf{k} + c\mathbf{i} = a\mathbf{i} + b\mathbf{j} + c\mathbf{k},$$

and $a = b$, $b = c$, $c = a$, that is, $a = b = c$. Thus, $\mathbf{x}f = \mathbf{x}$ iff $\mathbf{x} = a(\mathbf{i} + \mathbf{j} + \mathbf{k})$ for some $a \in \mathbb{R}$. Perhaps the reader can now describe f geometrically as a rotation about the line $\mathbb{R}(\mathbf{i} + \mathbf{j} + \mathbf{k})$ passing through the origin.

EXERCISES

Tell whether or not each of the following mappings is a l.t.

1. $\mathbb{Q}^3 \xrightarrow{f} \mathbb{Q}^2$; $(a, b, c)f = (c, b)$, $a, b, c \in \mathbb{Q}$.
2. $\mathbb{Q}^3 \xrightarrow{g} \mathbb{Q}^3$; $(a, b, c)g = (1, a - b, c)$, $a, b, c \in \mathbb{Q}$.
3. $\mathbb{Q}^2 \xrightarrow{g} \mathbb{Q}^3$; $(a, b)g = (0, a - b, a + b)$, $a, b \in \mathbb{Q}$.
4. $E_3 \xrightarrow{f} E_3$; $(a\mathbf{i} + b\mathbf{j} + c\mathbf{k})f = \mathbf{i} - a\mathbf{j} + (b + c)\mathbf{k}$, $a, b, c \in \mathbb{R}$.
5. $E_2 \xrightarrow{h} E_2$; $(a\mathbf{i} + b\mathbf{j})h = a\mathbf{i} - b\mathbf{j}$, $a, b \in \mathbb{R}$.
6. $E_2 \xrightarrow{g} E_3$; $(a\mathbf{i} + b\mathbf{j})g = \mathbf{i} + \mathbf{j} + (a + b)\mathbf{k}$, $a, b \in \mathbb{R}$.
7. Let U and V be finite-dimensional vector spaces over a field F, $\{\mathbf{u}_1, \mathbf{u}_2, \ldots, \mathbf{u}_n\}$ be a basis of U, and $\mathbf{v}_1, \mathbf{v}_2, \ldots, \mathbf{v}_n \in V$. Prove that the mapping $U \xrightarrow{f} V$ defined by

$$\left(\sum_{i=1}^{n} a_i\mathbf{u}_i\right)f = \sum_{i=1}^{n} a_i\mathbf{v}_i, \qquad a_i \in F,$$

is a l.t.

2. REPRESENTATION OF LINEAR TRANSFORMATIONS BY MATRICES

Let U and V be finite-dimensional vector spaces over a field F, $(\mathbf{u}_1, \mathbf{u}_2, \ldots, \mathbf{u}_n)$ be an ordered basis of U, and $(\mathbf{v}_1, \mathbf{v}_2, \ldots, \mathbf{v}_m)$ be an ordered basis of V. For each l.t. $U \xrightarrow{f} V$, there exist unique $a_{ij} \in F$ such that

3.3 $$\mathbf{u}_i f = \sum_{j=1}^{m} a_{ij}\mathbf{v}_j, \qquad i = 1, 2, \ldots, n.$$

The n equations of 3.3 completely determine f, as we described in Section 1. Thus, if $\mathbf{x} = \sum_{i=1}^{n} c_i\mathbf{u}_i \in U$, then we have

$$\mathbf{x}f = \sum_{i=1}^{n} c_i(\mathbf{u}_i f) = \sum_{i=1}^{n}\sum_{j=1}^{m} c_i a_{ij}\mathbf{v}_j.$$

Evidently the mn scalars a_{ij}, $i = 1, 2, \ldots, n$, $j = 1, 2, \ldots, m$ determine f, or, in other words, the $n \times m$ matrix

$$A = (a_{ij})$$

over F determines f. We shall say that the l.t. f is *represented* by the matrix $A = (a_{ij})$ relative to the given ordered bases of U and V.

EXAMPLE 1: The projection $E_3 \xrightarrow{p} E_2$ defined by

$$(a\mathbf{i} + b\mathbf{j} + c\mathbf{k})p = a\mathbf{i} + b\mathbf{j}, \; a, b, c \in \mathbb{R}$$

maps the basis $\{\mathbf{i}, \mathbf{j}, \mathbf{k}\}$ of E_3 into E_2 as follows:

$$\mathbf{i}p = 1\mathbf{i} + 0\mathbf{j},$$
$$\mathbf{j}p = 0\mathbf{i} + 1\mathbf{j},$$
$$\mathbf{k}p = 0\mathbf{i} + 0\mathbf{j}.$$

Thus, p is represented by the 3×2 matrix

$$A = \begin{pmatrix} 1 & 0 \\ 0 & 1 \\ 0 & 0 \end{pmatrix}$$

relative to the ordered bases $(\mathbf{i}, \mathbf{j}, \mathbf{k})$ of E_3 and $(\mathbf{i}, \mathbf{j})$ of E_2.

If we change either or both of the bases above, then the matrix representing p might also change. For example, if we take the ordered basis $(\mathbf{i}, \mathbf{j}, \mathbf{k})$ of E_3 and $(\mathbf{i} + \mathbf{j}, \mathbf{i} - \mathbf{j})$ of E_2, then we have

$$\mathbf{i}p = \tfrac{1}{2}(\mathbf{i} + \mathbf{j}) + \tfrac{1}{2}(\mathbf{i} - \mathbf{j}),$$
$$\mathbf{j}p = \tfrac{1}{2}(\mathbf{i} + \mathbf{j}) - \tfrac{1}{2}(\mathbf{i} - \mathbf{j}),$$
$$\mathbf{k}p = 0(\mathbf{i} + \mathbf{j}) + 0(\mathbf{i} - \mathbf{j}),$$

and p is represented by the 3×2 matrix

$$B = \begin{pmatrix} \frac{1}{2} & \frac{1}{2} \\ \frac{1}{2} & -\frac{1}{2} \\ 0 & 0 \end{pmatrix}$$

relative to the ordered bases $(\mathbf{i}, \mathbf{j}, \mathbf{k})$ of E_3 and $(\mathbf{i} + \mathbf{j}, \mathbf{i} - \mathbf{j})$ of E_2.

When we consider a l.t. of a vector space V into itself, $V \xrightarrow{f} V$, it is natural to select only one basis of V in representing f by a matrix rather than one basis for the domain of f and another basis for the image of f. We illustrate this fact below.

EXAMPLE 2: Let $\mathbf{u}_1 = (1, 0, 0)$, $\mathbf{u}_2 = (0, 1, 0)$, $\mathbf{u}_3 = (0, 0, 1)$ be the usual unit basis of $\mathbb{Q}^3$, and let the l.t. $\mathbb{Q}^3 \xrightarrow{f} \mathbb{Q}^3$ be defined by

$$\mathbf{u}_1 f = (1, -2, 1), \qquad \mathbf{u}_2 f = (1, 0, 5), \qquad \mathbf{u}_3 f = (0, 2, 0).$$

Then we have

$$\begin{aligned} \mathbf{u}_1 f &= 1\mathbf{u}_1 - 2\mathbf{u}_2 + 1\mathbf{u}_3, \\ \mathbf{u}_2 f &= 1\mathbf{u}_1 + 0\mathbf{u}_2 + 5\mathbf{u}_3, \\ \mathbf{u}_3 f &= 0\mathbf{u}_1 + 2\mathbf{u}_2 + 0\mathbf{u}_3, \end{aligned}$$

and f is represented by the 3×3 matrix

$$A = \begin{pmatrix} 1 & -2 & 1 \\ 1 & 0 & 5 \\ 0 & 2 & 0 \end{pmatrix}$$

relative to the ordered basis $(\mathbf{u}_1, \mathbf{u}_2, \mathbf{u}_3)$ of $\mathbb{Q}^3$.

We leave it to the reader to verify that f is represented by the matrix

$$B = \begin{pmatrix} 3 & -3 & 1 \\ 4 & -8 & 6 \\ 2 & -6 & 6 \end{pmatrix}$$

relative to the ordered basis $(\mathbf{u}_1, \mathbf{u}_1 + \mathbf{u}_2, \mathbf{u}_1 + \mathbf{u}_2 + \mathbf{u}_3)$ of $\mathbb{Q}^3$.

Often, a l.t. is described by giving its representing matrix relative to bases of the vector spaces involved, as illustrated below.

EXAMPLE 3: Let vector space $\mathbb{Q}^2$ have basis $\mathbf{u}_1 = (1, 0)$, $\mathbf{u}_2 = (0, 1)$ and vector space $\mathbb{Q}^3$ have basis $\mathbf{v}_1 = (1, 0, 0)$, $\mathbf{v}_2 = (0, 1, 0)$, $\mathbf{v}_3 = (0, 0, 1)$. Then the 2×3 matrix

$$A = \begin{pmatrix} -1 & 3 & 2 \\ 4 & 0 & -7 \end{pmatrix}$$

represents a unique l.t. $\mathbb{Q}^2 \xrightarrow{f} \mathbb{Q}^3$ relative to the given ordered bases $(\mathbf{u}_1, \mathbf{u}_2)$ of $\mathbb{Q}^2$ and $(\mathbf{v}_1, \mathbf{v}_2, \mathbf{v}_3)$ of $\mathbb{Q}^3$. Thus, we find that

$$\mathbf{u}_1 f = -\mathbf{v}_1 + 3\mathbf{v}_2 + 2\mathbf{v}_3 = (-1, 3, 2),$$
$$\mathbf{u}_2 f = 4\mathbf{v}_1 + 0\mathbf{v}_2 - 7\mathbf{v}_3 = (4, 0, -7),$$

and

$$(a, b)f = a(-1, 3, 2) + b(4, 0, -7) = (-a + 4b, 3a, 2a - 7b)$$

for all $a, b \in \mathbb{R}$. For example,

$$(-1, 3)f = -(-1, 3, 2) + 3(4, 0, -7) = (13, -3, -23).$$

EXERCISES

Represent each of the following l.t.'s by a matrix relative to the usual bases of the given vector spaces.

1. $\mathbb{Q}^3 \xrightarrow{f} \mathbb{Q}^3$, $(a, b, c)f = (2a + b, a - b, c)$.
2. $E_2 \xrightarrow{g} E_3$, $(a\mathbf{i} + b\mathbf{j})g = (a - b)\mathbf{i} + (a + 2b)\mathbf{j} + 4a\mathbf{k}$.
3. $\mathbb{Q}^4 \xrightarrow{f} \mathbb{Q}^3$, $(a, b, c, d)f = (a - 3b, 3a + b + c, -a - b + c + d)$.
4. $E_3 \xrightarrow{h} E_3$, $(a\mathbf{i} + b\mathbf{j} + c\mathbf{k})h = a\mathbf{j} + b\mathbf{k} + c\mathbf{i}$.
5. $\mathbb{R}^2 \xrightarrow{g} \mathbb{R}^4$, $(a, b)g = (a - b, 0, a + 2b, 3a - 4b)$.
6. $E_2 \xrightarrow{h} E_2$, $(a\mathbf{i} + b\mathbf{j})h = a\mathbf{j} - b\mathbf{i}$.
7. $\mathbb{Q}^3 \xrightarrow{f} \mathbb{Q}^4$, $(a, b, c)f = (0, a + b, b + c, 0)$.
8. $\mathbb{Q}^4 \xrightarrow{g} \mathbb{Q}^4$, $(a, b, c, d)g = (a - 2b, 2a - b, c - 2d, 2c - d)$.

3. THE VECTOR SPACE OF LINEAR TRANSFORMATIONS

If U and V are vector spaces over a field F and $U \xrightarrow{f} V$, $U \xrightarrow{g} V$ are any two mappings of U into V, then a new mapping

$$U \xrightarrow{f+g} V$$

can be defined in a natural way as follows:

3.4 $$\mathbf{x}(f + g) = \mathbf{x}f + \mathbf{x}g \qquad \text{for all } \mathbf{x} \in U.$$

Thus, $f + g$ is defined in terms of addition in V. We note that $f + g$ is defined whether or not f and g are l.t. If f and g are l.t., then we can prove the following result.

3.5. THEOREM. If $U \xrightarrow{f} V$ and $U \xrightarrow{g} V$ are l.t., then $U \xrightarrow{f+g} V$ is a l.t.

Outline of proof: We must show that

(1) $(\mathbf{x}+\mathbf{y})(f+g) = \mathbf{x}(f+g) + \mathbf{y}(f+g)$ for all $\mathbf{x}, \mathbf{y} \in U$.

(2) $(a\mathbf{x})(f+g) = a[\mathbf{x}(f+g)]$ for all $a \in F$, $\mathbf{x} \in U$.

The proof of (1) is given below. We leave the proof of (2) as an exercise.

$$\begin{aligned}(\mathbf{x}+\mathbf{y})(f+g) &= (\mathbf{x}+\mathbf{y})f + (\mathbf{x}+\mathbf{y})g && \text{(by 3.4)}\\ &= (\mathbf{x}f+\mathbf{y}f) + (\mathbf{x}g+\mathbf{y}g) && \text{(by 3.1(1))}\\ &= (\mathbf{x}f+\mathbf{x}g) + (\mathbf{y}f+\mathbf{y}g)\\ &= \mathbf{x}(f+g) + \mathbf{y}(f+g) && \text{(by 3.4).}\end{aligned}$$

For any three sets U, V, and W and any two mappings $U \xrightarrow{f} V$ and $V \xrightarrow{g} W$, the *composite* mapping

$$U \xrightarrow{fg} W$$

is defined as follows.

3.6 $$x(fg) = (xf)g \qquad \text{for all } x \in U.$$

For example, if $\mathbb{Z} \xrightarrow{f} \mathbb{Q}$ and $\mathbb{Q} \xrightarrow{g} \mathbb{R}$ are defined by

$$xf = \tfrac{1}{3}x - 5, \qquad yg = \sqrt{3y+10},$$

then $\mathbb{Z} \xrightarrow{fg} \mathbb{R}$ is defined by

$$x(fg) = \sqrt{3(xf)+10} = \sqrt{x-5} \qquad \text{for all } x \in \mathbb{Z}.$$

If U, V, and W are vector spaces over a field F and $U \xrightarrow{f} V$ and $V \xrightarrow{g} W$ are l.t., is $U \xrightarrow{fg} W$ also a l.t.? We can answer this question by computing $(\mathbf{x}+\mathbf{y})(fg)$ and $(a\mathbf{x})(fg)$ as shown below.

$$\begin{aligned}(\mathbf{x}+\mathbf{y})(fg) &= [(\mathbf{x}+\mathbf{y})f]g = (\mathbf{x}f+\mathbf{y}f)g = (\mathbf{x}f)g + (\mathbf{y}f)g\\ &= \mathbf{x}(fg) + \mathbf{y}(fg),\\ (a\mathbf{x})(fg) &= [(a\mathbf{x})f]g = [a(\mathbf{x}f)]g = a[(\mathbf{x}f)g] = a[\mathbf{x}(fg)].\end{aligned}$$

Since properties 3.1(1) and (2) are satisfied by fg, we have proved that fg is a l.t.

3.7. THEOREM. If $U \xrightarrow{f} V$ and $V \xrightarrow{g} W$ are l.t., then $U \xrightarrow{fg} W$ is a l.t.

If U and V are vector spaces over a field F and $U \xrightarrow{f} V$ is a mapping, then we can multiply f by a scalar $c \in F$ to obtain the mapping $U \xrightarrow{cf} V$ defined as follows.

3.8 $$\mathbf{x}(cf) = c(\mathbf{x}f) \qquad \text{for all } \mathbf{x} \in U.$$

The reader should have no trouble proving that if f is a l.t., then cf is also a l.t. for each $c \in F$.

For convenience, let us denote the set of all l.t. of a vector space U into a vector space V by

$$L(U, V).$$

Just as in a vector space, there are two operations in $L(U, V)$, addition and scalar multiplication. The composite of two elements of $L(U, V)$ is not defined unless $U = V$, a case which we shall discuss later.

It should not be too surprising to learn that many of the properties of addition and scalar multiplication in a vector space carry over to $L(U, V)$. For example, if $f, g, h \in L(U, V)$ and $\mathbf{x} \in U$, then we have

$$\mathbf{x}[(f + g) + h] = \mathbf{x}(f + g) + \mathbf{x}h = (\mathbf{x}f + \mathbf{x}g) + \mathbf{x}h,$$
$$\mathbf{x}[f + (g + h)] = \mathbf{x}f + \mathbf{x}(g + h) = \mathbf{x}f + (\mathbf{x}g + \mathbf{x}h).$$

Since the associative law holds in V, we have $(\mathbf{x}f + \mathbf{x}g) + \mathbf{x}h = \mathbf{x}f + (\mathbf{x}g + \mathbf{x}h)$. Hence, $\mathbf{x}[(f + g) + h] = \mathbf{x}[f + (g + h)]$ for all $\mathbf{x} \in U$, and $(f + g) + h = f + (g + h)$. Thus, addition in $L(U, V)$ is associative. The reader can show, similarly, that addition in $L(U, V)$ is commutative.

The *zero mapping* $U \xrightarrow{0} V$ maps every element of U into the zero element of V:

$$\mathbf{x}0 = \mathbf{0} \qquad \text{for all } \mathbf{x} \in U.$$

We use the symbol "0" in three different ways: as the zero element of the field of scalars F, as the zero vector of every vector space, and as the zero mapping. We rely on the context to tell us in which way the symbol is being used at any particular instance. Since $(\mathbf{x} + \mathbf{y})0 = \mathbf{x}0 + \mathbf{y}0 = \mathbf{0} + \mathbf{0} = \mathbf{0}$ and $\mathbf{0} = (a\mathbf{x})0 = a(\mathbf{x}0)$, evidently the zero mapping $U \xrightarrow{0} V$ is in $L(U, V)$.

The zero mapping $U \xrightarrow{0} V$ is the additive identity element of $L(U, V)$. That is, we have

$$f + 0 = 0 + f = f \qquad \text{for all } f \in L(U, V),$$

as the reader can easily verify.

Each mapping $U \xrightarrow{f} V$ has a *negative* $U \xrightarrow{-f} V$ defined by

$$\mathbf{x}(-f) = -(\mathbf{x}f) \qquad \text{for all } \mathbf{x} \in U.$$

If $f \in L(U, V)$, then $-f \in L(U, V)$ also, since

$$(\mathbf{x} + \mathbf{y})(-f) = -[(\mathbf{x} + \mathbf{y})f] = -(\mathbf{x}f + \mathbf{y}f)$$
$$= -(\mathbf{x}f) - (\mathbf{y}f) = \mathbf{x}(-f) + \mathbf{y}(-f)$$

and

$$(a\mathbf{x})(-f) = -[(a\mathbf{x})f] = -[a(\mathbf{x}f)] = a[-(\mathbf{x}f)] = a[\mathbf{x}(-f)]$$

for all $\mathbf{x}, \mathbf{y} \in U$, $a \in F$. We leave it for the reader to prove that the negative of each $f \in L(U, V)$ has the same property as the negative of an element in a field or vector space, namely

$$f + (-f) = (-f) + f = 0 \qquad \text{for all } f \in L(U, V).$$

Scalar multiplication in $L(U, V)$ has the four usual properties, which we list below.

(1) $\quad a(f + g) = af + ag \quad$ for all $a \in F, f, g \in L(U, V)$.

(2) $\quad (a + b)f = af + bf \quad$ for all $a, b \in F, f \in L(U, V)$.

(3) $\quad (ab)f = a(bf) \quad$ for all $a, b \in F, f \in L(U, V)$.

(4) $\quad 1f = f \quad$ for all $f \in L(U, V)$.

The proof of (3) is as follows:

$$\mathbf{x}[(ab)f] = (ab)(\mathbf{x}f) = a[b(\mathbf{x}f)] = a[\mathbf{x}(bf)] = \mathbf{x}[a(bf)]$$

for all $\mathbf{x} \in U$. Hence, $(ab)f = a(bf)$. We leave the proofs of (1), (2), and (4) as exercises.

The properties of addition and scalar multiplication in $L(U, V)$ are precisely the properties of a vector space (1.19). Hence, we have the following theorem.

3.9. THEOREM. If U and V are vector spaces over a field F, then $L(U, V)$ is also a vector space over F.

If U and V have ordered bases $(\mathbf{u}_1, \mathbf{u}_2, \ldots, \mathbf{u}_n)$ and $(\mathbf{v}_1, \mathbf{v}_2, \ldots, \mathbf{v}_m)$, respectively, then let us define $e_{ij} \in L(U, V)$ as follows:

$$\mathbf{u}_k e_{ij} = \mathbf{0} \quad \text{if} \quad k \neq i, \qquad \mathbf{u}_k e_{ij} = \mathbf{v}_j \quad \text{if} \quad k = i,\ k = 1, 2, \ldots, n.$$

Using the Kronecker delta, the above definition has the form

3.10 $$\mathbf{u}_k e_{ij} = \delta_{ki}\mathbf{v}_j, \qquad k = 1, 2, \ldots, n.$$

Since 3.10 describes the effect of e_{ij} on a basis of U, it uniquely defines a l.t. of U into V. Thus, we have defined a set of mn l.t. of U into V,

$$\{e_{ij} \mid i = 1, 2, \ldots, n, j = 1, 2, \ldots, m\}.$$

Let E_{ij} denote the matrix representing e_{ij} relative to the given bases of U and V. According to 3.10, the matrix E_{ij} has 1 in the (i, j)th position and zeros elsewhere. Using the Kronecker delta, we find that E_{rs} is the $n \times m$ matrix over F of the form

3.11 $$E_{rs} = (\delta_{ir}\delta_{sj}).$$

That is, the (i, j)th element of matrix E_{rs} is $\delta_{ir}\delta_{sj}$.

For example, let $\mathbb{Q}^3$ and $\mathbb{Q}^2$ have their usual ordered bases, which we denote by $(\mathbf{u}_1, \mathbf{u}_2, \mathbf{u}_3)$ and $(\mathbf{v}_1, \mathbf{v}_2)$. Then the E_{ij} are as follows:

$$E_{11} = \begin{pmatrix} 1 & 0 \\ 0 & 0 \\ 0 & 0 \end{pmatrix}, \qquad E_{21} = \begin{pmatrix} 0 & 0 \\ 1 & 0 \\ 0 & 0 \end{pmatrix}, \qquad E_{31} = \begin{pmatrix} 0 & 0 \\ 0 & 0 \\ 1 & 0 \end{pmatrix},$$

$$E_{12} = \begin{pmatrix} 0 & 1 \\ 0 & 0 \\ 0 & 0 \end{pmatrix}, \qquad E_{22} = \begin{pmatrix} 0 & 0 \\ 0 & 1 \\ 0 & 0 \end{pmatrix}, \qquad E_{32} = \begin{pmatrix} 0 & 0 \\ 0 & 0 \\ 0 & 1 \end{pmatrix}.$$

The e_{ij} are defined accordingly. For example, e_{32} is defined by:

$$\mathbf{u}_1 e_{32} = \mathbf{0}, \qquad \mathbf{u}_2 e_{32} = \mathbf{0}, \qquad \mathbf{u}_3 e_{32} = \mathbf{v}_2.$$

Hence, we have

$$(a, b, c)e_{32} = (a\mathbf{u}_1 + b\mathbf{u}_2 + c\mathbf{u}_3)e_{32} = c\mathbf{v}_2 = (0, c)$$

for all $a, b, c \in \mathbb{Q}$.

3.12. THEOREM. If U and V are vector spaces over a field F of dimensions n and m, respectively, then $L(U, V)$ is a vector space over F of dimension mn. If $(\mathbf{u}_1, \mathbf{u}_2, \ldots, \mathbf{u}_n)$ is a basis of U and $(\mathbf{v}_1, \mathbf{v}_2, \ldots, \mathbf{v}_m)$ of V, then $S = \{e_{ij} \mid i = 1, 2, \ldots, n, j = 1, 2, \ldots, m\}$ defined by 3.10 is a basis of $L(U, V)$.

Proof: If $f \in L(U, V)$ is represented by the $n \times m$ matrix $A = (a_{ij})$ relative to the given bases, then we have

$$f = \sum_{i=1}^{n} \sum_{j=1}^{m} a_{ij} e_{ij},$$

because

$$\mathbf{u}_r f = \mathbf{u}_r \left(\sum_{i=1}^{n} \sum_{j=1}^{m} a_{ij} e_{ij} \right) = \sum_{j=1}^{m} a_{rj} \mathbf{v}_j, \qquad r = 1, 2, \ldots, n.$$

Hence, S is a set of generators of $L(U, V)$. The e_{ij} are l.i., for if we have

$$f = \sum_{i=1}^{n} \sum_{j=1}^{m} a_{ij} e_{ij} = 0,$$

then $\mathbf{u}_r f = \sum_j a_{rj} \mathbf{v}_j = 0$ for each r, and $a_{rj} = 0$ because the $\mathbf{v}_i$ are l.i. We conclude that the e_{ij} are l.i., and hence that S is a basis of $L(U, V)$. This proves 3.12.

For example, for any field F, the vector space $L(F^n, F^m)$ has dimension mn.

EXERCISES

In the following exercises, U and V are finite-dimensional vector spaces over a field F.

1. Finish the proof of 3.5.
2. Prove that $cf \in L(U, V)$ for all $c \in F, f \in L(U, V)$.
3. Describe the matrix which represents the zero mapping.
4. Prove that addition in $L(U, V)$ is commutative.
5. Prove that $0 + f = f$ for every $f \in L(U, V)$.
6. Prove that $f + (-f) = 0$ for every $f \in L(U, V)$.
7. Prove properties (1), (2), and (4) of scalar multiplication in $L(U, V)$.

4. THE ALGEBRA OF LINEAR TRANSFORMATIONS

Given mappings

$$U \xrightarrow{f} V \xrightarrow{g} W \xrightarrow{h} X,$$

then there is defined a natural mapping $U \xrightarrow{s} X$, where

$$\mathbf{x}s = ((\mathbf{x}f)g)h \qquad \text{for all } \mathbf{x} \in U.$$

Since $(\mathbf{x}f)g = \mathbf{x}(fg)$ and $((\mathbf{x}f)g)h = (\mathbf{x}f)(gh)$, evidently we have

$$s = (fg)h = f(gh).$$

In other words, the composite operation is associative.

If U, V, and W are vector spaces over a field F, then the composite operation has the following properties for l.t.

(1) $f(g + h) = fg + fh$ for all $f \in L(U, V)$, $g, h \in L(V, W)$.

(2) $(f + g)h = fh + gh$ for all $f, g \in L(U, V)$, $h \in L(V, W)$.

(3) $c(fg) = (cf)g = f(cg)$ for all $c \in F, f \in L(U, V)$, $g \in L(V, W)$.

The proof of (1) is as follows:

$$\begin{aligned} \mathbf{x}[f(g + h)] &= (\mathbf{x}f)(g + h) = (\mathbf{x}f)g + (\mathbf{x}f)h \\ &= \mathbf{x}(fg) + \mathbf{x}(fh) = \mathbf{x}(fg + fh) \qquad \text{for all } \mathbf{x} \in U. \end{aligned}$$

Hence, $f(g + h) = fg + fh$. The proofs of (2) and (3) are left as exercises for the reader.

For each vector space U over a field F, the *identity mapping* 1 is defined by

$$\mathbf{x}1 = \mathbf{x} \qquad \text{for all } \mathbf{x} \in U.$$

Clearly $U \xrightarrow{1} U$ is a l.t. Of course, different vector spaces have different identity elements. If we wish to emphasize that 1 is the identity mapping of U, we will write 1_U.

The identity mapping is the identity element relative to the composite operation. That is,

3.13 $$1_U f = f, \qquad f 1_V = f \qquad \text{for all } f \in L(U, V).$$

These follow from the equations below:

$$\left.\begin{aligned} \mathbf{x}(1_U f) &= (\mathbf{x}1_U)f = \mathbf{x}f \\ \mathbf{x}(f 1_V) &= (\mathbf{x}f)1_V = \mathbf{x}f \end{aligned}\right\} \text{for all } \mathbf{x} \in U.$$

In the special case when $U = V$, the vector space $L(U, V)$ is closed under the composite operation; for, if $V \xrightarrow{f} V$ and $V \xrightarrow{g} V$, then also $V \xrightarrow{fg} V$. In this case, we call the composite operation *multiplication* in V. Let us denote by $L(V)$ the vector space $L(V, V)$:

$$L(V) = L(V, V).$$

The algebraic system $L(V)$ having operations of addition, scalar multiplication, and multiplication which possess the properties given in this section is called a *linear algebra*.

3.14. THEOREM. If V is a vector space over a field F, then the set of all linear transformations of V, $L(V)$, is a linear algebra. That is:

(1) $L(V)$ is a vector space.

(2) $(fg)h = f(gh)$ for all $f, g, h \in L(V)$.

(3) $f(g + h) = fg + fh, \quad (g + h)f = gf + hf$ for all $f, g, h \in L(V)$.

(4) $c(fg) = (cf)g = f(cg)$ for all $c \in F, f, g \in L(V)$.

(5) $1f = f1 = f$ for all $f \in L(V)$, where $1 = 1_V$.

EXERCISES

In the exercises, U, V, and W are vector spaces over a field F.

1. Prove that $(f + g)h = fh + gh$ for all $f, g \in L(U, V), h \in L(V, W)$.
2. Prove that $c(fg) = (cf)g = f(cg)$ for all $c \in F$, $f \in L(U, V)$, $g \in L(V, W)$.
3. If V is finite-dimensional, describe the matrix representing 1_V relative to any basis of V.
4. If $\dim V = 1$, show that $L(V)$ is isomorphic to F.
5. If $\dim V > 1$, show that the operation of multiplication in $L(V)$ is noncommutative.

5. THE ALGEBRA OF MATRICES

For convenience, let us denote by

$$F(n, m)$$

the set of all $n \times m$ matrices over a field F. We can make this set into a vector space by considering the matrices as representing l.t. and then defining operations in $F(n, m)$ to correspond to the operations in some $L(U, V)$. To be more precise, let U be an n-dimensional and V an m-dimensional vector space over F. Thus, we could select $U = F^n$ and $V = F^m$. Also, let $(\mathbf{u}_1, \mathbf{u}_2, \ldots, \mathbf{u}_n)$ be a basis of U and $(\mathbf{v}_1, \mathbf{v}_2, \ldots, \mathbf{v}_m)$ be a basis of V. Now each $f \in L(U, V)$ is represented by a unique matrix $A = (a_{ij}) \in F(n, m)$:

$$(1) \qquad \mathbf{u}_i f = \sum_{j=1}^{m} a_{ij}\mathbf{v}_j, \qquad i = 1, 2, \ldots, n.$$

Conversely, each $B = (b_{ij}) \in F(n, m)$ represents a unique $g \in L(U, V)$, namely the l.t. g defined by

$$(2) \qquad \mathbf{u}_i g = \sum_{j=1}^{m} b_{ij}\mathbf{v}_j, \qquad i = 1, 2, \ldots, n.$$

In this way, there is defined a 1–1 mapping

$$(3) \qquad L(U, V) \xrightarrow{\varphi} F(n, m),$$

where $\varphi(f) = A$ as defined in (1) above and im $\varphi = F(n, m)$.

Since the sets $L(U, V)$ and $F(n, m)$ above are in a 1–1 correspondence, the operations in $L(U, V)$ naturally induce operations in $F(n, m)$. Thus, if f and g are given by (1) and (2) above, so that $\varphi(f) = A$ and $\varphi(g) = B$, then we have

$$\mathbf{u}_i(f + g) = \mathbf{u}_i f + \mathbf{u}_i g = \sum_{j=1}^{m} a_{ij}\mathbf{v}_j + \sum_{j=1}^{m} b_{ij}\mathbf{v}_j$$

$$= \sum_{j=1}^{m} (a_{ij} + b_{ij})\mathbf{v}_j, \qquad i = 1, 2, \ldots, n.$$

Consequently, $f + g$ is represented by the matrix $(a_{ij} + b_{ij})$ which we *define* to be $A + B$:

$$3.15 \qquad (a_{ij}) + (b_{ij}) = (a_{ij} + b_{ij}).$$

For example, addition in $F(3, 2)$ is defined as follows according to 3.15.

$$\begin{pmatrix} a_{11} & a_{12} \\ a_{21} & a_{22} \\ a_{31} & a_{32} \end{pmatrix} + \begin{pmatrix} b_{11} & b_{12} \\ b_{21} & b_{22} \\ b_{31} & b_{32} \end{pmatrix} = \begin{pmatrix} a_{11} + b_{11} & a_{12} + b_{12} \\ a_{21} + b_{21} & a_{22} + b_{22} \\ a_{31} + b_{31} & a_{32} + b_{32} \end{pmatrix}.$$

If $f \in L(U, V)$ is given by (1) above and $c \in F$, then we have

$$\mathbf{u}_i(cf) = c(\mathbf{u}_i f) = \sum_{j=1}^{m} (ca_{ij})\mathbf{v}_j, \qquad i = 1, 2, \ldots, n.$$

Thus, cf is represented by the matrix (ca_{ij}), which we *define* to be cA:

3.16 $$c(a_{ij}) = (ca_{ij}).$$

For example, scalar multiplication in $F(3, 2)$ is defined as follows according to 3.16.

$$c\begin{pmatrix} a_{11} & a_{12} \\ a_{21} & a_{22} \\ a_{31} & a_{32} \end{pmatrix} = \begin{pmatrix} ca_{11} & ca_{12} \\ ca_{21} & ca_{22} \\ ca_{31} & ca_{32} \end{pmatrix}.$$

Having defined addition and scalar multiplication in $F(n, m)$ by 3.15 and 3.16, we can immediately assert that $F(n, m)$ is a vector space. This is true because $L(U, V)$ is a vector space, and the mapping $L(U, V) \xrightarrow{\varphi} F(n, m)$ is an isomorphism, that is, $\varphi(f + g) = \varphi(f) + \varphi(g)$ and $\varphi(cf) = c\varphi(f)$ for all $f, g \in L(U, V)$ and $c \in F$.

Corresponding to the zero l.t. in $L(U, V)$ is the zero matrix having 0's in all its coordinates. For example,

$$\begin{pmatrix} 0 & 0 \\ 0 & 0 \\ 0 & 0 \end{pmatrix}$$

is the zero matrix in $F(3, 2)$. We usually denote this matrix by 0 also. If f is given by (1) above, then $-f$ is given by

$$\mathbf{u}_i(-f) = \sum_{j=1}^{m} (-a_{ij})\mathbf{v}_j, \qquad i = 1, 2, \ldots, n.$$

Therefore, in $F(n, m)$ we have

3.17 $$-(a_{ij}) = (-a_{ij}).$$

For example, in $F(3, 2)$ we have

$$-\begin{pmatrix} a_{11} & a_{12} \\ a_{21} & a_{22} \\ a_{31} & a_{32} \end{pmatrix} = \begin{pmatrix} -a_{11} & -a_{12} \\ -a_{21} & -a_{22} \\ -a_{31} & -a_{32} \end{pmatrix}.$$

Corresponding to the composite operation for l.t. is a multiplication for matrices. To describe this correspondence, let U, V, and W be vector spaces over a field F of dimensions n, m, and l, respectively, and let $(\mathbf{u}_1, \mathbf{u}_2, \ldots, \mathbf{u}_n)$, $(\mathbf{v}_1, \mathbf{v}_2, \ldots, \mathbf{v}_m)$, and $(\mathbf{w}_1, \mathbf{w}_2, \ldots, \mathbf{w}_l)$ be ordered bases of U, V, and W, respectively. If $U \xrightarrow{f} V$ and $V \xrightarrow{g} W$ are l.t., then so is their composite $U \xrightarrow{fg} W$. Now f and g are represented by matrices $A = (a_{ij}) \in F(n, m)$ and $B = (b_{ij}) \in F(m, l)$, where we have

$$\mathbf{u}_i f = \sum_{k=1}^{m} a_{ik}\mathbf{v}_k, \qquad i = 1, 2, \ldots, n,$$

$$\mathbf{v}_k g = \sum_{j=1}^{l} b_{kj}\mathbf{w}_j, \qquad k = 1, 2, \ldots, m.$$

Therefore, we find that

$$\begin{aligned} \mathbf{u}_i(fg) = (\mathbf{u}_i f)g &= \sum_{k=1}^{m} a_{ik}(\mathbf{v}_k g) = \sum_{k=1}^{m} a_{ik} \sum_{j=1}^{l} b_{kj}\mathbf{w}_j \\ &= \sum_{j=1}^{l} \left(\sum_{k=1}^{m} a_{ik}b_{kj} \right) \mathbf{w}_j, \qquad i = 1, 2, \ldots, n, \end{aligned}$$

and the l.t. fg is represented by the matrix $C = (c_{ij}) \in F(n, l)$, where

$$c_{ij} = \sum_{k=1}^{m} a_{ik}b_{kj}, \qquad i = 1, 2, \ldots, n, \qquad j = 1, 2, \ldots, l.$$

We *define* matrix C to be the product of A and B:

3.18
$$(a_{ij})(b_{ij}) = \left(\sum_{k=1}^{m} a_{ik}b_{kj} \right).$$

Note that the product of an $n \times m$ matrix and an $m \times l$ matrix is an $n \times l$ matrix. *We never multiply A on the right by B unless the number of columns of A equals the number of rows of B.*

For example, the product of a 2×3 matrix and a 3×2 matrix is as given below:

$$\begin{pmatrix} a_{11} & a_{12} & a_{13} \\ a_{21} & a_{22} & a_{23} \end{pmatrix} \begin{pmatrix} b_{11} & b_{12} \\ b_{21} & b_{22} \\ b_{31} & b_{32} \end{pmatrix} = \begin{pmatrix} \sum_{k=1}^{3} a_{1k}b_{k1} & \sum_{k=1}^{3} a_{1k}b_{k2} \\ \sum_{k=1}^{3} a_{2k}b_{k1} & \sum_{k=1}^{3} a_{2k}b_{k2} \end{pmatrix}.$$

An interesting special case of 3.18 is the product of a $1 \times n$ matrix by an $n \times 1$ matrix as follows:

3.19 $$(a_{11}, a_{12}, \ldots, a_{1n})\begin{pmatrix} b_{11} \\ b_{21} \\ \cdot \\ \cdot \\ \cdot \\ b_{n1} \end{pmatrix} = \sum_{k=1}^{n} a_{1k}b_{k1}.$$

The product is a 1–1 matrix, that is, an element of F. In fact, the product is simply the inner product of two n-tuples as defined in 1.41.

All matrix multiplications consist of a series of simple multiplications of the form 3.19. That is, if the $n \times m$ matrix $A = (a_{ij})$ has rows $A_1, A_2, \ldots, A_n$ and the $m \times l$ matrix $B = (b_{ij})$ has columns $B^1, B^2, \ldots, B^l$, then each A_i is a $1 \times m$ matrix, each B^j is a $m \times 1$ matrix, and

$$A_iB^j = \sum_{k=1}^{m} a_{ik}b_{kj}.$$

Therefore, by 3.18 and 3.19, we find that

$$AB = \begin{pmatrix} A_1 \\ A_2 \\ \cdot \\ \cdot \\ \cdot \\ A_n \end{pmatrix}(B^1, B^2, \ldots, B^l) = (A_iB^j).$$

In other words, the (i, j)th element of AB is the product of the ith row A_i of A by the jth column B^j of B.

Since the multiplication of matrices was made to correspond to the composite operation of l.t., the properties of the composite operation necessarily carry over to the multiplication of matrices. Therefore, matrix multiplication is associative,

$$(AB)C = A(BC),$$

distributive with respect to addition,

$$A(B + B') = AB + AB', \qquad (A + A')B = AB + A'B,$$

and "compatible" with scalar multiplication,

$$c(AB) = (cA)B = A(cB).$$

If V is an n-dimensional vector space over a field F, the identity l.t. 1 maps each $\mathbf{x} \in V$ into itself, $\mathbf{x}1 = \mathbf{x}$. Hence, $\mathbf{u}_i 1 = \mathbf{u}_i = \sum_{j=1}^{n} \delta_{ij}\mathbf{u}_j$ for each $\mathbf{u}_i$ in a basis $(\mathbf{u}_1, \mathbf{u}_2, \ldots, \mathbf{u}_n)$ of V, and 1 is represented by the matrix (δ_{ij}) relative to every basis of V. We call the $n \times n$ matrix (δ_{ij}) the *identity matrix* of $F(n, n)$ and denote it by I:

$$I = (\delta_{ij}).$$

For example, in $F(3, 3)$ we have

$$I = \begin{pmatrix} 1 & 0 & 0 \\ 0 & 1 & 0 \\ 0 & 0 & 1 \end{pmatrix}.$$

The matrix I is an identity element relative to multiplication. That is, if $I \in F(n, n)$ and $A \in F(n, m)$, we have

$$IA = A.$$

Also, if $I \in F(m, m)$ and $A \in f(n, m)$, we have

$$AI = A.$$

These follow directly from 3.13.

If we restrict ourselves to *square matrices*, that is, $n \times n$ matrices, then the product of two $n \times n$ matrices is again an $n \times n$ matrix. Let us denote the set of all $n \times n$ matrices over a field F by $F(n)$ for short. Thus we have

$$F(n) = F(n, n).$$

Then $F(n)$ is closed under addition, scalar multiplication, and multiplication, and $F(n)$ is isomorphic to $L(F^n)$ relative to a given basis of F^n. This isomorphism preserves multiplication as well as addition and scalar multiplication. Thus, the following theorem is a direct consequence of 3.14.

3.20. THEOREM. The set $F(n)$ of all $n \times n$ matrices over a field F is a linear algebra. That is:

(1) $F(n)$ is a vector space.
(2) $(AB)C = A(BC)$ for all $A, B, C \in F(n)$.
(3) $A(B + C) = AB + AC$, $(A + B)C = AC + BC$ for all $A, B, C \in F(n)$.
(4) $c(AB) = (cA)B = A(cB)$ for all $c \in F$, $A, B \in F(n)$.
(5) $IA = AI = A$ for all $A \in F(n)$.

EXERCISES

1. Let matrices A, B, C, and D over $\mathbb{Q}$ be defined as follows:

$$A = \begin{pmatrix} 2 & -1 & 4 \\ 3 & 0 & 5 \end{pmatrix}, \quad B = \begin{pmatrix} 2 & 1 & -1 \\ -3 & 5 & 2 \\ 4 & 0 & 1 \\ -1 & 5 & 3 \end{pmatrix},$$

$$C = \begin{pmatrix} 7 & -2 & 3 & 5 \\ 4 & 0 & -4 & 0 \\ 2 & 6 & -3 & 7 \end{pmatrix}, \quad D = \begin{pmatrix} 6 & 2 \\ -2 & -1 \\ 3 & 4 \\ 5 & 7 \end{pmatrix}.$$

Find, if possible:

(a) AC. (b) DA. (c) CB.
(d) BC. (e) AD. (f) BA.
(g) $A(CB)$. (h) $(DA)C$. (i) $(CD)A$.

2. Let matrices $A, B, C, D \in \mathbb{Q}(3)$ be defined as follows:

$$A = \begin{pmatrix} 1 & 2 & -1 \\ 3 & 1 & 2 \\ -1 & -1 & -2 \end{pmatrix}, \quad B = \begin{pmatrix} 0 & 4 & -1 \\ 0 & 0 & 3 \\ 0 & 0 & 0 \end{pmatrix},$$

$$C = \begin{pmatrix} 0 & 5 & 5 \\ 4 & -3 & -5 \\ -2 & -1 & -5 \end{pmatrix}, \quad D = \begin{pmatrix} 1 & 2 & -5 \\ -1 & 3 & 2 \\ -4 & 0 & 0 \end{pmatrix}.$$

Find:

(a) $AB + BA$. (b) $\frac{1}{10}(AC)$. (c) $\frac{1}{10}(CA)$.
(d) B^2. (e) B^3. (f) $(A + B)C$.
(g) BD. (h) DB. (i) $(A - D)(A + 2D)$.
(j) $(2A - C)(A + 3C)$. (k) $3(CD)$. (l) $AB - CD$.

6. THE RANK OF A LINEAR TRANSFORMATION

Let U and V be finite-dimensional vector spaces over a field F and $f \in L(U, V)$. The *image* of f defined by

$$\text{im}\, f = \{\mathbf{x}f \mid \mathbf{x} \in U\}$$

is easily shown to be a subspace of V, while the *kernel* of f defined by

$$\ker f = \{\mathbf{x} \in U \mid \mathbf{x}f = \mathbf{0}\}$$

is a subspace of U. Thus, if $\mathbf{x}, \mathbf{y} \in \ker f$ and $a \in F$, then $(\mathbf{x} + \mathbf{y})f = \mathbf{x}f + \mathbf{y}f = \mathbf{0}$, and $(a\mathbf{x})f = a(\mathbf{x}f) = a\mathbf{0} = \mathbf{0}$. Hence, $\mathbf{x} + \mathbf{y}$ and $a\mathbf{x}$ are in $\ker f$, and $\ker f$ is a subspace. Evidently, $\ker f = U$ iff $f = 0$.

3.21. DEFINITION OF RANK OF A LINEAR TRANSFORMATION. The rank of a l.t. $U \xrightarrow{f} V$ is denoted by $\text{r}(f)$ and defined by

$$\text{r}(f) = \dim(\text{im}\, f).$$

If $\{\mathbf{u}_1, \mathbf{u}_2, \ldots, \mathbf{u}_n\}$ is a basis of U, then each $\mathbf{x} \in U$ has the form $\mathbf{x} = \sum_{i=1}^{n} c_i\mathbf{u}_i$ for some $c_i \in F$. Consequently, if $f \in L(U, V)$, then we have

$$\mathbf{x}f = \sum_{i=1}^{n} c_i(\mathbf{u}_i f).$$

Therefore, $\{\mathbf{u}_1 f, \mathbf{u}_2 f, \ldots, \mathbf{u}_n f\}$ is a set of generators of $\operatorname{im} f$. If this set is l.i., then $\mathrm{r}(f) = n$; otherwise, $\mathrm{r}(f) < n$. Since $\operatorname{im} f \subset V$, always $\dim(\operatorname{im} f) \leq \dim V$. Thus, we see that

$$\mathrm{r}(f) \leq \min(\dim U, \dim V).$$

A l.t. $U \xrightarrow{f} V$ for which $\ker f \neq \{\mathbf{0}\}$ is not a 1–1 mapping. For $\mathbf{x}f = \mathbf{0}f = \mathbf{0}$ if $\mathbf{x} \in \ker f$, although $\mathbf{x} \neq \mathbf{0}$ for some $\mathbf{x} \in \ker f$. On the other hand, if $U \xrightarrow{f} V$ is a l.t. for which $\ker f = \{\mathbf{0}\}$ and if $\mathbf{x}, \mathbf{y} \in U, \mathbf{x} \neq \mathbf{y}$, then $f(\mathbf{x} - \mathbf{y}) = f(\mathbf{x}) - f(\mathbf{y}) \neq \mathbf{0}$, and $f(\mathbf{x}) \neq f(\mathbf{y})$. Hence, f is a 1–1 mapping. If $\{\mathbf{u}_1, \mathbf{u}_2, \ldots, \mathbf{u}_n\}$ is a basis of U and $\ker f = \{\mathbf{0}\}$, then $\{\mathbf{u}_1 f, \mathbf{u}_2 f, \ldots, \mathbf{u}_n f\}$ is a basis of $\operatorname{im} f$. For if $\sum_{i=1}^{n} c_i(\mathbf{u}_i f) = \mathbf{0}$ for some $c_i \in F$, then $(\sum_{i=1}^{n} c_i\mathbf{u}_i)f = \mathbf{0}$ and

$$\sum_{i=1}^{n} c_i\mathbf{u}_i = \mathbf{0}.$$

Therefore, all $c_i = 0$, and the vectors $\mathbf{u}_1 f, \mathbf{u}_2 f, \ldots, \mathbf{u}_n f$ are l.i.

If $U \xrightarrow{f} V$ is a l.t. such that $f \neq 0$ and $\ker f \neq \{\mathbf{0}\}$, then we can select a basis $\{\mathbf{x}_1, \mathbf{x}_2, \ldots, \mathbf{x}_k\}$ of $\ker f$ and then extend this set to a basis of U, say $\{\mathbf{x}_1, \mathbf{x}_2, \ldots, \mathbf{x}_k, \mathbf{x}_{k+1}, \ldots, \mathbf{x}_n\}$. Since the vectors $\mathbf{x}_1 f, \mathbf{x}_2 f, \ldots, \mathbf{x}_n f$ are generators of $\operatorname{im} f$ and $\mathbf{x}_i f = \mathbf{0}$ if $i \leq k$, evidently the vectors $\mathbf{x}_{k+1} f, \ldots, \mathbf{x}_n f$ generate $\operatorname{im} f$. These vectors are l.i.; for if $\sum_{i=k+1}^{n} c_i(\mathbf{x}_i f) = \mathbf{0}$ for some $c_i \in F$, then $\sum_{i=k+1}^{n} c_i\mathbf{x}_i \in \ker f$ and $\sum_{i=k+1}^{n} c_i\mathbf{x}_i = \sum_{i=1}^{k} a_i\mathbf{x}_i$ for some $a_i \in F$. Since the vectors $\mathbf{x}_1, \mathbf{x}_2, \ldots, \mathbf{x}_n$ are l.i., necessarily $c_i = 0$ (and $a_i = 0$) for all i. Therefore, $\{\mathbf{x}_{k+1} f, \ldots, \mathbf{x}_n f\}$ is a basis of $\operatorname{im} f$, and $\dim(\operatorname{im} f) = n - k$. This proves the following theorem.

3.22. THEOREM. If U and V are finite-dimensional vector spaces over a field F and $f \in L(U, V)$, then we have

$$\mathrm{r}(f) + \dim(\ker f) = \dim U.$$

The number $\dim(\ker f)$ is often called the *nullity* of f and denoted by $\operatorname{nul}(f)$. In this notation, 3.22 has the form $r(f) + \operatorname{nul}(f) = \dim U$.

We recall that the rank of an $n \times n$ matrix $A = (a_{ij})$ over a field F is the dimension of the row (or column) space of A. How is the rank of a matrix related to the rank of a linear transformation? To answer this question, let vector spaces U and V over a field F have dimensions n and m, respectively, and let $U \xrightarrow{f} V$ be a l.t. which is represented by A relative to some bases of U and V. Then f has the same rank as the l.t. $F^n \xrightarrow{g} F^m$ defined by

$$\mathbf{u}_i g = \sum_{j=1}^{m} a_{ij}\mathbf{v}_j, \qquad i = 1, 2, \ldots, n,$$

relative to the usual bases of F^n and F^m. Thus, if matrix A has rows A_1, A_2, . . . , A_n, then $\mathbf{u}_i g$ is simply A_i for each i. Hence, im g is the row space of matrix A, and $r(g) = r(A)$. These remarks give the following answer to our question above.

3.23. THEOREM. If a linear transformation f is represented by a matrix A, then $r(f) = r(A)$.

Let V be an n-dimensional vector space over a field F and $f \in L(V)$. We shall call f *singular* if $r(f) < n$ and *nonsingular* if $r(f) = n$. By 3.22, f is nonsingular iff $\ker f = \{\mathbf{0}\}$. Hence, f is nonsingular iff f is a 1–1 mapping and $\operatorname{im} f = V$, that is, iff f is an isomorphism of V.

Each isomorphism f of V has an inverse f^{-1} defined by

$$(\mathbf{x}f)f^{-1} = \mathbf{x} \qquad \text{for all } \mathbf{x} \in V.$$

Since we have

$$(\mathbf{x}f + \mathbf{y}f)f^{-1} = [(\mathbf{x} + \mathbf{y})f]f^{-1} = \mathbf{x} + \mathbf{y} = (\mathbf{x}f)f^{-1} + (\mathbf{y}f)f^{-1}$$
$$[a(\mathbf{x}f)]f^{-1} = [(a\mathbf{x})f]f^{-1} = a\mathbf{x} = a[(\mathbf{x}f)f^{-1}]$$

for all $\mathbf{x}, \mathbf{y} \in V$ and $a \in F$, f^{-1} is also a l.t. of V. By the definition of f^{-1}, we have $ff^{-1} = 1$. Therefore, $Vf^{-1} = (Vf)f^{-1} = V1 = V$, and $\operatorname{im} f^{-1} = V$. This shows that $r(f^{-1}) = n$ and hence that f^{-1} is nonsingular. Since f^{-1} is a 1–1 mapping and $[(\mathbf{x}f^{-1})f]f^{-1} = \mathbf{x}f^{-1}$, we must have $(\mathbf{x}f^{-1})f = \mathbf{x}$ for all $\mathbf{x} \in V$. Hence, $f^{-1}f$ is also equal to 1. Therefore, we have

$$ff^{-1} = f^{-1}f = 1,$$

and f^{-1} is the multiplicative inverse of f.

If f is a l.t. of V which has a multiplicative inverse f^{-1}, then $V = (Vf^{-1})f$ and, necessarily, $r(f) = \dim V$. Thus, we have proved the following result.

3.24. THEOREM. A linear transformation f of a vector space V is nonsingular iff f has a multiplicative inverse.

Similarly, an $n \times n$ matrix A over a field F is called *singular* if $r(A) < n$ and *nonsingular* if $r(A) = n$. Since the algebra $F(n)$ is isomorphic to the algebra of l.t. of an n-dimensional vector space over F, the following result is a corollary of 3.23 and 3.24.

3.25. THEOREM. An $n \times n$ matrix A over a field F is nonsingular iff A has a multiplicative inverse.

A system of n linear equations in n unknowns over a field F has the form

$$\sum_{j=1}^{n} a_{ij}x_j = b_i, \qquad i = 1, 2, \ldots, n.$$

If we let $A = (a_{ij}) \in F(n)$ and

$$X = \begin{pmatrix} x_1 \\ x_2 \\ \cdot \\ \cdot \\ \cdot \\ x_n \end{pmatrix}, \qquad B = \begin{pmatrix} b_1 \\ b_2 \\ \cdot \\ \cdot \\ \cdot \\ b_n \end{pmatrix}$$

be in $F(n, 1)$, then the above system can be put in the form

$$AX = B.$$

If A is nonsingular, so that A has an inverse A^{-1}, then $A^{-1}(AX) = A^{-1}B$, $IX = A^{-1}B$, and

3.26
$$X = A^{-1}B$$

is the unique solution of $AX = B$. Conversely, if $AX = B$ has a unique solution, then $\mathrm{r}(A) = n$ by 2.15 and 2.16. This proves the following result.

3.27. THEOREM. A system of n linear equations in n unknowns over a field F has a unique solution iff its matrix of coefficients is nonsingular.

We cannot effectively use 3.26 to solve a system of linear equations, because we do not have a method of finding A^{-1}. Such a method will be given in the next chapter. However, it is clear that for 2×2 matrices, we have

$$\begin{pmatrix} a & b \\ c & d \end{pmatrix}\begin{pmatrix} d & -b \\ -c & a \end{pmatrix} = \begin{pmatrix} d & -b \\ -c & a \end{pmatrix}\begin{pmatrix} a & b \\ c & d \end{pmatrix}$$
$$= \begin{pmatrix} k & 0 \\ 0 & k \end{pmatrix}, \qquad \text{where } k = ad - bc.$$

Hence, if $k \neq 0$, then we have

$$\begin{pmatrix} a & b \\ c & d \end{pmatrix}^{-1} = \frac{1}{k}\begin{pmatrix} d & -b \\ -c & a \end{pmatrix}.$$

For example, let us solve the system of linear equations

$$3x + 4y = 4,$$
$$2x + 4y = 5.$$

If we let

$$A = \begin{pmatrix} 3 & 4 \\ 2 & 4 \end{pmatrix}, \qquad X = \begin{pmatrix} x \\ y \end{pmatrix}, \qquad B = \begin{pmatrix} 4 \\ 5 \end{pmatrix},$$

then the system above has the form $AX = B$. Now $k = 3 \cdot 4 - 4 \cdot 2 = 4$. Hence, we have

$$A^{-1} = \frac{1}{4}\begin{pmatrix} 4 & -4 \\ -2 & 3 \end{pmatrix},$$

and, by 3.26, we find that

$$X = \frac{1}{4}\begin{pmatrix} 4 & -4 \\ -2 & 3 \end{pmatrix}\begin{pmatrix} 4 \\ 5 \end{pmatrix} = \frac{1}{4}\begin{pmatrix} -4 \\ 7 \end{pmatrix} = \begin{pmatrix} -1 \\ \frac{7}{4} \end{pmatrix}.$$

Thus, the unique solution of the given system is $x = -1$ and $y = \frac{7}{4}$.

EXERCISES

In the following exercises, U, V, and W are finite-dimensional vector spaces over a field F.

1. Prove that for all $f \in L(U, V)$ and $g \in L(V, W)$, $\mathrm{r}(fg) \leq \mathrm{r}(g)$ and $\mathrm{r}(fg) \leq \mathrm{r}(f)$.
2. Prove that for all $f, g \in L(U, V)$, $\mathrm{r}(f + g) \leq \mathrm{r}(f) + \mathrm{r}(g)$. Give an example in which $f \neq 0$, $g \neq 0$, and $\mathrm{r}(f + g) = \mathrm{r}(f) + \mathrm{r}(g)$.
3. Assume that $\dim V = n > 1$. For each integer k such that $0 < k < n$, give an example of an $f \in L(V)$ such that $f^2 = f$ and $\mathrm{r}(f) = k$.
4. For each $f \in L(V)$ such that $\ker f \neq \{\mathbf{0}\}$, describe some $g \in L(V)$ having the property that $\mathrm{r}(g) = \mathrm{nul}\,(f)$ and $gf = 0$.
5. Prove that the product AB of two nonsingular $n \times n$ matrices A and B over F is nonsingular, and that $(AB)^{-1} = B^{-1}A^{-1}$. Is the set of all nonsingular $n \times n$ matrices over a field F a multiplicative group?
6. For each $A \in F(n, m)$, the *transpose* A^T of A is in $F(m, n)$ and is defined as follows: the ith row of A is the ith column of A^T and the jth column of A is the jth row of A^T. Prove the following:

   (1) $(A^T)^T = A$ for each $A \in F(n, m)$.

   (2) $(aA + bB)^T = aA^T + bB^T$ for all $a, b \in F$, $A, B \in F(n, m)$.

   (3) $(AB)^T = B^T A^T$ for all $A \in F(n, m)$, $B \in F(m, k)$.

   (4) If $A \in F(n)$ is nonsingular, then A^T is nonsingular, and $(A^T)^{-1} = (A^{-1})^T$.

7. CHANGE OF BASIS

Let V be an n-dimensional vector space over a field F. Each $f \in L(V)$ is represented by a matrix $A = (a_{ij})$ relative to a basis $(\mathbf{u}_1, \mathbf{u}_2, \ldots, \mathbf{u}_n)$ of V. Thus, we have

(1) $$\mathbf{u}_i f = \sum_{j=1}^{n} a_{ij}\mathbf{u}_j, \qquad i = 1, 2, \ldots, n.$$

If we select another basis $(\mathbf{v}_1, \mathbf{v}_2, \ldots, \mathbf{v}_n)$ of V, then f is represented by another matrix $B = (b_{ij})$. Thus, we have

(2) $$\mathbf{v}_i f = \sum_{j=1}^{n} b_{ij}\mathbf{v}_j, \qquad i = 1, 2, \ldots, n.$$

How are matrices A and B related? Given a matrix C, how can we tell if C represents f relative to some basis of V?

To answer these questions, let g be the l.t. which maps the $\mathbf{u}$-basis into the $\mathbf{v}$-basis,

$$\mathbf{v}_i g = \mathbf{u}_i, \qquad i = 1, 2, \ldots, n,$$

and let $P = (p_{ij})$ be the matrix which represents g relative to the $\mathbf{v}$-basis:

(3) $$\mathbf{v}_i g = \mathbf{u}_i = \sum_{j=1}^{n} p_{ij}\mathbf{v}_j, \qquad i = 1, 2, \ldots, n.$$

Since $\mathrm{r}(g) = n$, P is a nonsingular matrix. From (1) and (3), we have that

$$\mathbf{u}_i f = \sum_{k=1}^{n} a_{ik}\mathbf{u}_k = \sum_{k=1}^{n} a_{ik}\left(\sum_{j=1}^{n} p_{kj}\mathbf{v}_j\right) = \sum_{j=1}^{n}\left(\sum_{k=1}^{n} a_{ik}p_{kj}\right)\mathbf{v}_j,$$

whereas from (2) and (3), we see that

$$\mathbf{u}_i f = \sum_{k=1}^{n} p_{ik}(\mathbf{v}_k f) = \sum_{k=1}^{n} p_{ik}\left(\sum_{j=1}^{n} b_{kj}\mathbf{v}_j\right) = \sum_{j=1}^{n}\left(\sum_{k=1}^{n} p_{ik}b_{kj}\right)\mathbf{v}_j$$

for $i = 1, 2, \ldots, n$. On equating the coefficients of $\mathbf{v}_j$ in these two equations, we get

$$\sum_{k=1}^{n} a_{ik}p_{kj} = \sum_{k=1}^{n} p_{ik}b_{kj}, \qquad i, j = 1, 2, \ldots, n.$$

In matrix form, we have

$$AP = PB.$$

Since P is nonsingular, it has an inverse P^{-1}, and

3.28 $$B = P^{-1}AP.$$

We now have answered one of our questions: A and B are related by Equation 3.28.

If $A, B \in F(n)$, then matrix B is said to be *similar* to matrix A iff there exists a nonsingular matrix P such that $B = P^{-1}AP$. Since $A = PBP^{-1} = (P^{-1})^{-1}BP^{-1}$, evidently A is similar to B whenever B is similar to A. Thus, the relation of similarity in $F(n)$ is symmetric. Since $A = I^{-1}AI$, where I is the identity matrix, A is similar to itself. Hence, the similarity relation is reflexive. Finally, if B is similar to A and C to B, so that we have

$$B = P^{-1}AP, \qquad C = Q^{-1}BQ$$

for some nonsingular $P, Q \in F(n)$, then C is similar to A because

$$C = (PQ)^{-1}A(PQ).$$

That is, the similarity relation is transitive. Since the similarity relation in $F(n)$ is reflexive, symmetric, and transitive, it is an *equivalence relation.*

If $f \in L(V)$ is represented by matrix $A = (a_{ij})$ relative to the basis $(\mathbf{u}_1, \mathbf{u}_2, \ldots, \mathbf{u}_n)$ of V and if $C = (c_{ij})$ is similar to A, then $C = P^{-1}AP$ for some nonsingular matrix P. If $P^{-1} = (q_{ij})$ and

$$\mathbf{v}_i = \sum_{j=1}^{n} q_{ij}\mathbf{u}_j, \qquad i = 1, 2, \ldots, n,$$

then we can easily show, as above, that

$$\mathbf{v}_i f = \sum_{j=1}^{n} c_{ij}\mathbf{v}_j, \qquad i = 1, 2, \ldots, n.$$

Therefore, f is represented by the matrix C relative to the $\mathbf{v}$-basis. We have proved the following theorem.

3.29. THEOREM. Let V be a vector space over a field F and $(\mathbf{u}_1, \mathbf{u}_2, \ldots, \mathbf{u}_n)$ be a basis of V. If $f \in L(V)$ is represented by the matrix A relative to the $\mathbf{u}$-basis and if $B \in F(n)$, then B represents f relative to some basis of V iff B is similar to A.

We have now answered both questions which we posed in the first paragraph of this section.

EXAMPLE: Let $f \in L(\mathbb{Q}^3)$ be defined as follows:

$$(a, b, c)f = (b + c, a - b - c, 2a + b), \; a, b, c \in \mathbb{Q}.$$

Let us find the matrices A and B of f relative to the ordered bases ((1, 0, 0), (0, 1, 0), (0, 0, 1)) and ((1, 0, −1), (0, 1, 0), (1, 1, 1)), respectively, of $\mathbb{Q}^3$. Also, let us find the nonsingular matrix P such that $B = P^{-1}AP$.

If $\mathbf{u}_1 = (1, 0, 0)$, $\mathbf{u}_2 = (0, 1, 0)$, $\mathbf{u}_3 = (0, 0, 1)$ as usual, then we have

$$\mathbf{u}_1 f = (0, 1, 2) = \mathbf{u}_2 + 2\mathbf{u}_3,$$
$$\mathbf{u}_2 f = (1, -1, 1) = \mathbf{u}_1 - \mathbf{u}_2 + \mathbf{u}_3,$$
$$\mathbf{u}_3 f = (1, -1, 0) = \mathbf{u}_1 - \mathbf{u}_2,$$

and f is represented by the following matrix A relative to the $\mathbf{u}$-basis:

$$A = \begin{pmatrix} 0 & 1 & 2 \\ 1 & -1 & 1 \\ 1 & -1 & 0 \end{pmatrix}.$$

If we let $\mathbf{v}_1 = (1, 0, -1) = \mathbf{u}_1 - \mathbf{u}_3$, $\mathbf{v}_2 = (0, 1, 0) = \mathbf{u}_2$, and $\mathbf{v}_3 = (1, 1, 1) = \mathbf{u}_1 + \mathbf{u}_2 + \mathbf{u}_3$, then $\{\mathbf{v}_1, \mathbf{v}_2, \mathbf{v}_3\}$ is a basis of V, and we have

$$\mathbf{u}_1 = \tfrac{1}{2}\mathbf{v}_1 - \tfrac{1}{2}\mathbf{v}_2 + \tfrac{1}{2}\mathbf{v}_3, \qquad \mathbf{u}_2 = \mathbf{v}_2, \qquad \mathbf{u}_3 = -\tfrac{1}{2}\mathbf{v}_1 - \tfrac{1}{2}\mathbf{v}_2 + \tfrac{1}{2}\mathbf{v}_3.$$

Hence, we can easily compute

$$\mathbf{v}_1 f = \mathbf{u}_1 f - \mathbf{u}_3 f = -\mathbf{u}_1 + 2\mathbf{u}_2 + 2\mathbf{u}_3 = -\tfrac{3}{2}\mathbf{v}_1 + \tfrac{3}{2}\mathbf{v}_2 + \tfrac{1}{2}\mathbf{v}_3,$$
$$\mathbf{v}_2 f = \mathbf{u}_2 f = \mathbf{u}_1 - \mathbf{u}_2 + \mathbf{u}_3 = -2\mathbf{v}_2 + \mathbf{v}_3,$$
$$\mathbf{v}_3 f = \mathbf{u}_1 f + \mathbf{u}_2 f + \mathbf{u}_3 f = 2\mathbf{u}_1 - \mathbf{u}_2 + 3\mathbf{u}_3 = -\tfrac{1}{2}\mathbf{v}_1 - \tfrac{7}{2}\mathbf{v}_2 + \tfrac{5}{2}\mathbf{v}_3.$$

Thus, f is represented by the following matrix B relative to the $\mathbf{v}$-basis:

$$B = \begin{pmatrix} -\frac{3}{2} & \frac{3}{2} & \frac{1}{2} \\ 0 & -2 & 1 \\ -\frac{1}{2} & -\frac{7}{2} & \frac{5}{2} \end{pmatrix}.$$

We also see from equations above that the l.t. $V \xrightarrow{g} V$ defined by $\mathbf{v}_i g = \mathbf{u}_i$ has the matrix

$$P = \begin{pmatrix} \frac{1}{2} & -\frac{1}{2} & \frac{1}{2} \\ 0 & 1 & 0 \\ -\frac{1}{2} & -\frac{1}{2} & \frac{1}{2} \end{pmatrix}$$

relative to the $\mathbf{v}$-basis. Therefore, by the work of this section, we find that

$$B = P^{-1}AP.$$

The reader may wish to verify that

$$P^{-1} = \begin{pmatrix} 1 & 0 & -1 \\ 0 & 1 & 0 \\ 1 & 1 & 1 \end{pmatrix},$$

and then to check that $P^{-1}AP$ actually equals B.

EXERCISES

In each of the following exercises, find the matrices A and B representing the given l.t. relative to the bases $((1, 0, 0), (0, 1, 0), (0, 0, 1))$ and $((1, 1, 0), (1, 0, 1), (0, 1, 1))$ of $\mathbb{Q}^3$. Then find the nonsingular matrix P such that $B = P^{-1}AP$.

1. $(a, b, c)f = (b, c, a)$, $a, b, c \in \mathbb{Q}$.
2. $(a, b, c)f = (2a + 3c, a - b, 3b - 2c)$, $a, b, c \in \mathbb{Q}$.
3. $(a, b, c)f = (a + b + c, b + c, c)$, $a, b, c \in \mathbb{Q}$.
4. $(a, b, c)f = (5a, 3a - b, 2a + 3b + c)$, $a, b, c \in \mathbb{Q}$.
5. $(a, b, c)f = (2a + 2b - c, 3b - 4c, c)$, $a, b, c \in \mathbb{Q}$.
6. If F is a field and $A = (a_{ij}) \in F(n)$, then the *trace* of A, $\mathrm{T}(A)$, is defined by $\mathrm{T}(A) = a_{11} + a_{22} + \cdots + a_{nn}$. Prove the following:

   (1) $\mathrm{T}(aA + bB) = a\mathrm{T}(A) + b\mathrm{T}(B)$ for all $a, b \in F$, $A, B \in F(n)$.
   (2) $\mathrm{T}(AB) = \mathrm{T}(BA)$ for all $A, B \in F(n)$.
   (3) $\mathrm{T}(A) = \mathrm{T}(P^{-1}AP)$ for all $A \in F(n)$ and all nonsingular $P \in F(n)$. Hence, conclude that the trace of a l.t. may be meaningfully defined.
   (4) If $A \in F(n)$ is nonsingular, is $\mathrm{T}(A)$ necessarily nonzero? Give examples.

Chapter Four

Determinants

1. PERMUTATIONS

A 1–1 mapping $A \xrightarrow{\varphi} A$ such that im $\varphi = A$ is called a *permutation* of A. If set A has n elements, φ is called a *permutation on n letters*. For example, if $A = \{1, 2, 3, 4\}$ and φ is defined by

$$1\varphi = 3, \qquad 2\varphi = 1, \qquad 3\varphi = 4, \qquad 4\varphi = 2,$$

then φ is a permutation on four letters.

If $A \xrightarrow{\varphi} A$ and $A \xrightarrow{\theta} A$ are permutations, then their composite $A \xrightarrow{\varphi\theta} A$ is also a permutation. Each permutation $A \xrightarrow{\varphi} A$ has an inverse $A \xrightarrow{\varphi^{-1}} A$, which is also a permutation, defined by $b\varphi^{-1} = a$ iff $a\varphi = b$. For example, if φ is the permutation on four letters defined above, then φ^{-1} is given by

$$1\varphi^{-1} = 2, \qquad 2\varphi^{-1} = 4, \qquad 3\varphi^{-1} = 1, \qquad 4\varphi^{-1} = 3.$$

The identity mapping $A \xrightarrow{\epsilon} A$ defined by $x\epsilon = x$ for all $x \in A$ is clearly a permutation.

If A is a set with n elements, then the set of all permutations of A is denoted by

$$S_n.$$

Evidently S_n only depends on the number n of elements of A and not on the nature of these elements. We shall usually take A to be the set $\{1, 2, \ldots, n\}$.

4.1. THEOREM. The set S_n is a group under the composite operation. That is, the following properties hold.

(1) $(\alpha\beta)\gamma = \alpha(\beta\gamma)$ for all $\alpha, \beta, \gamma \in S_n$ (Associative law),

(2) $\alpha\epsilon = \epsilon\alpha = \alpha$ for all $\alpha \in S_n$ (Identity element),

(3) $\alpha\alpha^{-1} = \alpha^{-1}\alpha = \epsilon$ for all $\alpha \in S_n$ (Inverse elements).

The group S_n is called the *symmetric group on n letters*. A common notation for $\varphi \in S_n$ is

$$\varphi = \begin{pmatrix} 1 & 2 & 3 & \dots & n \\ i_1 & i_2 & i_3 & \dots & i_n \end{pmatrix},$$

where it is understood that φ maps each element of the first row into the element directly below it: that is, $k\varphi = i_k$. Since φ is a 1–1 mapping, the elements $i_1, i_2, \dots, i_n$ are the n integers $1, 2, \dots, n$ in some order. Since there are n possible choices for i_1, having chosen i_1, there are $n - 1$ choices for i_2, and having chosen i_1 and i_2, there are $n - 2$ choices for i_3, and so on, evidently there are $n!$ elements in S_n.

For example, S_4 has $4! = 24$ elements, one of which is

$$\varphi = \begin{pmatrix} 1 & 2 & 3 & 4 \\ 3 & 1 & 4 & 2 \end{pmatrix}$$

given above.

A permutation $\alpha \in S_n$ is called a *transposition* iff there exist distinct integers j and k in $\{1, 2, \dots, n\}$ such that

(1) $j\varphi = k, \quad k\varphi = j, \quad \text{and} \quad x\varphi = x \quad \text{if} \quad x \neq j \quad \text{and} \quad x \neq k.$

For example, we know that

$$\alpha = \begin{pmatrix} 1 & 2 & 3 & 4 \\ 1 & 4 & 3 & 2 \end{pmatrix}, \qquad \beta = \begin{pmatrix} 1 & 2 & 3 & 4 \\ 1 & 3 & 2 & 4 \end{pmatrix}$$

are transpositions in S_4. We shall use the abbreviated notation $(j\,k)$ for transposition (1) above. Thus, $\alpha = (2\,4)$ and $\beta = (2\,3)$ in this notation. Each transposition is its own inverse, since $(i\,j)^2 = \epsilon$. Thus, $(2\,4)^{-1} = (2\,4)$ and $(2\,3)^{-1} = (2\,3)$ in S_4.

Every element of S_n can be expressed as a product of transpositions. We won't prove this fact but indicate by examples how to express any permutation as a product of transpositions.

For example, if we have

$$\varphi = \begin{pmatrix} 1 & 2 & 3 & 4 \\ 3 & 1 & 4 & 2 \end{pmatrix} \in S_4,$$

then $1\varphi = 3$, and we take $(1\,3)$ as the first transposition. Since $3\varphi = 4$, we take $(1\,4)$ as the second transposition. Note that $1\,(1\,3)(1\,4) = 3$, $3\,(1\,3)(1\,4) = 1\,(1\,4) = 4$. Next, we see that $4\varphi = 2$, and therefore we take $(1\,2)$ as the third transposition. Finally, $2\varphi = 1$, and we are back to 1, the element with which we started. Hence, we have

$$\varphi = (1\,3)(1\,4)(1\,2).$$

As a second example, consider

$$\theta = \begin{pmatrix} 1 & 2 & 3 & 4 & 5 & 6 & 7 \\ 1 & 6 & 2 & 4 & 7 & 3 & 5 \end{pmatrix} \in S_7.$$

Since $1\theta = 1$ and $4\theta = 4$, we need not consider 1 or 4. Now we know that $2\theta = 6$, $6\theta = 3$, and $3\theta = 2$, so we take $(2\ 6)(2\ 3)$ as the first two transpositions. We now have finished with the elements 1, 2, 3, 4, and 6. Since $5\theta = 7$ and $7\theta = 5$, we find that $(5\ 7)$ is the final transposition. Thus, we have

$$\theta = (2\ 6)(2\ 3)(5\ 7).$$

There are many ways of expressing a permutation as a product of transpositions. For example, in S_3, we have

$$(2\ 3) = (1\ 2)(2\ 3)(1\ 3).$$

Thus, we have

$$1\,(1\ 2)(2\ 3)(1\ 3) = 2\,(2\ 3)(1\ 3) = 3\,(1\ 3) = 1,$$
$$2\,(1\ 2)(2\ 3)(1\ 3) = 1\,(2\ 3)(1\ 3) = 1\,(1\ 3) = 3,$$
$$3\,(1\ 2)(2\ 3)(1\ 3) = 3\,(2\ 3)(1\ 3) = 2\,(1\ 3) = 2.$$

However, there is some uniqueness about the expression as follows.

4.2. THEOREM. If a permutation can be expressed as a product of k transpositions and also as a product of m transpositions, then k and m are either both even integers or both odd integers.

We shall not prove this theorem but rather refer the reader to almost any book on higher algebra for a proof.

According to 4.2, every permutation is either *even* (that is, can be expressed as a product of an even number of transpositions) or *odd* (that is, can be expressed as a product of an odd number of transpositions). It is convenient to introduce the *sign of a permutation* φ to be 1 if φ is even and -1 if φ is odd:

$$\operatorname{sgn} \varphi = \begin{cases} 1 & \text{if } \ \varphi \text{ is even}, \\ -1 & \text{if } \ \varphi \text{ is odd}. \end{cases}$$

If $\varphi \in S_n$ is expressed as a product of transpositions $\varphi = \alpha_1\alpha_2\cdots\alpha_m$, then we have

$$\varphi^{-1} = \alpha_m\alpha_{m-1}\cdots\alpha_1.$$

Hence, $\operatorname{sgn} \varphi = \operatorname{sgn} \varphi^{-1}$ for every $\varphi \in S_n$.

EXERCISES

1. Express each element of S_3 as a product of transpositions.
2. Express each element of S_4 as a product of transpositions.

3. Find the sign of each element of S_6 below.

$$\alpha = \begin{pmatrix} 1 & 2 & 3 & 4 & 5 & 6 \\ 4 & 2 & 5 & 3 & 6 & 1 \end{pmatrix}, \quad \beta = \begin{pmatrix} 1 & 2 & 3 & 4 & 5 & 6 \\ 5 & 4 & 6 & 1 & 2 & 3 \end{pmatrix},$$

$$\gamma = \begin{pmatrix} 1 & 2 & 3 & 4 & 5 & 6 \\ 2 & 1 & 4 & 3 & 6 & 5 \end{pmatrix}, \quad \delta = \begin{pmatrix} 1 & 2 & 3 & 4 & 5 & 6 \\ 4 & 1 & 3 & 6 & 5 & 2 \end{pmatrix}.$$

4. Prove that $\operatorname{sgn}(\alpha\beta) = (\operatorname{sgn}\alpha)(\operatorname{sgn}\beta)$ for all $\alpha, \beta \in S_n$.

2. DETERMINANTS

If F is a field and n is a positive integer, then the determinant of each $n \times n$ matrix in $F(n)$ is defined as follows.

4.3. DEFINITION OF DETERMINANT. For each $A = (a_{ij}) \in F(n)$, the determinant of A is denoted by $\det A$ and defined by

$$\det A = \sum_{\varphi \in S_n} (\operatorname{sgn}\varphi) a_{1\,1\varphi} a_{2\,2\varphi} \cdots a_{n\,n\varphi}.$$

According to 4.3, $\det A$ is an element of F, in fact, it is a sum of $n!$ elements of F, each of which is plus or minus a product of n elements of F.

The case $n = 1$ is trivial: $\det(a) = a$, since $S_1 = \{\epsilon\}$ and $\operatorname{sgn}\epsilon = 1$ (ϵ is a product of 0 transpositions).

If $n = 2$, then $S_2 = \{\epsilon, (1\ 2)\}$ and $\operatorname{sgn}\epsilon = 1$, $\operatorname{sgn}(1\ 2) = -1$. Hence, for any $A = (a_{ij}) \in F(2)$, we have

$$\begin{aligned} \det A &= a_{1\,1\epsilon} a_{2\,2\epsilon} - a_{1\,1(12)} a_{2\,2(12)} \\ &= a_{11}a_{22} - a_{12}a_{21}. \end{aligned}$$

If $n = 3$, then $S_3 = \{\epsilon, \varphi_1, \varphi_2, \varphi_3, \varphi_4, \varphi_5\}$, where $\varphi_1 = (1\ 2)$, $\varphi_2 = (1\ 3)$, $\varphi_3 = (2\ 3)$, $\varphi_4 = (1\ 2)(1\ 3)$, and $\varphi_5 = (1\ 3)(1\ 2)$. Also, $\operatorname{sgn}\epsilon = \operatorname{sgn}\varphi_4 = \operatorname{sgn}\varphi_5 = 1$, and $\operatorname{sgn}\varphi_1 = \operatorname{sgn}\varphi_2 = \operatorname{sgn}\varphi_3 = -1$. Hence, for any $A = (a_{ij}) \in F(3)$, we have

$$\det A = a_{11}a_{22}a_{33} - a_{12}a_{21}a_{33} - a_{13}a_{22}a_{31} - a_{11}a_{23}a_{32} + a_{12}a_{23}a_{31} + a_{13}a_{21}a_{32}.$$

For example, in $\mathbb{Q}(3)$ we have

$$\begin{aligned} \det \begin{pmatrix} 1 & 2 & -3 \\ 4 & -1 & 2 \\ 5 & 2 & 3 \end{pmatrix} &= 1\cdot(-1)\cdot 3 - 2\cdot 4\cdot 3 - (-3)\cdot(-1)\cdot 5 - 1\cdot 2\cdot 2 \\ &\quad + 2\cdot 2\cdot 5 + (-3)\cdot 4\cdot 2 \\ &= -50. \end{aligned}$$

If $I \in F(n)$ is the identity matrix, then only one of the $n!$ terms of $\det A$ in 4.3 is nonzero, namely $a_{11}a_{22}\cdots a_{nn}$. Therefore, we find that

$$\det I = 1.$$

More generally, if $A = (a_{ij}) \in F(n)$ is a *diagonal matrix* (that is, $a_{ij} = 0$ if $i \neq j$), then we have

$$\det A = a_{11}a_{22}\cdots a_{nn}.$$

We notice that each term of det A in 4.3,

$$(1) \qquad (\operatorname{sgn} \varphi)a_{1\,1\varphi}a_{2\,2\varphi}\cdots a_{n\,n\varphi},$$

consists of a product of n elements, one from each row and one from each column of the matrix A. Thus, $a_{i\,i\varphi}$ is in the ith row and $i\varphi$th column of A, and as i ranges from 1 to n so does $i\varphi$. If a_{ij} is one of the factors appearing in (1), then $j = i\varphi$ and also $i = j\varphi^{-1}$. Therefore, in view of the fact that $\operatorname{sgn} \varphi = \operatorname{sgn} \varphi^{-1}$, the term (1) can also be expressed in the form

$$(2) \qquad (\operatorname{sgn} \theta)a_{1\theta\,1}a_{2\theta\,2}\cdots a_{n\theta\,n},$$

where $\theta = \varphi^{-1}$. Since $S_n = \{\varphi^{-1} \mid \varphi \in S_n\}$, we also have, by the equality of (1) and (2), that

$$4.4 \qquad \det A = \sum_{\theta \in S_n} (\operatorname{sgn} \theta)a_{1\theta\,1}a_{2\theta\,2}\cdots a_{n\theta\,n}.$$

Associated with each $n \times m$ matrix $A = (a_{ij})$ is an $m \times n$ matrix (a_{ji}) having a_{ji} in the ith row and jth column. This new matrix is called the *transpose* of A and is denoted by A^T. Thus,

$$\text{if} \quad A = (a_{ij}), \qquad \text{then} \quad A^T = (a_{ji}).$$

For example, we have

$$A = \begin{pmatrix} a_{11} & a_{12} \\ a_{21} & a_{22} \\ a_{31} & a_{32} \end{pmatrix}, \qquad A^T = \begin{pmatrix} a_{11} & a_{21} & a_{31} \\ a_{12} & a_{22} & a_{32} \end{pmatrix}.$$

The rows of A are the columns of A^T, and vice versa.

If $A \in F(n)$, then the right-hand side of 4.4 is simply det A^T according to 4.3. Hence, we find that

$$4.5 \qquad \det A = \det A^T \qquad \text{for all } A \in F(n).$$

It is often convenient to consider the determinant as a function of the row vectors of a matrix. If $A \in F(n)$ has rows $A_1, A_2, \ldots, A_n$, then we will write

$$\det A = \det(A_1, A_2, \ldots, A_n)$$

when we wish to consider the determinant as a function of the rows of A.

Let F be a field, $A = (a_{ij}) \in F(n)$, and $A_1, A_2, \ldots, A_n$ be the row vectors of A. Assume that

$$A_1 = rA_1' + sA_1'',$$

where

$$A'_1 = (a'_{11}, a'_{12}, \ldots, a'_{1n}), \qquad A''_1 = (a''_{11}, a''_{12}, \ldots, a''_{1n}).$$

Then we have

$$\begin{aligned}\det A &= \det(rA'_1 + sA''_1, A_2, \ldots, A_n)\\ &= \sum_{\varphi \in S_n} (\operatorname{sgn} \varphi)(ra'_{1\,1\varphi} + sa''_{1\,1\varphi})a_{2\,2\varphi}\cdots a_{n\,n\varphi}\\ &= r \sum_{\varphi \in S_n} (\operatorname{sgn} \varphi)a'_{1\,1\varphi}a_{2\,2\varphi}\cdots a_{n\,n\varphi} + s \sum_{\varphi \in S_n} (\operatorname{sgn} \varphi)a''_{1\,1\varphi}a_{2\,2\varphi}\cdots a_{n\,n\varphi}.\end{aligned}$$

If we let A' be the matrix having row vectors $A'_1, A_2, \ldots, A_n$ and A'' the matrix having row vectors $A''_1, A_2, \ldots, A_n$, then we find that

$$\det A = r \det A' + s \det A''$$

by our work above. A similar argument proves the following result.

4.6. THEOREM. Let F be a field and $A \in F(n)$ have row vectors $A_1, A_2, \ldots, A_n$. If for some i, $1 \leq i \leq n$, $A_i = rA'_i + sA''_i$, where $A'_i, A''_i \in F^n$, and if matrix A' has row vectors $A_1, \ldots, A_{i-1}, A'_i, A_{i+1}, \ldots, A_n$ and matrix A'' has row vectors $A_1, \ldots, A_{i-1}, A''_i, A_{i+1}, \ldots, A_n$, then we have

$$\det A = r \det A' + s \det A''.$$

We can extend 4.6 by induction as follows.

4.7. THEOREM. Let F be a field and $A_1, A_2, \ldots, A_n, B_1, B_2, \ldots, B_k$ be in F^n. Then, for each i, $1 \leq i \leq n$, and all $r_1, r_2, \ldots, r_k \in F$, we have

$$\det\left(A_1, \ldots, A_{i-1}, \sum_{j=1}^{k} r_j B_j, A_{i+1}, \ldots, A_n\right) = \sum_{j=1}^{k} r_j \det(A_1, \ldots, A_{i-1}, B_j, A_{i+1}, \ldots, A_n).$$

If $A \in F(n)$ has rows $A_1, A_2, \ldots, A_n$ and if $\sigma \in S_n$, let $A\sigma$ denote the matrix with rows $A_{1\sigma}, A_{2\sigma}, \ldots, A_{n\sigma}$. For example, if we have

$$A = \begin{pmatrix} 1 & 2 & -1 \\ 3 & 0 & 1 \\ 2 & 1 & 4 \end{pmatrix} \in \mathbb{Q}(3), \qquad \sigma = \begin{pmatrix} 1 & 2 & 3 \\ 3 & 1 & 2 \end{pmatrix} \in S_3,$$

then $A\sigma$ is the 3×3 matrix

$$A\sigma = \begin{pmatrix} 2 & 1 & 4 \\ 1 & 2 & -1 \\ 3 & 0 & 1 \end{pmatrix}.$$

Since the rows of $A\sigma$ are $A_{1\sigma}, A_{2\sigma}, \ldots, A_{n\sigma}$, by 4.3 we have

$$\det A\sigma = \sum_{\varphi \in S_n} (\operatorname{sgn} \varphi) a_{1\sigma\, 1\varphi} a_{2\sigma\, 2\varphi} \cdots a_{n\sigma\, n\varphi}.$$

We can rewrite the right-hand side above as follows. For each i, $1 \leq i \leq n$, there exists some j, $1 \leq j \leq n$, such that $j\sigma = i$. Then, we have $j = i\sigma^{-1}$ and $j\varphi = i\theta$, where $\theta = \sigma^{-1}\varphi$. Hence, we have $a_{j\sigma\, j\varphi} = a_{i\, i\theta}$. Since $S_n = \{\sigma^{-1}\varphi \mid \varphi \in S_n\}$ and $\sigma\theta = \varphi$, we find that $(\operatorname{sgn} \sigma)(\operatorname{sgn} \theta) = \operatorname{sgn} \varphi$ and

$$\det A\sigma = \sum_{\theta \in S_n} (\operatorname{sgn} \sigma)(\operatorname{sgn} \theta) a_{1\, 1\theta} a_{2\, 2\theta} \cdots a_{n\, n\theta}.$$

This proves the following theorem.

4.8. THEOREM. For all $A \in F(n)$ and $\sigma \in S_n$,

$$\det A\sigma = (\operatorname{sgn} \sigma) \det A.$$

A special case of interest of 4.8 is that in which σ is a transposition. Then $\operatorname{sgn} \sigma = -1$, and $A\sigma$ is simply A with two rows interchanged.

4.9. THEOREM. If matrix $B \in F(n)$ is obtained from $A \in F(n)$ by interchanging two rows of A, then $\det B = -\det A$.

For example, we have

$$\det \begin{pmatrix} 1 & -1 & 3 \\ 2 & 0 & 4 \\ 5 & 7 & -1 \end{pmatrix} = -\det \begin{pmatrix} 2 & 0 & 4 \\ 1 & -1 & 3 \\ 5 & 7 & -1 \end{pmatrix}.$$

If two rows of a matrix $A \in F(n)$ are equal, then an interchange of these two rows does not change A. However, by 4.9, the determinant changes sign, so that $\det A = -\det A$. Hence, $2 \det A = 0$, and* $\det A = 0$. We state this result below.

4.10. THEOREM. If two rows of a matrix $A \in F(n)$ are equal, then $\det A = 0$.

Another result, whose proof we leave to the reader as an exercise, is as follows.

4.11. THEOREM. If a matrix $A \in F(n)$ contains a row of zeros, then $\det A = 0$.

An important property of the determinant is as follows.

4.12. THEOREM. If F is a field, then

$$\det AB = \det A \det B \qquad \text{for all } A, B \in F(n).$$

* If field F has characteristic 2, that is, $x + x = 0$ for all $x \in F$, then our argument is not valid. However, the result may then be proved directly from 4.3.

Proof: If matrix B has row vectors $B_1, B_2, \ldots, B_n$ and if $A = (a_{ij})$, then matrix $C = AB$ has row vectors $C_1, C_2, \ldots, C_n$, where

$$C_i = \sum_{k=1}^{n} a_{ik}B_k, \qquad i = 1, 2, \ldots, n.$$

Therefore, using 4.7 in each of the n rows of C, we obtain

$$\det C = \det\left(\sum_{k_1=1}^{n} a_{1k_1}B_{k_1}, \sum_{k_2=1}^{n} a_{2k_2}B_{k_2}, \ldots, \sum_{k_n=1}^{n} a_{nk_n}B_{k_n}\right)$$

$$= \sum_{k_1=1}^{n}\sum_{k_2=1}^{n}\cdots\sum_{k_n=1}^{n} a_{1k_1}a_{2k_2}\cdots a_{nk_n} \det(B_{k_1}, B_{k_2}, \ldots, B_{k_n}).$$

Now, $\det(B_{k_1}, B_{k_2}, \ldots, B_{k_n}) = 0$ if $k_i = k_j$ for any $i \neq j$ by 4.10. Hence, we need only consider those terms in $\det C$ above for which $(k_1, k_2, \ldots, k_n)$ is a permutation of $(1, 2, \ldots, n)$. Thus, we have

$$\det C = \sum_{\sigma \in S_n} a_{1\,1\sigma}a_{2\,2\sigma}\cdots a_{n\,n\sigma} \det(B_{1\sigma}, B_{2\sigma}, \ldots, B_{n\sigma}).$$

Therefore, by 4.8, we have

$$\det C = \sum_{\sigma \in S_n} (a_{1\,1\sigma}a_{2\,2\sigma}\cdots a_{n\,n\sigma})(\operatorname{sgn}\sigma) \det(B_1, B_2, \ldots, B_n)$$

$$= \det B \sum_{\sigma \in S_n} (\operatorname{sgn}\sigma)a_{1\,1\sigma}a_{2\,2\sigma}\cdots a_{n\,n\sigma}$$

$$= \det B \det A.$$

This proves 4.12.

If A is nonsingular, so that A has an inverse A^{-1}, then $AA^{-1} = I$ and $\det A \det A^{-1} = \det I = 1$. Hence, we have

4.13 $\qquad \det A^{-1} = (\det A)^{-1} \qquad$ if A is nonsingular.

Theorems 4.6 through 4.11 which pertain to the row vectors of a matrix also hold for the column vectors. This is true because $\det A = \det A^T$ by 4.5, and the column vectors of A are the row vectors of A^T. For example, if $A^1, A^2, \ldots, A^n$ are the column vectors of $A \in F(n)$ and if matrix B has $A^{1\sigma}, A^{2\sigma}, \ldots, A^{n\sigma}$ as its column vectors for some $\sigma \in S_n$, then $\det B^T = (\operatorname{sgn}\sigma) \det A^T$ by 4.8, and hence $\det B = (\operatorname{sgn}\sigma) \det A$ by 4.5.

EXERCISES

1. Prove 4.11.
2. The matrices

$$A = \begin{pmatrix} 1 & 0 & 0 \\ 2 & -3 & 0 \\ 4 & -1 & 2 \end{pmatrix}, \quad \text{and} \quad B = \begin{pmatrix} 3 & 0 & 0 & 0 \\ 2 & 5 & 0 & 0 \\ -1 & 3 & 2 & 0 \\ 4 & -1 & 2 & 7 \end{pmatrix}$$

are called *lower triangular matrices over* $\mathbb{Q}$, because $a_{ij} = 0$ and $b_{ij} = 0$ if $i < j$. Find det A and det B. Describe det C for every lower triangular matrix C over a field F.

3. The matrices

$$A = \begin{pmatrix} 3 & 5 \\ 0 & 4 \end{pmatrix}, \quad \text{and} \quad B = \begin{pmatrix} 5 & 4 & 2 & 3 \\ 0 & 3 & -1 & 7 \\ 0 & 0 & 4 & 9 \\ 0 & 0 & 0 & 2 \end{pmatrix}$$

are called *upper triangular matrices* over $\mathbb{Q}$. Find det A and det B. Describe det C for every upper triangular matrix C over a field F.

4. If an $n \times n$ matrix A over a field F has only n nonzero elements, under what conditions is det $A \neq 0$?
5. If $A = (a_{ij}) \in F(n)$ is such that $a_{i1} = 0$ for all $i > 1$ and if B is the $(n-1) \times (n-1)$ matrix $(a_{ij} \mid i, j = 2, 3, \ldots, n)$, then prove that det $A = a_{11}$ det B. Use this fact to find det A, where $A \in \mathbb{Q}(4)$ is given by

$$A = \begin{pmatrix} 3 & -2 & 1 & 4 \\ 0 & 2 & 1 & -2 \\ 0 & 3 & 2 & 5 \\ 0 & 1 & -1 & 0 \end{pmatrix}.$$

6. If $A \in F(n)$ is a nonsingular matrix such that $A^{-1} = A^T$, then show that det $A = \pm 1$.
7. Prove that $A \in F(n)$ is singular iff det $A = 0$.
8. If $A \in \mathbb{Q}(4)$ is given by

$$A = \begin{pmatrix} x & 1 & 1 & 1 \\ 1 & x & 1 & 1 \\ 1 & 1 & x & 1 \\ 1 & 1 & 1 & x \end{pmatrix},$$

show that det $A = (x-1)^3(x+3)$.

9. If $B \in \mathbb{Q}(3)$ is given by

$$B = \begin{pmatrix} 1 & a & a^2 \\ 1 & b & b^2 \\ 1 & c & c^2 \end{pmatrix},$$

show that det $B = (a-b)(b-c)(c-a)$.

3. EXPANSION BY MINORS

Let F be a field and $A = (a_{ij})$ be an $n \times n$ matrix over F. The expression for det A in 4.3 can be written in the form

$$\text{4.14} \qquad \det A = \sum_{s=1}^{n} a_{rs}a'_{rs}$$

for each integer r, $1 \leq r \leq n$, where

$$\text{4.15} \qquad a'_{rs} = \sum_{\substack{\varphi \in S_n \\ r\varphi = s}} (\operatorname{sgn} \varphi) a_{1\,1\varphi} \cdots a_{r-1\,(r-1)\varphi} a_{r+1\,(r+1)\varphi} \cdots a_{n\,n\varphi}.$$

Thus, the sum in 4.15 is taken over all $\varphi \in S_n$ for which $r\varphi = s$. Clearly this sum has $(n-1)!$ terms. We call a'_{rs} the *cofactor* of a_{rs} in A.

If, in matrix $A = (a_{ij}) \in F(n)$, we strike out the rth row and sth column, the resulting $(n-1) \times (n-1)$ matrix is called a *minor matrix* of A and is denoted by A_{rs}. Thus, A_{rs} is as follows:

$$A_{rs} = \begin{pmatrix} a_{11} & \cdots & a_{1\,s-1} a_{1\,s+1} & \cdots & a_{1n} \\ & & \cdots\cdots & & \\ & & \cdots\cdots & & \\ a_{r-1\,1} & \cdots & a_{r-1\,s-1} a_{r-1\,s+1} & \cdots & a_{r-1\,n} \\ a_{r+1\,1} & \cdots & a_{r+1\,s-1} a_{r+1\,s+1} & \cdots & a_{r+1\,n} \\ & & \cdots\cdots & & \\ & & \cdots\cdots & & \\ a_{n1} & \cdots & a_{n\,s-1} a_{n\,s+1} & \cdots & a_{nn} \end{pmatrix}.$$

What is det A_{rs}? To answer this question, we first observe that if

$$B = \begin{pmatrix} a_{r1} & a_{r2} & \cdots & a_{rn} \\ a_{11} & a_{12} & \cdots & a_{1n} \\ & \cdots\cdots & & \\ & \cdots\cdots & & \\ a_{r-1\,1} & a_{r-1\,2} & \cdots & a_{r-1\,n} \\ a_{r+1\,1} & a_{r+1\,2} & \cdots & a_{r+1\,n} \\ & \cdots\cdots & & \\ & \cdots\cdots & & \\ a_{n1} & a_{n2} & \cdots & a_{nn} \end{pmatrix} = (b_{ij}) \in F(n),$$

then $a_{rs} = b_{1s}$ and $A_{rs} = B_{1s}$. If $\sigma \in S_n$ is defined by

$$\sigma = \begin{pmatrix} 1 & 2 & \cdots & r-1 & r & r+1 & \cdots & n \\ 2 & 3 & \cdots & r & 1 & r+1 & \cdots & n \end{pmatrix} = (1\ 2)(1\ 3)\cdots(1\ r),$$

then $B = A\sigma$ and

$$\det B = (\operatorname{sgn} \sigma) \det A$$

by 4.8. Evidently $\operatorname{sgn} \sigma = (-1)^{r-1}$. If we collect the terms of $\det B$ containing b_{1s}, these must equal the terms of $(\operatorname{sgn} \sigma) \det A$ containing a_{rs}, that is,

$$b'_{1s} = (-1)^{r-1} a'_{rs}.$$

Starting with matrix B above, we can form matrix $C = (c_{ij})$ having as its columns $(B^s, B^1, \ldots, B^{s-1}, B^{s+1}, \ldots, B^n)$, where B^i denotes the ith column of B. Then we have

$$\det C = (-1)^{s-1} \det B$$

by the same argument as above, using column vectors this time. Now, $C_{11} = A_{rs}$, and we have

$$\begin{aligned} c'_{11} &= \sum_{\substack{\varphi \in S_n \\ 1\varphi = 1}} (\operatorname{sgn} \varphi) c_{2\,2\varphi} \cdots c_{n\,n\varphi} = \det C_{11} \\ &= \det A_{rs}. \end{aligned}$$

Also, we find that $c_{11} = b_{1s}$ and $c'_{11} = (-1)^{s-1} b'_{1s}$. Hence, we have

$$\det A_{rs} = (-1)^{s-1} b'_{1s} = (-1)^{r+s-2} a'_{rs},$$

and we have proved the following result.

4.16 $$a'_{rs} = (-1)^{r+s} \det A_{rs}, \qquad r, s = 1, 2, \ldots, n.$$

If we replace $A = (a_{ij})$ by its transpose in 4.14, we obtain

4.17 $$\det A = \sum_{r=1}^{n} a_{rs} a'_{rs}, \qquad s = 1, 2, \ldots, n.$$

We call 4.14 the *expansion of* $\det A$ *by minors of the* rth *row*, and 4.17 the *expansion of* $\det A$ *by minors of the* sth *column*.

For example, if $A \in \mathbb{Q}(3)$ is given by

$$A = \begin{pmatrix} 2 & -1 & 3 \\ 1 & 2 & -1 \\ -3 & 0 & 2 \end{pmatrix},$$

then the expansion of $\det A$ by minors of the second row is as follows:

$$\begin{aligned} \det A &= 1a'_{21} + 2a'_{22} - 1a'_{23} \\ &= 1(-1)^{2+1} \det A_{21} + 2(-1)^{2+2} \det A_{22} - 1(-1)^{2+3} \det A_{23} \\ &= -\det \begin{pmatrix} -1 & 3 \\ 0 & 2 \end{pmatrix} + 2 \det \begin{pmatrix} 2 & 3 \\ -3 & 2 \end{pmatrix} + \det \begin{pmatrix} 2 & -1 \\ -3 & 0 \end{pmatrix} \\ &= 2 + 26 - 3 = 25. \end{aligned}$$

The expansion of det A by minors of the third column is accomplished as follows.

$$\begin{aligned}\det A &= 3a'_{13} - 1a'_{23} + 2a'_{33} \\ &= 3(-1)^{1+3}\det A_{13} - 1(-1)^{2+3}\det A_{23} + 2(-1)^{3+3}\det A_{33} \\ &= 3\det\begin{pmatrix}1 & 2\\ -3 & 0\end{pmatrix} + \det\begin{pmatrix}2 & -1\\ -3 & 0\end{pmatrix} + 2\det\begin{pmatrix}2 & -1\\ 1 & 2\end{pmatrix} \\ &= 18 - 3 + 10 = 25.\end{aligned}$$

If a row or a column of a matrix $A \in F(n)$ has $n - 1$ zeros, then det A is immediately given in terms of a single determinant of an $(n - 1) \times (n - 1)$ matrix by 4.14 or 4.17. For example, if

$$A = \begin{pmatrix} -1 & 1 & 0 & 2\\ 2 & 3 & 4 & -2\\ 5 & -3 & 0 & 0\\ 2 & 1 & 0 & -4\end{pmatrix}$$

is in $\mathbb{Q}(4)$, then expanding det A by minors of the third column yields

$$\det A = 4(-1)^{2+3}\det A_{23}, \qquad \text{where} \quad A_{23} = \begin{pmatrix} -1 & 1 & 2\\ 5 & -3 & 0\\ 2 & 1 & -4\end{pmatrix}.$$

Given a matrix $A \in F(n)$, we can find some $B \in F(n)$ having a row or column containing $n - 1$ zeros, such that det B = det A. Thus, if $A = (a_{ij})$ has row vectors $A_1, A_2, \ldots, A_n$ and if, for simplicity, $a_{11} \neq 0$, then we let matrix B have row vectors

$$(A_1, A_2 - b_2A_1, \ldots, A_n - b_nA_1), \qquad \text{where} \quad b_i = a_{i1}a_{11}^{-1}.$$

Using 4.6 and 4.10, we see that det B = det A. Clearly, the first column of B has $n - 1$ zeros.

For example, if $A \in \mathbb{Q}(4)$ is given by

$$A = \begin{pmatrix} 3 & -1 & 1 & 2\\ 2 & 0 & -1 & 1\\ 1 & 2 & 0 & 4\\ 3 & -3 & 2 & 5\end{pmatrix}$$

and if A has rows A_1, A_2, A_3, A_4, then

$$B = \begin{pmatrix} 0 & -7 & 1 & -10\\ 0 & -4 & -1 & -7\\ 1 & 2 & 0 & 4\\ 0 & -9 & 2 & -7\end{pmatrix}$$

has rows $A_1 - 3A_3$, $A_2 - 2A_3$, A_3, $A_4 - 3A_3$, and hence we have

$$\det B = \det A.$$

Expanding det B by minors of the first column, we obtain

$$\det A = \det B = (-1)^{3+1} \det B_{31}, \qquad \text{where} \quad B_{31} = \begin{pmatrix} -7 & 1 & -10 \\ -4 & -1 & -7 \\ -9 & 2 & -7 \end{pmatrix}.$$

In turn, denoting the row vectors of B_{31} by B_1', B_2', B_3', we obtain

$$\det B_{31} = \det C,$$

where matrix C has rows B_1', $B_2' + B_1'$, $B_3' - 2B_1'$:

$$C = \begin{pmatrix} -7 & 1 & -10 \\ -11 & 0 & -17 \\ 5 & 0 & 13 \end{pmatrix}.$$

Expanding det C by minors of the second column, we get

$$\det C = (-1)^{1+2} \det C_{12} = -\det \begin{pmatrix} -11 & -17 \\ 5 & 13 \end{pmatrix} = 58.$$

Therefore, we have

$$\det A = \det B_{31} = \det C = 58.$$

If a matrix has a triangular block form, then its determinant can be found by using the following theorem.

4.18. THEOREM. Let F be a field and A be an $n \times n$ matrix over F. If A has the triangular block matrix form

$$A = \begin{pmatrix} A_{11} & A_{12} & A_{13} & \cdots & A_{1k} \\ 0 & A_{22} & A_{23} & \cdots & A_{2k} \\ & & \cdots\cdots & & \\ & & \cdots\cdots & & \\ 0 & 0 & \cdots & 0 & A_{kk} \end{pmatrix},$$

where each A_{ii} is a square matrix, then we have

$$\det A = \det A_{11} \det A_{22} \cdots \det A_{kk}.$$

Proof: We shall prove the theorem for $k = 2$. The general case then follows by mathematical induction. Thus, let

$$A = \begin{pmatrix} B & D \\ 0 & C \end{pmatrix},$$

where $B = (b_{ij}) \in F(r)$, $C = (c_{ij}) \in F(s)$, $D \in F(r, s)$, and $r + s = n$. If $A = (a_{ij})$, we see that then $a_{ij} = b_{ij}$ and $a_{r+i\,r+j} = c_{ij}$ if $1 \leq i \leq r$ and $1 \leq j \leq r$. Also, $a_{ij} = 0$ if $i > r$ and $j \leq r$. By definition, we have

$$\det A = \sum_{\varphi \in S_n} (\text{sgn } \varphi) a_{1\,1\varphi} \cdots a_{r\,r\varphi} a_{r+1\,(r+1)\varphi} \cdots a_{n\,n\varphi}.$$

For each $\varphi \in S_n$ such that $i\varphi > r$ for some $i \le r$, we see that necessarily $i'\varphi \le r$ for some $i' > r$. Since $a_{i'i'\varphi} = 0$, each such term of $\det A$ is zero. Thus, each nonzero term of $\det A$ above has the form

$$k = (\text{sgn } \varphi) a_{1\,1\varphi} \cdots a_{r\,r\varphi} a_{r+1\,(r+1)\varphi} \cdots a_{n\,n\varphi},$$

where $i\varphi \le r$ if $i \le r$ and $i\varphi > r$ if $i > r$. If we define $\alpha \in S_r$, $\beta \in S_s$ by $i\alpha = i\varphi$ if $1 \le i \le r$, $i\beta = (i + r)\varphi - r$ if $1 \le i \le s$, then we find that $\text{sgn } \varphi = (\text{sgn } \alpha)(\text{sgn } \beta)$, and k has the form

$$(\text{sgn } \alpha) b_{1\,1\alpha} b_{2\,2\alpha} \cdots b_{r\,r\alpha} (\text{sgn } \beta) c_{1\,1\beta} c_{2\,2\beta} \cdots c_{s\,s\beta}.$$

Conversely, each term of the above form is in the sum defining $\det A$. We conclude that $\det A = (\det B)(\det C)$. This proves 4.18.

For example, the matrix $A \in \mathbb{Q}(5)$,

$$A = \left(\begin{array}{cc|cc|c} 2 & 1 & -1 & 3 & 4 \\ 1 & -1 & 0 & 2 & 3 \\ \hline 0 & 0 & 3 & 2 & 5 \\ 0 & 0 & 1 & -5 & 1 \\ \hline 0 & 0 & 0 & 0 & 2 \end{array}\right),$$

has triangular block matrix form as indicated. Therefore, we have

$$\begin{aligned} \det A &= \det \begin{pmatrix} 2 & 1 \\ 1 & -1 \end{pmatrix} \cdot \det \begin{pmatrix} 3 & 2 \\ 1 & -5 \end{pmatrix} \cdot \det (2) \\ &= (-3) \cdot (-17) \cdot 2 = 102. \end{aligned}$$

EXERCISES

Find the determinant of each of the following matrices over $\mathbb{Q}$.

1. $\begin{pmatrix} 2 & -1 & 5 \\ 0 & 3 & 4 \\ 1 & 2 & -3 \end{pmatrix}$.

2. $\begin{pmatrix} 4 & 1 & 2 & -1 \\ 3 & 5 & 1 & 2 \\ 2 & -2 & 2 & 7 \\ 3 & 1 & -2 & 3 \end{pmatrix}$.

3. $\begin{pmatrix} 1 & 0 & -1 & 3 \\ 2 & 1 & 0 & 5 \\ -3 & 2 & 1 & 0 \\ 0 & 4 & 2 & 1 \end{pmatrix}$.

4. $\begin{pmatrix} 2 & 1 & -1 & 3 \\ 4 & 2 & 3 & 2 \\ 7 & -2 & 2 & 5 \\ 4 & 3 & 0 & 5 \end{pmatrix}$.

5. $\begin{pmatrix} 1 & -1 & 1 & 1 & 1 \\ 1 & 1 & -1 & 1 & -1 \\ -1 & -1 & 1 & 1 & -1 \\ 1 & -1 & 1 & -1 & 1 \\ 1 & 1 & 1 & 1 & 1 \end{pmatrix}.$

6. $\begin{pmatrix} 2 & 0 & 2 & 0 & 2 \\ 0 & 3 & 0 & 3 & 0 \\ 1 & 1 & 0 & 1 & 1 \\ -1 & 0 & 1 & 0 & -1 \\ 3 & -3 & 0 & -3 & 3 \end{pmatrix}.$

7. $\begin{pmatrix} 2 & -5 & 4 & 1 & 3 \\ 1 & 0 & 2 & 1 & 0 \\ 0 & 0 & 3 & 5 & 2 \\ 0 & 0 & 1 & -1 & 4 \\ 0 & 0 & 0 & 0 & 3 \end{pmatrix}.$

8. $\begin{pmatrix} 3 & 1 & 0 & 4 & 2 & 1 \\ 2 & 0 & 1 & 0 & 5 & 1 \\ 0 & 4 & -1 & 1 & -1 & 2 \\ 0 & 0 & 0 & 2 & 0 & 1 \\ 0 & 0 & 0 & 0 & 1 & -1 \\ 0 & 0 & 0 & 1 & 0 & 1 \end{pmatrix}.$

9. If $A \in F(n)$ has zeros down the main diagonal and ones elsewhere, prove that $\det A = n - 1$ if n is odd and $\det A = 1 - n$ if n is even.
10. An $n \times n$ matrix A over the field $\mathbb{R}$ is called *skew symmetric* iff $A^T = -A$. Give some examples of 3×3 and 4×4 skew symmetric matrices. Show that $\det A = 0$ for every 3×3 skew symmetric matrix A. Is this also true for every 4×4 skew symmetric matrix?

4. INVERSES

Let $A = (a_{ij})$ be an $n \times$ n matrix over a field F and $A_1, A_2, \ldots, A_n$ be the row vectors of A. If we replace the rth row of A by the kth row, where $k \neq r$, then the resulting matrix $B = (b_{ij})$ has two equal rows and hence has zero determinant. Expanding $\det B$ by minors of the rth row, we get

$$0 = \det B = \sum_{s=1}^{n} a_{ks}a'_{rs}, \qquad k \neq r,$$

since $b'_{rs} = a'_{rs}$ for each s. We can combine this result with 4.14 to obtain

4.19 $$\sum_{s=1}^{n} a_{ks}a'_{rs} = (\det A)\delta_{kr}, \qquad k, r = 1, 2, \ldots, n.$$

Similarly, interchanging rows and columns, we have

4.20 $$\sum_{r=1}^{n} a_{rk}a'_{rs} = (\det A)\delta_{ks}, \qquad k, s = 1, 2, \ldots, n.$$

The cofactors of the elements of a matrix $A = (a_{ij}) \in F(n)$ can be used to form a matrix $(a'_{ij}) \in F(n)$. The transpose of the matrix (a'_{ij}) is called the *adjoint* of A and is denoted by adj A:

4.21
$$\text{adj } A = (a'_{ij})^T.$$

Using the fact that

$$((\det A)\delta_{ij}) = (\det A)I,$$

where $I \in F(n)$ is the identity matrix, we can express 4.19 in the form $A \cdot \text{adj } A = (\det A)I$, and 4.20 in the form $\text{adj } A \cdot A = (\det A)I$. Hence, the following equation is true for every $A \in F(n)$.

4.22
$$A \cdot \text{adj } A = \text{adj } A \cdot A = (\det A)I.$$

If $\det A \neq 0$, then 4.22 shows that A has an inverse given by

4.23
$$A^{-1} = \frac{1}{\det A} \text{adj } A.$$

This result, together with 4.13, proves that a matrix is nonsingular iff its determinant is nonzero.

For example, let us find the inverse, if it exists, of the matrix

$$A = \begin{pmatrix} -1 & 2 & 1 \\ 0 & 3 & -2 \\ 2 & -1 & 0 \end{pmatrix}$$

over $\mathbb{Q}$. We first find adj A by finding all cofactors.

$$\begin{aligned} a'_{11} &= \det A_{11} = -2, & a'_{12} &= -\det A_{12} = -4, & a'_{13} &= \det A_{13} = -6, \\ a'_{21} &= -\det A_{21} = -1, & a'_{22} &= \det A_{22} = -2, & a'_{23} &= -\det A_{23} = 3, \\ a'_{31} &= \det A_{31} = -7, & a'_{32} &= -\det A_{32} = -2, & a'_{33} &= \det A_{33} = -3. \end{aligned}$$

Hence, we have

$$\text{adj } A = \begin{pmatrix} -2 & -1 & -7 \\ -4 & -2 & -2 \\ -6 & 3 & -3 \end{pmatrix}.$$

On multiplying A by adj A, we get

$$A \cdot \text{adj } A = \text{adj } A \cdot A = \begin{pmatrix} -12 & 0 & 0 \\ 0 & -12 & 0 \\ 0 & 0 & -12 \end{pmatrix}.$$

Hence, $\det A = -12$ and we have

$$A^{-1} = -\tfrac{1}{12}\operatorname{adj} A = \begin{pmatrix} \frac{1}{6} & \frac{1}{12} & \frac{7}{12} \\ \frac{1}{3} & \frac{1}{6} & \frac{1}{6} \\ \frac{1}{2} & -\frac{1}{4} & \frac{1}{4} \end{pmatrix}.$$

If $A \in F(n)$ and $\mathrm{r}(A) = n$, then $\det A \neq 0$, by our remarks above. For any $m \times n$ matrix A over a field F, the rank and determinant functions are related as follows.

4.24. THEOREM. Let $A = (a_{ij})$ be an $m \times n$ matrix over a field F and k be the largest integer such that some $k \times k$ submatrix B of A has a nonzero determinant. Then we have $\mathrm{r}(A) = k$.

Proof: We may assume that the $k \times k$ submatrix B of A is in the upper left-hand corner of A. For, otherwise, we could interchange rows or columns of A to obtain a new matrix A' having B in the upper left-hand corner. Clearly, $\mathrm{r}(A') = \mathrm{r}(A)$. Thus, by assumption, $B = (a_{ij}) \in F(k)$. Since B is nonsingular, the rows of B are linearly independent and, hence, so are the first k rows of A. Therefore, $\mathrm{r}(A) = \mathrm{rr}(A) \geq k$.

If $k = m$ or $k = n$, then necessarily $\mathrm{r}(A) = k$, and the theorem is proved. So let us assume that $k < m$ and $k < n$, and form the $(k + 1) \times (k + 1)$ matrix C_{rs}:

$$C_{rs} = \begin{pmatrix} a_{11} & a_{12} & \dots & a_{1k} & a_{1s} \\ a_{21} & a_{22} & \dots & a_{2k} & a_{2s} \\ & & \cdots\cdots & & \\ & & \cdots\cdots & & \\ a_{k1} & a_{k2} & \dots & a_{kk} & a_{ks} \\ a_{r1} & a_{r2} & \dots & a_{rk} & a_{rs} \end{pmatrix}, \quad r = k + 1, \dots, m, \quad s = 1, 2, \dots, n.$$

If $s \leq k$, then $\det C_{rs} = 0$, since two columns of C_{rs} are equal, whereas if $s > k$, then $\det C_{rs} = 0$, since C_{rs} is a $(k + 1) \times (k + 1)$ submatrix of A. Expanding $\det C_{rs}$ by minors of the last column, we obtain

$$(1) \qquad 0 = \sum_{i=1}^{k} c_i a_{is} + (\det B) a_{rs},$$

where c_i is the cofactor of a_{is} in C_{rs}. Evidently, the c_i depend on r but not on s. Thus, for each r, Equation (1) is true for $s = 1, 2, \dots, n$. Hence, we have

$$(2) \qquad A_r = -\frac{1}{\det B} \sum_{i=1}^{k} c_i A_i.$$

Since A_r is a linear combination of the rows $A_1, \dots, A_k$ for $r = k + 1, \dots, m$ according to (2), we must have $\mathrm{r}(A) = \mathrm{rr}(A) \leq k$. Therefore, we have that $\mathrm{r}(A) = k$. This proves 4.24.

Let us find the rank of the matrix

$$A = \begin{pmatrix} 2 & -1 & 3 & 1 \\ 1 & 4 & -2 & 0 \\ 4 & -11 & 13 & 3 \end{pmatrix}$$

over $\mathbb{Q}$, using 4.24. Since we have

$$\det \begin{pmatrix} 2 & -1 \\ 1 & 4 \end{pmatrix} = 9 \neq 0,$$

$r(A) \geq 2$ by 4.24. We can add multiples of one row (column) to another row (column) without changing the determinant of any submatrix. If B is the matrix with rows $(A_1 - 2A_2, A_2, A_3 - 4A_2)$, where A_1, A_2, A_3 are the rows of A, then we have

$$B = \begin{pmatrix} 0 & -9 & 7 & 1 \\ 1 & 4 & -2 & 0 \\ 0 & -27 & 21 & 3 \end{pmatrix}.$$

Clearly, $r(B) = r(A)$. Since the third row of B is three times the first row, evidently $r(B) < 3$. Therefore, $r(B) = r(A) = 2$.

EXERCISES

Find, if possible, the inverse of each of the following matrices over $\mathbb{Q}$.

1. $\begin{pmatrix} 4 & 1 & 3 \\ 0 & 2 & -1 \\ 3 & 1 & 0 \end{pmatrix}$.

2. $\begin{pmatrix} 2 & -1 & 1 \\ 1 & 3 & -4 \\ 1 & -11 & 14 \end{pmatrix}$.

3. $\begin{pmatrix} 2 & 0 & 0 \\ 1 & -1 & 0 \\ 0 & 3 & 3 \end{pmatrix}$.

4. $\begin{pmatrix} 8 & 2 & 5 \\ -7 & 3 & -4 \\ 9 & -6 & 4 \end{pmatrix}$.

5. $\begin{pmatrix} 1 & 0 & 1 & 0 \\ 0 & 1 & 1 & 0 \\ 1 & 1 & 0 & 1 \\ 1 & 0 & 0 & 1 \end{pmatrix}$.

6. $\begin{pmatrix} 0 & 0 & 1 & 0 \\ 1 & 0 & 0 & 0 \\ 0 & 1 & 0 & 0 \\ 0 & 0 & 0 & 1 \end{pmatrix}$.

7. $\begin{pmatrix} 2 & 0 & 1 & -2 \\ 1 & 1 & 0 & 0 \\ -1 & 0 & 1 & 3 \\ 2 & -1 & 0 & 1 \end{pmatrix}$.

8. $\begin{pmatrix} 1 & -1 & 2 & 1 \\ 0 & 1 & 3 & 2 \\ 0 & 0 & 1 & 4 \\ 0 & 0 & 0 & 1 \end{pmatrix}$.

9. Let $A = (a_{ij}) \in F(n)$ be a lower triangular matrix (see p. 107). Prove that A is nonsingular iff $a_{ii} \neq 0$ for $i = 1, 2, \ldots, n$. If A is nonsingular, prove that its inverse is also lower triangular.
10. A matrix $N \in F(n)$ is called *nilpotent* iff $N^k = 0$ for some integer $k > 0$. If N is nilpotent, prove that $I + N$ is nonsingular, where I is the identity matrix of $F(n)$. What is the inverse of $I + N$? [*Hint:* $(I + N)(I - N) = I - N^2$, etc.]

5. SYSTEMS OF LINEAR EQUATIONS

Let

4.25 $$\sum_{j=1}^{n} a_{ij}x_j = b_i, \qquad i = 1, 2, \ldots, m$$

be a system of m linear equations in n unknowns $x_1, x_2, \ldots, x_n$ over a field F. If $A = (a_{ij}) \in F(m, n)$ is the matrix of coefficients of the system and if $\mathrm{r}(A) = k$, then we can rearrange the equations of 4.25 and possibly relabel the unknowns until the $k \times k$ matrix C in the upper left-hand corner of A is nonsingular. Let us assume that 4.25 has a solution, so that $\mathrm{r}(A) = \mathrm{r}(\mathrm{aug}\ A)$ by 2.10. Then, each equation of 4.25 with $i > k$ is a linear combination of the first k equations. Hence, 4.25 has the same solution set as the system

4.26 $$\sum_{j=1}^{n} a_{ij}x_j = b_i, \qquad i = 1, 2, \ldots, k$$

of k equations in n unknowns.

To solve system 4.26, let us express it in the form

4.27 $$\sum_{j=1}^{k} a_{ij}x_j = b_i - \sum_{j=k+1}^{n} a_{ij}x_j, \qquad i = 1, 2, \ldots, k.$$

If we let

$$X = \begin{pmatrix} x_1 \\ x_2 \\ \cdot \\ \cdot \\ \cdot \\ x_k \end{pmatrix}, \quad B = \begin{pmatrix} c_1 \\ c_2 \\ \cdot \\ \cdot \\ \cdot \\ c_k \end{pmatrix}, \quad \text{where} \quad c_i = b_i - \sum_{j=k+1}^{n} a_{ij}x_j,$$

then 4.27 can be put in the form

$$CX = B.$$

Since C has an inverse, we can solve this equation for X,

4.28
$$X = C^{-1}B,$$

as we did in 3.25.

Equation 4.28 gives the complete solution of 4.25. Thus, if $(t_1, t_2, \ldots, t_n) \in F^n$ is a solution of 4.25, then

(1)
$$X = \begin{pmatrix} t_1 \\ t_2 \\ \cdot \\ \cdot \\ \cdot \\ t_k \end{pmatrix}$$

is a solution of 4.28 if we let $x_{k+1} = t_{k+1}, \ldots, x_n = t_n$ in B. Conversely, for any values of $x_{k+1}, \ldots, x_n$ in F, say $x_{k+1} = t_{k+1}, \ldots, x_n = t_n$, we can solve 4.28 for X. Say X is given by (1) above, then $(t_1, t_2, \ldots, t_n)$ is a solution of 4.26 and, hence, also of 4.25.

As the remarks above attest, we can reduce the problem of solving a system of linear equations to that of solving a system having the same number of equations as unknowns and also having a nonsingular matrix of coefficients. Such a system is most often solved by using determinants as shown below.

Let

$$\sum_{j=1}^{n} a_{ij}x_j = b_i, \qquad i = 1, 2, \ldots, n$$

be a system of n linear equations in n unknowns over a field F for which the matrix of coefficients $A = (a_{ij})$ is nonsingular. If

$$X = \begin{pmatrix} x_1 \\ x_2 \\ \cdot \\ \cdot \\ \cdot \\ x_n \end{pmatrix}, \qquad B = \begin{pmatrix} b_1 \\ b_2 \\ \cdot \\ \cdot \\ \cdot \\ b_n \end{pmatrix},$$

then the solution of this system is given by 4.28 as

$$X = A^{-1}B$$

or

$$X = \frac{1}{\det A}(\text{adj } A)B.$$

Since adj $A = (a'_{ij})^T$, where a'_{ij} is the cofactor of a_{ij} in A, we have

$$x_j = \left(\frac{1}{\det A}\right) \sum_{i=1}^{n} a'_{ij}b_i.$$

The summation above is the expansion by minors of the jth column of the matrix C_j, whose column vectors are $A^1, \ldots, A^{j-1}, B, A^{j+1}, \ldots, A^n$:

4.29
$$C_j = \begin{pmatrix} a_{11} & \cdots & a_{1\,j-1} & b_1 & a_{1\,j+1} & \cdots & a_{1n} \\ a_{21} & \cdots & a_{2\,j-1} & b_2 & a_{2\,j+1} & \cdots & a_{2n} \\ & & & \cdots\cdots & & & \\ & & & \cdots\cdots & & & \\ a_{n1} & \cdots & a_{n\,j-1} & b_n & a_{n\,j+1} & \cdots & a_{nn} \end{pmatrix}.$$

Thus, we have proved the following theorem attributed to an 18th-century French mathematician.

4.30. CRAMER'S RULE. The system of linear equations

$$\sum_{i=1}^{n} a_{ij}x_j = b_i, \qquad i = 1, 2, \ldots, n,$$

over a field F for which the matrix $A = (a_{ij})$ is nonsingular has the unique solution

$$x_j = \frac{\det C_j}{\det A}, \qquad j = 1, 2, \ldots, n,$$

where C_j is the matrix of 4.29.

For example, let us solve the following system of linear equations over $\mathbb{Q}$ by Cramer's rule:

$$\begin{aligned} 5x + 2y + z &= 3, \\ 2x - y + 2z &= 7, \\ x + 5y - z &= 6. \end{aligned}$$

It is easily verified that the matrix of coefficients

$$A = \begin{pmatrix} 5 & 2 & 1 \\ 2 & -1 & 2 \\ 1 & 5 & -1 \end{pmatrix}$$

is nonsingular. In fact, we have

$$\det A = -26.$$

The matrices C_1, C_2, and C_3 of 4.29 are as follows:

$$C_1 = \begin{pmatrix} 3 & 2 & 1 \\ 7 & -1 & 2 \\ 6 & 5 & -1 \end{pmatrix}, \quad C_2 = \begin{pmatrix} 5 & 3 & 1 \\ 2 & 7 & 2 \\ 1 & 6 & -1 \end{pmatrix}, \quad C_3 = \begin{pmatrix} 5 & 2 & 3 \\ 2 & -1 & 7 \\ 1 & 5 & 6 \end{pmatrix}.$$

Then, we have

$$\det C_1 = 52, \qquad \det C_2 = -78, \qquad \det C_3 = -182.$$

Therefore,

$$x = \frac{52}{-26} = -2, \qquad y = \frac{-78}{-26} = 3, \qquad z = \frac{-182}{-26} = 7$$

is the unique solution of the system.

EXERCISES

Solve, if possible, each of the following systems of linear equations over $\mathbb{Q}$ by Cramer's rule.

1. $3x - y = 2,$
   $2x + 3y = 5.$

2. $7x + 4y = 12,$
   $9x - 5y = 23.$

3. $2x + y + z = 1,$
   $x - 2y + z = -1,$
   $3x + 3y - 4z = 2.$

4. $x - 3y + 5z = 2,$
   $2x + y - 7z = -3,$
   $3x + 2y - 2z = 5.$

5. $w + x + y + z = 0,$
   $w - x + y + z = 6,$
   $w + x - y + z = -10,$
   $w + x + y - z = 8.$

6. $w + x = -2,$
   $x - y = -1,$
   $w - z = 1,$
   $y + 2z = 4.$

7. $w - x + z = 3,$
   $x + y - z = -3,$
   $w - 2x + 3z = 0,$
   $-w + 3y - 2z = -6.$

8. $w + y + z = 3,$
   $w + x - y = -3,$
   $x + 2y - 2z = -1,$
   $2w + x - 3z = -4.$

6. DETERMINANT OF A LINEAR TRANSFORMATION

If V is an n-dimensional vector space over a field F and f is a l.t. of V, then f is represented by a matrix relative to each basis of V. If A and B are two $n \times n$ matrices representing f relative to two bases of V, then A and B are similar by 3.28. Thus, we have that

$$B = P^{-1}AP$$

for some nonsingular matrix $P \in F(n)$. By 4.12 and 4.13, we get

$$\begin{aligned}\det B &= (\det P^{-1})(\det A)(\det P)\\ &= (\det P)^{-1}(\det P)(\det A) = \det A.\end{aligned}$$

That is, all the matrices which represent f have the same determinant. This fact allows us to make the following definition.

4.31. DEFINITION OF THE DETERMINANT OF A LINEAR TRANSFORMATION. For each $f \in L(V)$, $\det f = \det A$, where A is any matrix representing f.

EXAMPLE: Let $f \in L(\mathbb{Q}^3)$ be defined by

$$(a, b, c)f = (3a - b, a + 2b - c, 2b + 5c), \qquad a, b, c \in \mathbb{Q}.$$

To find $\det f$, we note that if

$$\mathbf{u}_1 = (1, 0, 0), \qquad \mathbf{u}_2 = (0, 1, 0), \qquad \mathbf{u}_3 = (0, 0, 1)$$

is the usual basis of $\mathbb{Q}^3$, then we have

$$\begin{aligned} \mathbf{u}_1 f &= (3, 1, 0) &&= 3\mathbf{u}_1 + \mathbf{u}_2, \\ \mathbf{u}_2 f &= (-1, 2, 2) &&= -\mathbf{u}_1 + 2\mathbf{u}_2 + 2\mathbf{u}_3, \\ \mathbf{u}_3 f &= (0, -1, 5) &&= -\mathbf{u}_2 + 5\mathbf{u}_3. \end{aligned}$$

Hence, f is represented by the matrix A relative to the $\mathbf{u}$-basis, where

$$A = \begin{pmatrix} 3 & 1 & 0 \\ -1 & 2 & 2 \\ 0 & -1 & 5 \end{pmatrix}.$$

We can easily show that $\det A = 41$. Hence, by 4.31, $\det f = 41$.

EXERCISES

Find the determinant of each of the following linear transformations:

1. $f \in L(\mathbb{Q}^2)$, $(a, b)f = (4a - 5b, 3a + 7b)$, $a, b \in \mathbb{Q}$.
2. $f \in L(\mathbb{Q}^3)$, $(a, b, c)f = (2a + c, 3a - 2b + c, -4b + c)$, $a, b, c \in \mathbb{Q}$.
3. $f \in L(\mathbb{Q}^3)$, $(a, b, c)f = (a - b - c, b + 2c, 3a - 2b)$, $a, b, c \in \mathbb{Q}$.
4. $f \in L(\mathbb{Q}^4)$, $(a, b, c, d)f = (a + c, a + d, b - c, b + d)$, $a, b, c, d \in \mathbb{Q}$.
5. $f \in L(\mathbb{Q}^4)$, $(a, b, c, d)f = (a - b - c + d, b - c - d, a + b - d, a + c - d)$, $a, b, c, d \in \mathbb{Q}$.
6. If f is a l.t. of a vector space V, prove that $\det f = 0$ iff f is singular.

Chapter Five

Polynomials and Matrices

1. POLYNOMIALS

Let F be a field. An expression of the form

$$a_0 + a_1\lambda + a_2\lambda^2 + \cdots + a_n\lambda^n,$$

where n is a nonnegative integer and $a_0, a_1, \ldots, a_n$ are in F, is called a *polynomial in* λ *over* F. We think of λ as an unknown element not in F, and consider $\lambda^2 = \lambda\cdot\lambda$, $\lambda^3 = \lambda\cdot\lambda\cdot\lambda$, and so on. We use the Greek letter λ in place of the more conventional symbol x, because we have been using $\mathbf{x}$ to denote a vector. The elements $a_0, a_1, \ldots, a_n$ are called the *coefficients* of the polynomial above, with a_0 called the *constant term* and a_n the *leading coefficient* if $a_n \neq 0$. If $a_n \neq 0$, then n is called the *degree* of this polynomial. The zero polynomial does not have a degree.

The set of all polynomials in λ over F is called a *polynomial domain* and is denoted by

$$F[\lambda].$$

We shall denote elements of $F[\lambda]$ by $f(\lambda)$, $g(\lambda)$, $h(\lambda)$, and so on. Two polynomials are equal iff corresponding coefficients are equal. The field F is contained in $F[\lambda]$, once we identify the constant polynomial a_0 with the element a_0 of F.

Polynomials are added and multiplied in the familiar way. Thus, if

$$f(\lambda) = a_0 + a_1\lambda + \cdots + a_m\lambda^m, \qquad g(\lambda) = b_0 + b_1\lambda + \cdots + b_n\lambda^n$$

with $m \leq n$ (for convenience of notation), then we have

$$f(\lambda) + g(\lambda) = (a_0 + b_0) + (a_1 + b_1)\lambda + \cdots + (a_n + b_n)\lambda^n$$

and

$$f(\lambda)g(\lambda) = c_0 + c_1\lambda + \cdots + c_{m+n}\lambda^{m+n},$$

where

$$c_i = a_0b_i + a_1b_{i-1} + \cdots + a_{i-1}b_1 + a_ib_0, \qquad i = 0, 1, \ldots, m + n,$$

and we understand that $a_i = 0$ and $b_j = 0$ whenever $i > m$ or $j > n$. The set $F[\lambda]$ is closed under these operations, and properties 1.1 through 1.5 of a field hold. The identity elements of $F[\lambda]$ are simply the identity elements 0 and 1 of F. The negative of $f(\lambda)$ is given by

$$-f(\lambda) = (-a_0) + (-a_1)\lambda + \cdots + (-a_m)\lambda^m.$$

Each nonzero constant polynomial $a \in F$ has an inverse a^{-1}, whereas no polynomial $f(\lambda)$ of degree $m > 0$ has a multiplicative inverse. Hence, $F[\lambda]$ is not a field. However, $F[\lambda]$ does have the following useful property:

5.1 $\quad f(\lambda)g(\lambda) = 0 \quad$ iff either $\quad f(\lambda) = 0 \quad$ or $\quad g(\lambda) = 0.$

This follows from the fact that if $f(\lambda) \neq 0$ and $g(\lambda) \neq 0$, then we have

$$\deg\,[f(\lambda)g(\lambda)] = \deg f(\lambda) + \deg g(\lambda),$$

where "deg" means "degree." An algebraic system with operations of addition and multiplication satisfying 1.1 through 1.5 and 5.1 is called an *integral domain*. Thus, $F[\lambda]$ is an integral domain. Another example of an integral domain is $\mathbb{Z}$, the system of integers.

The familiar long-division process can be used to show that each polynomial $f(\lambda)$ can be divided by a nonzero polynomial $g(\lambda)$, yielding a quotient $q(\lambda)$ and a remainder $r(\lambda)$ of smaller degree than $g(\lambda)$ [or, $r(\lambda) = 0$]. Thus, we have

5.2 $\quad f(\lambda) = g(\lambda)q(\lambda) + r(\lambda), \qquad$ where $\quad r(\lambda) = 0 \qquad$ or $\quad \deg r(\lambda) < \deg g(\lambda).$

We shall use 5.2 without formally proving it.

For example, if $f(\lambda), g(\lambda) \in \mathbb{Q}[\lambda]$ are given by

$$f(\lambda) = \lambda^3 - 3\lambda^2 + 2\lambda + 5, \qquad g(\lambda) = \lambda^2 + 2\lambda - 3,$$

then, by long division, we have

$$\begin{array}{r|l} & \lambda - 5 \\ \hline \lambda^2 + 2\lambda - 3 & \lambda^3 - 3\lambda^2 + 2\lambda + 5 \\ & \lambda^3 + 2\lambda^2 - 3\lambda \\ \hline & \quad - 5\lambda^2 + 5\lambda + 5 \\ & \quad - 5\lambda^2 - 10\lambda + 15 \\ \hline & \qquad\qquad 15\lambda - 10. \end{array}$$

Thus, the quotient on dividing $f(\lambda)$ by $g(\lambda)$ is $q(\lambda) = \lambda - 5$, and the remainder is $r(\lambda) = 15\lambda - 10$:

$$\lambda^3 - 3\lambda^2 + 2\lambda + 5 = (\lambda^2 + 2\lambda - 3)(\lambda - 5) + (15\lambda - 10).$$

Observe that $\deg r(\lambda) = 1$, which is less than $\deg g(\lambda) = 2$.

If $r(\lambda) = 0$ in 5.2, we call $g(\lambda)$ a *divisor*, or *factor*, of $f(\lambda)$ and $f(\lambda)$ a *multiple* of $g(\lambda)$. Every polynomial $f(\lambda)$ has a *trivial factorization*

$$f(\lambda) = c\left(\frac{1}{c}f(\lambda)\right)$$

for any nonzero $c \in F$. In turn, c and $(1/c)f(\lambda)$ are called *trivial factors* of $f(\lambda)$. A polynomial $p(\lambda)$ in $F[\lambda]$ is called *prime*, or *irreducible*, iff $\deg p(\lambda) \geq 1$ and $p(\lambda)$ has only trivial factors. Thus, if $p(\lambda)$ is prime and $p(\lambda) = f(\lambda)g(\lambda)$, then either $f(\lambda)$ or $g(\lambda)$ is a constant (that is, an element of F). Clearly, every polynomial of degree 1 is prime.

A polynomial having leading coefficient 1 is called a *monic polynomial.* Every nonzero polynomial is a constant times a monic polynomial. Thus, we have

$$a_0 + a_1\lambda + \cdots + a_n\lambda^n = a_n(a_n^{-1}a_0 + a_n^{-1}a_1\lambda + \cdots + \lambda^n).$$

Every integer $a > 1$ has a unique factorization into primes. For example, $60 = 2\cdot 2\cdot 3\cdot 5$. Similarly, every monic polynomial of positive degree has a unique factorization into monic primes. For example, we see that

$$\lambda^2 - 3\lambda - 10 = (\lambda - 5)(\lambda + 2)$$

in $\mathbb{Q}[\lambda]$. Proofs of these facts can be found in any book on modern algebra.

If $F[\lambda]$ is a polynomial domain over a field F, then a nonempty subset A of $F[\lambda]$ is called an *ideal* iff the following properties hold:

(1) $\quad f(\lambda) + g(\lambda), f(\lambda) - g(\lambda) \in A \quad$ for all $f(\lambda), g(\lambda) \in A$.

(2) $\quad f(\lambda)g(\lambda) \in A \quad$ for all $f(\lambda) \in A$, $g(\lambda) \in F[\lambda]$.

An example of an ideal in $\mathbb{Q}[\lambda]$ is the set of all multiples of $\lambda^2 + 2$:

$$A = (\lambda^2 + 2)F[\lambda] = \{(\lambda^2 + 2)h(\lambda) \mid h(\lambda) \in F[\lambda]\}.$$

Thus, we have

(1) $\quad (\lambda^2 + 2)h(\lambda) \pm (\lambda^2 + 2)k(\lambda) = (\lambda^2 + 2)[h(\lambda) \pm k(\lambda)] \in A,$

and

(2) $\quad [(\lambda^2 + 2)h(\lambda)]g(\lambda) = (\lambda^2 + 2)[h(\lambda)g(\lambda)] \in A$

for all $g(\lambda)$, $h(\lambda)$, $k(\lambda) \in \mathbb{Q}[\lambda]$.

In general, if $f(\lambda) \in F[\lambda]$, then the set of all multiples of $f(\lambda)$ is an ideal A of $F[\lambda]$:

$$A = f(\lambda)F[\lambda] = \{f(\lambda)g(\lambda) \mid g(\lambda) \in F[\lambda]\}.$$

Such an ideal is called a *principal ideal* of $F[\lambda]$, and $f(\lambda)$ is called a *generator* of A. If $A = f(\lambda)F[\lambda]$, then also $A = cf(\lambda)F[\lambda]$ for every nonzero c in F. On the other hand, if $f(\lambda)F[\lambda] = g(\lambda)F[\lambda]$, then necessarily $g(\lambda) = cf(\lambda)$ for some c in F. By selecting $c = a^{-1}$, where a is the leading coefficient of

$f(\lambda)$, we see that the nonzero ideal $A = f(\lambda)F[\lambda]$ is generated by a unique monic polynomial $cf(\lambda)$. An important property of $F[\lambda]$ is described below.

5.3. THEOREM. If $F[\lambda]$ is a polynomial domain over a field F, then every ideal A of $F[\lambda]$ is principal.

Proof: If $A = \{0\}$, then A is principal with generator 0. If $A \neq \{0\}$, then let $g(\lambda)$ be a nonzero polynomial in A of minimal degree. If $f(\lambda)$ is any other polynomial in A, then, by 5.2, there exist $q(\lambda), r(\lambda) \in F[\lambda]$ such that

$$f(\lambda) = g(\lambda)q(\lambda) + r(\lambda), \quad \text{where} \quad r(\lambda) = 0 \quad \text{or} \quad \deg r(\lambda) < \deg g(\lambda).$$

Since $f(\lambda)$ and $g(\lambda)q(\lambda)$ are in A, so is $r(\lambda) = f(\lambda) - g(\lambda)q(\lambda)$. If $r(\lambda) \neq 0$, $\deg r(\lambda) < \deg g(\lambda)$, contrary to the fact that $g(\lambda)$ is a polynomial of minimal degree in A. Hence, we find that $r(\lambda) = 0$, and $f(\lambda) = g(\lambda)q(\lambda)$. Therefore, we have $A = g(\lambda)F[\lambda]$, and 5.3 is proved.

If A and B are ideals of $F[\lambda]$, then it is easily proved that $A \cap B$ and $A + B = \{f(\lambda) + g(\lambda) \mid f(\lambda) \in A, g(\lambda) \in B\}$ are also ideals of $F[\lambda]$. If

$$A = h(\lambda)F[\lambda], \qquad B = k(\lambda)F[\lambda],$$

and

$$A \cap B = m(\lambda)F[\lambda], \qquad A + B = d(\lambda)F[\lambda],$$

where $m(\lambda)$ and $d(\lambda)$ are monic polynomials, then it can be proved that $m(\lambda)$ is the *least common multiple* (l.c.m.) and $d(\lambda)$ is the *greatest common divisor* (g.c.d.) of $h(\lambda)$ and $k(\lambda)$. The monic g.c.d. of $h(\lambda)$ and $k(\lambda)$ is commonly denoted by

$$(h(\lambda), k(\lambda)),$$

and the monic l.c.m. by

$$[h(\lambda), k(\lambda)].$$

For example, if $h(\lambda), k(\lambda) \in \mathbb{Q}[\lambda]$ are given by

$$h(\lambda) = (\lambda + 3)(\lambda^2 + 1), \qquad k(\lambda) = (\lambda - 2)(\lambda + 3)(\lambda + 7),$$

then we have

$$(h(\lambda), k(\lambda)) = \lambda + 3, \qquad [h(\lambda), k(\lambda)] = (\lambda + 3)(\lambda - 2)(\lambda + 7)(\lambda^2 + 1).$$

Polynomials $h(\lambda), k(\lambda) \in F[\lambda]$ are called *relatively prime* iff $(h(\lambda), k(\lambda)) = 1$. If $(h(\lambda), k(\lambda)) = 1$, then $[h(\lambda), k(\lambda)] = h(\lambda)k(\lambda)$. In any case, we have

$$[h(\lambda), k(\lambda)] = \frac{h(\lambda)k(\lambda)}{(h(\lambda), k(\lambda))}.$$

A useful property is that the g.c.d. of $h(\lambda)$ and $k(\lambda)$ can be expressed as a linear combination of $h(\lambda)$ and $k(\lambda)$; that is, there exist $h_1(\lambda), k_1(\lambda) \in F[\lambda]$ such that

5.4 $$h(\lambda)k_1(\lambda) + k(\lambda)h_1(\lambda) = (h(\lambda), k(\lambda)).$$

This follows directly from the fact that $A + B = d(\lambda)F[\lambda]$, where $A = h(\lambda)F[\lambda]$, $B = k(\lambda)F[\lambda]$, and $d(\lambda) = (h(\lambda), k(\lambda))$.

2. MINIMAL POLYNOMIALS

Let V be a finite-dimensional vector space over a field F, $L(V)$ be the algebra of l.t. of V, and $F[\lambda]$ be the polynomial domain in λ over F. Throughout this section, we will focus our attention on a fixed but arbitrary

$$t \in L(V).$$

For every $f(\lambda) = a_0 + a_1\lambda + \cdots + a_m\lambda^m \in F[\lambda]$, let

$$f(t) = a_0 + a_1 t + \cdots + a_m t^m.$$

Since $L(V)$ is a linear algebra over F, every polynomial in t is also in $L(V)$, that is, $f(t) \in L(V)$. If $f(\lambda), g(\lambda) \in F[\lambda]$ and $f(\lambda) + g(\lambda) = h(\lambda), f(\lambda)g(\lambda) = k(\lambda)$, then we see that $f(t) + g(t) = h(t)$ and $f(t)g(t) = k(t)$. Also, if $cf(\lambda) = d(\lambda)$ for $c \in F$, then $cf(t) = d(t)$. If t has matrix representation A relative to some basis of V, then $f(t)$ has matrix representation

$$f(A) = a_0 I + a_1 A + \cdots + a_m A^m.$$

Since the algebras $L(V)$ and $F(n)$ are isomorphic, every algebraic property of t is also a property of A.

For example, if $t \in L(\mathbb{Q}^3)$ has matrix representation

$$A = \begin{pmatrix} -1 & 2 & 1 \\ 0 & 3 & 7 \\ 2 & 5 & 0 \end{pmatrix}$$

relative to the usual basis of $\mathbb{Q}^3$, and if $f(\lambda) = \lambda^2 - 2\lambda + 3$, then

$$f(t) = t^2 - 2t + 3$$

is a l.t. of $\mathbb{Q}^3$ having matrix representation $f(A) = A^2 - 2A + 3I$. Thus, we have

$$f(A) = \begin{pmatrix} 3 & 9 & 13 \\ 14 & 44 & 21 \\ -2 & 19 & 37 \end{pmatrix} - 2\begin{pmatrix} -1 & 2 & 1 \\ 0 & 3 & 7 \\ 2 & 5 & 0 \end{pmatrix} + 3\begin{pmatrix} 1 & 0 & 0 \\ 0 & 1 & 0 \\ 0 & 0 & 1 \end{pmatrix},$$

or

$$f(A) = \begin{pmatrix} 8 & 5 & 11 \\ 14 & 41 & 7 \\ -6 & 9 & 40 \end{pmatrix}.$$

For each $\mathbf{x} \in V$, the $n + 1$ vectors $\mathbf{x}, \mathbf{x}t, \mathbf{x}t^2, \ldots, \mathbf{x}t^n$ are necessarily l.d., since dim $V = n$. Hence, there exist $a_0, a_1, \ldots, a_n \in F$, not all zero, such that

$$\sum_{i=0}^{n} a_i(\mathbf{x}t^i) = \mathbf{0}.$$

This equation can be expressed in the form

$$\mathbf{x}f(t) = \mathbf{0}, \qquad \text{where } f(\lambda) = \sum_{i=0}^{n} a_i\lambda^i.$$

Thus, $\mathbf{x}f(t) = \mathbf{0}$ for some nonzero polynomial $f(\lambda)$, with $\deg f(\lambda) \leq n$.

Let

5.5 $$N(\mathbf{x}) = \{f(\lambda) \in F[\lambda] \mid \mathbf{x}f(t) = \mathbf{0}\}, \qquad \mathbf{x} \in V.$$

We call $N(\mathbf{x})$ the *annihilator* of $\mathbf{x}$. If $f_1(\lambda), f_2(\lambda) \in N(\mathbf{x})$ and $g(\lambda) \in F[\lambda]$, then $f_1(\lambda) \pm f_2(\lambda), f_1(\lambda)g(\lambda) \in N(\mathbf{x})$, because we have

$$\mathbf{x}[f_1(t) \pm f_2(t)] = \mathbf{x}f_1(t) \pm \mathbf{x}f_2(t) = \mathbf{0}, \quad \text{and} \quad \mathbf{x}[f_1(t)g(t)] = [\mathbf{x}f_1(t)]g(t) = \mathbf{0}.$$

Hence, *$N(\mathbf{x})$ is an ideal of $F[\lambda]$*. Since $\deg f(\lambda) \leq n$ for some $f(\lambda) \in N(\mathbf{x})$, and $N(\mathbf{x})$ is a principal ideal by 5.3, $N(\mathbf{x})$ has a unique monic generator $h(\lambda)$ of degree $\leq n$:

$$N(\mathbf{x}) = h(\lambda)F[\lambda].$$

5.6. DEFINITION OF MINIMAL POLYNOMIAL OF A VECTOR. For each $\mathbf{x} \in V$, the unique monic generator $h(\lambda)$ of $N(\mathbf{x})$ is called the minimal polynomial of $\mathbf{x}$.

In other words, the minimal polynomial of $\mathbf{x}$ is the monic polynomial $h(\lambda)$ of minimal degree such that $\mathbf{x}h(t) = \mathbf{0}$.

If $\mathbf{x} = \mathbf{0}$, then $h(\lambda) = 1$. If $\mathbf{x} \neq \mathbf{0}$, let k be the least positive integer such that the vectors $\mathbf{x}, \mathbf{x}t, \ldots, \mathbf{x}t^{k-1}$ are l.i., whereas the vectors $\mathbf{x}, \mathbf{x}t, \ldots, \mathbf{x}t^{k-1}$, $\mathbf{x}t^k$ are l.d. Then, there exist $a_0, a_1, \ldots, a_k \in F$, with $a_k \neq 0$, such that

(1) $$\sum_{i=0}^{k} a_i(\mathbf{x}t^i) = \mathbf{x}h(t) = \mathbf{0}, \qquad \text{where } h(\lambda) = \sum_{i=0}^{k} a_i\lambda^i.$$

Evidently we can choose $a_k = 1$, since we can multiply both sides of (1) by a_k^{-1}. Thus, $h(\lambda)$ is monic. It is clear from the way $h(\lambda)$ was chosen that it is the minimal polynomial of $\mathbf{x}$.

EXAMPLE 1: Let $V = \mathbb{Q}^3$ and $t \in L(V)$ be defined relative to the usual basis of V as follows:

$$\mathbf{u}_1t = \mathbf{u}_1 + \mathbf{u}_3, \qquad \mathbf{u}_2t = 2\mathbf{u}_1 + 3\mathbf{u}_2 - \mathbf{u}_3, \qquad \mathbf{u}_3t = 4\mathbf{u}_1 + \mathbf{u}_3.$$

Now we have

$$\mathbf{u}_1t^2 = (\mathbf{u}_1t)t = (\mathbf{u}_1 + \mathbf{u}_3)t = \mathbf{u}_1t + \mathbf{u}_3t = 5\mathbf{u}_1 + 2\mathbf{u}_3.$$

The vectors $\mathbf{u}_1$ and $\mathbf{u}_1t$ are l.i., whereas the vectors $\mathbf{u}_1$, $\mathbf{u}_1t$, $\mathbf{u}_1t^2$ are dependent:

$$\mathbf{u}_1t^2 - 2(\mathbf{u}_1t) - 3\mathbf{u}_1 = (5\mathbf{u}_1 + 2\mathbf{u}_3) - 2(\mathbf{u}_1 + \mathbf{u}_3) - 3\mathbf{u}_1 = \mathbf{0}.$$

Therefore, $\mathbf{u}_1(t^2 - 2t - 3) = \mathbf{0}$, and the minimal polynomial of $\mathbf{u}_1$ is

$$h(\lambda) = \lambda^2 - 2\lambda - 3.$$

If the minimal polynomial $h(\lambda)$ of some $\mathbf{x} \in V$ is factorable, say

$$h(\lambda) = h_1(\lambda)h_2(\lambda),$$

where $h_1(\lambda)$ and $h_2(\lambda)$ are monic and of positive degree, then $\mathbf{y} = \mathbf{x}h_1(t)$ has $h_2(\lambda)$ as its minimal polynomial. For we see that $\mathbf{y}h_2(t) = \mathbf{0}$, and if $\mathbf{y}f(t) = \mathbf{0}$ for some nonzero $f(\lambda) \in F[\lambda]$, then $\mathbf{x}h_1(t)f(t) = \mathbf{0}$, and $h_1(\lambda)f(\lambda) \in N(\mathbf{x})$. Hence, $\deg h_1(\lambda)f(\lambda) \geq \deg h(\lambda)$, and $\deg f(\lambda) \geq \deg h_2(\lambda)$. We state this result below.

5.7. THEOREM. If $\mathbf{x} \in V$ has minimal polynomial $h(\lambda)$ and if $h(\lambda) = h_1(\lambda)h_2(\lambda)$, where $h_1(\lambda)$ and $h_2(\lambda)$ are monic and of positive degree, then $\mathbf{y} = \mathbf{x}h_1(t)$ has minimal polynomial $h_2(\lambda)$.

For example, the minimal polynomial of $\mathbf{u}_1$ in Example 1 is factorable; $\lambda^2 - 2\lambda - 3 = (\lambda + 1)(\lambda - 3)$. Hence, we find that

$$\mathbf{y} = \mathbf{u}_1(t + 1) = \mathbf{u}_1t + \mathbf{u}_1 = 2\mathbf{u}_1 + \mathbf{u}_3$$

has minimal polynomial $\lambda - 3$.

Another useful fact about minimal polynomials is as follows.

5.8. THEOREM. If $h(\lambda)$ and $k(\lambda)$ are minimal polynomials of two vectors of V, then their l.c.m. $[h(\lambda), k(\lambda)]$ is also the minimal polynomial of a vector of V.

Proof: We shall prove the theorem under the assumption that $h(\lambda)$ and $k(\lambda)$ are relatively prime, in which case $[h(\lambda), k(\lambda)] = h(\lambda)k(\lambda)$. From this, the general proof follows easily by use of 5.7. We leave the details to the reader.

Let $h(\lambda)$ and $k(\lambda)$ be the minimal polynomials of $\mathbf{x}$ and $\mathbf{y}$, respectively. Since $(h(\lambda), k(\lambda)) = 1$, we have by 5.4 that

(1) $\quad h(\lambda)k_1(\lambda) + k(\lambda)h_1(\lambda) = 1 \quad$ for some $h_1(\lambda), k_1(\lambda) \in F[\lambda]$.

Hence, we have $h(t)k_1(t) + k(t)h_1(t) = 1$. If we let

(2) $$\mathbf{z} = \mathbf{x}h_1(t) + \mathbf{y}k_1(t),$$

then we obtain

(3) $$\mathbf{z}h(t) = \mathbf{y}, \qquad \text{and} \qquad \mathbf{z}k(t) = \mathbf{x}.$$

Thus, from (1) and (2), we find that $\mathbf{z}h(t) = \mathbf{x}h(t)h_1(t) + \mathbf{y}h(t)k_1(t) = \mathbf{y}h(t)k_1(t) = \mathbf{y}[1 - k(t)h_1(t)] = \mathbf{y} - \mathbf{y}k(t)h_1(t) = \mathbf{y}$, and similarly that $\mathbf{z}k(t) = \mathbf{x}$. Consequently, $\mathbf{z}h(t)k(t) = \mathbf{y}k(t) = \mathbf{0}$. Thus, we see that $h(\lambda)k(\lambda) \in N(\mathbf{z})$.

If $f(\lambda)$ is the minimal polynomial of $\mathbf{z}$, that is, $N(\mathbf{z}) = f(\lambda)F[\lambda]$, then, by (3), $\mathbf{y}f(t) = \mathbf{z}f(t)h(t) = \mathbf{0}$, and $\mathbf{x}f(t) = \mathbf{z}f(t)k(t) = \mathbf{0}$. Hence, we have that $f(\lambda) \in N(\mathbf{x}) \cap N(\mathbf{y})$, and $f(\lambda)$ is a multiple of both $h(\lambda)$ and $k(\lambda)$. Therefore, $f(\lambda)$ is a multiple of $h(\lambda)k(\lambda)$, the l.c.m. of $h(\lambda)$ and $k(\lambda)$. On the other hand, $h(\lambda)k(\lambda) \in N(\mathbf{z})$, and hence $f(\lambda)$ is a factor of $h(\lambda)k(\lambda)$. It follows that $f(\lambda) = h(\lambda)k(\lambda)$. This proves 5.8.

Theorem 5.8 is easily extended to any finite number of polynomials by induction. Thus, if $h_i(\lambda)$ is the minimal polynomial of vector $\mathbf{x}_i$, $i = 1, 2, \ldots, m$, there exists some vector $\mathbf{z}$ whose minimal polynomial is

$$h(\lambda) = [h_1(\lambda), h_2(\lambda), \ldots, h_m(\lambda)],$$

the l.c.m. of the $h_i(\lambda)$.

EXAMPLE 2: Let $t \in L(\mathbb{Q}^4)$ be defined by

$$\mathbf{u}_1 t = \mathbf{u}_1 + \mathbf{u}_3, \qquad \mathbf{u}_2 t = 3\mathbf{u}_2 - \mathbf{u}_4, \qquad \mathbf{u}_3 t = 3\mathbf{u}_1 - \mathbf{u}_3, \qquad \mathbf{u}_4 t = 3\mathbf{u}_2 - \mathbf{u}_4$$

relative to the usual basis of $\mathbb{Q}^4$. Then we have

$$\mathbf{u}_1 t^2 = \mathbf{u}_1 t + \mathbf{u}_3 t = 4\mathbf{u}_1, \qquad \text{so that} \quad \mathbf{u}_1(t^2 - 4) = \mathbf{0},$$

and

$$\mathbf{u}_2 t^2 = 3\mathbf{u}_2 t - \mathbf{u}_4 t = 2\mathbf{u}_2 t, \qquad \text{so that} \quad \mathbf{u}_2(t^2 - 2t) = \mathbf{0}.$$

It is clear that $\lambda^2 - 4$ is the minimal polynomial of $\mathbf{u}_1$ as is $\lambda^2 - 2\lambda$ of $\mathbf{u}_2$. Hence, $[\lambda^2 - 4, \lambda^2 - 2\lambda] = \lambda(\lambda^2 - 4)$ is the minimal polynomial of some vector $\mathbf{z}$ by 5.8. To find $\mathbf{z}$, we have, by 5.7, that $\mathbf{y} = \mathbf{u}_2(t - 2) = \mathbf{u}_2 - \mathbf{u}_4$ has minimal polynomial λ. Now λ and $\lambda^2 - 4$ are relatively prime, and

$$\lambda(\tfrac{1}{4}\lambda) + (\lambda^2 - 4)(-\tfrac{1}{4}) = 1.$$

Hence, we find that

$$\mathbf{z} = \mathbf{u}_1(\tfrac{1}{4}t) + \mathbf{y}(-\tfrac{1}{4}) = \tfrac{1}{4}(\mathbf{u}_1 - \mathbf{u}_2 + \mathbf{u}_3 + \mathbf{u}_4)$$

has minimal polynomial $\lambda(\lambda^2 - 4)$ by the proof of 5.8.

Continuing, we can easily show that $\mathbf{u}_3 t^2 = 4\mathbf{u}_3$ and $\mathbf{u}_4 t^2 = 2\mathbf{u}_4 t$, from which it follows (since $\mathbf{u}_3$ and $\mathbf{u}_3 t$ are l.i., and $\mathbf{u}_4$ and $\mathbf{u}_4 t$ are l.i.) that $\lambda^2 - 4$ is the minimal polynomial of $\mathbf{u}_3$ as is $\lambda^2 - 2\lambda$ of $\mathbf{u}_4$. Hence, we see that $\mathbf{u}_i t(t^2 - 4) = \mathbf{0}$ for each i. A l.t. which maps every element of a basis into $\mathbf{0}$ must be the zero l.t. Thus, $t^3 - 4t = 0$, and t is a root of the polynomial $\lambda^3 - 4\lambda$.

To return to the general case, let vector space V have basis $\{\mathbf{v}_1, \mathbf{v}_2, \ldots, \mathbf{v}_n\}$, let $t \in L(V)$, and let $h_i(\lambda)$ be the minimal polynomial of $\mathbf{v}_i$, $i = 1, 2, \ldots, n$. The l.c.m. $h(\lambda)$ of the $h_i(\lambda)$ is the minimal polynomial of some vector $\mathbf{z}$ by 5.8, and hence $\deg h(\lambda) \leq \dim V = n$. Since $h(\lambda) = h_i(\lambda)k_i(\lambda)$ for some $k_i(\lambda) \in$

$F[\lambda]$, $i = 1, 2, \ldots, n$, evidently $\mathbf{v}_i h(t) = [\mathbf{v}_i h_i(t)]k_i(t) = 0$, $i = 1, 2, \ldots, n$. Therefore, we have

$$h(t) = 0.$$

Thus, each $t \in L(V)$ is a root of some monic polynomial $h(\lambda)$ of degree $\leq$ dim V. If we let

5.9 $$N = \{g(\lambda) \in F[\lambda] \mid g(t) = 0\},$$

then it is easily shown that N is a nonzero ideal of $F[\lambda]$; in fact, N is the intersection of all $N(\mathbf{x})$, $\mathbf{x} \in V$. Thus, we have

5.10 $$N = \bigcap_{\mathbf{x} \in V} N(\mathbf{x}).$$

By 5.3, N is a principal ideal of $F[\lambda]$.

5.11. DEFINITION OF THE MINIMAL POLYNOMIAL OF $t \in L(V)$. The minimal polynomial of t is the unique monic generator of the ideal N of 5.9.

From our remarks above, we see that for each $t \in L(V)$ there exists a monic polynomial $h(\lambda)$, such that (1) deg $h(\lambda) \leq$ dim V, (2) $h(t) = 0$, and (3) $h(\lambda)$ is the minimal polynomial of some $\mathbf{z} \in V$. Hence, we have $N(\mathbf{z}) = h(\lambda)F[\lambda]$, $h(\lambda) \in N(\mathbf{x})$ for every $\mathbf{x} \in V$, and, by 5.10,

$$N = N(\mathbf{z}) = h(\lambda)F[\lambda].$$

Thus, $h(\lambda)$ is the minimal polynomial of t. We normally find the minimal polynomial of t as we did $h(\lambda)$ above: that is, $h(\lambda) = [h_1(\lambda), h_2(\lambda), \ldots, h_n(\lambda)]$, where $h_1(\lambda), h_2(\lambda), \ldots, h_n(\lambda)$ are the minimal polynomials of a basis of V. As the name suggests, the minimal polynomial of t is the monic polynomial $h(\lambda)$ of minimal degree such that $h(t) = 0$.

For example, in Example 2 the l.c.m. of the minimal polynomials of the $\mathbf{u}$-basis of $\mathbb{Q}^4$ is $\lambda^3 - 4\lambda$. Thus, $\lambda^3 - 4\lambda$ is the minimal polynomial of t.

The algebras $L(V)$ and $F(n)$ are isomorphic, where $n = \dim V$. Hence, each $n \times n$ matrix A over F also has a minimal polynomial $h(\lambda)$ of degree $\leq n$. To find the minimal polynomial of A, we need only find the minimal polynomial of any l.t. which A represents.

For example,

$$A = \begin{pmatrix} 1 & 0 & 1 & 0 \\ 0 & 3 & 0 & -1 \\ 3 & 0 & -1 & 0 \\ 0 & 3 & 0 & -1 \end{pmatrix}$$

represents t in Example 2. Hence, the minimal polynomial of A is the minimal polynomial of t, namely $\lambda^3 - 4\lambda$. Thus, we find that $A^3 - 4A = 0$, whereas A is not a root of any linear or quadratic polynomial.

EXAMPLE 3: Let us find the minimal polynomial of the following matrix over $\mathbb{Q}$:

$$A = \begin{pmatrix} 2 & 1 & 0 \\ -1 & 0 & 1 \\ 0 & -2 & 1 \end{pmatrix}.$$

This matrix represents $t \in L(V)$ defined by

$$\mathbf{u}_1 t = 2\mathbf{u}_1 + \mathbf{u}_2, \qquad \mathbf{u}_2 t = -\mathbf{u}_1 + \mathbf{u}_3, \qquad \mathbf{u}_3 t = -2\mathbf{u}_2 + \mathbf{u}_3,$$

relative to the usual basis of $\mathbb{Q}^3$. We easily compute that $\mathbf{u}_1 t^2 = 3\mathbf{u}_1 + 2\mathbf{u}_2 + \mathbf{u}_3$, and $\mathbf{u}_1 t^3 = 4\mathbf{u}_1 + \mathbf{u}_2 + 3\mathbf{u}_3$. Clearly, $\mathbf{u}_1$, $\mathbf{u}_1 t$, $\mathbf{u}_1 t^2$ are l.i., whereas $\mathbf{u}_1$, $\mathbf{u}_1 t$, $\mathbf{u}_1 t^2$, $\mathbf{u}_1 t^3$ are dependent. Evidently, we have

$$a\mathbf{u}_1 + b(\mathbf{u}_1 t) + c(\mathbf{u}_1 t^2) + d(\mathbf{u}_1 t^3) = \mathbf{0}$$

iff

$$\begin{cases} a + 2b + 3c + 4d = 0, \\ \qquad b + 2c + \ d = 0, \\ \qquad\qquad c + 3d = 0. \end{cases}$$

One solution of this system is $a = -5$, $b = 5$, $c = -3$, $d = 1$. Hence,

$$h(\lambda) = \lambda^3 - 3\lambda^2 + 5\lambda - 5$$

is the minimal polynomial of $\mathbf{u}_1$. Since the l.c.m. of the minimal polynomials of $\mathbf{u}_1$, $\mathbf{u}_2$, $\mathbf{u}_3$ is of degree ≤ 3, evidently $h(\lambda)$ is this l.c.m. Hence, $h(\lambda)$ is the minimal polynomial of both t and A. Thus, we have

$$A^3 - 3A^2 + 5A - 5I = 0,$$

and A is not a root of any linear or quadratic polynomial. We observe that the inverse of A can be found from this equation. Thus, we have

$$A(A^2 - 3A + 5I) = 5I, \qquad \text{and} \qquad A^{-1} = \tfrac{1}{5}(A^2 - 3A + 5I).$$

Using this equation, we compute

$$A^{-1} = \frac{1}{5}\begin{pmatrix} 2 & -1 & 1 \\ 1 & 2 & -2 \\ 2 & 4 & 1 \end{pmatrix}.$$

As is illustrated by this example, the following theorem is true.

5.12. THEOREM. The $n \times n$ matrix A over a field F is nonsingular iff the minimal polynomial $h(\lambda)$ of A has a nonzero constant term. If

$$h(\lambda) = \lambda^m + a_{m-1}\lambda^{m-1} + \cdots + a_1\lambda + a_0, \qquad a_0 \neq 0,$$

then we have

$$A^{-1} = -a_0^{-1}(A^{m-1} + a_{m-1}A^{m-2} + \cdots + a_1 I).$$

Proof: If $a_0 \neq 0$, then clearly A^{-1} is as given above. On the other hand, if A is nonsingular and $a_0 = 0$, then we have

$$A^{-1}(A^m + a_{m-1}A^{m-1} + \cdots + a_1 A) = A^{m-1} + a_{m-1}A^{m-2} + \cdots + a_1 I = 0,$$

and A is a root of a polynomial of degree $m - 1$. This contradicts the fact that the minimal polynomial of A has degree m. Hence, $a_0 \neq 0$ whenever A is nonsingular. This proves the theorem.

Since $L(V)$ and $F(n)$ are isomorphic if $\dim V = n$, Theorem 5.12 is valid for linear transformations as well as matrices.

EXERCISES

In each of Exercises 1 through 6, find the minimal polynomial of each of the usual basis vectors. Also, find the minimal polynomial of the linear transformation t, and then find a vector whose minimal polynomial is the same as that of t.

1. $t \in L(\mathbb{Q}^2)$; $\mathbf{u}_1 t = \mathbf{u}_2$, $\mathbf{u}_2 t = \mathbf{u}_1 + \mathbf{u}_2$.
2. $t \in L(\mathbb{Q}^2)$; $\mathbf{u}_1 t = 2\mathbf{u}_1 - 3\mathbf{u}_2$, $\mathbf{u}_2 t = \mathbf{u}_1 + 5\mathbf{u}_2$.
3. $t \in L(\mathbb{Q}^3)$; $\mathbf{u}_1 t = \mathbf{u}_1 - \mathbf{u}_2 + \mathbf{u}_3$, $\mathbf{u}_2 t = -2\mathbf{u}_2 + 5\mathbf{u}_3$, $\mathbf{u}_3 t = 2\mathbf{u}_1 + 3\mathbf{u}_2$.
4. $t \in L(\mathbb{Q}^3)$; $\mathbf{u}_1 t = 2\mathbf{u}_2$, $\mathbf{u}_2 t = 2\mathbf{u}_1$, $\mathbf{u}_3 t = 2\mathbf{u}_3$.
5. $t \in L(\mathbb{Q}^4)$; $\mathbf{u}_1 t = \mathbf{u}_1 + \mathbf{u}_3$, $\mathbf{u}_2 t = 3\mathbf{u}_4$, $\mathbf{u}_3 t = \mathbf{u}_1 - \mathbf{u}_3$, $\mathbf{u}_4 t = \mathbf{u}_2$.
6. $t \in L(\mathbb{Q}^4)$; $\mathbf{u}_1 t = \mathbf{u}_1 + \mathbf{u}_2$, $\mathbf{u}_2 t = \mathbf{u}_2 - \mathbf{u}_3$, $\mathbf{u}_3 t = \mathbf{u}_3 + \mathbf{u}_4$, $\mathbf{u}_4 t = \mathbf{u}_1 - \mathbf{u}_4$.

In each of Exercises 7 through 12, find the minimal polynomial of the matrix over $\mathbb{Q}$, and find its inverse if it is nonsingular.

7. $\begin{pmatrix} 2 & 1 \\ -1 & 3 \end{pmatrix}$.

8. $\begin{pmatrix} 4 & -4 \\ -1 & 1 \end{pmatrix}$.

9. $\begin{pmatrix} 0 & 1 & 0 \\ 0 & 0 & 1 \\ 1 & -2 & 3 \end{pmatrix}$.

10. $\begin{pmatrix} 2 & 0 & 0 \\ -1 & 3 & 0 \\ 5 & 2 & 1 \end{pmatrix}$.

11. $\begin{pmatrix} 1 & 4 & 0 & 0 \\ 1 & 1 & 0 & 0 \\ 0 & 0 & 0 & 1 \\ 0 & 0 & -3 & 4 \end{pmatrix}$.

12. $\begin{pmatrix} 1 & 0 & -1 & 0 \\ 0 & 1 & 1 & 0 \\ -1 & 0 & 0 & 1 \\ 0 & 1 & 0 & 1 \end{pmatrix}$.

13. Prove that N in 5.9 is an ideal.
14. Prove Equation 5.10.
15. Complete the proof of Theorem 5.8.

3. THE COMPANION MATRIX

Given a field F and a monic polynomial

$$h(\lambda) = \lambda^n - c_{n-1}\lambda^{n-1} - \cdots - c_1\lambda - c_0$$

in $F[\lambda]$, we can always find an $n \times n$ matrix A over F having $h(\lambda)$ as its minimal polynomial. To prove this, we select a basis $(\mathbf{u}_1, \mathbf{u}_2, \ldots, \mathbf{u}_n)$ of F^n, and let $t \in L(F^n)$ be defined by

$$\begin{aligned}
\mathbf{u}_1 t &= \mathbf{u}_2,\\
\mathbf{u}_2 t &= \mathbf{u}_3,\\
&\cdots\cdots\\
&\cdots\cdots\\
\mathbf{u}_{n-1} t &= \mathbf{u}_n,\\
\mathbf{u}_n t &= \sum_{i=0}^{n-1} c_i \mathbf{u}_{1+i}.
\end{aligned}$$

Since $\mathbf{u}_1 t^i = \mathbf{u}_{1+i}$ for $i = 1, 2, \ldots, n-1$, evidently $\mathbf{u}_1, \mathbf{u}_1 t, \ldots, \mathbf{u}_1 t^{n-1}$ are l.i. vectors. On the other hand, we find that

$$\mathbf{u}_1 t^n = \mathbf{u}_n t = \sum_{i=0}^{n-1} c_i \mathbf{u}_1 t^i,$$

and hence we have

$$\mathbf{u}_1 \left(t^n - \sum_{i=0}^{n-1} c_i t^i \right) = \mathbf{0}.$$

Therefore, $h(\lambda)$ is the minimal polynomial of $\mathbf{u}_1$. In fact, since $\deg h(\lambda) = \dim F^n = n$, $h(\lambda)$ is also the minimal polynomial of t. The matrix representing t relative to the given basis has a special name as follows.

5.13. DEFINITION OF THE COMPANION MATRIX. The companion matrix of the monic polynomial

$$h(\lambda) = \lambda^n - \sum_{i=0}^{n-1} c_i \lambda^i$$

in $F[\lambda]$ is the $n \times n$ matrix C over F given below.

$$C = \begin{pmatrix}
0 & 1 & 0 & 0 & \ldots & 0 & 0\\
0 & 0 & 1 & 0 & \ldots & 0 & 0\\
 & & & & \cdots\cdots & & \\
 & & & & \cdots\cdots & & \\
0 & 0 & & & \ldots & 1 & 0\\
0 & 0 & & & \ldots & 0 & 1\\
c_0 & c_1 & & & \ldots & c_{n-2} & c_{n-1}
\end{pmatrix}.$$

Since C represents $t \in L(F^n)$ defined above, and t has $h(\lambda)$ as its minimal polynomial, the following result is true.

5.14. THEOREM. The companion matrix of each monic $h(\lambda) \in F[\lambda]$ has $h(\lambda)$ as its minimal polynomial.

EXAMPLE 1: Let us find the companion matrix C of the monic polynomial

$$h(\lambda) = \lambda^3 - 5\lambda^2 + 2\lambda + 3$$

in $\mathbb{Q}[\lambda]$. By 5.13, we have

$$C = \begin{pmatrix} 0 & 1 & 0 \\ 0 & 0 & 1 \\ -3 & -2 & 5 \end{pmatrix}.$$

This matrix represents $t \in L(\mathbb{Q}^3)$ defined by

$$\mathbf{u}_1 t = \mathbf{u}_2, \qquad \mathbf{u}_2 t = \mathbf{u}_3, \qquad \mathbf{u}_3 t = -3\mathbf{u}_1 - 2\mathbf{u}_2 + 5\mathbf{u}_3.$$

Our discussion above also has the following consequence.

5.15. THEOREM. If V is an n-dimensional vector space over a field F and if $t \in L(V)$ has minimal polynomial $h(\lambda)$ of degree n, then the companion matrix of $h(\lambda)$ represents t relative to some basis of V.

Since $h(\lambda)$ is the minimal polynomial of some $\mathbf{x} \in V$, t is represented by the companion matrix of $h(\lambda)$ relative to the basis $(\mathbf{x}, \mathbf{x}t, \ldots, \mathbf{x}t^{n-1})$.

EXAMPLE 2: Let $t \in L(\mathbb{Q}^4)$ be defined as follows:

$$\mathbf{u}_1 t = 2\mathbf{u}_2, \qquad \mathbf{u}_2 t = -\mathbf{u}_1 - \mathbf{u}_2 - \mathbf{u}_3 - 3\mathbf{u}_4,$$

$$\mathbf{u}_3 t = 2\mathbf{u}_1 - 2\mathbf{u}_3, \qquad \mathbf{u}_4 t = \mathbf{u}_1 + \mathbf{u}_2 + \mathbf{u}_3 + 5\mathbf{u}_4.$$

Then, we have $\mathbf{u}_1 t^2 = -2(\mathbf{u}_1 + \mathbf{u}_2 + \mathbf{u}_3 + 3\mathbf{u}_4)$, $\mathbf{u}_1 t^3 = -8(\mathbf{u}_1 + \mathbf{u}_2 + 3\mathbf{u}_4)$, $\mathbf{u}_1 t^4 = -16(\mathbf{u}_1 + 2\mathbf{u}_2 + \mathbf{u}_3 + 6\mathbf{u}_4)$. It is not hard to show that the vectors $\mathbf{u}_1, \mathbf{u}_1 t, \mathbf{u}_1 t^2, \mathbf{u}_1 t^3$ are l.i. Hence, the minimal polynomial $h(\lambda)$ of $\mathbf{u}_1$ is of degree 4. Since $-16\mathbf{u}_1 - 8(\mathbf{u}_1 t^2) - 2(\mathbf{u}_1 t^3) + \mathbf{u}_1 t^4 = \mathbf{0}$, we have

$$h(\lambda) = \lambda^4 - 2\lambda^3 - 8\lambda^2 - 16.$$

That $h(\lambda)$ is also the minimal polynomial of t follows from the fact that $\deg h(\lambda) = \dim \mathbb{Q}^4$. The companion matrix C of $h(\lambda)$ is given by

$$C = \begin{pmatrix} 0 & 1 & 0 & 0 \\ 0 & 0 & 1 & 0 \\ 0 & 0 & 0 & 1 \\ 16 & 0 & 8 & 2 \end{pmatrix}.$$

The matrix C represents t relative to the basis $(\mathbf{u}_1, \mathbf{u}_1 t, \mathbf{u}_1 t^2, \mathbf{u}_1 t^3)$ of $\mathbb{Q}^4$.

If F is a field and C is the companion matrix of

$$h(\lambda) = \lambda^n - c_{n-1}\lambda^{n-1} - \cdots - c_1\lambda - c_0$$

in $F[\lambda]$, then we can form the matrix $\lambda I - C$ having elements* in $F[\lambda]$:

$$\lambda I - C = \begin{pmatrix} \lambda & -1 & 0 \; 0 & \dots & 0 & 0 \\ 0 & \lambda & -1 \; 0 & \dots & 0 & 0 \\ & & \cdots\cdots & & & \\ & & \cdots\cdots & & & \\ 0 & 0 & & \dots & -1 & 0 \\ 0 & 0 & & \dots & \lambda & -1 \\ -c_0 & -c_1 & & \dots & -c_{n-2} & \lambda - c_{n-1} \end{pmatrix}.$$

The importance of the matrix $\lambda I - C$ stems from the following fact.

5.16 $$\det(\lambda I - C) = h(\lambda).$$

The proof of 5.16 is by induction. If $n = 1$, then we have that $h(\lambda) = \lambda - c_0$, $C = (c_0)$, $\lambda I - C = (\lambda - c_0)$, and $\det(\lambda I - C) = h(\lambda)$. Thus, 5.16 is true if $n = 1$. Assume the truth of 5.16 for every polynomial in $F[\lambda]$ of degree less than n, and let $h(\lambda)$ have degree $n > 1$ as shown above. Expanding $\det(\lambda I - C)$ by minors of the first column, we obtain

$$\det(\lambda I - C) = \lambda \det C_{11} - (-1)^{n+1}c_0 \det C_{n1},$$

where

$$C_{11} = \begin{pmatrix} \lambda & -1 & 0 & \dots & 0 & 0 \\ 0 & \lambda & -1 & \dots & 0 & 0 \\ & & \cdots\cdots & & & \\ & & \cdots\cdots & & & \\ 0 & 0 & 0 & \dots & \lambda & -1 \\ -c_1 & -c_2 & -c_3 & \dots & -c_{n-2} & \lambda - c_{n-1} \end{pmatrix},$$

$$C_{n1} = \begin{pmatrix} -1 & 0 & 0 & \dots & 0 & 0 \\ \lambda & -1 & 0 & \dots & 0 & 0 \\ 0 & \lambda & -1 & \dots & 0 & 0 \\ & & \cdots\cdots & & & \\ & & \cdots\cdots & & & \\ 0 & 0 & 0 & \dots & \lambda & -1 \end{pmatrix}.$$

Evidently, $C_{11} = \lambda I - C'$, where C' is the companion matrix of the polynomial

* Such matrices are well-defined in view of the fact that $F[\lambda]$ is contained in the field $F(\lambda)$ of all rational expressions of the form $f(\lambda)/g(\lambda)$, $f(\lambda), g(\lambda) \in F[\lambda]$. The determinant of each matrix with elements from $F[\lambda]$ is defined as usual.

$$f(\lambda) = \lambda^{n-1} - c_{n-1}\lambda^{n-2} - \cdots - c_2\lambda - c_1$$

of degree $n - 1$. By the induction assumption, we see that

$$\det C_{11} = \det(\lambda I - C') = f(\lambda).$$

Since C_{n1} is a lower triangular matrix, $\det C_{n1}$ is the product of its diagonal elements, $\det C_{n1} = (-1)^{n-1}$. Hence, we have

$$\det(\lambda I - C) = \lambda f(\lambda) - (-1)^{2n}c_0 = h(\lambda).$$

This proves 5.16.

If A is any $n \times n$ matrix over a field F having its minimal polynomial $h(\lambda)$ of degree n, then A is similar to the companion matrix C of $h(\lambda)$ by 3.29 and 5.15. Thus, $C = P^{-1}AP$ for some nonsingular matrix $P \in F(n)$, and we have

$$P^{-1}(\lambda I - A)P = \lambda P^{-1}IP - P^{-1}AP = \lambda I - C.$$

Hence, the matrices $\lambda I - A$ and $\lambda I - C$ are also similar. Since similar matrices have the same determinant, we have proved the following result.

5.17. THEOREM. If A is an $n \times n$ matrix over a field F and if the minimal polynomial $h(\lambda)$ of A has degree n, then we have

$$h(\lambda) = \det(\lambda I - A).$$

The main flaw in trying to use this theorem to find the minimal polynomial $h(\lambda)$ of A is that we must be able to show that $\deg h(\lambda) = n$.

EXAMPLE 3: Let us find the minimal polynomial $h(\lambda)$ of

$$A = \begin{pmatrix} -1 & 3 & 2 \\ 2 & 0 & 1 \\ 1 & 1 & 2 \end{pmatrix}$$

in $\mathbb{Q}(3)$. If $t \in L(\mathbb{Q}^3)$ is represented by A relative to the usual basis of $\mathbb{Q}^3$, then it is easy to show that the vectors $\mathbf{u}_1$, $\mathbf{u}_1t = -\mathbf{u}_1 + 3\mathbf{u}_2 + 2\mathbf{u}_3$, $\mathbf{u}_1t^2 = 9\mathbf{u}_1 - \mathbf{u}_2 + 5\mathbf{u}_3$ are l.i. Hence, the minimal polynomial of $\mathbf{u}_1$, and also of t and A, is of degree 3. Therefore, by 5.17, we find that

$$h(\lambda) = \det \begin{pmatrix} \lambda + 1 & -3 & -2 \\ -2 & \lambda & -1 \\ -1 & -1 & \lambda - 2 \end{pmatrix}$$

$$= \lambda(\lambda + 1)(\lambda - 2) - 3 - 4 - 2\lambda - (\lambda + 1) - 6(\lambda - 2)$$

$$= \lambda^3 - \lambda^2 - 11\lambda + 4.$$

EXERCISES

In each of Exercises 1 through 6, find the companion matrix of the given polynomial in $\mathbb{Q}[\lambda]$.

1. $\lambda^2 + 1$.
2. $\lambda^3 + 5\lambda^2 + 8\lambda - 3$.
3. $\lambda^5 - 5\lambda + 1$.
4. λ^4.
5. $\lambda^4 - 7\lambda^2 + 1$.
6. $(\lambda - 1)^4$.

In each of Exercises 7 through 12, find the minimal polynomial of the matrix over $\mathbb{Q}$.

7. $\begin{pmatrix} 0 & 1 & 0 \\ 0 & 0 & 1 \\ -5 & 1 & 5 \end{pmatrix}$.

8. $\begin{pmatrix} 0 & 0 & 1 \\ 1 & 0 & 0 \\ 0 & 1 & -1 \end{pmatrix}$.

9. $\begin{pmatrix} 1 & 1 & 0 & 0 \\ 0 & 1 & 1 & 0 \\ 0 & 0 & 1 & 1 \\ 1 & 0 & 0 & 1 \end{pmatrix}$.

10. $\begin{pmatrix} 2 & 0 & 1 & 0 \\ 0 & 1 & 0 & 1 \\ 0 & -1 & 0 & 1 \\ 3 & 1 & 4 & -1 \end{pmatrix}$.

11. $\begin{pmatrix} 0 & 1 & 0 & 0 & 0 \\ 0 & 0 & 1 & 0 & 0 \\ 0 & 0 & 1 & 1 & 0 \\ 0 & 0 & 0 & 0 & 1 \\ 0 & 0 & 0 & 0 & 0 \end{pmatrix}$.

12. $\begin{pmatrix} 1 & 1 & 0 & 0 & 0 \\ 0 & 1 & 1 & 0 & 0 \\ 0 & 0 & 1 & 1 & 0 \\ 0 & 0 & 0 & 1 & 1 \\ 0 & 0 & 0 & 0 & 1 \end{pmatrix}$.

4. THE JORDAN MATRIX

An nth degree polynomial $h(\lambda) \in F[\lambda]$, which is a power of a monic polynomial $f(\lambda)$ of degree k, has associated with it an $n \times n$ matrix J closely related to the companion matrix C of $f(\lambda)$.

We describe J by defining a l.t. of the vector space F^n which is represented by J. Let

$$h(\lambda) = f^m(\lambda), \qquad f(\lambda) = \lambda^k - \sum_{i=0}^{k-1} c_i\lambda^i, \qquad \text{where} \quad n = mk,$$

and let $(\mathbf{u}_1, \mathbf{u}_2, \ldots, \mathbf{u}_n)$ be a basis of F^n. We define $t \in L(F^n)$ as follows: $\mathbf{u}_1 t = \mathbf{u}_2$, $\mathbf{u}_2 t = \mathbf{u}_3, \ldots, \mathbf{u}_{k-1} t = \mathbf{u}_k$, and, in general, let

$$\mathbf{u}_i t = \mathbf{u}_{i+1} \qquad \text{if} \quad i \neq jk.$$

Also, let

$$\mathbf{u}_{jk}t = \mathbf{u}_{jk+1} + \sum_{i=0}^{k-1} c_i \mathbf{u}_{(j-1)k+i+1} \qquad \text{if} \quad 1 \le j < m,$$

$$\mathbf{u}_n t = \sum_{i=0}^{k-1} c_i \mathbf{u}_{(m-1)k+i+1}.$$

Then, we have

$$\mathbf{u}_1 t^i = \mathbf{u}_{i+1} \qquad \text{if} \quad 0 \le i < k,$$

$$\mathbf{u}_1 t^k = \mathbf{u}_{k+1} + \sum_{i=0}^{k-1} c_i \mathbf{u}_1 t^i, \qquad \text{so that} \quad \mathbf{u}_1 f(t) = \mathbf{u}_{k+1},$$

$$\mathbf{u}_1 f(t) t^i = \mathbf{u}_{k+i+1} \qquad \text{if} \quad 0 \le i < k,$$

$$\mathbf{u}_1 f(t) t^k = \mathbf{u}_{2k+1} + \sum_{i=0}^{k-1} c_i \mathbf{u}_1 f(t) t^i, \qquad \text{so that} \quad \mathbf{u}_1 f^2(t) = \mathbf{u}_{2k+1},$$

and so on, with

$$\mathbf{u}_1 f^j(t) = \mathbf{u}_{jk+1} \qquad \text{if} \quad 1 \le j < m,$$

and finally

$$\mathbf{u}_1 f^m(t) = \mathbf{0}.$$

The vectors $\mathbf{u}_1, \mathbf{u}_1 t, \ldots, \mathbf{u}_1 t^{n-1}$ are l.i., because $\mathbf{u}_1 t^i$ is either $\mathbf{u}_{i+1}$ or $\mathbf{u}_{i+1}$ plus a linear combination of $\mathbf{u}_r$ with $r < i + 1$. Hence, the minimal polynomial of $\mathbf{u}_1$ has degree n. In fact, $f^m(\lambda)$ is the minimal polynomial of $\mathbf{u}_1$, since $\deg f^m(\lambda) = n$ and $\mathbf{u}_1 f^m(t) = \mathbf{0}$. Also, $f^m(\lambda)$ is the minimal polynomial of t, because $\deg f^m(\lambda) = \dim F^n$.

The reader can easily convince himself that t is represented by the $n \times n$ matrix J shown below relative to the $\mathbf{u}$-basis of F^n.

5.18
$$J = \begin{pmatrix} C & N & 0 & 0 & \ldots & 0 \\ 0 & C & N & 0 & \ldots & 0 \\ & & \cdots\cdots & & & \\ & & \cdots\cdots & & & \\ 0 & & \ldots & 0 & C & N \\ 0 & & \ldots & 0 & 0 & C \end{pmatrix}.$$

The matrix J has triangular block matrix form, where C is the companion matrix of $f(\lambda)$ and N is the $k \times k$ matrix having 1 in the $(k, 1)$ position and zeros elsewhere:

5.19
$$N = \begin{pmatrix} 0 & 0 & \dots & 0 \\ 0 & 0 & \dots & 0 \\ & \cdot\cdot\cdot\cdot\cdot & & \\ & \cdot\cdot\cdot\cdot\cdot & & \\ 0 & 0 & \dots & 0 \\ 1 & 0 & \dots & 0 \end{pmatrix}.$$

5.20. DEFINITION OF THE JORDAN MATRIX OF $f^m(\lambda)$. If $f(\lambda) \in F[\lambda]$ is a monic polynomial of degree k, having C as its companion matrix, and N is the $k \times k$ matrix of 5.19, then the $mk \times mk$ matrix J of 5.18 is called the Jordan matrix of $f^m(\lambda)$.

Since J represents $t \in L(F^n)$ defined above and t has minimal polynomial $f^m(\lambda)$, J also has minimal polynomial $f^m(\lambda)$. We state this below as a theorem.

5.21. THEOREM. The Jordan matrix of $f^m(\lambda)$ has $f^m(\lambda)$ as its minimal polynomial.

If $m = 1$, then the Jordan matrix of $f^m(\lambda)$ is simply the companion matrix of $f(\lambda)$. Ordinarily, we insist that $m > 1$ before we call J of 5.18 the Jordan matrix of $f^m(\lambda)$.

EXAMPLE 1: Let us find the Jordan matrix of the polynomial $(\lambda^2 - 2\lambda + 3)^3$ in $\mathbb{Q}[\lambda]$. The companion matrix C of $\lambda^2 - 2\lambda + 3$ and the matrix N of 5.19 are given by

$$C = \begin{pmatrix} 0 & 1 \\ -3 & 2 \end{pmatrix}, \qquad N = \begin{pmatrix} 0 & 0 \\ 1 & 0 \end{pmatrix}.$$

Therefore, the Jordan matrix J is given by

$$J = \begin{pmatrix} C & N & 0 \\ 0 & C & N \\ 0 & 0 & C \end{pmatrix}$$

or

$$J = \left(\begin{array}{cc|cc|cc} 0 & 1 & 0 & 0 & 0 & 0 \\ -3 & 2 & 1 & 0 & 0 & 0 \\ \hline 0 & 0 & 0 & 1 & 0 & 0 \\ 0 & 0 & -3 & 2 & 1 & 0 \\ \hline 0 & 0 & 0 & 0 & 0 & 1 \\ 0 & 0 & 0 & 0 & -3 & 2 \end{array}\right).$$

EXAMPLE 2: To find the Jordan matrix J of a power of a linear polynomial, say of $(\lambda - a)^4 \in \mathbb{Q}[\lambda]$, we observe that C and N are 1×1 matrices: $C = (a)$, $N = (1)$. Hence, we have

$$J = \begin{pmatrix} a & 1 & 0 & 0 \\ 0 & a & 1 & 0 \\ 0 & 0 & a & 1 \\ 0 & 0 & 0 & a \end{pmatrix}.$$

On the other hand, we find that $(\lambda - a)^4 = \lambda^4 - 4a\lambda^3 + 6a^2\lambda^2 - 4a^3\lambda + a^4$, and the companion matrix of $(\lambda - a)^4$ is as given below:

$$\begin{pmatrix} 0 & 1 & 0 & 0 \\ 0 & 0 & 1 & 0 \\ 0 & 0 & 0 & 1 \\ -a^4 & 4a^3 & -6a^2 & 4a \end{pmatrix}.$$

If $J \in F(n)$ is the Jordan matrix of $f^m(\lambda)$, then we have

$$f^m(\lambda) = \det(\lambda I - J)$$

by 5.17. Thus, in Example 2 above, we obtain

$$\lambda I - J = \begin{pmatrix} \lambda - a & -1 & 0 & 0 \\ 0 & \lambda - a & -1 & 0 \\ 0 & 0 & \lambda - a & -1 \\ 0 & 0 & 0 & \lambda - a \end{pmatrix},$$

and clearly $\det(\lambda I - J) = (\lambda - a)^4$.

EXERCISES

Find the Jordan matrix of each of the following polynomials of $\mathbb{Q}[\lambda]$.

1. $(\lambda^3 + 1)^3$.
2. $(\lambda^2 + \lambda + 1)^2$.
3. $(\lambda^4 + 2)^2$.
4. $(\lambda - 4)^5$.
5. $(\lambda^2 - 2\lambda + 1)^3$.
6. $(\lambda^3 - 3\lambda^2 + 2\lambda - 1)^3$
7. λ^6.
8. $(\lambda + \frac{1}{2})^4$.
9. Let V be an n-dimensional vector space over a field F and $t \in L(V)$ have minimal polynomial $h(\lambda)$ of degree n. We know that t commutes with each $f(t) \in F[t]$, that is, $t \cdot f(t) = f(t) \cdot t$. Prove that

$$\{s \in L(V) \mid ts = st\} = F[t].$$

[*Hint:* Observe the action of s on a basis of V of the form $(\mathbf{x}, \mathbf{x}t, \ldots, \mathbf{x}t^{n-1})$.]

10. For each $n \times n$ matrix A over a field F, prove that $\det(\lambda I - A)$ is a monic polynomial in λ of degree n.

Chapter Six

Invariant Subspaces and Characteristic Values

1. INVARIANT SUBSPACES

The linear transformation t of $\mathbb{Q}^3$ defined by

$$\mathbf{u}_1 t = \mathbf{u}_1 - \mathbf{u}_2, \qquad \mathbf{u}_2 t = \mathbf{u}_1 + \mathbf{u}_2, \qquad \mathbf{u}_3 t = \mathbf{u}_1 + \mathbf{u}_2 - \mathbf{u}_3$$

relative to the usual basis $\{\mathbf{u}_1, \mathbf{u}_2, \mathbf{u}_3\}$ of $\mathbb{Q}^3$ maps the subspace $W = \mathbb{Q}\mathbf{u}_1 + \mathbb{Q}\mathbf{u}_2$ of $\mathbb{Q}^3$ into itself. That is, we have

$$(a\mathbf{u}_1 + b\mathbf{u}_2)t = (a + b)\mathbf{u}_1 + (-a + b)\mathbf{u}_2 \in W$$

for every $a\mathbf{u}_1 + b\mathbf{u}_2 \in W$. Using the notation

$$Wt = \{\mathbf{x}t \mid \mathbf{x} \in W\},$$

we have shown that $Wt \subset W$. This example illustrates the following definition.

6.1. DEFINITION OF AN INVARIANT SUBSPACE. Let V be a vector space and t a linear transformation of V. A subspace W of V is called a t-invariant subspace iff $Wt \subset W$.

In the example above, $W = \mathbb{Q}\mathbf{u}_1 + \mathbb{Q}\mathbf{u}_2$ is a t-invariant subspace of $\mathbb{Q}^3$.

If W is a t-invariant subspace of a vector space V, then $Wt \subset W$, $(Wt)t \subset Wt$, $(Wt^2)t \subset Wt^2$, and so on. That is, $W \supset Wt \supset Wt^2 \supset Wt^3 \supset \ldots$, so that we have

$$Wf(t) \subset W \qquad \text{for every } f(\lambda) \in F[\lambda].$$

Using the notation

$$F[t] = \{f(t) \mid f(\lambda) \in F[\lambda]\},$$

we have $WF[t] \subset W$ for every t-invariant subspace W of V, in the sense that $\mathbf{x}f(t) \in W$ for all $\mathbf{x} \in W, f(t) \in F[t]$.

Whenever we have a t-invariant subspace W of V, then we can restrict the mapping $V \xrightarrow{t} V$ to a mapping $W \xrightarrow{t'} W$ in the obvious way: $\mathbf{x}t' = \mathbf{x}t$ for all $\mathbf{x} \in W$. Clearly, t' is a l.t. of W. We call t' the *restriction of t to W* and denote it by

$$t' = t \mid W.$$

In the example above, $t' = t \mid (\mathbb{Q}\mathbf{u}_1 + \mathbb{Q}\mathbf{u}_2)$ is defined by $\mathbf{u}_1t' = \mathbf{u}_1 - \mathbf{u}_2$, $\mathbf{u}_2t' = \mathbf{u}_1 + \mathbf{u}_2$. Note that t' is a l.t. of a two-dimensional vector space, whereas t is l.t. of a three-dimensional vector space.

Each basis $(\mathbf{x}_1, \mathbf{x}_2, \ldots, \mathbf{x}_k)$ of a subspace W of an n-dimensional vector space V can be extended to a basis of V, say $(\mathbf{x}_1, \ldots, \mathbf{x}_k, \mathbf{x}_{k+1}, \ldots, \mathbf{x}_n)$. If $t \in L(V)$ and W is a t-invariant subspace of V, then let $A = (a_{ij})$ be the matrix representing t relative to the $\mathbf{x}$-basis of V. Since $Wt \subset W$, we see that $a_{ij} = 0$ whenever $i \leq k$ and $j > k$. Hence, A has the block form

6.2 $$A = \left(\begin{array}{ccc|ccc} a_{11} & \cdots & a_{1k} & 0 & \cdots & 0 \\ \vdots & & \vdots & \vdots & & \vdots \\ a_{k1} & \cdots & a_{kk} & 0 & \cdots & 0 \\ \hline a_{k+1\,1} & \cdots & a_{k+1\,k} & a_{k+1\,k+1} & \cdots & a_{k+1\,n} \\ \vdots & & \vdots & \vdots & & \vdots \\ a_{n1} & \cdots & a_{nk} & a_{n\,k+1} & \cdots & a_{nn} \end{array}\right) = \begin{pmatrix} B & 0 \\ C & D \end{pmatrix},$$

where B is a $k \times k$ submatrix, C an $(n - k) \times k$ submatrix, and D an $(n - k) \times (n - k)$ submatrix of A. By definition, matrix B represents the restriction $t \mid W$ relative to the basis $(\mathbf{x}_1, \mathbf{x}_2, \ldots, \mathbf{x}_k)$.

It is true, conversely, that if the matrix A representing a l.t. t relative to a basis $(\mathbf{x}_1, \mathbf{x}_2, \ldots, \mathbf{x}_n)$ of V has the form 6.2, then $W = F\mathbf{x}_1 + F\mathbf{x}_2 + \cdots + F\mathbf{x}_k$ is a t-invariant subspace of V. We state these results as follows.

6.3. THEOREM. Let W be a subspace of a vector space V over a field F, $(\mathbf{x}_1, \mathbf{x}_2, \ldots, \mathbf{x}_k)$ be a basis of W, and $(\mathbf{x}_1, \ldots, \mathbf{x}_k, \mathbf{x}_{k+1}, \ldots, \mathbf{x}_n)$ be an extension of this basis to a basis of V. If $t \in L(V)$ is represented by the matrix A relative to the $\mathbf{x}$-basis, then W is a t-invariant subspace of V iff A has the block form

$$A = \begin{pmatrix} B & 0 \\ C & D \end{pmatrix},$$

where B is a $k \times k$ submatrix.

One way to obtain a t-invariant subspace of V is to start with any $\mathbf{x} \in V$ and form the set W of all multiples of $\mathbf{x}$ by polynomials in t. Thus, we have

$$W = \mathbf{x}F[t] = \{\mathbf{x}f(t) \mid f(\lambda) \in F[\lambda]\}.$$

If $\mathbf{x}f(t)$, $\mathbf{x}g(t) \in W$ and $c \in F$, then $\mathbf{x}f(t) + \mathbf{x}g(t) = \mathbf{x}[f(t) + g(t)]$ and $c[\mathbf{x}f(t)] = \mathbf{x}[cf(t)]$ are in W. Thus, W is a subspace of V. Since $[\mathbf{x}f(t)]t = \mathbf{x}[f(t)t] \in W$, it is evident that W is t-invariant. Actually, W is a cyclic according to the following definition.

6.4. DEFINITION OF A CYCLIC INVARIANT SUBSPACE. Let V be a vector space over a field F and $t \in L(V)$. A t-invariant subspace W of V is called cyclic with generator $\mathbf{x}$ iff $W = \mathbf{x}F[t]$ for some $\mathbf{x} \in V$.

Let us consider $t \in L(V)$ and a cyclic t-invariant subspace

$$W = \mathbf{x}F[t].$$

If

$$h(\lambda) = \lambda^m - c_{m-1}\lambda^{m-1} - \cdots - c_1\lambda - c_0$$

is the minimal polynomial of $\mathbf{x}$, then $\{\mathbf{x}, \mathbf{x}t, \ldots, \mathbf{x}t^{m-1}\}$ is a l.i. set of vectors. Since $\mathbf{x}h(t) = \mathbf{0}$, we see that $\mathbf{x}t^m$ is a linear combination of $\mathbf{x}, \mathbf{x}t, \ldots, \mathbf{x}t^{m-1}$. Thus, we have

$$\mathbf{x}t^m = \sum_{i=0}^{m-1} c_i\mathbf{x}t^i.$$

In turn, we have

$$\begin{aligned} \mathbf{x}t^{m+1} &= \sum_{i=0}^{m-2} c_i\mathbf{x}t^{i+1} + c_{m-1}\mathbf{x}t^m \\ &= \sum_{i=0}^{m-2} c_i\mathbf{x}t^{i+1} + c_{m-1}\sum_{i=0}^{m-1} c_i\mathbf{x}t^i, \end{aligned}$$

and $\mathbf{x}t^{m+1}$ is also a linear combination of $\mathbf{x}, \mathbf{x}t, \ldots, \mathbf{x}t^{m-1}$. On continuing this process, we see that $\mathbf{x}t^k$ is a linear combination of $\mathbf{x}, \mathbf{x}t, \ldots, \mathbf{x}t^{m-1}$ for every integer $k > m - 1$. Therefore, $\mathbf{x}f(t)$ is a linear combination of $\mathbf{x}, \mathbf{x}t, \ldots, \mathbf{x}t^{m-1}$ for every $f(\lambda) \in F[\lambda]$. We have proved the following result.

6.5. THEOREM. Let V be a vector space over a field F, $t \in L(V)$, $\mathbf{x} \in V$, and $h(\lambda) \in F[\lambda]$ be the minimal polynomial of $\mathbf{x}$. Then the cyclic t-invariant subspace $W = \mathbf{x}F[t]$ of V generated by $\mathbf{x}$ has dimension $m = \deg h(\lambda)$ and basis $\{\mathbf{x}, \mathbf{x}t, \ldots, \mathbf{x}t^{m-1}\}$.

For each $t \in L(V)$, there are two trivial t-invariant subspaces of V, $\{\mathbf{0}\}$ and V. The subspace $\{\mathbf{0}\}$ is cyclic with generator $\mathbf{0}$. It is evident that V is cyclic iff the minimal polynomial of t has degree $n = \dim V$.

EXAMPLE: Let $t \in L(\mathbb{Q}^3)$ be defined by

$$\mathbf{u}_1 t = \mathbf{u}_1 + \mathbf{u}_2, \qquad \mathbf{u}_2 t = \mathbf{u}_2 - 2\mathbf{u}_3, \qquad \mathbf{u}_3 t = \mathbf{u}_1 - \mathbf{u}_2 + 2\mathbf{u}_3$$

relative to the usual basis. Thus, t is represented by the matrix

$$A = \begin{pmatrix} 1 & 1 & 0 \\ 0 & 1 & -2 \\ 1 & -1 & 2 \end{pmatrix}$$

relative to this basis. Let us find the cyclic t-invariant subspace W of $\mathbb{Q}^3$ generated by

$$\mathbf{x} = \mathbf{u}_1 - \mathbf{u}_2.$$

We have

$$\mathbf{x}t = \mathbf{u}_1 t - \mathbf{u}_2 t = \mathbf{u}_1 + 2\mathbf{u}_3,$$
$$\mathbf{x}t^2 = \mathbf{u}_1 t + 2\mathbf{u}_3 t = 3\mathbf{u}_1 - \mathbf{u}_2 + 4\mathbf{u}_3.$$

Since

$$\mathbf{x}t^2 - 2\mathbf{x}t - \mathbf{x} = (3\mathbf{u}_1 - \mathbf{u}_2 + 4\mathbf{u}_3) - 2(\mathbf{u}_1 + 2\mathbf{u}_3) - (\mathbf{u}_1 - \mathbf{u}_2) = \mathbf{0},$$

whereas the vectors $\mathbf{x}$ and $\mathbf{x}t$ are l.i., we find that $\mathbf{x}$ has minimal polynomial

$$h(\lambda) = \lambda^2 - 2\lambda - 1.$$

Therefore, W has dimension 2 and basis $(\mathbf{x}, \mathbf{x}t)$. We can extend $(\mathbf{x}, \mathbf{x}t)$ to a basis of $\mathbb{Q}^3$ in many ways. For example, $(\mathbf{x}, \mathbf{x}t, \mathbf{u}_3)$ is a basis of $\mathbb{Q}^3$. Now, we have

$$\mathbf{x}t = -\mathbf{x} + 1(\mathbf{x}t) + 0\mathbf{u}_3,$$
$$(\mathbf{x}t)t = 1\mathbf{x} + 2(\mathbf{x}t) + 0\mathbf{u}_3,$$
$$\mathbf{u}_3 t = 1\mathbf{x} + 0(\mathbf{x}t) + 2\mathbf{u}_3,$$

and therefore t has matrix

$$A' = \begin{pmatrix} 0 & 1 & 0 \\ 1 & 2 & 0 \\ 1 & 0 & 2 \end{pmatrix}$$

relative to the basis $(\mathbf{x}, \mathbf{x}t, \mathbf{u}_3)$. Note that A' has the form

$$A' = \begin{pmatrix} B & 0 \\ C & D \end{pmatrix},$$

where

$$B = \begin{pmatrix} 0 & 1 \\ 1 & 2 \end{pmatrix}, \qquad C = (1 \quad 0), \qquad D = (2).$$

The restriction of t to W, $t \mid W$, is represented by matrix B relative to the basis $(\mathbf{x}, \mathbf{x}t)$ of W. Evidently B is the companion matrix of $h(\lambda)$.

EXERCISES

In each of the following exercises, find two nonzero cyclic t-invariant subspaces of the given space. (The usual **u**-basis is used.)

1. $V = \mathbb{Q}^3$, $t \in L(V)$ defined by: $\mathbf{u}_1 t = \mathbf{u}_2$, $\mathbf{u}_2 t = \mathbf{u}_1$, $\mathbf{u}_3 t = \mathbf{u}_1 + \mathbf{u}_2$.
2. $V = \mathbb{Q}^3$, $t \in L(V)$ defined by: $\mathbf{u}_1 t = \mathbf{u}_1 + 3\mathbf{u}_2$, $\mathbf{u}_2 t = 2\mathbf{u}_1 - \mathbf{u}_2$, $\mathbf{u}_3 t = \mathbf{u}_1 - 4\mathbf{u}_2 + 2\mathbf{u}_3$.
3. $V = \mathbb{Q}^3$, $t \in L(V)$ defined by: $\mathbf{u}_1 t = 3\mathbf{u}_1$, $\mathbf{u}_2 t = \mathbf{u}_1 - \mathbf{u}_2$, $\mathbf{u}_3 t = \mathbf{u}_1 + 3\mathbf{u}_3$.
4. $V = \mathbb{Q}^4$, $t \in L(V)$ defined by: $\mathbf{u}_1 t = \mathbf{u}_2 - \mathbf{u}_3$, $\mathbf{u}_2 t = \mathbf{u}_1 + \mathbf{u}_3$, $\mathbf{u}_3 t = \mathbf{u}_1 + \mathbf{u}_2 + \mathbf{u}_3$, $\mathbf{u}_4 t = \mathbf{u}_1 - \mathbf{u}_4$.
5. $V = \mathbb{Q}^4$, $t \in L(V)$ defined by: $\mathbf{u}_1 t = \mathbf{u}_1 + \mathbf{u}_4$, $\mathbf{u}_2 t = \mathbf{u}_2 - \mathbf{u}_4$, $\mathbf{u}_3 t = \mathbf{u}_3 + 2\mathbf{u}_4$, $\mathbf{u}_4 t = -\mathbf{u}_4$.
6. $V = \mathbb{Q}^5$, $t \in L(V)$ defined by: $\mathbf{u}_1 t = \mathbf{u}_1 - \mathbf{u}_3 + \mathbf{u}_5$, $\mathbf{u}_2 t = 2\mathbf{u}_2 - \mathbf{u}_4$, $\mathbf{u}_3 t = -\mathbf{u}_1 + \mathbf{u}_5$, $\mathbf{u}_4 t = -\mathbf{u}_2 + 2\mathbf{u}_4$, $\mathbf{u}_5 t = \mathbf{u}_3 - \mathbf{u}_5$.
7. Prove the statement that a vector space V of dimension n is cyclic relative to some $t \in L(V)$ iff the minimal polynomial of t has degree n.
8. If W_1 and W_2 are t-invariant subspaces of V for some $t \in L(V)$, prove that $W_1 + W_2$ and $W_1 \cap W_2$ are also t-invariant subspaces.

2. DIRECT SUMS OF SUBSPACES

In this section, let V be an n-dimensional vector space over a field F.

6.6. DEFINITION OF DIRECT SUM. The vector space V is said to be a direct sum of subspaces $W_1, W_2, \ldots, W_r$, and we write

$$V = W_1 \oplus W_2 \oplus \cdots \oplus W_r,$$

iff

(1) $W_i \neq \{\mathbf{0}\}, \qquad i = 1, 2, \ldots, r.$

(2) $W_i \cap (W_1 + \cdots + W_{i-1} + W_{i+1} + \cdots + W_r) = \{\mathbf{0}\}, \quad i = 1, 2, \ldots, r.$

(3) $W_1 + W_2 + \cdots + W_r = V.$

Conditions (1) and (2) above state that $\{W_1, W_2, \ldots, W_r\}$ is an independent set of subspaces of V (see 1.27), whereas (3) states that every vector of V is a linear combination of the vectors of the W_i. The following result is an immediate consequence of 1.28.

6.7. THEOREM. If $\{W_1, W_2, \ldots, W_r\}$ is a set of subspaces of V, then we have

$$V = W_1 \oplus W_2 \oplus \cdots \oplus W_r$$

iff every $\mathbf{x} \in V$ has a unique representation

$$\mathbf{x} = \sum_{i=1}^{r} \mathbf{x}_i \qquad \text{for some } \mathbf{x}_i \in W_i, \qquad i = 1, 2, \ldots, r.$$

We state some simple facts about direct sums below. Proofs of these facts are left as exercises.

6.8. $\{\mathbf{x}_1, \mathbf{x}_2, \ldots, \mathbf{x}_n\}$ is a basis of V iff $V = F\mathbf{x}_1 \oplus F\mathbf{x}_2 \oplus \cdots \oplus F\mathbf{x}_n$.

6.9. $V = W_1 \oplus W_2 \oplus \cdots \oplus W_r$ iff $V = W_1 + W_2 + \cdots + W_r$, all $W_i \neq \{\mathbf{0}\}$, and $\dim V = \sum_{i=1}^{r} \dim W_i$.

6.10. If $V = W_1 \oplus W_2 \oplus \cdots \oplus W_r$ and $\{\mathbf{x}_{i1}, \mathbf{x}_{i2}, \ldots, \mathbf{x}_{in_i}\}$ is a basis of W_i, then $\{\mathbf{x}_{11}, \ldots, \mathbf{x}_{1n_1}, \mathbf{x}_{21}, \ldots, \mathbf{x}_{2n_2}, \ldots, \mathbf{x}_{r1}, \ldots, \mathbf{x}_{rn_r}\}$ is a basis of V.

Our primary interest is with direct sums of t-invariant subspaces for some $t \in L(V)$. We shall eventually describe ways of deciding whether V can be expressed as a direct sum of t-invariant subspaces. Meanwhile, we shall give some properties of such direct sums if they exist.

Let us assume that $t \in L(V)$ and that $W_1, W_2, \ldots, W_r$ are t-invariant subspaces of V, such that

$$V = W_1 \oplus W_2 \oplus \cdots \oplus W_r.$$

Then we can define the restrictions of t to the various W_i:

$$t_i = t \mid W_i, \qquad i = 1, 2, \ldots, r.$$

Thus, $\mathbf{x}_i t_i = \mathbf{x}_i t$ for each $\mathbf{x}_i \in W_i$. Since every $\mathbf{x} \in V$ has the unique representation

$$\mathbf{x} = \sum_{i=1}^{r} \mathbf{x}_i \qquad \text{for some } \mathbf{x}_i \in W_i,$$

we have

$$\mathbf{x}t = \sum_{i=1}^{r} \mathbf{x}_i t = \sum_{i=1}^{r} \mathbf{x}_i t_i.$$

Hence, the effect of t on V is completely determined by the effects of the t_i on W_i. We write

$$t = t_1 \oplus t_2 \oplus \cdots \oplus t_r$$

to indicate this relationship, and we call t the *direct sum* of $t_1, t_2, \ldots, t_r$.

EXAMPLE 1: Define $t \in L(\mathbb{Q}^3)$ by

$$\mathbf{u}_1 t = 2\mathbf{u}_1 - 3\mathbf{u}_2, \qquad \mathbf{u}_2 t_1 = \mathbf{u}_1 + 2\mathbf{u}_2, \qquad \mathbf{u}_3 t = 5\mathbf{u}_3$$

relative to the usual basis of $\mathbb{Q}^3$. If $W_1 = \mathbb{Q}\mathbf{u}_1 + \mathbb{Q}\mathbf{u}_2$ and $W_2 = \mathbb{Q}\mathbf{u}_3$, then clearly we have

$$\mathbb{Q}^3 = W_1 \oplus W_2, \qquad t = t_1 \oplus t_2,$$

where

$$\mathbf{u}_1 t_1 = 2\mathbf{u}_1 - 3\mathbf{u}_2, \qquad \mathbf{u}_2 t_1 = \mathbf{u}_1 + 2\mathbf{u}_2, \qquad \mathbf{u}_3 t_2 = 5\mathbf{u}_3.$$

That is, we have that $t_1 = t \mid W_1 \in L(W_1)$ and $t_2 = t \mid W_2 \in L(W_2)$.

If $t \in L(V)$, W_i are t-invariant subspaces of V, and

$$V = W_1 \oplus W_2 \oplus \cdots \oplus W_r, \quad t = t_1 \oplus t_2 \oplus \cdots \oplus t_r,$$

where $t_i = t \mid W_i$, as above, then matrix representations of the t_i determine a unique matrix representation of t. To describe what we mean, let $n_k = \dim W_k$, $(\mathbf{x}_{k1}, \mathbf{x}_{k2}, \ldots, \mathbf{x}_{kn_k})$ be a basis of W_k, and $A_k = (a_{kij})$ be the matrix representation of t_k relative to this basis, $k = 1, 2, \ldots, r$. Then

$$(\mathbf{x}_{11}, \ldots, \mathbf{x}_{1n_1}, \mathbf{x}_{21}, \ldots, \mathbf{x}_{2n_2}, \ldots, \mathbf{x}_{r1}, \ldots, \mathbf{x}_{rn_r})$$

is a basis of V by 6.10. If $A \in F(n)$ represents t relative to this basis, then we have

$$\mathbf{x}_{ki} t = \mathbf{x}_{ki} t_k = \sum_{j=1}^{n_k} a_{kij}\, \mathbf{x}_{kj}, \qquad i = 1, \ldots, n_k,\ k = 1, \ldots, r.$$

Hence, matrix A has the block matrix form

$$A = \begin{pmatrix} A_1 & 0 & 0 & \ldots & 0 \\ 0 & A_2 & 0 & \ldots & 0 \\ & & \cdots\cdots & & \\ & & \cdots\cdots & & \\ 0 & 0 & 0 & \ldots & A_r \end{pmatrix}.$$

We call A the *direct sum* of matrices $A_1, A_2, \ldots, A_r$ and write

$$A = A_1 \oplus A_2 \oplus \cdots \oplus A_r.$$

Our remarks above may be summarized as follows.

6.11. THEOREM. Let V be an n-dimensional vector space over a field F, $t \in L(V)$, and $V = W_1 \oplus W_2 \oplus \cdots \oplus W_r$, where each W_k is a t-invariant subspace of V. If A_k is a matrix representation of $t_k = t \mid W_k$ relative to a basis of W_k, $k = 1, 2, \ldots, r$, then

$$A = A_1 \oplus A_2 \oplus \cdots \oplus A_r$$

is a matrix representation of t.

Thus, in Example 1, we have $r = 2$, W_1 has a basis $(\mathbf{u}_1, \mathbf{u}_2)$, and W_2 a basis $(\mathbf{u}_3)$. Relative to these bases, t_1 and t_2 are represented by $A_1 \in \mathbb{Q}(2)$ and $A_2 \in \mathbb{Q}(1)$ given by

$$A_1 = \begin{pmatrix} 2 & -3 \\ 1 & 2 \end{pmatrix}, \qquad A_2 = (5).$$

Hence, the matrix A of t relative to the basis $(\mathbf{u}_1, \mathbf{u}_2, \mathbf{u}_3)$ is given by

$$A = A_1 \oplus A_2 = \left(\begin{array}{cc|c} 2 & -3 & 0 \\ 1 & 2 & 0 \\ \hline 0 & 0 & 5 \end{array}\right).$$

We obtain a representation of V as a direct sum of t-invariant subspaces relative to some $t \in L(V)$ whenever the minimal polynomial $h(\lambda)$ of t can be factored into relatively prime factors of positive degree. For, if

$$h(\lambda) = h_1(\lambda)h_2(\lambda), \qquad (h_1(\lambda), h_2(\lambda)) = 1,$$

then, by 5.4, there exist polynomials $g_1(\lambda)$ and $g_2(\lambda)$ in $F[\lambda]$ such that

(1) $$h_1(\lambda)g_1(\lambda) + h_2(\lambda)g_2(\lambda) = 1.$$

If we let

$$W_1 = Vh_2(t), \qquad W_2 = Vh_1(t),$$

then we claim that W_1 and W_2 are t-invariant subspaces of V and that

(2) $$V = W_1 \oplus W_2.$$

To prove that W_1 is a t-invariant subspace of V, we observe, first of all, that W_1 is closed under addition and scalar multiplication, and hence that W_1 is a subspace. Since we have

$$W_1t = (Vh_2(t))t = (Vt)h_2(t) \subset Vh_2(t) = W_1,$$

W_1 is a t-invariant subspace. Similarly, W_2 is a t-invariant subspace of V. By (1), for each $\mathbf{x} \in V$, we have

$$\mathbf{x} = [\mathbf{x}g_1(t)]h_1(t) + [\mathbf{x}g_2(t)]h_2(t) \in W_2 + W_1.$$

Hence, we find that

(3) $$V = W_1 + W_2.$$

If $\mathbf{x} \in W_1 \cap W_2$, then $\mathbf{x} = \mathbf{x}_1h_2(t) = \mathbf{x}_2h_1(t)$ for some $\mathbf{x}_1, \mathbf{x}_2 \in V$, by the definitions of W_1 and W_2. Now, we have

$$\mathbf{x}h_1(t) = \mathbf{x}_1h_1(t)h_2(t) = \mathbf{x}_1h(t) = \mathbf{x}_1 0 = \mathbf{0},$$

and, similarly, $\mathbf{x}h_2(t) = \mathbf{0}$. Hence, by (1), we have

$$\mathbf{x} = \mathbf{x}h_1(t)g_1(t) + \mathbf{x}h_2(t)g_2(t) = \mathbf{0}g_1(t) + \mathbf{0}g_2(t) = \mathbf{0}.$$

Thus, we find that

(4) $$W_1 \cap W_2 = \{\mathbf{0}\}.$$

The fact that $V = W_1 \oplus W_2$ follows from (3) and (4). Clearly, $t = t_1 \oplus t_2$, where $t_i = t \mid W_i$, and the minimal polynomial of t_1 is $h_1(\lambda)$, and of t_2 is $h_2(\lambda)$.

Every polynomial $h(\lambda) \in F[\lambda]$ can be factored uniquely in the form

$$h(\lambda) = p_1^{s_1}(\lambda)p_2^{s_2}(\lambda) \cdots p_r^{s_r}(\lambda),$$

where $p_1(\lambda), p_2(\lambda), \ldots, p_r(\lambda)$ are the distinct monic prime factors of $h(\lambda)$, and $s_1, s_2, \ldots, s_r$ are positive integers. If $r > 1$ and

$$h_1(\lambda) = p_1^{s_1}(\lambda), \qquad h_2(\lambda) = p_2^{s_2}(\lambda) \cdots p_r^{s_r}(\lambda),$$

then $(h_1(\lambda), h_2(\lambda)) = 1$, and our results above apply. Thus, we have $V = W_1 \oplus W_2$ and $t = t_1 \oplus t_2$, where $t_i = t \mid W_i$ has minimal polynomial $h_i(\lambda)$, $i = 1, 2$. If $r > 2$, we can factor $h_2(\lambda)$ further. In r such steps, we can prove the following basic theorem.

6.12. THEOREM. Let V be a vector space over a field F, $t \in L(V)$, and $h(\lambda)$ be the minimal polynomial of t. If

$$h(\lambda) = p_1^{s_1}(\lambda)p_2^{s_2}(\lambda) \cdots p_r^{s_r}(\lambda),$$

where $p_1(\lambda), p_2(\lambda), \ldots, p_r(\lambda)$ are the distinct monic prime factors of $h(\lambda)$ and $s_1, s_2, \ldots, s_r$ are positive integers, then there exist unique t-invariant subspaces $V_1, V_2, \ldots, V_r$ of V such that

$$V = V_1 \oplus V_2 \oplus \cdots \oplus V_r,$$

$$t = t_1 \oplus t_2 \oplus \cdots \oplus t_r, \qquad \text{where} \quad t_i = t \mid V_i,$$

and each t_i has minimal polynomial $p_i^{s_i}(\lambda)$.

As in the proof for two factors, the V_i of 6.12 can be defined by

$$V_i = Vg_i(t), \qquad \text{where} \quad g_i(\lambda) = \frac{h(\lambda)}{p_i^{s_i}(\lambda)} \qquad i = 1, 2, \ldots, r.$$

Thus, $g_i(\lambda)$ is a product of $r - 1$ prime powers, with $p_i^{s_i}(\lambda)$ excluded from $h(\lambda)$. Also, $\mathbf{x}g_i(t)p_i^{s_i}(t) = \mathbf{x}h(t) = \mathbf{0}$ for each $\mathbf{x} \in V$, that is, $V_ip_i^{s_i}(t) = \mathbf{0}$. On the other hand, if $\mathbf{y} = \mathbf{y}_1 + \mathbf{y}_2 + \cdots + \mathbf{y}_r \in V$, with $\mathbf{y}_j \in V_j$ for each j, and if $\mathbf{y}p_i^{s_i}(t) = \mathbf{0}$, then $\mathbf{y}_jp_i^{s_i}(t) = \mathbf{0}$, $j = 1, 2, \ldots, r$. Since the minimal polynomial of $\mathbf{y}_j$ is a factor of $p_j^{s_j}(\lambda)$ and $p_i^{s_i}(\lambda)$, the minimal polynomial of $\mathbf{y}_j$ must be 1 if $i \neq j$. That is, $\mathbf{y}_j = \mathbf{0}$ if $j \neq i$. Hence, we have $\mathbf{y} = \mathbf{y}_i \in V_i$. This proves that

$$V_i = \{\mathbf{y} \in V \mid \mathbf{y}p_i^{s_i}(t) = \mathbf{0}\}, \qquad i = 1, 2, \ldots, r.$$

The fact that each V_i is given as above in terms of V and the prime power factors of $h(\lambda)$ alone means that the V_i are unique in 6.12.

EXAMPLE 2: Let $t \in L(\mathbb{Q}^8)$ be defined by

$$\mathbf{u}_1t = 2\mathbf{u}_1, \quad \mathbf{u}_2t = 2\mathbf{u}_2, \quad \mathbf{u}_3t = 2\mathbf{u}_3, \quad \mathbf{u}_4t = \mathbf{u}_5,$$

$$\mathbf{u}_5t = -\mathbf{u}_4 + 3\mathbf{u}_5, \quad \mathbf{u}_6t = \mathbf{u}_7, \quad \mathbf{u}_7t = \mathbf{u}_8, \quad \mathbf{u}_8t = 5\mathbf{u}_6 - 2\mathbf{u}_7.$$

Then, we have

$$V = V_1 \oplus V_2 \oplus V_3, \qquad t = t_1 \oplus t_2 \oplus t_3,$$

where

$$V_1 = \mathbb{Q}\mathbf{u}_1 + \mathbb{Q}\mathbf{u}_3 + \mathbb{Q}\mathbf{u}_3, \quad V_2 = \mathbb{Q}\mathbf{u}_4 + \mathbb{Q}\mathbf{u}_5, \quad V_3 = \mathbb{Q}\mathbf{u}_6 + \mathbb{Q}\mathbf{u}_7 + \mathbb{Q}\mathbf{u}_8,$$

and

$$t_1\colon\quad \mathbf{u}_1t_1 = 2\mathbf{u}_1, \qquad \mathbf{u}_2t_1 = 2\mathbf{u}_2, \qquad \mathbf{u}_3t_1 = 2\mathbf{u}_3,$$

$$t_2\colon\quad \mathbf{u}_4t_2 = \mathbf{u}_5, \qquad \mathbf{u}_5t_2 = -\mathbf{u}_4 + 3\mathbf{u}_5,$$

$$t_3\colon\quad \mathbf{u}_6t_3 = \mathbf{u}_7, \qquad \mathbf{u}_7t_3 = \mathbf{u}_8, \qquad \mathbf{u}_8t_3 = 5\mathbf{u}_6 - 2\mathbf{u}_7.$$

It is not hard to show that $\lambda - 2$, $\lambda^2 - 3\lambda + 1$, and $\lambda^3 + 2\lambda - 5$ are the minimal polynomials of t_1, t_2, and t_3, respectively. Since these polynomials are primes, evidently

$$h(\lambda) = (\lambda - 2)(\lambda^2 - 3\lambda + 1)(\lambda^3 + 2\lambda - 5)$$

is the minimal polynomial of t. The matrix representation of t relative to the **u**-basis is given by

$$A = \begin{pmatrix} 2 & 0 & 0 & 0 & 0 & 0 & 0 & 0 \\ 0 & 2 & 0 & 0 & 0 & 0 & 0 & 0 \\ 0 & 0 & 2 & 0 & 0 & 0 & 0 & 0 \\ 0 & 0 & 0 & 0 & 1 & 0 & 0 & 0 \\ 0 & 0 & 0 & -1 & 3 & 0 & 0 & 0 \\ 0 & 0 & 0 & 0 & 0 & 0 & 1 & 0 \\ 0 & 0 & 0 & 0 & 0 & 0 & 0 & 1 \\ 0 & 0 & 0 & 0 & 0 & 5 & -2 & 0 \end{pmatrix} = A_1 \oplus A_2 \oplus A_3,$$

where

$$A_1 = \begin{pmatrix} 2 & 0 & 0 \\ 0 & 2 & 0 \\ 0 & 0 & 2 \end{pmatrix}, \qquad A_2 = \begin{pmatrix} 0 & 1 \\ -1 & 3 \end{pmatrix}, \qquad A_3 = \begin{pmatrix} 0 & 1 & 0 \\ 0 & 0 & 1 \\ 5 & -2 & 0 \end{pmatrix}.$$

Evidently, A_2 and A_3 are the companion matrices of $\lambda^2 - 3\lambda + 1$ and $\lambda^3 + 2\lambda - 5$, respectively. However, A_1 is not the companion matrix of $\lambda - 2$. In fact, V_1 is itself a direct sum

$$V_1 = \mathbb{Q}\mathbf{u}_1 \oplus \mathbb{Q}\mathbf{u}_2 \oplus \mathbb{Q}\mathbf{u}_3,$$

and t_1 is a direct sum of three l.t., each of which has minimal polynomial $\lambda - 2$. Also, A_1 is a direct sum of three 1×1 matrices,

$$A_1 = (2) \oplus (2) \oplus (2),$$

each of which is the companion matrix of $\lambda - 2$.

EXAMPLE 3: Let $t \in L(\mathbb{Q}^3)$ be defined by

$$\mathbf{u}_1t = \mathbf{u}_2, \qquad \mathbf{u}_2t = \mathbf{u}_3, \qquad \mathbf{u}_3t = -2\mathbf{u}_1 + 3\mathbf{u}_2.$$

Then, we have

$$\mathbf{u}_1t^3 = -2\mathbf{u}_1 + 3\mathbf{u}_1t,$$

and $\mathbf{u}_1$ has minimal polynomial $h(\lambda) = \lambda^3 - 3\lambda + 2$. Since $\deg h(\lambda) = 3 = \dim \mathbb{Q}^3$, we see that $h(\lambda)$ is the minimal polynomial of t. We can factor $h(\lambda)$ into primes as follows:

$$h(\lambda) = (\lambda - 1)^2(\lambda + 2).$$

Hence, by 6.12, $V = V_1 \oplus V_2$, and $t = t_1 \oplus t_2$, where $t_i = t \mid V_i$ and

$$V_1 = V(t + 2), \qquad V_2 = V(t - 1)^2.$$

Since $\mathbf{u}_1(t + 2) = 2\mathbf{u}_1 + \mathbf{u}_2$, $\mathbf{u}_2(t + 2) = 2\mathbf{u}_2 + \mathbf{u}_3$, and $\mathbf{u}_1(t - 1)^2 = \mathbf{u}_1 - 2\mathbf{u}_2 + \mathbf{u}_3$, it is evident that

$$V_1 = \mathbb{Q}(2\mathbf{u}_1 + \mathbf{u}_2) + \mathbb{Q}(2\mathbf{u}_2 + \mathbf{u}_3), \qquad V_2 = \mathbb{Q}(\mathbf{u}_1 - 2\mathbf{u}_2 + \mathbf{u}_3).$$

Using the bases $\{2\mathbf{u}_1 + \mathbf{u}_2, 2\mathbf{u}_2 + \mathbf{u}_3\}$ and $\{\mathbf{u}_1 - 2\mathbf{u}_2 + \mathbf{u}_3\}$ for V_1 and V_2, we have

$$(2\mathbf{u}_1 + \mathbf{u}_2)t_1 = 2\mathbf{u}_2 + \mathbf{u}_3, \qquad (2\mathbf{u}_2 + \mathbf{u}_3)t_1 = -(2\mathbf{u}_1 + \mathbf{u}_2) + 2(2\mathbf{u}_2 + \mathbf{u}_3),$$

$$(\mathbf{u}_1 - 2\mathbf{u}_2 + \mathbf{u}_3)t_2 = -2(\mathbf{u}_1 - 2\mathbf{u}_2 + \mathbf{u}_3).$$

Thus, t_1 is represented by matrix A_1, and t_2 by A_2, where

$$A_1 = \begin{pmatrix} 0 & 1 \\ -1 & 2 \end{pmatrix}, \qquad A_2 = (-2),$$

and t is represented by A, where

$$A = A_1 \oplus A_2 = \left(\begin{array}{cc|c} 0 & 1 & 0 \\ -1 & 2 & 0 \\ \hline 0 & 0 & -2 \end{array}\right).$$

EXERCISES

Express each of the following linear transformations as a direct sum of linear transformations whose minimal polynomials are powers of primes (as in 6.12).

1. $t \in L(\mathbb{Q}^2)$: $\mathbf{u}_1t = \mathbf{u}_2$, $\mathbf{u}_2t = 3\mathbf{u}_1 + 2\mathbf{u}_2$.
2. $t \in L(\mathbb{Q}^2)$: $\mathbf{u}_1t = -4\mathbf{u}_1 + 4\mathbf{u}_2$, $\mathbf{u}_2t = \mathbf{u}_2$.
3. $t \in L(\mathbb{Q}^3)$: $\mathbf{u}_1t = \mathbf{u}_2$, $\mathbf{u}_2t = \mathbf{u}_3$, $\mathbf{u}_3t = 2\mathbf{u}_1 - \mathbf{u}_2 + 2\mathbf{u}_3$.
4. $t \in L(\mathbb{Q}^3)$: $\mathbf{u}_1t = 3\mathbf{u}_1$, $\mathbf{u}_2t = \mathbf{u}_2 - \mathbf{u}_3$, $\mathbf{u}_3t = \mathbf{u}_1 + 3\mathbf{u}_2$.
5. $t \in L(\mathbb{Q}^3)$: $\mathbf{u}_1t = 3\mathbf{u}_1 + \mathbf{u}_2$, $\mathbf{u}_2t = \mathbf{u}_2 - 5\mathbf{u}_3$, $\mathbf{u}_3t = 2\mathbf{u}_1 + 2\mathbf{u}_2 + 2\mathbf{u}_3$.
6. $t \in L(\mathbb{Q}^4)$: $\mathbf{u}_1t = \mathbf{u}_2 + \mathbf{u}_3$, $\mathbf{u}_2t = \mathbf{u}_1 + \mathbf{u}_4$, $\mathbf{u}_3t = -\mathbf{u}_2 + \mathbf{u}_4$, $\mathbf{u}_4t = -\mathbf{u}_1 - \mathbf{u}_2 - \mathbf{u}_3 + \mathbf{u}_4$.
7. $t \in L(\mathbb{Q}^4)$: $\mathbf{u}_1t = \mathbf{u}_2$, $\mathbf{u}_2t = \mathbf{u}_3$, $\mathbf{u}_3t = \mathbf{u}_4$, $\mathbf{u}_4t = -2\mathbf{u}_3$.
8. $t \in L(\mathbb{Q}^4)$: $\mathbf{u}_1t = 2\mathbf{u}_1 - \mathbf{u}_2$, $\mathbf{u}_2t = 3\mathbf{u}_2 + \mathbf{u}_4$, $\mathbf{u}_3t = -5\mathbf{u}_3 + \mathbf{u}_4$, $\mathbf{u}_4t = -2\mathbf{u}_4$.
9. If $W_1, W_2, \ldots, W_m$ are nonzero subspaces of a vector space V, prove

that $V = W_1 \oplus W_2 \oplus \cdots \oplus W_m$ iff $V = W_1 + W_2 + \cdots + W_m$ and $(W_1 + \cdots + W_{i-1}) \cap W_i = \{\mathbf{0}\}$, $i = 2, 3, \cdots, m$.

10. If V is an n-dimensional vector space over a field F and if $t \in L(V)$ has minimal polynomial $h(\lambda) = (\lambda - a_1)(\lambda - a_2) \cdots (\lambda - a_n)$, where $a_1, a_2, \ldots, a_n$ are distinct elements of F, then prove that t is represented by the $n \times n$ matrix $(a_1) \oplus (a_2) \oplus \cdots \oplus (a_n)$, a diagonal matrix. If $t \in L(V)$ can be represented by a diagonal matrix, what can be said about the minimal polynomial of t?

3. REDUCIBLE SPACES

Let us call a vector space V over a field F *reducible* relative to $t \in L(V)$ iff V can be expressed as a direct sum of two or more proper t-invariant subspaces, and *irreducible* otherwise. Similarly, we shall call a proper t-invariant subspace W of V reducible (irreducible) iff W is reducible (irreducible) relative to $t \mid W$. If the minimal polynomial $h(\lambda)$ of t has two or more distinct prime factors, then V is reducible by 6.12. We shall show in Chapter 8 that every finite-dimensional vector space V can be expressed as a direct sum of irreducible t-invariant subspaces in an essentially unique way. However, we shall now prove a special case of this general result.

In the following discussion, V is an n-dimensional vector space over a field F. If $t \in L(V)$ has a prime $p(\lambda)$ as its minimal polynomial, then each nonzero vector $\mathbf{x}$ in V must also have $p(\lambda)$ as its minimal polynomial. Therefore, if $\deg p(\lambda) = k$, we find that $\mathbf{x}$ generates a t-invariant subspace $W = \mathbf{x}F[t]$ of dimension k by 6.5. Since every nonzero vector in W also generates W, evidently W contains no t-invariant subspaces of V other than $\{\mathbf{0}\}$ and W. Thus, in particular, W is irreducible. If U is any other t-invariant subspace of V, then $W \cap U$ is also t-invariant. Hence, either $W \cap U = \{\mathbf{0}\}$ or $W \cap U = W$ (that is, $W \subset U$). With these remarks in mind, it is now clear that we can find irreducible t-invariant subspaces $W_1, W_2, \ldots, W_m$, such that

$$V = W_1 \oplus W_2 \oplus \cdots \oplus W_m,$$

where each W_i has the form $W_i = \mathbf{x}_i F[t]$ for some nonzero $\mathbf{x}_i \in V$.

Thus, $W_1 = \mathbf{x}_1 F[t]$ for any nonzero $\mathbf{x}_1 \in V$; and $W_2 = \mathbf{x}_2 F[t]$ for any vector $\mathbf{x}_2 \notin W_1$; and $W_3 = \mathbf{x}_3 F[t]$ for any vector $\mathbf{x}_3 \notin W_1 + W_2$; and so on. We state this result below.

6.13. THEOREM. If $t \in L(V)$ has a prime $p(\lambda)$ as its minimal polynomial, then there exist vectors $\mathbf{x}_1, \mathbf{x}_2, \ldots, \mathbf{x}_m$ in V such that $W_i = \mathbf{x}_i F[t]$ is irreducible for each i and

$$V = W_1 \oplus W_2 \oplus \cdots \oplus W_m.$$

EXAMPLE 1: Let $V = \mathbb{R}^4$, and let $t \in L(V)$ be represented by the matrix

$$A = \begin{pmatrix} -1 & 0 & 6 & -3 \\ -1 & 1 & -3 & 0 \\ 0 & 1 & -3 & 1 \\ 1 & 2 & -8 & 3 \end{pmatrix}$$

relative to the usual basis of V. We can easily show that $\mathbf{u}_i(t^2 + 2) = 0$ for each i. Hence, the minimal polynomial of t is the prime $\lambda^2 + 2$. Let $W_1 = \mathbf{u}_1F[t] = \mathbb{R}\mathbf{u}_1 + \mathbb{R}(\mathbf{u}_1t)$. Since $\mathbf{u}_2 \notin W_1$, let $W_2 = \mathbf{u}_2F[t] = \mathbb{R}\mathbf{u}_2 + \mathbb{R}(\mathbf{u}_2t)$. Thus, W_1 and W_2 are two-dimensional subspaces of V, such that $W_1 \cap W_2 = \{\mathbf{0}\}$. Clearly, W_1 and W_2 are irreducible t-invariant subspaces of V, such that

$$V = W_1 \oplus W_2$$

as in 6.13.

If we combine 6.12 and 6.13, then we obtain the following result.

6.14. THEOREM. If $t \in L(V)$ has minimal polynomial

$$h(\lambda) = p_1(\lambda)p_2(\lambda) \cdots p_r(\lambda),$$

where $p_1(\lambda), p_2(\lambda), \ldots, p_r(\lambda)$ are distinct monic primes, then there exist irreducible t-invariant subspaces $W_1, W_2, \ldots, W_s$ of V, such that

$$V = W_1 \oplus W_2 \oplus \cdots \oplus W_s,$$

and each $t \mid W_i$ has some $p_j(\lambda)$ as its minimal polynomial.

Proof: By 6.12, we have

$$V = V_1 \oplus V_2 \oplus \cdots \oplus V_r, \qquad t = t_1 \oplus t_2 \oplus \cdots \oplus t_r,$$

where $t_i = t \mid V_i$ has $p_i(\lambda)$ as its minimal polynomial for each i. In turn, we may apply 6.13 to each V_i and t_i, obtaining

$$V_i = W_{i1} \oplus W_{i2} \oplus \cdots \oplus W_{im_i},$$

where each W_{ij} is an irreducible t_i-invariant subspace of V_i. Hence, each W_{ij} is an irreducible t-invariant subspace of V, and the direct sum of all the W_{ij}'s is V. This proves 6.14.

We point out in passing that each of the primes $p_i(\lambda)$ of 6.14 is the minimal polynomial of $t \mid W_j$ for some j. Of course, some of the $p_i(\lambda)$ might be associated with several W_j.

Each W_i of 6.14 is cyclic; that is, $W_i = \mathbf{x}_iF[t]$ for some $\mathbf{x}_i \in V$, with the minimal polynomial $h_i(\lambda)$ of $\mathbf{x}_i$ being one of the prime factors of $h(\lambda)$. If $\deg h_i(\lambda) = n_i$, then $(\mathbf{x}_i, \mathbf{x}_it, \ldots, \mathbf{x}_it^j)$ is a basis of W_i, where $j = n_i - 1$, and $(\mathbf{x}_it^j \mid i = 1, 2, \ldots, s, j = 1, 2, \ldots, n_i - 1)$ is a basis of V. Relative to this basis, t is represented by the matrix

$$C = C_1 \oplus C_2 \oplus \cdots \oplus C_s,$$

where C_i is the companion matrix of $h_i(\lambda)$ for each i. Hence, we have

$$\lambda I - C = (\lambda I_1 - C_1) \oplus (\lambda I_2 - C_2) \oplus \cdots \oplus (\lambda I_s - C_s),$$

where I is the $n \times n$ identity matrix and I_j is the $n_j \times n_j$ identity matrix for each j. Therefore, we have

$$\begin{aligned}\det(\lambda I - C) &= \det(\lambda I_1 - C_1)\det(\lambda I_2 - C_2)\cdots\det(\lambda I_s - C_s)\\ &= h_1(\lambda)h_2(\lambda)\cdots h_s(\lambda)\end{aligned}$$

by 4.18 and 5.16. If we recall that every $p_j(\lambda)$ occurs in the above product, then it is evident that $h(\lambda) = p_1(\lambda)p_2(\lambda)\cdots p_r(\lambda)$ is a factor of the polynomial $\det(\lambda I - C)$.

Before continuing this discussion, let us make the following definition.

6.15. DEFINITION OF CHARACTERISTIC POLYNOMIAL. For each $n \times n$ matrix A over a field F, the polynomial

$$f(\lambda) = \det(\lambda I - A)$$

is called the characteristic polynomial of A.

According to 6.15, $f(\lambda)$ is a monic polynomial of degree n. One of the famous theorems of mathematical history is as follows.

6.16. HAMILTON–CAYLEY THEOREM. Every $n \times n$ matrix A over a field F is a root of its characteristic polynomial $f(\lambda)$.

Proof: This theorem says that if $f(\lambda) = a_0 + a_1\lambda + a_2\lambda^2 + \cdots + \lambda^n$, then we have

$$a_0 I + a_1 A + a_2 A^2 + \cdots + A^n = 0.$$

If $h(\lambda)$ is the minimal polynomial of A, then $h(A) = 0$. Hence, whenever $h(\lambda)$ is a factor of $f(\lambda)$, that is, when $f(\lambda) = h(\lambda)k(\lambda)$ for some $k(\lambda) \in F[\lambda]$, then $f(A) = h(A)k(A) = 0$, and the theorem is proved. We shall postpone until Chapter 8 the proof that $h(\lambda)$ is always a factor of $f(\lambda)$. However, we can observe now that if $h(\lambda) = p_1(\lambda)p_2(\lambda)\cdots p_r(\lambda)$, where the $p_i(\lambda)$ are distinct monic primes and t is a l.t. which is represented by A, then t is also represented by the matrix $C = C_1 \oplus C_2 \oplus \cdots \oplus C_s$ described above. Hence, A is similar to C, and $\lambda I - A$ is similar to $\lambda I - C$. Therefore, we find that $f(\lambda) = \det(\lambda I - C)$. Consequently, $h(\lambda)$ is a factor of $f(\lambda)$, as we showed above.

Although we will not complete the proof of 6.16 until Chapter 8, we shall use it whenever necessary.

In Example 1, $h(\lambda) = \lambda^2 + 2$ has companion matrix

$$C = \begin{pmatrix} 0 & 1 \\ -2 & 0 \end{pmatrix}.$$

Hence, t is represented by

$$C \oplus C = \begin{pmatrix} 0 & 1 & 0 & 0 \\ -2 & 0 & 0 & 0 \\ 0 & 0 & 0 & 1 \\ 0 & 0 & -2 & 0 \end{pmatrix}$$

relative to the basis $(\mathbf{u}_1, \mathbf{u}_1 t, \mathbf{u}_2, \mathbf{u}_2 t)$ of $\mathbb{R}^4$.

EXAMPLE 2: Let us find the characteristic polynomial of $A \in \mathbb{Q}(3)$ given below. We have

$$A = \begin{pmatrix} 4 & -5 & 3 \\ 2 & -3 & 2 \\ -1 & 1 & 0 \end{pmatrix}.$$

Now, we see that

$$\lambda I - A = \begin{pmatrix} \lambda - 4 & 5 & -3 \\ -2 & \lambda + 3 & -2 \\ 1 & -1 & \lambda \end{pmatrix},$$

and therefore

$$\det(\lambda I - A) = \lambda^3 - \lambda^2 - \lambda + 1 = (\lambda - 1)^2(\lambda + 1).$$

We can readily verify that $A^3 - A^2 - A + I = 0$. Hence, the minimal polynomial of A is a factor of $(\lambda - 1)^2(\lambda + 1)$. By trial, we find out that it actually is $(\lambda - 1)^2(\lambda + 1)$.

EXERCISES

In each of Exercises 1 through 6, express the vector space as a direct sum of irreducible t-invariant subspaces.

1. $t \in L(\mathbb{Q}^2)$; $\mathbf{u}_1 t = \mathbf{u}_1 + 2\mathbf{u}_2$, $\mathbf{u}_2 t = -\mathbf{u}_1 + \mathbf{u}_2$.
2. $t \in L(\mathbb{Q}^2)$; $\mathbf{u}_1 t = 2\mathbf{u}_1 + 3\mathbf{u}_2$, $\mathbf{u}_2 t = \mathbf{u}_1 - 2\mathbf{u}_2$.
3. $t \in L(\mathbb{R}^2)$; $\mathbf{u}_1 t = 2\mathbf{u}_1 + 3\mathbf{u}_2$, $\mathbf{u}_2 t = \mathbf{u}_1 - 2\mathbf{u}_2$.
4. $t \in L(\mathbb{Q}^4)$; $\mathbf{u}_1 t = \mathbf{u}_1 + 3\mathbf{u}_3$, $\mathbf{u}_2 t = -2\mathbf{u}_1 - 2\mathbf{u}_3 - \mathbf{u}_4$, $\mathbf{u}_3 t = -\mathbf{u}_1 - 2\mathbf{u}_3$, $\mathbf{u}_4 t = -2\mathbf{u}_1 + \mathbf{u}_2 - 4\mathbf{u}_3 - \mathbf{u}_4$.
5. $t \in L(\mathbb{Q}^4)$; $\mathbf{u}_1 t = \mathbf{u}_1 - \mathbf{u}_2 - \mathbf{u}_3 + 2\mathbf{u}_4$, $\mathbf{u}_2 t = -\mathbf{u}_1 - \mathbf{u}_4$, $\mathbf{u}_3 t = -\mathbf{u}_1 - \mathbf{u}_4$, $\mathbf{u}_4 t = -2\mathbf{u}_1 + \mathbf{u}_2 + \mathbf{u}_3 - 3\mathbf{u}_4$.
6. $t \in L(\mathbb{R}^6)$; $\mathbf{u}_1 t = \mathbf{u}_2 - \mathbf{u}_3 - \mathbf{u}_5 + \mathbf{u}_6$, $\mathbf{u}_2 t = -\mathbf{u}_1 + \mathbf{u}_4 + \mathbf{u}_6$, $\mathbf{u}_3 t = \mathbf{u}_4 - \mathbf{u}_5$, $\mathbf{u}_4 t = -\mathbf{u}_3 + \mathbf{u}_6$, $\mathbf{u}_5 t = \mathbf{u}_6$, $\mathbf{u}_6 t = -\mathbf{u}_5$.

Find the characteristic polynomial and minimal polynomial of each of the following matrices over $\mathbb{Q}$.

7. $\begin{pmatrix} 1 & 0 & 0 \\ 2 & 3 & 0 \\ -2 & -2 & 1 \end{pmatrix}.$

8. $\begin{pmatrix} 0 & 0 & 1 \\ 0 & 0 & 0 \\ 0 & 0 & 0 \end{pmatrix}.$

9. $\begin{pmatrix} -10 & 13 & -7 \\ -6 & 9 & -6 \\ 1 & -1 & -2 \end{pmatrix}.$

10. $\begin{pmatrix} 1 & 1 & 1 \\ 1 & 1 & 1 \\ 1 & 1 & 1 \end{pmatrix}.$

11. $\begin{pmatrix} 0 & 1 & 0 & 0 \\ 0 & 0 & 0 & 0 \\ 0 & 0 & 1 & 1 \\ 0 & 0 & 0 & 1 \end{pmatrix}.$

12. $\begin{pmatrix} -1 & -1 & 1 & 1 \\ 0 & 0 & -1 & -1 \\ 0 & 0 & -1 & 0 \\ 0 & 1 & -1 & -2 \end{pmatrix}.$

4. CHARACTERISTIC VALUES

Of special interest in a vector space are the one-dimensional invariant subspaces. If V is a vector space over a field F and $t \in L(V)$, then each one-dimensional t-invariant subspace of V has the form $F\mathbf{x}$ for some nonzero vector $\mathbf{x}$. Since $\mathbf{x}t \in F\mathbf{x}$, we see that

$$\mathbf{x}t = c\mathbf{x}$$

for some $c \in F$. That is, $\mathbf{x}(t - c) = \mathbf{0}$, and $\lambda - c$ is the minimal polynomial of $\mathbf{x}$. Conversely, if $\mathbf{y} \in V$ has minimal polynomial $\lambda - d \in F[\lambda]$, then $\mathbf{y}t = d\mathbf{y}$, and $F\mathbf{y}$ is a one-dimensional t-invariant subspace of V. Vectors such as $\mathbf{x}$ and $\mathbf{y}$ and scalars such as c and d have special names as follows.

6.17. DEFINITION OF CHARACTERISTIC VECTORS AND VALUES. If $F\mathbf{x}$ is a one-dimensional invariant subspace of V relative to some $t \in L(V)$, so that $\mathbf{x}t = c\mathbf{x}$ for some $c \in F$, then $\mathbf{x}$ is called a characteristic vector of t, and c the characteristic value of t belonging to $\mathbf{x}$.

EXAMPLE 1: Let us find the characteristic values of $t \in L(\mathbb{R}^2)$ represented by the matrix

$$A = \begin{pmatrix} -1 & 2 \\ 3 & 0 \end{pmatrix}$$

relative to the basis $(\mathbf{u}_1, \mathbf{u}_2)$ of $\mathbb{R}^2$. Since $\mathbf{u}_1 t = -\mathbf{u}_1 + 2\mathbf{u}_2$ and $\mathbf{u}_1 t^2 = 7\mathbf{u}_1 - 2\mathbf{u}_2$, it is evident that $\mathbf{u}_1(t^2 + t - 6) = \mathbf{0}$ and

$$h(\lambda) = \lambda^2 + \lambda - 6 = (\lambda + 3)(\lambda - 2)$$

is the minimal polynomial of both $\mathbf{u}_1$ and t. By 5.7, we see that

$$\mathbf{x} = \mathbf{u}_1(t + 3) = 2(\mathbf{u}_1 + \mathbf{u}_2)$$

has minimal polynomial $\lambda - 2$, and that

$$\mathbf{y} = \mathbf{u}_1(t - 2) = -3\mathbf{u}_1 + 2\mathbf{u}_2$$

has minimal polynomial $\lambda + 3$. Thus, $F\mathbf{x}$ and $F\mathbf{y}$ are one-dimensional t-invariant subspaces of $\mathbb{R}^2$. Since we have

$$\mathbf{x}t = 2\mathbf{x}, \qquad \mathbf{y}t = -3\mathbf{y},$$

$\mathbf{x}$ and $\mathbf{y}$ are characteristic vectors of t, and 2 and -3 are characteristic values of t belonging to $\mathbf{x}$ and $\mathbf{y}$, respectively.

In the literature, the German–English words *eigenvalue* and *eigenvector* are often used in place of characteristic value and characteristic vector, and the set of all characteristic values of $t \in L(V)$ is called the *spectrum* of t.

Let V be a vector space over a field F and $t \in L(V)$ have minimal polynomial $h(\lambda)$. If c is a root of $h(\lambda)$ (that is, $h(c) = 0$), then $\lambda - c$ is a factor of $h(\lambda)$, and

$$h(\lambda) = f(\lambda)(\lambda - c) \qquad \text{for some } f(\lambda) \in F[\lambda].$$

We know that some vector $\mathbf{x}$ has $h(\lambda)$ as its minimal polynomial. Hence, $\mathbf{y} = \mathbf{x}f(t)$ has $\lambda - c$ as its minimal polynomial by 5.7. Thus, we have

$$\mathbf{y}t = c\mathbf{y},$$

and c is a characteristic value of t. On the other hand, if d is a characteristic value of $t \in L(V)$, then $\mathbf{z}t = d\mathbf{z}$ for some nonzero $\mathbf{z} \in V$, and $\lambda - d$ is the minimal polynomial of $\mathbf{z}$. Therefore, $\lambda - d$ is a factor of the minimal polynomial $h(\lambda)$ of t, and d is a root of $h(\lambda)$. This proves the following theorem.

6.18. THEOREM. The spectrum of each $t \in L(V)$ is the set of roots of the minimal polynomial $h(\lambda)$ of t.

If $\dim V = n$, then $\deg h(\lambda) \leq n$, and $h(\lambda)$ has at most n roots. Thus, each $t \in L(V)$ has at most n characteristic values.

In Example 1, $t \in L(\mathbb{R}^2)$ has minimal polynomial $h(\lambda) = (\lambda + 3)(\lambda - 2)$. Hence, the roots of $h(\lambda)$ are -3 and 2, and $\{-3, 2\}$ is the spectrum of t.

If $c \in F$ is a characteristic value of $t \in L(V)$, then $\mathbf{x}(t - c) = \mathbf{0}$ for some nonzero $\mathbf{x} \in V$. Therefore, $\ker (t - c) \neq \{\mathbf{0}\}$, and the linear transformation $t - c$ is singular. Conversely, if $t - c$ is singular, then $\mathbf{x}(t - c) = \mathbf{0}$ for some nonzero $\mathbf{x} \in V$. Hence, c is a characteristic value of t. In other words, c is a characteristic value of t iff $t - c$ is singular. Since $t - c$ is singular iff $\det (t - c) = 0$, we have proved the following result.

6.19. THEOREM. The linear transformation t has c as a characteristic value iff $\det (t - c) = 0$.

Practically, we apply 6.19 by going to matrix representations of linear transformations. If $t \in L(V)$ is represented by $A \in F(n)$ relative to some basis of V, then, for each $c \in F$, the linear transformation $t - c$ is represented by $A - cI$ relative to the same basis. Since $\det(t - c) = \det(A - cI)$ by definition (4.31), we have by 6.19 that c is a characteristic value of t iff $\det(A - cI) = 0$, or equivalently, $\det(cI - A) = 0$. Thus, c is a characteristic value of t, or of A, iff c is a root of the characteristic polynomial $f(\lambda) = \det(\lambda I - A)$ of A. We state this result in matrix form as follows.

6.20. THEOREM. For each $n \times n$ matrix A over a field F, the spectrum of A is the set of roots of its characteristic polynomial.

EXAMPLE 2: Let us find the spectrum of $A \in \mathbb{R}(3)$ given by

$$A = \begin{pmatrix} 1 & 0 & 1 \\ 2 & -1 & 2 \\ 0 & 1 & 0 \end{pmatrix}.$$

We first find the matrix $\lambda I - A$. Thus, we have

$$\lambda I - A = \begin{pmatrix} \lambda - 1 & 0 & -1 \\ -2 & \lambda + 1 & -2 \\ 0 & -1 & \lambda \end{pmatrix}.$$

The characteristic polynomial of A is given by

$$\begin{aligned} f(\lambda) = \det(\lambda I - A) &= \lambda(\lambda - 1)(\lambda + 1) - 2 - 2(\lambda - 1) \\ &= \lambda^3 - 3\lambda. \end{aligned}$$

Since $f(\lambda) = \lambda(\lambda - \sqrt{3})(\lambda + \sqrt{3})$, the spectrum of A is $\{0, \sqrt{3}, -\sqrt{3}\}$.

It is natural to wonder which $n \times n$ matrices over a field F are similar to diagonal matrices, that is, to matrices of the form

$$D = (d_{ij}), \qquad \text{where} \quad d_{ij} = 0 \qquad \text{whenever} \quad i \neq j.$$

In other words, D is a direct sum of 1×1 matrices,

$$D = (d_{11}) \oplus (d_{22}) \oplus \cdots \oplus (d_{nn}).$$

If $A \in F(n)$ is similar to D and $t \in L(V)$ is represented by A, then t is also represented by D. Hence, there exists a basis $(\mathbf{u}_1, \mathbf{u}_2, \ldots, \mathbf{u}_n)$ of V such that

$$\mathbf{u}_i t = d_{ii}\mathbf{u}_i, \qquad i = 1, 2, \ldots, n.$$

Thus, $F\mathbf{u}_i$ is a t-invariant subspace of V for each i, and we have

$$V = F\mathbf{u}_1 \oplus F\mathbf{u}_2 \oplus \cdots \oplus F\mathbf{u}_n. \tag{1}$$

Each d_{ii} is a characteristic value of t belonging to $\mathbf{u}_i$, and $\lambda - d_{ii}$ is the minimal polynomial of $\mathbf{u}_i$. Therefore, the minimal polynomial $h(\lambda)$ of t, and also of A, is the l.c.m. of the polynomials $\lambda - d_{11}, \lambda - d_{22}, \ldots, \lambda - d_{nn}$ associated with the basis $(\mathbf{u}_1, \mathbf{u}_2, \ldots, \mathbf{u}_n)$ of V. Thus, we have

(2) $$h(\lambda) = (\lambda - c_1)(\lambda - c_2) \ldots (\lambda - c_m),$$

where $c_1, c_2, \ldots, c_m$ are the different d_{ii}, $i = 1, 2, \ldots, n$.

We already know from 6.14 that if the minimal polynomial $h(\lambda)$ of $t \in L(V)$ has form (2) above for distinct $c_1, c_2, \ldots, c_m$ in F, then V has form (1), where each $F\mathbf{u}_i$ is a t-invariant subspace of V of dimension 1. Hence, $\mathbf{u}_i t = d_{ii}\mathbf{u}_i$ for some $d_{ii} \in \{c_1, c_2, \ldots, c_m\}$, and t is represented by the diagonal matrix $D = (d_{11}) \oplus (d_{22}) \oplus \cdots \oplus (d_{nn})$ relative to the basis $(\mathbf{u}_1, \mathbf{u}_2, \ldots, \mathbf{u}_n)$. Thus, we have proved the following theorem.

6.21. THEOREM. An $n \times n$ matrix A over a field F is similar to a diagonal matrix iff the minimal polynomial $h(\lambda)$ of A has the form

$$h(\lambda) = (\lambda - c_1)(\lambda - c_2) \cdots (\lambda - c_m)$$

for some m distinct elements $c_1, c_2, \ldots, c_m$ of F.

For example, the matrix A of Example 1 has minimal polynomial $h(\lambda) = (\lambda + 3)(\lambda - 2)$. Thus, A is similar to a diagonal matrix by 6.21. Since $\deg h(\lambda) = 2$ and A is a 2×2 matrix, evidently A is similar to the diagonal matrix

$$D = \begin{pmatrix} -3 & 0 \\ 0 & 2 \end{pmatrix}.$$

The matrix A of Example 2 has spectrum $\{0, \sqrt{3}, -\sqrt{3}\}$. By 6.18, we find that 0, $\sqrt{3}$, and $-\sqrt{3}$ are roots of the minimal polynomial $h(\lambda)$ of A. Since $\deg h(\lambda) \leq 3$, evidently $h(\lambda) = \lambda(\lambda - \sqrt{3})(\lambda + \sqrt{3})$. Hence, by 6.21, A is similar to the diagonal matrix

$$\begin{pmatrix} 0 & 0 & 0 \\ 0 & \sqrt{3} & 0 \\ 0 & 0 & -\sqrt{3} \end{pmatrix}.$$

EXAMPLE 3: Let us check the matrix

$$A = \begin{pmatrix} -4 & 3 & 3 & -6 \\ 3 & -1 & 0 & 3 \\ 3 & 0 & -1 & 3 \\ 6 & -3 & -3 & 8 \end{pmatrix}$$

in $\mathbb{R}(4)$ to see if it is similar to a diagonal matrix. We first compute the characteristic polynomial of A, which we find to be

$$\det(\lambda I - A) = (\lambda + 1)^2(\lambda - 2)^2.$$

Hence, $\{-1, 2\}$ is the spectrum of A. Hence, by 6.14 and 6.18, A is similar to a diagonal matrix iff its minimal polynomial is

$$h(\lambda) = (\lambda + 1)(\lambda - 2).$$

Since we have

$$A^2 = \begin{pmatrix} -2 & 3 & 3 & -6 \\ 3 & 1 & 0 & 3 \\ 3 & 0 & 1 & 3 \\ 6 & -3 & -3 & 10 \end{pmatrix},$$

we see that $A^2 - A - 2I = 0$. Therefore, $h(\lambda)$ is the minimal polynomial of A, and A is similar to a diagonal matrix D. Since $\lambda I - D$ is also similar to $\lambda I - A$, we have $\det(\lambda I - D) = (\lambda + 1)^2(\lambda - 2)^2$. Hence, we have

$$D = \begin{pmatrix} -1 & 0 & 0 & 0 \\ 0 & -1 & 0 & 0 \\ 0 & 0 & 2 & 0 \\ 0 & 0 & 0 & 2 \end{pmatrix}.$$

If we wish to find the nonsingular matrix P such that $D = P^{-1}AP$, then we proceed as follows. Let $V = \mathbb{R}^4$ and $t \in L(V)$ be represented by A relative to the usual basis of V. By 6.12, $V = V_1 \oplus V_2$, where $V_1 = V(t - 2)$ and $V_2 = V(t + 1)$.

The reader can quickly compute $\mathbf{u}_i(t - 2)$ and $\mathbf{u}_i(t + 1)$, $i = 1, 2, 3, 4$, and then conclude that

$$V_1 = \mathbb{R}\mathbf{x}_1 + \mathbb{R}\mathbf{x}_2, \quad \text{where } \mathbf{x}_1 = \mathbf{u}_1 - \mathbf{u}_2 + \mathbf{u}_4, \quad \mathbf{x}_2 = \mathbf{u}_1 - \mathbf{u}_3 + \mathbf{u}_4,$$
$$V_2 = \mathbb{R}\mathbf{x}_3 + \mathbb{R}\mathbf{x}_4, \quad \text{where } \mathbf{x}_3 = \mathbf{u}_1 + \mathbf{u}_4, \quad \mathbf{x}_4 = \mathbf{u}_2 + \mathbf{u}_3 - \mathbf{u}_4.$$

The vectors $\mathbf{x}_1$, $\mathbf{x}_2$, $\mathbf{x}_3$, and $\mathbf{x}_4$ are characteristic vectors of t, with -1 being the characteristic value of t belonging to $\mathbf{x}_1$ and $\mathbf{x}_2$, and 2 being the characteristic value of t belonging to $\mathbf{x}_3$ and $\mathbf{x}_4$. That is, we have

$$\mathbf{x}_1 t = -\mathbf{x}_1, \quad \mathbf{x}_2 t = -\mathbf{x}_2, \quad \mathbf{x}_3 t = 2\mathbf{x}_3, \quad \mathbf{x}_4 t = 2\mathbf{x}_4.$$

Thus, t is represented by the diagonal matrix D relative to the basis $(\mathbf{x}_1, \mathbf{x}_2, \mathbf{x}_3, \mathbf{x}_4)$ of V.

To find the nonsingular matrix P, we know that P^{-1} transforms the $\mathbf{u}$-basis into the $\mathbf{x}$-basis, that is, we know that

$$P^{-1} = \begin{pmatrix} 1 & -1 & 0 & 1 \\ 1 & 0 & -1 & 1 \\ 1 & 0 & 0 & 1 \\ 0 & 1 & 1 & -1 \end{pmatrix}.$$

Then $P = (P^{-1})^{-1}$ can be computed in the usual way, and we find that

$$P = \begin{pmatrix} 1 & 1 & -1 & 1 \\ -1 & 0 & 1 & 0 \\ 0 & -1 & 1 & 0 \\ -1 & -1 & 2 & -1 \end{pmatrix}.$$

The reader may now wish to check that

$$D = P^{-1}AP.$$

EXAMPLE 4: To see that not all matrices are similar to diagonal matrices, consider the following 2×2 matrix over $\mathbb{R}$:

$$A = \begin{pmatrix} -16 & 9 \\ -16 & 8 \end{pmatrix}.$$

If $t \in L(\mathbb{R}^2)$ is represented by A relative to the usual basis, then $\mathbf{u}_1 t = -16\mathbf{u}_1 + 9\mathbf{u}_2$ and $\mathbf{u}_1 t^2 = -16(-16\mathbf{u}_1 + 9\mathbf{u}_2) + 9(-16\mathbf{u}_1 + 8\mathbf{u}_2) = 112\mathbf{u}_1 - 72\mathbf{u}_2$. Hence, we find that $\mathbf{u}_1(t^2 + 8t + 16) = \mathbf{0}$, and $h(\lambda) = \lambda^2 + 8\lambda + 16$ is the minimal polynomial of $\mathbf{u}_1$. Since $\deg h(\lambda) = \dim \mathbb{R}^2$, $h(\lambda)$ is also the minimal polynomial of t and of A. Now, we have

$$h(\lambda) = (\lambda + 4)^2,$$

so that $h(\lambda)$ does not have the form stated in 6.21. Hence, A is not similar to any diagonal matrix. The best we can say is that A is similar to the Jordan matrix J of $h(\lambda)$,

$$J = \begin{pmatrix} -4 & 1 \\ 0 & -4 \end{pmatrix}.$$

EXERCISES

In each of Exercises 1 through 4, find the spectrum of the l.t., and, if possible, represent it by a diagonal matrix.

1. $t \in L(\mathbb{R}^2)$; $\mathbf{u}_1 t = -\mathbf{u}_1 + 2\mathbf{u}_2$, $\mathbf{u}_2 t = \mathbf{u}_1 - \mathbf{u}_2$.
2. $t \in L(\mathbb{C}^2)$; $\mathbf{u}_1 t = \mathbf{u}_1 - \mathbf{u}_2$, $\mathbf{u}_2 t = \mathbf{u}_1 + 2\mathbf{u}_2$.
3. $t \in L(\mathbb{R}^3)$; $\mathbf{u}_1 t = \mathbf{u}_1 - \mathbf{u}_3$, $\mathbf{u}_2 t = -2\mathbf{u}_1 + 4\mathbf{u}_2 + 4\mathbf{u}_3$, $\mathbf{u}_3 t = 3\mathbf{u}_1 - 3\mathbf{u}_2 - 4\mathbf{u}_3$.
4. $t \in L(\mathbb{C}^4)$; $\mathbf{u}_1 t = -\mathbf{u}_1 + 2\mathbf{u}_3 - 2\mathbf{u}_4$, $\mathbf{u}_2 t = \mathbf{u}_2$, $\mathbf{u}_3 t = 2\mathbf{u}_1 - \mathbf{u}_3 + 2\mathbf{u}_4$, $\mathbf{u}_4 t = 2\mathbf{u}_1 - 2\mathbf{u}_3 + 3\mathbf{u}_4$.

In each of Exercises 5 through 8, find the spectrum of the given matrix over $\mathbb{R}$ and, if possible, find a similar diagonal matrix.

5. $\begin{pmatrix} 2 & 2 \\ 1 & 3 \end{pmatrix}$.

6. $\begin{pmatrix} -1 & -1 & -1 \\ 3 & 3 & 1 \\ -3 & -4 & -2 \end{pmatrix}$.

7. $\begin{pmatrix} -3 & 3 & -3 \\ -3 & 3 & -3 \\ -3 & 3 & -3 \end{pmatrix}$.

8. $\begin{pmatrix} -7 & 8 & -4 & -12 \\ 0 & 3 & -6 & -6 \\ -4 & 2 & -1 & -6 \\ 4 & -2 & -2 & 3 \end{pmatrix}$.

9. If $A \in \mathbb{R}(2)$ has the form

$$A = \begin{pmatrix} a & b \\ c & d \end{pmatrix}, \qquad \text{with either } b \neq 0 \quad \text{or} \quad c \neq 0,$$

then show that

$$h(\lambda) = \lambda^2 - (a + d)\lambda + ad - bc$$

is the minimal polynomial of A. Prove that A is similar to a diagonal matrix iff $(a - d)^2 + 4bc > 0$.

10. If $A \in \mathbb{R}(n)$ is similar to a diagonal matrix, prove that A has a square root (that is, there exists a matrix B such that $B^2 = A$) if the characteristic values of A are nonnegative.

11. Let $A = (a_{ij}) \in F(n)$ be a lower triangular matrix (that is, $a_{ij} = 0$, whenever $j > i$) such that the diagonal elements $a_{11}, a_{22}, \ldots, a_{nn}$ are all different. Is A similar to a diagonal matrix? Prove your answer.

12. If $A \in \mathbb{R}(n)$ is similar to a diagonal matrix, prove that there exists some $B \in \mathbb{R}(n)$ such that $B^3 = A$.

13. For each $A \in F(n)$, prove that A and A^T have the same spectrum. Do A and A^T necessarily have the same minimal polynomial?

Chapter 7

Geometric Applications

1. EUCLIDEAN SPACES

We recall from Section 9 of Chapter 1 that a finite-dimensional vector space V over the real field $\mathbb{R}$ is called a *Euclidean space* iff it has an inner-product operation (1.39). The inner product of vectors $\mathbf{x}$ and $\mathbf{y}$ is a real number denoted by $\mathbf{x}\cdot\mathbf{y}$. Each vector $\mathbf{x}$ in a Euclidean space V has *length* denoted by $|\mathbf{x}|$ and defined by (1.43)

$$|\mathbf{x}| = \sqrt{\mathbf{x}\cdot\mathbf{x}}.$$

Any two nonzero vectors $\mathbf{x}$ and $\mathbf{y}$ in V have a unique *angle* between them defined by (1.48)

$$\cos\theta = \frac{\mathbf{x}\cdot\mathbf{y}}{|\mathbf{x}|\,|\mathbf{y}|}, \qquad 0 \leq \theta \leq \pi.$$

If $\theta = \pi/2$, a right angle, then $\mathbf{x}$ and $\mathbf{y}$ are said to be *orthogonal.* Since $\cos \pi/2 = 0$, we have the following test for orthogonality.

7.1. THEOREM. Two nonzero vectors $\mathbf{x}$ and $\mathbf{y}$ of a Euclidean space V are orthogonal iff $\mathbf{x}\cdot\mathbf{y} = 0$.

It is customary to say that the zero vector is orthogonal to every vector, since $\mathbf{0}\cdot\mathbf{x} = 0$ for all $\mathbf{x} \in V$.

The geometric spaces E_2 and E_3 defined in Section 3 of Chapter 1 are examples of Euclidean spaces (1.47). Another example is $\mathbb{R}^n$ for every positive integer n, where the inner product is defined by 1.41.

Let us call a set $\{\mathbf{x}_1, \mathbf{x}_2, \ldots, \mathbf{x}_k\}$ of vectors of a Euclidean space V *orthogonal* iff (1) $\mathbf{x}_i \neq \mathbf{0}$, $i = 1, 2, \ldots, k$, and (2) $\mathbf{x}_i\cdot\mathbf{x}_j = 0$ if $i \neq j$, $i, j = 1, 2, \ldots, k$. If $\{\mathbf{x}_1, \mathbf{x}_2, \ldots, \mathbf{x}_k\}$ is an orthogonal set and $a_1, a_2, \ldots, a_k \in \mathbb{R}$ are such that

$$\sum_{i=1}^{k} a_i\mathbf{x}_i = \mathbf{0},$$

then, by 1.40, we have

$$0 = \mathbf{x}_j \cdot \mathbf{0} = \mathbf{x}_j \cdot \sum_{i=1}^{k} a_i\mathbf{x}_i = \sum_{i=1}^{k} a_i(\mathbf{x}_j \cdot \mathbf{x}_i) = a_j(\mathbf{x}_j \cdot \mathbf{x}_j)$$

for $j = 1, 2, \ldots, k$. Since $\mathbf{x}_j \neq \mathbf{0}$ and hence $\mathbf{x}_j \cdot \mathbf{x}_j \neq 0$, evidently $a_j = 0$ for $j = 1, 2, \ldots, k$. Thus, $\{\mathbf{x}_1, \mathbf{x}_2, \ldots, \mathbf{x}_k\}$ is l.i. by 1.29. We state this result below.

7.2. THEOREM. Every orthogonal set of vectors of a Euclidean space is independent.

Given an independent set $\{\mathbf{x}_1, \mathbf{x}_2, \ldots, \mathbf{x}_k\}$ of vectors, the set $\{c_1\mathbf{x}_1, c_2\mathbf{x}_2, \ldots, c_k\mathbf{x}_k\}$ is also independent for any nonzero real numbers $c_1, c_2, \ldots, c_k$. In particular, we can choose $c_i = 1/|\mathbf{x}_i|$ for each i, so that each vector $c_i\mathbf{x}_i$ is *normal* (that is, has length 1).

7.3. DEFINITION OF AN ORTHONORMAL SET. A set of vectors of a Euclidean space V is called orthonormal iff the set is orthogonal and all the vectors in the set are normal.

Thus, $\{\mathbf{x}_1, \mathbf{x}_2, \ldots, \mathbf{x}_k\} \subset V$ is orthonormal iff $\mathbf{x}_i \cdot \mathbf{x}_j = \delta_{ij}$, $i, j = 1, 2, \ldots, k$, where δ_{ij} is the Kronecker delta.

If V is an n-dimensional vector space and $\{\mathbf{x}_1, \mathbf{x}_2, \ldots, \mathbf{x}_k\} \subset V$ is orthogonal, with $k < n$, then it is always possible to find a vector $\mathbf{x}$ such that $\{\mathbf{x}_1, \mathbf{x}_2, \ldots, \mathbf{x}_k, \mathbf{x}\}$ is orthogonal. To test the truth of this statement, let

$$W = \mathbb{R}\mathbf{x}_1 + \mathbb{R}\mathbf{x}_2 + \cdots + \mathbb{R}\mathbf{x}_k,$$

and let $\mathbf{y} \in V$, $\mathbf{y} \notin W$. If we let

$$\mathbf{x} = \mathbf{y} - \sum_{i=1}^{k} a_i\mathbf{x}_i$$

for any $a_i \in \mathbb{R}$, then $\mathbf{x} \neq \mathbf{0}$, and we also have

$$\mathbf{x} \cdot \mathbf{x}_j = \mathbf{y} \cdot \mathbf{x}_j - a_j(\mathbf{x}_j \cdot \mathbf{x}_j), \qquad j = 1, 2, \ldots, k.$$

In particular, if we let

$$a_j = \frac{\mathbf{y} \cdot \mathbf{x}_j}{\mathbf{x}_j \cdot \mathbf{x}_j}, \qquad j = 1, 2, \ldots, k,$$

then $\mathbf{x} \cdot \mathbf{x}_j = 0$ for every j. For this choice of the a_j, the set $\{\mathbf{x}_1, \mathbf{x}_2, \ldots, \mathbf{x}_k, \mathbf{x}\}$ is orthogonal, which we wanted to show.

Starting with a single nonzero vector $\mathbf{x}_1$, we can build an orthogonal set of n vectors in $n - 1$ steps of the type described above. If we normalize the final set, then we obtain a proof of the following theorem.

7.4. THEOREM. Every Euclidean space has an orthonormal basis.

EXAMPLE 1: Let us start with the nonzero vector $\mathbf{x}_1 = \mathbf{i} - \mathbf{j} + \mathbf{k}$ and build an orthonormal basis $\{\mathbf{x}_1, \mathbf{x}_2, \mathbf{x}_3\}$ of E_3. First, we select some $\mathbf{y} \notin \mathbb{R}\mathbf{x}_1$, say $\mathbf{y} = \mathbf{i}$. Then, as above, let

$$\mathbf{x}_2 = \mathbf{y} - a\mathbf{x}_1, \qquad \text{where } a = \frac{\mathbf{y}\cdot\mathbf{x}_1}{\mathbf{x}_1\cdot\mathbf{x}_1}.$$

Since $\mathbf{x}_1\cdot\mathbf{x}_1 = 3$ and $\mathbf{i}\cdot(\mathbf{i} - \mathbf{j} + \mathbf{k}) = 1$, we see that $\mathbf{x}_2 = \mathbf{i} - a(\mathbf{i} - \mathbf{j} + \mathbf{k})$ or

$$\mathbf{x}_2 = \tfrac{1}{3}(2\mathbf{i} + \mathbf{j} - \mathbf{k}).$$

Next, we select some $\mathbf{y}_1 \notin \mathbb{R}\mathbf{x}_1 + \mathbb{R}\mathbf{x}_2$, say $\mathbf{y}_1 = \mathbf{j}$. Then, as above, let

$$\mathbf{x}_3 = \mathbf{y}_1 - a_1\mathbf{x}_1 - a_2\mathbf{x}_2,$$

where

$$a_1 = \frac{\mathbf{y}_1\cdot\mathbf{x}_1}{\mathbf{x}_1\cdot\mathbf{x}_1} = -\frac{1}{3}, \qquad a_2 = \frac{\mathbf{y}_1\cdot\mathbf{x}_2}{\mathbf{x}_2\cdot\mathbf{x}_2} = \frac{1}{2}.$$

Thus, we have

$$\mathbf{x}_3 = \tfrac{1}{2}(\mathbf{j} + \mathbf{k}).$$

It follows that $\{\mathbf{x}_1, \mathbf{x}_2, \mathbf{x}_3\}$ is an orthogonal basis of E_3. We can make this basis normal by multiplying each vector by the reciprocal of its length. Doing this, we get

$$\left\{\frac{1}{\sqrt{3}}(\mathbf{i} - \mathbf{j} + \mathbf{k}), \frac{1}{\sqrt{6}}(2\mathbf{i} + \mathbf{j} - \mathbf{k}), \frac{1}{\sqrt{2}}(\mathbf{j} + \mathbf{k})\right\}$$

as an orthonormal basis of E_3. Of course, $\{\mathbf{i}, \mathbf{j}, \mathbf{k}\}$ is the more commonly used orthonormal basis of E_3.

The Euclidean space $\mathbb{R}^n$ has orthonormal basis $\{\mathbf{u}_1, \mathbf{u}_2, \ldots, \mathbf{u}_n\}$, where

$$\mathbf{u}_i = (\delta_{i1}, \delta_{i2}, \ldots, \delta_{in}), \qquad i = 1, 2, \ldots, n.$$

For example, $\mathbb{R}^3$ has orthonormal basis $\{\mathbf{u}_1, \mathbf{u}_2, \mathbf{u}_3\}$, where

$$\mathbf{u}_1 = (1, 0, 0), \qquad \mathbf{u}_2 = (0, 1, 0), \qquad \mathbf{u}_3 = (0, 0, 1).$$

7.5. DEFINITION OF ORTHOGONAL COMPLEMENT. For each subspace S of a Euclidean space V, the orthogonal complement of S is denoted by $S^\perp$ and defined by

$$S^\perp = \{\mathbf{x} \in V \mid \mathbf{x}\cdot\mathbf{y} = 0 \quad \text{for all } \mathbf{y} \in S\}.$$

In words, $S^\perp$ is the set of all vectors of V which are orthogonal to every vector of S. If $S = \{\mathbf{0}\}$, then $S^\perp = V$; if $S = V$, then $S^\perp = \{\mathbf{0}\}$. More generally, we have the following result.

7.6. THEOREM. If S is a proper subspace of a Euclidean space V, then $S^\perp$ is also a proper subspace of V, and we have

$$V = S \oplus S^\perp.$$

Proof: The reader can easily verify that $S^\perp$ is a subspace of V. If $\mathbf{x} \in S \cap S^\perp$, then we see that $\mathbf{x}\cdot\mathbf{x} = 0$. Hence, we have $\mathbf{x} = \mathbf{0}$ by 1.39 (4). Thus, $S \cap S^\perp = \{\mathbf{0}\}$. By 7.4, we find that S has an orthogonal basis $\{\mathbf{x}_1, \mathbf{x}_2, \ldots, \mathbf{x}_k\}$, and by the proof of 7.4, that $\{\mathbf{x}_1, \mathbf{x}_2, \ldots, \mathbf{x}_k\}$ can be extended to an orthogonal basis $\{\mathbf{x}_1, \ldots, \mathbf{x}_k, \mathbf{x}_{k+1}, \ldots, \mathbf{x}_n\}$ of V.

Now, we have

$$\mathbf{x}_j\cdot\sum_{i=1}^{k} a_i\mathbf{x}_i = \sum_{i=1}^{k} a_i(\mathbf{x}_j\cdot\mathbf{x}_i) = 0, \qquad j = k+1, \ldots, n,$$

for all $a_1, a_2, \ldots, a_k \in \mathbb{R}$. Therefore, $\mathbf{x}_j \in S^\perp$ for $j = k+1, \ldots, n$. Since every element of the basis $\{\mathbf{x}_1, \mathbf{x}_2, \ldots, \mathbf{x}_n\}$ is in either S or $S^\perp$, we must have $V = S + S^\perp$. In fact, $V = S \oplus S^\perp$, because $S \cap S^\perp = \{\mathbf{0}\}$. This proves 7.6.

EXAMPLE 2: If we have

$$S = R(1, 0, 1, 0) + R(0, 1, 1, -1) \subset \mathbb{R}^4,$$

then we could find $S^\perp$ as in the proof of 7.6. Another way to do this is as follows. If $\mathbf{x} = (a, b, c, d) \in \mathbb{R}^4$, then $\mathbf{x} \in S^\perp$ iff $\mathbf{x}\cdot(1, 0, 1, 0) = 0$ and $\mathbf{x}\cdot(0, 1, 1, -1) = 0$. Since $\mathbf{x}\cdot(1, 0, 1, 0) = a + c$ and $\mathbf{x}\cdot(0, 1, 1, -1) = b + c - d$, we see that $\mathbf{x} \in S^\perp$ iff $a + c = 0$ and $b + c - d = 0$. Hence, we have

$$S^\perp = \{(a, b, -a, b-a) \mid a, b \in \mathbb{R}\}.$$

For example, if $a = 0$ and $b = 1$, we get $(0, 1, 0, 1) \in S^\perp$; and if $a = 1$ and $b = 0$, we get $(1, 0, -1, -1) \in S^\perp$. Since $\dim S^\perp = 4 - \dim S = 2$, we can also express $S^\perp$ in the form

$$S^\perp = R(0, 1, 0, 1) + R(1, 0, -1, -1).$$

EXERCISES

In Exercises 1 through 6, find orthogonal bases of S and $S^\perp$.

1. $V = \mathrm{E}_3$, $S = \mathbb{R}(\mathbf{i} + 2\mathbf{j})$.
2. $V = \mathrm{E}_3$, $S = \mathbb{R}(\mathbf{i} + \mathbf{j}) + \mathbb{R}(\mathbf{j} - \mathbf{k})$.
3. $V = \mathbb{R}^3$, $S = \mathbb{R}(1, -1, 1) + \mathbb{R}(1, 1, 1)$.
4. $V = \mathbb{R}^4$, $S = \mathbb{R}(1, 0, 0, 1) + \mathbb{R}(1, -1, 1, 0)$.
5. $V = \mathbb{R}^5$, $S = \mathbb{R}(1, 0, 0, 0, 0) + \mathbb{R}(1, 1, 0, 1, 1)$.
6. $V = \mathbb{R}^5$, $S = \mathbb{R}(1, 0, 0, 0, 1) + \mathbb{R}(1, 1, 0, 0, -1) + \mathbb{R}(0, 0, 1, 1, 1)$.
7. Prove that $(S^\perp)^\perp = S$ for every subspace S of a Euclidean space V.
8. If S_1 and S_2 are subspaces of a Euclidean space V, express $(S_1 + S_2)^\perp$ and $(S_1 \cap S_2)^\perp$ in terms of $S_1^\perp$ and $S_2^\perp$. Illustrate with an example.

2. ISOMETRIES

A geometric example of a linear transformation of E_2 is the mapping t which rotates each (position) vector about the origin through an angle θ. Thus, $\mathbf{i}t$ and $\mathbf{j}t$ are as shown in Fig. 7.1:

$$\mathbf{i}t = (\cos\theta)\mathbf{i} + (\sin\theta)\mathbf{j}, \qquad \mathbf{j}t = (-\sin\theta)\mathbf{i} + (\cos\theta)\mathbf{j}.$$

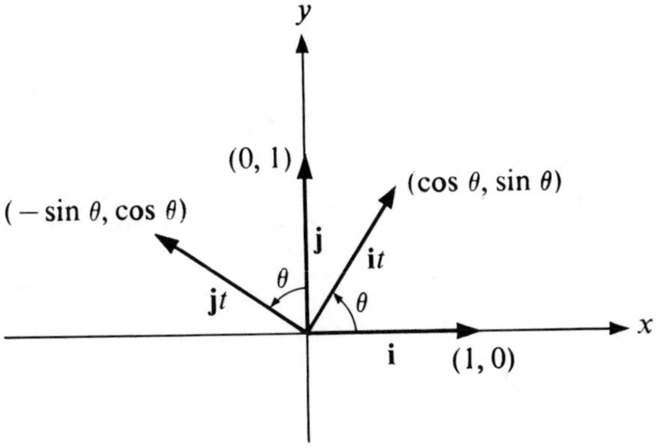

Figure 7.1

Hence, we have

$$(a\mathbf{i} + b\mathbf{j})t = (a\cos\theta - b\sin\theta)\mathbf{i} + (a\sin\theta + b\cos\theta)\mathbf{j}$$

for every $a\mathbf{i} + b\mathbf{j} \in E_2$. It is evident that t carries each vector $\mathbf{x}$ into a vector $\mathbf{x}t$ of the same length. That is, we have that

$$|(a\mathbf{i} + b\mathbf{j})t| = |a\mathbf{i} + b\mathbf{j}| = \sqrt{a^2 + b^2} \qquad \text{for all } a, b \in \mathbb{R}.$$

Another geometric example of a linear transformation of E_2 is the mapping t which reflects each (position) vector through the y-axis. Thus, we have

$$(a\mathbf{i} + b\mathbf{j})t = -a\mathbf{i} + b\mathbf{j} \qquad \text{for all } a, b \in \mathbb{R},$$

as indicated in Fig. 7.2. Again, t maps each vector $\mathbf{u}$ into a vector $\mathbf{u}t$ of the same length:

$$|(a\mathbf{i} + b\mathbf{j})t| = |-a\mathbf{i} + b\mathbf{j}| = \sqrt{a^2 + b^2} \qquad \text{for all } a, b \in \mathbb{R}.$$

Length-preserving linear transformations such as the two above occur often enough to be given a special name as follows.

7.7. DEFINITION OF AN ISOMETRY. A linear transformation t of a Euclidean space V is called an isometry iff $|\mathbf{x}t| = |\mathbf{x}|$ for all $\mathbf{x} \in V$.

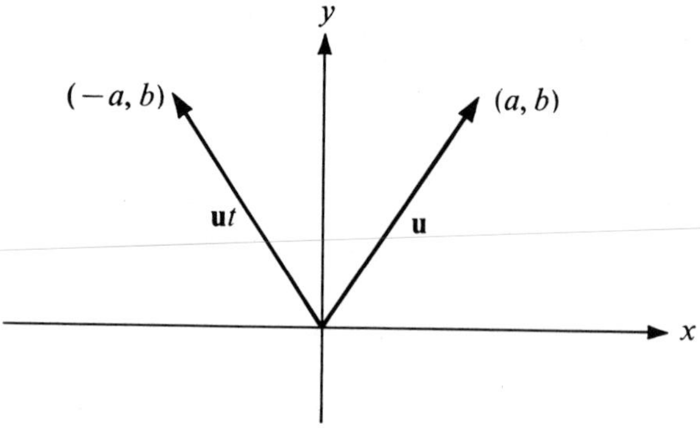

Figure 7.2

Since $|\mathbf{x}t| = |\mathbf{x}| = 0$ iff $\mathbf{x} = \mathbf{0}$, evidently $\ker t = \{\mathbf{0}\}$, and each isometry t is nonsingular.

If $\mathbf{x}$ is a characteristic vector of an isometry t, say $\mathbf{x}t = c\mathbf{x}$, then $|\mathbf{x}| = |\mathbf{x}t| = |c|\,|\mathbf{x}|$, and $c = \pm 1$. Thus, 1 and -1 are the only possible characteristic values of an isometry.

Clearly, condition 7.7 is equivalent to the following condition:

7.8 $$\mathbf{x}t\cdot\mathbf{x}t = \mathbf{x}\cdot\mathbf{x} \qquad \text{for all } \mathbf{x} \in V.$$

For convenience, let

$$I(V)$$

denote the set of all isometries of V. If $s, t \in I(V)$, then $st \in I(V)$, since we have

$$\mathbf{x}(st)\cdot\mathbf{x}(st) = (\mathbf{x}s)t\cdot(\mathbf{x}s)t = \mathbf{x}s\cdot\mathbf{x}s = \mathbf{x}\cdot\mathbf{x} \qquad \text{for all } \mathbf{x} \in V.$$

Also, if $t \in I(V)$, then $t^{-1} \in I(V)$, since we have

$$\mathbf{x}\cdot\mathbf{x} = \mathbf{x}(t^{-1}t)\cdot\mathbf{x}(t^{-1}t) = (\mathbf{x}t^{-1})t\cdot(\mathbf{x}t^{-1})t = \mathbf{x}t^{-1}\cdot\mathbf{x}t^{-1} \qquad \text{for all } \mathbf{x} \in V.$$

Since the identity l.t. is an isometry and multiplication in $L(V)$ is associative, $I(V)$ has the four properties of a *group:* (1) Closure under multiplication; (2) $1 \in I(V)$; (3) $t^{-1} \in I(V)$ for each $t \in I(V)$; (4) Multiplication is associative. We state this fact as a theorem.

7.9. THEOREM. For each Euclidean space V, the set $I(V)$ of all isometries of V is a group under multiplication.

If $t \in I(V)$ and $\mathbf{x}, \mathbf{y} \in V$, then $(\mathbf{x}+\mathbf{y})t\cdot(\mathbf{x}+\mathbf{y})t = (\mathbf{x}+\mathbf{y})\cdot(\mathbf{x}+\mathbf{y})$. Hence, $(\mathbf{x}t+\mathbf{y}t)\cdot(\mathbf{x}t+\mathbf{y}t) = (\mathbf{x}+\mathbf{y})\cdot(\mathbf{x}+\mathbf{y})$ and, on expanding, we have $\mathbf{x}t\cdot\mathbf{x}t + 2(\mathbf{x}t\cdot\mathbf{y}t) + \mathbf{y}t\cdot\mathbf{y}t = \mathbf{x}\cdot\mathbf{x} + 2(\mathbf{x}\cdot\mathbf{y}) + \mathbf{y}\cdot\mathbf{y}$. Since $\mathbf{x}t\cdot\mathbf{x}t = \mathbf{x}\cdot\mathbf{x}$ and $\mathbf{y}t\cdot\mathbf{y}t = \mathbf{y}\cdot\mathbf{y}$, it is also evident that $\mathbf{x}t\cdot\mathbf{y}t = \mathbf{x}\cdot\mathbf{y}$. We state this result below.

7.10. THEOREM. $\mathbf{x}t \cdot \mathbf{y}t = \mathbf{x} \cdot \mathbf{y}$ for all $\mathbf{x}, \mathbf{y} \in V$, $t \in I(V)$.

Another property of an isometry which follows immediately from 7.10 and from the definition 1.48 of the angle between two vectors is as follows.

7.11. THEOREM. An isometry of a Euclidean space preserves angles.

That is, if $t \in I(V)$ and $\mathbf{x}, \mathbf{y} \in V$, then the angle between $\mathbf{x}$ and $\mathbf{y}$ is the same as the angle between $\mathbf{x}t$ and $\mathbf{y}t$.

If $t \in I(V)$ and $\{\mathbf{u}_1, \mathbf{u}_2, \ldots, \mathbf{u}_n\}$ is an orthonormal basis of V, then, by 7.10, we have

$$\mathbf{u}_i t \cdot \mathbf{u}_j t = \mathbf{u}_i \cdot \mathbf{u}_j = \delta_{ij}, \qquad i, j = 1, 2, \ldots, n.$$

Therefore, $\{\mathbf{u}_1 t, \mathbf{u}_2 t, \ldots, \mathbf{u}_n t\}$ is also an orthonormal basis of V. Let t be represented by the matrix $A = (a_{ij}) \in \mathbb{R}(n)$ relative to the $\mathbf{u}$-basis:

$$\mathbf{u}_i t = \sum_{k=1}^{n} a_{ik} \mathbf{u}_k, \qquad i = 1, 2, \ldots, n.$$

Then, we have

$$\mathbf{u}_i t \cdot \mathbf{u}_j t = \left(\sum_{k=1}^{n} a_{ik} \mathbf{u}_k \right) \cdot \left(\sum_{l=1}^{n} a_{jl} \mathbf{u}_l \right) = \delta_{ij},$$

and, by 1.40,

$$\sum_{k=1}^{n} a_{ik} a_{jk} = \delta_{ij}, \qquad i, j = 1, 2, \ldots, n.$$

This equation has the matrix form

7.12 $$AA^T = I.$$

That is, the transpose A^T of A is also the inverse of A. A matrix A that has property 7.12 is called an *orthogonal matrix*. We have proved the following result.

7.13. THEOREM. An isometry is represented by an orthogonal matrix relative to an orthonormal basis.

If $A \in \mathbb{R}(n)$ is orthogonal, so that $AA^T = I$, then, by 4.5 and 4.12, we have

$$\det AA^T = \det A \det A^T = (\det A)^2 = 1.$$

Hence, $\det A = \pm 1$. Since the determinant of a l.t. equals the determinant of any representing matrix, we have proved the theorem below.

7.14. THEOREM. If t is an isometry, then $\det t = \pm 1$.

The rotation t given at the beginning of this section is represented by the matrix

$$A = \begin{pmatrix} \cos\theta & \sin\theta \\ -\sin\theta & \cos\theta \end{pmatrix}.$$

Hence, $\det t = \det A = \cos^2\theta + \sin^2\theta = 1$.

For the reflection t in Fig. 7.2, $\mathbf{i}t = -\mathbf{i}$ and $\mathbf{j}t = \mathbf{j}$. Hence, t is represented by the matrix

$$A = \begin{pmatrix} -1 & 0 \\ 0 & 1 \end{pmatrix}.$$

Therefore, $\det t = \det A = -1$.

With these examples in mind, we shall call an isometry t of a Euclidean space V a *rotation* if $\det t = 1$ and a *reflection* if $\det t = -1$.

EXERCISES

1. Prove that $A \in \mathbb{R}(n)$ is orthogonal iff the row vectors of A form an orthonormal basis of $\mathbb{R}^n$. Which of the following matrices over $\mathbb{R}$ are orthogonal? Find the inverse of each orthogonal matrix.

(a) $\begin{pmatrix} 1 & 1 \\ 1 & -1 \end{pmatrix}$. (b) $\begin{pmatrix} 0 & 1 \\ -1 & 0 \end{pmatrix}$.

(c) $\begin{pmatrix} \frac{3}{5} & \frac{4}{5} \\ \frac{4}{5} & -\frac{3}{5} \end{pmatrix}$. (d) $\begin{pmatrix} \frac{5}{13} & -\frac{12}{13} \\ -\frac{12}{13} & \frac{5}{13} \end{pmatrix}$.

(e) $\begin{pmatrix} 0 & 1 & 0 \\ 1 & 0 & 0 \\ 0 & 0 & -1 \end{pmatrix}$. (f) $\begin{pmatrix} \frac{1}{3} & \frac{2}{3} & \frac{2}{3} \\ -\frac{2}{3} & \frac{2}{3} & -\frac{1}{3} \\ \frac{2}{3} & \frac{1}{3} & -\frac{2}{3} \end{pmatrix}$.

(g) $\begin{pmatrix} 0 & 0 & 1 & 0 \\ 1 & 0 & 0 & 0 \\ 0 & 0 & 0 & 1 \\ 0 & 1 & 0 & 0 \end{pmatrix}$. (h) $\begin{pmatrix} \frac{1}{\sqrt{2}} & 0 & \frac{1}{\sqrt{2}} & 0 \\ 0 & \frac{1}{\sqrt{2}} & 0 & \frac{1}{\sqrt{2}} \\ \frac{1}{2} & \frac{1}{2} & -\frac{1}{2} & -\frac{1}{2} \\ \frac{1}{2} & -\frac{1}{2} & -\frac{1}{2} & \frac{1}{2} \end{pmatrix}$.

2. An isometry of a Euclidean space V maps an orthonormal basis into an orthonormal basis. Prove, conversely, that if $t \in L(V)$ maps an orthonormal basis of V into an orthonormal basis, then t is an isometry.
3. Prove that the set of all rotations of a Euclidean space is a group under multiplication. Is the set of reflections a group?
4. Prove that the set of all $n \times n$ orthogonal matrices is a group under multiplication.

3. INVARIANT SUBSPACES RELATIVE TO AN ISOMETRY

Let V be a Euclidean space and t be an isometry of V. If S is a t-invariant subspace of V, then $St = S$, since $St \subset S$ and t is nonsingular. Hence, the restriction of t to S, $t \mid S$, is an isometry of S. If S is t-invariant, is the orthogonal complement $S^\perp$ of S also a t-invariant subspace of V? To answer this question, we observe that $S^\perp t \subset S^\perp$ iff $\mathbf{y}\cdot\mathbf{z}t = 0$ for all $\mathbf{y} \in S$, $\mathbf{z} \in S^\perp$. Now, each $\mathbf{y} \in S$ has the form $\mathbf{y} = \mathbf{x}t$, where $\mathbf{x} = \mathbf{y}t^{-1} \in S$. Hence, $\mathbf{y}\cdot\mathbf{z}t = \mathbf{x}t\cdot\mathbf{z}t = \mathbf{x}\cdot\mathbf{z} = 0$ for all $\mathbf{y} \in S$, $\mathbf{z} \in S^\perp$, and $S^\perp$ is a t-invariant subspace of V. These remarks, together with 7.6, prove the result below.

7.15. THEOREM. If t is an isometry of V and S is a proper t-invariant subspace of V, then $S^\perp$ is also t-invariant, and we have

$$V = S \oplus S^\perp.$$

Let V be an n-dimensional Euclidean space, $t \in I(V)$, and $h(\lambda)$ be the minimal polynomial of t. If $p_1(\lambda)$ is a prime factor of $h(\lambda)$, then, by 5.7, there exists some $\mathbf{x}_1 \in V$ having $p_1(\lambda)$ as its minimal polynomial. Let $W_1 = \mathbf{x}_1\mathbb{R}[t]$ and $V_1 = W_1^\perp$. Then, by 7.15, $V = W_1 \oplus V_1$. Starting over with the isometry $t \mid V_1$ of V_1, we can find some $\mathbf{x}_2 \in V_2$ having a prime $p_2(\lambda)$ as its minimal polynomial, such that $V_1 = W_2 \oplus V_2$, where $W_2 = \mathbf{x}_2\mathbb{R}[t \mid V_1] = \mathbf{x}_2\mathbb{R}[t]$ and $V_2 = W_2^\perp$. Thus, $V = W_1 \oplus W_2 \oplus V_2$. In n such steps at the most, we can show that there exist $\mathbf{x}_1, \mathbf{x}_2, \ldots, \mathbf{x}_m \in V$, such that

$$V = W_1 \oplus W_2 \oplus \cdots \oplus W_m, \qquad \text{where } W_i = \mathbf{x}_iF[t],$$

and the minimal polynomial of each $\mathbf{x}_i$ is a prime $p_i(\lambda)$. The minimal polynomial $h(\lambda)$ is now seen to be the l.c.m. of the primes $p_1(\lambda), p_2(\lambda), \ldots, p_m(\lambda)$. That is, $h(\lambda)$ is the product of the distinct primes among $p_1(\lambda), p_2(\lambda), \ldots, p_m(\lambda)$. Thus, $h(\lambda)$ is of the form considered in 6.14.

The monic prime polynomials in $\mathbb{R}[\lambda]$ are of a particularly simple form, either being linear polynomials such as $\lambda - a$ or quadratic polynomials of the form

$$\lambda^2 + b\lambda + c, \qquad \text{with } b^2 - 4c < 0.$$

Hence, each prime $p_i(\lambda)$ encountered above is of degree 1 or 2, and the associated t-invariant subspace W_i of V is of dimension 1 or 2.

Our remarks above can be summarized in the following statement.

7.16. THEOREM. For each isometry t of a Euclidean space V, there exist irreducible t-invariant subspaces $W_1, W_2, \ldots, W_m$ of V, each of dimension 1 or 2, and $t_i \in I(W_i)$, such that

$$V = W_1 \oplus W_2 \oplus \cdots \oplus W_m \qquad \text{and} \qquad t = t_1 \oplus t_2 \oplus \cdots \oplus t_m.$$

If W is a one-dimensional invariant subspace of V relative to an isometry

t, then $t \mid W$ is an isometry and $t \mid W = \pm 1$, since $\det (t \mid W) = \pm 1$ by 7.14. Thus, $W = \mathbb{R}\mathbf{x}$ for some $\mathbf{x} \in V$, and either $\mathbf{x}t = \mathbf{x}$ or $\mathbf{x}t = -\mathbf{x}$. The minimal polynomial of $t \mid W$ is $\lambda - 1$ if $\mathbf{x}t = \mathbf{x}$ and $\lambda + 1$ if $\mathbf{x}t = -\mathbf{x}$.

The only other type of irreducible t-invariant subspace of V, according to 7.16, is a subspace W of dimension 2 for which the minimal polynomial $h(\lambda)$ is a prime of degree 2, $h(\lambda) = \lambda^2 + b\lambda + c$ with $b^2 - 4c < 0$. The companion matrix C of $h(\lambda)$ represents $t' = t \mid W$ relative to some basis of W, and, therefore, we have

$$\det t' = \det C = \det \begin{pmatrix} 0 & 1 \\ -c & -b \end{pmatrix} = c.$$

Since $\det t' = \pm 1$ and $c > 0$ (if $c < 0$, $b^2 - 4c > 0$), it is evident that $c = 1$ and $\det t' = 1$. Hence, t' is a rotation.

Let $(\mathbf{u}_1, \mathbf{u}_2)$ be an orthonormal basis of W and

$$A = \begin{pmatrix} a_1 & a_2 \\ a_3 & a_4 \end{pmatrix}$$

represent t' relative to $(\mathbf{u}_1, \mathbf{u}_2)$. Since t' is irreducible, $a_2 \neq 0$ and $a_3 \neq 0$. The matrix A is orthogonal by 7.13, and $\det A = 1$, since t is a rotation. Hence, $AA^T = I$, and the following equations are true.

(1) $a_1^2 + a_2^2 = 1$, (2) $a_3^2 + a_4^2 = 1$,

(3) $a_1a_3 + a_2a_4 = 0$, (4) $a_1a_4 - a_2a_3 = 1$.

If we multiply (1) by a_3^2, (2) by a_2^2, and then subtract the resulting equations, we get $(a_1a_3)^2 - (a_2a_4)^2 = a_3^2 - a_2^2$. Since $(a_1a_3)^2 = (a_2a_4)^2$ by (3), we see that $a_2^2 = a_3^2$ and $a_2 = \pm a_3$. Then, from (3) again, we have $a_1 = \mp a_4$. We cannot have $a_2 = a_3$ and $a_1 = -a_4$ in view of (4). Hence, we must have $a_2 = -a_3$ and $a_1 = a_4$. For convenience, let $a_1 = r$ and $a_2 = s$. Then, matrix A has the form

$$A = \begin{pmatrix} r & s \\ -s & r \end{pmatrix}, \qquad \text{with} \quad r^2 + s^2 = 1,\ s \neq 0.$$

The minimal polynomial of A, and also of t', is

$$\det (\lambda I - A) = \lambda^2 - 2r\lambda + 1.$$

Since $r^2 < 1$, this polynomial is prime.

We summarize our results above as follows.

7.17. THEOREM. Let V be a Euclidean space and t be an isometry of V. If W is an irreducible t-invariant subspace of V and $t' = t \mid W$, then either $\dim W = 1$ or $\dim W = 2$.

(1) If $\dim W = 1$, then either $t' = 1$ or $t' = -1$.
(2) If $\dim W = 2$, then t' is represented by an orthogonal matrix

$$A = \begin{pmatrix} r & s \\ -s & r \end{pmatrix}, \qquad \text{with} \quad r^2 + s^2 = 1 \qquad \text{and} \quad s \neq 0,$$

relative to an orthonormal basis of W. The isometry t' is a rotation with minimal polynomial $\lambda^2 - 2r\lambda + 1$.

Each isometry t of V leads to a representation of V as a direct sum of irreducible t-invariant subspaces $V = W_1 \oplus W_2 \oplus \cdots \oplus W_m$ and of t as a direct sum of isometries $t = t_1 \oplus t_2 \oplus \cdots \oplus t_m$, where $t_i = t \mid W_i$. This allows us to represent t by an orthogonal matrix A which is a direct sum of orthogonal matrices A_i representing the various t_i. Thus, we have

$$A = A_1 \oplus A_2 \oplus \cdots \oplus A_m.$$

In view of 7.17, we find that $A_i = (1)$ or (-1) if $\dim W_i = 1$, while

$$A_i = \begin{pmatrix} r_i & s_i \\ -s_i & r_i \end{pmatrix}, \qquad \text{with} \quad r_i^2 + s_i^2 = 1 \qquad \text{and} \quad s_i \neq 0$$

if $\dim W_i = 2$. The minimal polynomial $h_i(\lambda)$ of A_i is $\lambda \pm 1$ if $\dim W_i = 1$ and $\lambda^2 - 2r_i\lambda + 1$ if $\dim A_i = 2$. If I_i is the identity matrix of the same size as A_i, then we know that $\det(\lambda I_i - A_i) = h_i(\lambda)$ for each i. Hence, we have

$$\begin{aligned} \det(\lambda I - A) &= \det(\lambda I_1 - A_1)\det(\lambda I_2 - A_2) \cdots \det(\lambda I_m - A_m) \\ &= h_1(\lambda)h_2(\lambda) \ldots h_m(\lambda). \end{aligned}$$

Thus, we can completely describe the nature of an isometry t by looking at the characteristic polynomial of any matrix representing t, as follows.

7.18. THEOREM. Let V be a Euclidean space, t an isometry of V, and $f(\lambda)$ the characteristic polynomial of any matrix representing t. Then, $f(\lambda)$ has the form

$$f(\lambda) = (\lambda - 1)^k(\lambda + 1)^l q_{k+l+1}(\lambda) \cdots q_m(\lambda)$$

for some integers $k \geq 0$ and $l \geq 0$, and some quadratic polynomials $q_i(\lambda)$ of the form $q_i(\lambda) = \lambda^2 - 2r_i\lambda + 1$, where $r_i \in \mathbb{R}$ and $|r_i| < 1$, $i = k + l + 1, \ldots, m$. Every representation of V as a direct sum of irreducible t-invariant subspaces has the corresponding form

$$V = W_1 \oplus \cdots \oplus W_k \oplus W_{k+1} \oplus \cdots \oplus W_{k+l} \oplus W_{k+l+1} \oplus \cdots \oplus W_m$$

and t has the form

$$t = \overbrace{1 \oplus \cdots \oplus 1}^{k} \oplus \overbrace{-1 \oplus \cdots \oplus -1}^{l} + t_{k+l+1} \oplus \cdots \oplus t_m,$$

where $t_i = t \mid W_i$ when $i > k + l$.

We should realize, of course, that k, l, or $m - k - l$ might be zero for some $t \in I(V)$.

EXAMPLE: Let $V = \mathbb{R}^3$ and $t \in L(V)$ be defined by

$$(1, 0, 0)t = (\tfrac{1}{3}, \tfrac{2}{3}, \tfrac{2}{3}), \qquad (0, 1, 0)t = (-\tfrac{2}{3}, \tfrac{2}{3}, -\tfrac{1}{3}),$$
$$(0, 0, 1)t = (\tfrac{2}{3}, \tfrac{1}{3}, -\tfrac{2}{3}).$$

Since t is represented by the orthogonal matrix

$$A = \begin{pmatrix} \tfrac{1}{3} & \tfrac{2}{3} & \tfrac{2}{3} \\ -\tfrac{2}{3} & \tfrac{2}{3} & -\tfrac{1}{3} \\ \tfrac{2}{3} & \tfrac{1}{3} & -\tfrac{2}{3} \end{pmatrix},$$

t is an isometry (Example 2, p. 170). We can easily show that A has characteristic polynomial

$$f(\lambda) = \det(\lambda I - A) = \lambda^3 - \tfrac{1}{3}\lambda^2 - \tfrac{1}{3}\lambda + 1,$$

or

$$f(\lambda) = (\lambda + 1)(\lambda^2 - \tfrac{4}{3}\lambda + 1),$$

where $\lambda^2 - \frac{4}{3}\lambda + 1$ is prime. Hence, by 6.12, $V = W_1 \oplus W_2$, where $W_1 = V(t^2 - \frac{4}{3}t + 1)$ and $W_2 = V(t + 1)$. We find that

$$W_1 = \mathbb{R}(1, 0, -2), \qquad W_2 = \mathbb{R}(2, 1, 1) + \mathbb{R}(-2, 5, -1),$$

and the minimal polynomial of $t \mid W_1$ is $\lambda + 1$, of $t \mid W_2$ is $\lambda^2 - \frac{4}{3}\lambda + 1$. Thus, $t = -1 \oplus t_2$, where $-1 = t \mid W_1$ and $t_2 = t \mid W_2$. If we let $\mathbf{x}_1 = (1/\sqrt{5})(1, 0, -2)$, $\mathbf{x}_2 = (1/\sqrt{6})(2, 1, 1)$, $\mathbf{x}_3 = (1/\sqrt{30})(-2, 5, -1)$, then $\{\mathbf{x}_1\}$ is an orthonormal basis of W_1 and $\{\mathbf{x}_2, \mathbf{x}_3\}$ of W_2.

Since we have

$$\mathbf{x}_1(-1) = -\mathbf{x}_1, \qquad \mathbf{x}_2 t_2 = \frac{2}{3}\mathbf{x}_2 + \frac{\sqrt{5}}{3}\mathbf{x}_3, \qquad \mathbf{x}_3 t_2 = -\frac{\sqrt{5}}{3}\mathbf{x}_2 + \frac{2}{3}\mathbf{x}_3,$$

t_2 is represented by the orthogonal matrix

$$A_2 = \begin{pmatrix} \frac{2}{3} & \frac{\sqrt{5}}{3} \\ -\frac{\sqrt{5}}{3} & \frac{2}{3} \end{pmatrix},$$

and t by the orthogonal matrix

$$B = (-1) \oplus A_2 = \begin{pmatrix} -1 & 0 & 0 \\ 0 & \frac{2}{3} & \frac{\sqrt{5}}{3} \\ 0 & -\frac{\sqrt{5}}{3} & \frac{2}{3} \end{pmatrix}$$

relative to the basis $(\mathbf{x}_1, \mathbf{x}_2, \mathbf{x}_3)$. Evidently, t is a reflection, because $\det t = \det B = -1$.

EXERCISES

In Exercises 1 through 6, show that each $n \times n$ matrix represents an isometry t relative to the usual basis of $\mathbb{R}^n$, and express $\mathbb{R}^n$ as a direct sum of irreducible t-invariant subspaces.

1. $\frac{1}{13}\begin{pmatrix} 5 & 12 \\ 12 & -5 \end{pmatrix}$.

2. $\frac{1}{13}\begin{pmatrix} 5 & -12 \\ 12 & 5 \end{pmatrix}$.

3. $\begin{pmatrix} \frac{1}{\sqrt{2}} & 0 & \frac{1}{\sqrt{2}} \\ -\frac{1}{\sqrt{3}} & \frac{1}{\sqrt{3}} & \frac{1}{\sqrt{3}} \\ \frac{1}{\sqrt{6}} & \frac{2}{\sqrt{6}} & -\frac{1}{\sqrt{6}} \end{pmatrix}$.

4. $\begin{pmatrix} 0 & 1 & 0 \\ 0 & 0 & 1 \\ 1 & 0 & 0 \end{pmatrix}$.

5. $\begin{pmatrix} \frac{1}{2} & -\frac{1}{2} & \frac{1}{2} & -\frac{1}{2} \\ 0 & \frac{1}{\sqrt{2}} & \frac{1}{\sqrt{2}} & 0 \\ \frac{1}{\sqrt{2}} & 0 & 0 & \frac{1}{\sqrt{2}} \\ \frac{1}{2} & \frac{1}{2} & -\frac{1}{2} & -\frac{1}{2} \end{pmatrix}$.

6. $\begin{pmatrix} 0 & 1 & 0 & 0 \\ 0 & 0 & 1 & 0 \\ 0 & 0 & 0 & 1 \\ 1 & 0 & 0 & 0 \end{pmatrix}$.

7. If V is an n-dimensional Euclidean space, where n is an odd integer, and $t \in I(V)$, prove that either $t + 1$ or $t - 1$ is a singular l.t.

4. ISOMETRIES OF E_2

According to 7.18, each isometry t of the two-dimensional Euclidean space E_2 is of one of the following four types: (1) $t = 1 \oplus 1$; (2) $t = 1 \oplus -1$; (3) $t = -1 \oplus -1$; (4) t has matrix representation

$$A = \begin{pmatrix} r & s \\ -s & r \end{pmatrix}, \qquad \text{where} \quad r^2 + s^2 = 1 \quad \text{and} \quad s \neq 0.$$

If t is of the first type, then $\mathbf{u}_1 t = \mathbf{u}_1$ and $\mathbf{u}_2 t = \mathbf{u}_2$ for some orthonormal basis $(\mathbf{u}_1, \mathbf{u}_2)$ of E_2. However, in this case $\mathbf{x}t = \mathbf{x}$ for all $\mathbf{x} \in E_2$, and t is the identity l.t.

If $t = 1 \oplus -1$ relative to an orthonormal basis $(\mathbf{u}_1, \mathbf{u}_2)$ of E_2, then $\mathbf{u}_1 t = \mathbf{u}_1$ and $\mathbf{u}_2 t = -\mathbf{u}_2$. Hence, we have

$$(a\mathbf{u}_1 + b\mathbf{u}_2)t = a\mathbf{u}_1 - b\mathbf{u}_2 \qquad \text{for all } a, b \in \mathbb{R},$$

and t is a reflection of the plane in the axis along the vector $\mathbf{u}_1$ as shown in Fig. 7.3. This agrees with the fact that det $t = -1$.

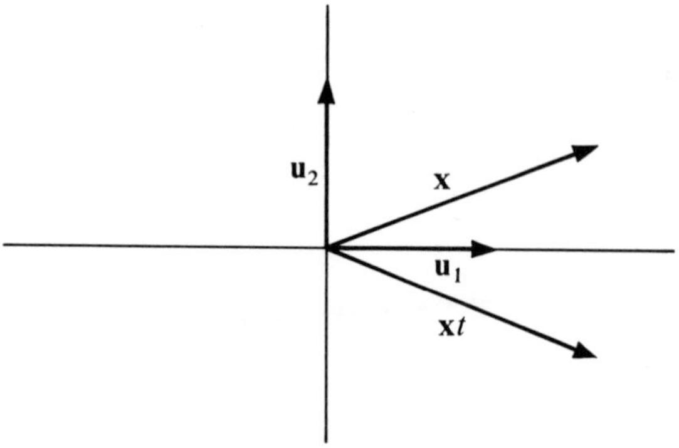

Figure 7.3

In the third case, $t = -1 \oplus -1$ relative to an orthonormal basis $(\mathbf{u}_1, \mathbf{u}_2)$ of E_2. Then, $\mathbf{u}_1 t = -\mathbf{u}_1$, $\mathbf{u}_2 t = -\mathbf{u}_2$, and

$$(a\mathbf{u}_1 + b\mathbf{u}_2)t = -(a\mathbf{u}_1 + b\mathbf{u}_2) \qquad \text{for all } a, b \in \mathbb{R}.$$

Geometrically, t is a rotation of the plane about the origin through an angle π as shown in Fig. 7.4. This agrees with the fact that det $t = 1$.

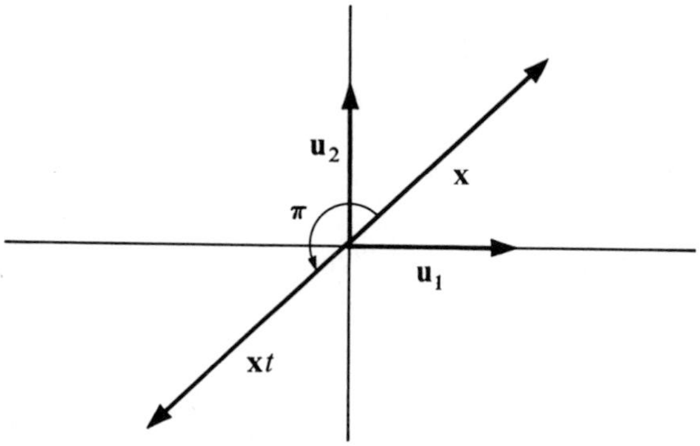

Figure 7.4

In the fourth case, t has matrix representation

$$A = \begin{pmatrix} r & s \\ -s & r \end{pmatrix}, \qquad r^2 + s^2 = 1, \qquad \text{and} \qquad s \neq 0,$$

relative to an orthonormal basis $(\mathbf{u}_1, \mathbf{u}_2)$ of E_2. Now, there exists a unique angle θ such that

$$r = \cos\theta, \qquad s = \sin\theta, \qquad 0 < \theta < 2\pi.$$

Hence, we have

$$\mathbf{u}_1 t = (\cos\theta)\mathbf{u}_1 + (\sin\theta)\mathbf{u}_2, \qquad \mathbf{u}_2 t = (-\sin\theta)\mathbf{u}_1 + (\cos\theta)\mathbf{u}_2.$$

Every vector $\mathbf{x} = a\mathbf{u}_1 + b\mathbf{u}_2$ in E_2 has the trigonometric form

$$\mathbf{x} = c(\cos\alpha)\mathbf{u}_1 + c(\sin\alpha)\mathbf{u}_2, \qquad \text{where} \quad c = |\mathbf{x}| = \sqrt{a^2 + b^2},$$

for a unique angle α, $0 \leq \alpha < 2\pi$, given by $\cos\alpha = a/c$, $\sin\alpha = b/c$. Then, we have

$$\begin{aligned} \mathbf{x}t &= c(\cos\alpha)(\mathbf{u}_1 t) + c(\sin\alpha)(\mathbf{u}_2 t) \\ &= c\cos\alpha[(\cos\theta)\mathbf{u}_1 + (\sin\theta)\mathbf{u}_2] + c\sin\alpha[(-\sin\theta)\mathbf{u}_1 + (\cos\theta)\mathbf{u}_2] \\ &= c(\cos\alpha\cos\theta - \sin\alpha\sin\theta)\mathbf{u}_1 + c(\cos\alpha\sin\theta + \sin\alpha\cos\theta)\mathbf{u}_2 \\ &= c\cos(\alpha + \theta)\mathbf{u}_1 + c\sin(\alpha + \theta)\mathbf{u}_2. \end{aligned}$$

This shows that geometrically t is a rotation of the plane about the origin through an angle θ as shown in Fig. 7.5. Since $s = \sin\theta \neq 0$, we find that

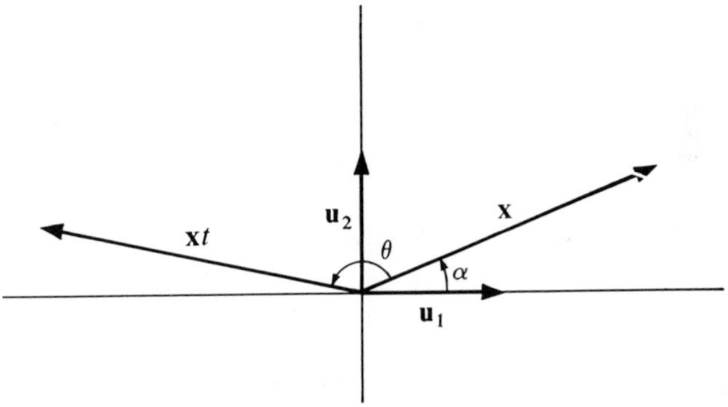

Figure 7.5

$\theta \neq \pi$. Thus, the fourth type is different from the third type, although both are rotations. Again, in this case, $\det t = 1$.

EXAMPLE 1: Let $t \in I(E_2)$ be represented by the orthogonal matrix

$$A = \begin{pmatrix} \frac{1}{2} & \frac{\sqrt{3}}{2} \\ \frac{\sqrt{3}}{2} & -\frac{1}{2} \end{pmatrix}$$

relative to the usual basis $(\mathbf{i}, \mathbf{j})$. Then the characteristic polynomial of A is

$$\det(\lambda I - A) = \lambda^2 - 1 = (\lambda - 1)(\lambda + 1).$$

We know from 6.12 that $E_2 = W_1 \oplus W_2$, where $W_1 = E_2(t+1) = \mathbb{R}\mathbf{i}(t+1)$ and $W_2 = E_2(t-1) = \mathbb{R}\mathbf{i}(t-1)$. We can easily find that $W_1 = \mathbb{R}\mathbf{x}_1$ and $W_2 = \mathbb{R}\mathbf{x}_2$, where

$$\mathbf{x}_1 = \frac{\sqrt{3}}{2}\mathbf{i} + \frac{1}{2}\mathbf{j}, \qquad \mathbf{x}_2 = -\frac{1}{2}\mathbf{i} + \frac{\sqrt{3}}{2}\mathbf{j},$$

and $(\mathbf{x}_1, \mathbf{x}_2)$ is an orthonormal basis of E_2. Since $\mathbf{x}_1 t = \mathbf{x}_1$ and $\mathbf{x}_2 t = -\mathbf{x}_2$, we see that $t = 1 \oplus -1$ relative to the basis $(\mathbf{x}_1, \mathbf{x}_2)$. The basis $(\mathbf{x}_1, \mathbf{x}_2)$ is shown

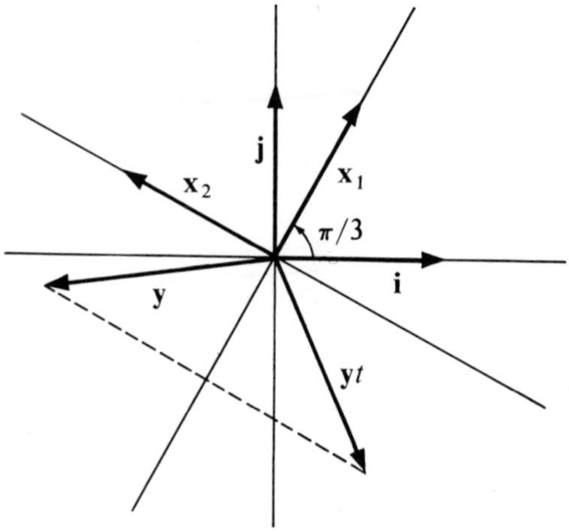

Figure 7.6

in Fig. 7.6. By the second type above, t is a reflection in the axis along the vector $\mathbf{x}_1$.

EXAMPLE 2: Let $t \in I(E_2)$ be represented by the orthogonal matrix

$$A = \frac{1}{\sqrt{2}}\begin{pmatrix} 1 & 1 \\ -1 & 1 \end{pmatrix}$$

relative to the basis $(\mathbf{i}, \mathbf{j})$. The characteristic polynomial of A is

$$\det(\lambda I - A) = \lambda^2 - \sqrt{2}\,\lambda + 1.$$

Since $\lambda^2 - \sqrt{2}\,\lambda + 1$ is prime, t is a rotation of the fourth type. By our remarks above, we can see that $1/\sqrt{2} = \cos\theta = \sin\theta$, and $\theta = \pi/4$. Thus, t is a rotation of the plane about the origin through an angle $\pi/4$.

EXERCISES

Tell which of the following $t \in L(E_2)$ are isometries. If t is an isometry, describe it geometrically.

1. $\mathbf{i}t = \dfrac{1}{\sqrt{2}}(\mathbf{i} + \mathbf{j}),\ \mathbf{j}t = \dfrac{1}{\sqrt{2}}(\mathbf{i} - \mathbf{j})$.
2. $\mathbf{i}t = \dfrac{1}{\sqrt{2}}(\mathbf{i} - \mathbf{j}),\ \mathbf{j}t = \dfrac{1}{\sqrt{5}}(2\mathbf{i} + \mathbf{j})$.
3. $\mathbf{i}t = \frac{1}{2}(-\sqrt{3}\,\mathbf{i} + \mathbf{j}),\ \mathbf{j}t = \frac{1}{2}(\mathbf{i} + \sqrt{3}\,\mathbf{j})$.
4. $\mathbf{i}t = \mathbf{j},\ \mathbf{j}t = -\mathbf{i}$.
5. $\mathbf{i}t = 2\mathbf{i} - 3\mathbf{j},\ \mathbf{j}t = 3\mathbf{i} + 2\mathbf{j}$.
6. $\mathbf{i}t = \frac{1}{5}(3\mathbf{i} + 4\mathbf{j}),\ \mathbf{j}t = \frac{1}{5}(4\mathbf{i} - 3\mathbf{j})$.
7. $\mathbf{i}t = \dfrac{1}{\sqrt{10}}(3\mathbf{i} - \mathbf{j}),\ \mathbf{j}t = \dfrac{1}{\sqrt{10}}(-3\mathbf{i} + \mathbf{j})$.
8. $\mathbf{i}t = \dfrac{1}{\sqrt{2}}(-\mathbf{i} - \mathbf{j}),\ \mathbf{j}t = \dfrac{1}{\sqrt{2}}(\mathbf{i} - \mathbf{j})$.

5. ISOMETRIES OF E_3

The isometries of E_3 are somewhat more complicated than those of E_2. According to 7.18, an isometry t of E_3 is of one of the following six types. In describing these types, we shall assume for simplicity that the orthonormal basis with respect to which each is described is the usual basis $(\mathbf{i}, \mathbf{j}, \mathbf{k})$.

Type 1. $t = 1 \oplus 1 \oplus 1$. Then $\mathbf{v}t = \mathbf{v}$, for all $\mathbf{v} \in E_3$, and t is the identity l.t.

Type 2. $t = 1 \oplus 1 \oplus -1$. Then $\det t = -1$, and t is a reflection. If $\mathbf{v} = a\mathbf{i} + b\mathbf{j} + c\mathbf{k}$ for some $a, b, c \in \mathbb{R}$, then $\mathbf{v}t = a\mathbf{i} + b\mathbf{j} - c\mathbf{k}$. Geometrically, t is a reflection of space in the xy-plane, as indicated in Fig. 7.7.

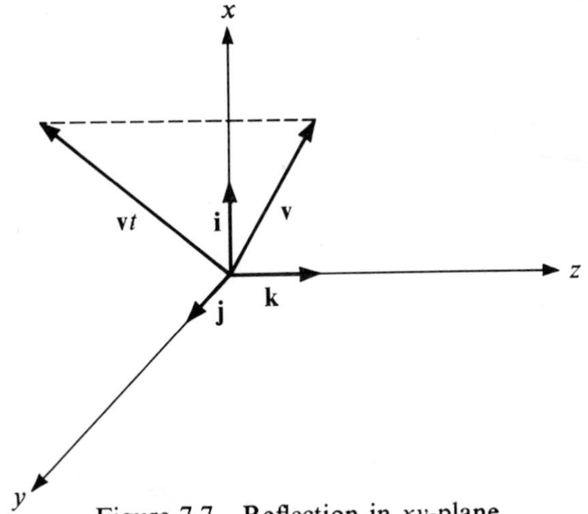

Figure 7.7 Reflection in xy-plane.

Type 3. $t = 1 \oplus -1 \oplus -1$. Since $\det t = 1$, t is a rotation. If $\mathbf{v} = a\mathbf{i} + b\mathbf{j} + c\mathbf{k}$ for some $a, b, c \in \mathbb{R}$, then $\mathbf{v}t = a\mathbf{i} - b\mathbf{j} - c\mathbf{k}$. Thus, t is a rotation of space about the x-axis through an angle π, as shown in Fig. 7.8.

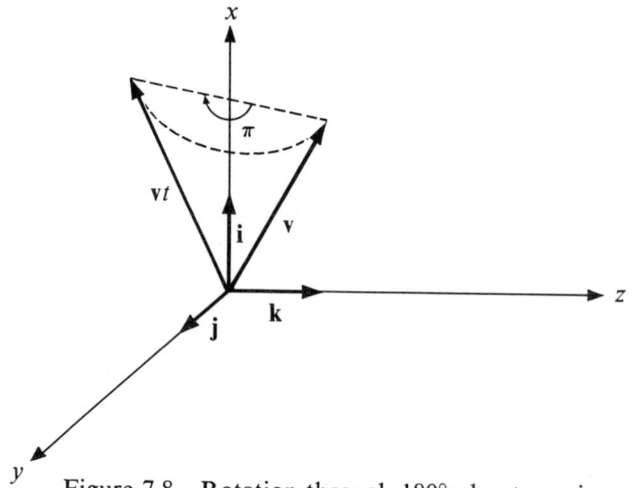

Figure 7.8 Rotation through 180° about x-axis.

Type 4. $t = -1 \oplus -1 \oplus -1$. In this case, $\det t = -1$, and t is a reflection. Clearly, $\mathbf{v}t = -\mathbf{v}$ for every $\mathbf{v} \in E_3$. Therefore, t is a reflection of space through the origin, as indicated in Fig. 7.9.

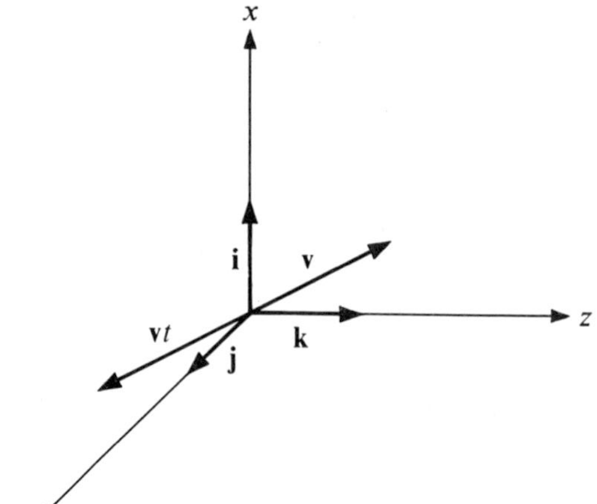

Figure 7.9 Reflection in origin.

Type 5. $t = 1 \oplus t'$, where t' has matrix

$$A = \begin{pmatrix} r & s \\ -s & r \end{pmatrix}, \qquad r^2 + s^2 = 1, \qquad s \neq 0,$$

relative to the basis $(\mathbf{j}, \mathbf{k})$. Since $\det t = 1 \cdot \det t' = 1$, t is a rotation. There is a unique angle θ, such that

$$r = \cos\theta, \qquad s = \sin\theta, \qquad 0 < \theta < 2\pi, \qquad \theta \neq \pi.$$

Hence, t is a rotation of space about the x-axis through an angle θ, as indicated in Fig. 7.10.

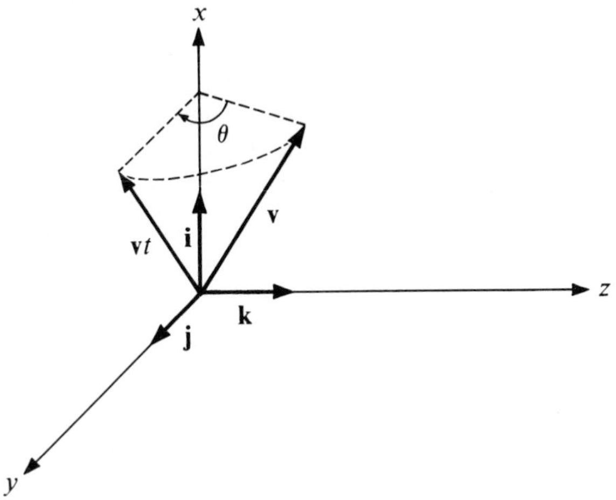

Figure 7.10 Rotation through θ about x-axis.

Type 6. $t = -1 \oplus t'$, where t' is as defined above. Evidently, $\det t = -1$, and t is a reflection. To visualize t, let $t_1 = -1 \oplus 1 \oplus 1$ and $t_2 = 1 \oplus t'$. Then, we have

$$t = t_1 t_2,$$

and t is the product of a reflection in the yz-plane and a rotation about the x-axis. Thus, a reflection in the yz-plane is followed by a rotation about the x-axis (or vice versa).

EXAMPLE: If $t \in I(E_3)$ is represented by the orthogonal matrix

$$A = \begin{pmatrix} \frac{1}{\sqrt{2}} & \frac{1}{\sqrt{2}} & 0 \\ -\frac{1}{2} & \frac{1}{2} & \frac{-1}{\sqrt{2}} \\ -\frac{1}{2} & \frac{1}{2} & \frac{1}{\sqrt{2}} \end{pmatrix}$$

relative to the basis (**i**, **j**, **k**), then we have

$$\det(\lambda I - A) = \lambda^3 - (\tfrac{1}{2} + \sqrt{2})\lambda^2 + (\tfrac{1}{2} + \sqrt{2})\lambda - 1$$
$$= (\lambda - 1)(\lambda^2 + (\tfrac{1}{2} - \sqrt{2})\lambda + 1).$$

Hence, by 6.12, we have $E_3 = W_1 \oplus W_2$, where

$$W_1 = E_3[t^2 + (\tfrac{1}{2} - \sqrt{2})t + 1], \qquad W_2 = E_3(t - 1).$$

We now compute

$$W_1 = \mathbb{R}[\mathbf{i} + (\sqrt{2} - 1)\mathbf{j} - \mathbf{k}],$$
$$W_2 = \mathbb{R}[(\sqrt{2} - 1)\mathbf{i} - \mathbf{j}] + \mathbb{R}[\mathbf{i} + \mathbf{j} + \sqrt{2}\mathbf{k}].$$

Thus, $t = 1 \oplus t'$, where $1 = t \mid W_1$ and $t' = t \mid W_2$. The minimal polynomial of t' is the prime $\lambda^2 + (\frac{1}{2} - \sqrt{2})\lambda + 1$, and therefore t' is a rotation. Clearly, t is of Type 5. Hence, t is a rotation about the axis containing the vector $\mathbf{i} + (\sqrt{2} - 1)\mathbf{j} - \mathbf{k}$ through an angle θ. We shall not compute θ but point out that this can be done by finding the matrix representation of t' relative to an orthonormal basis of W_2.

EXERCISES

Tell which of the following $t \in L(E_3)$ are isometries. If t is an isometry, describe it geometrically.

1. $\mathbf{i}t = \mathbf{j}$, $\mathbf{j}t = \mathbf{i}$, $\mathbf{k}t = \mathbf{k}$.
2. $\mathbf{i}t = \mathbf{j}$, $\mathbf{j}t = \mathbf{k}$, $\mathbf{k}t = \mathbf{i}$.
3. $\mathbf{i}t = \dfrac{\sqrt{2}}{2}(\mathbf{i} + \mathbf{j})$, $\mathbf{j}t = \dfrac{\sqrt{2}}{2}(\mathbf{j} + \mathbf{k})$, $\mathbf{k}t = \dfrac{\sqrt{2}}{2}(\mathbf{i} + \mathbf{k})$.
4. $\mathbf{i}t = \dfrac{1}{3}(2\mathbf{i} - \mathbf{j} + 2\mathbf{k})$, $\mathbf{j}t = \dfrac{\sqrt{5}}{5}(\mathbf{i} + 2\mathbf{j})$, $\mathbf{k}t = \dfrac{\sqrt{5}}{5}(2\mathbf{j} + \mathbf{k})$.
5. $\mathbf{i}t = \dfrac{1}{3}(2\mathbf{i} - \mathbf{j} + 2\mathbf{k})$, $\mathbf{j}t = \dfrac{\sqrt{5}}{5}(\mathbf{i} + 2\mathbf{j})$, $\mathbf{k}t = \dfrac{\sqrt{5}}{15}(-4\mathbf{i} + 2\mathbf{j} + 5\mathbf{k})$.
6. $\mathbf{i}t = \dfrac{\sqrt{2}}{2}(\mathbf{i} - \mathbf{k})$, $\mathbf{j}t = \dfrac{\sqrt{2}}{2}(\mathbf{i} + \mathbf{k})$, $\mathbf{k}t = \mathbf{j}$.
7. $\mathbf{i}t = \frac{1}{3}(-\mathbf{i} + 2\mathbf{j} + 2\mathbf{k})$, $\mathbf{j}t = \frac{1}{3}(2\mathbf{i} - \mathbf{j} + 2\mathbf{k})$, $\mathbf{k}t = \frac{1}{3}(2\mathbf{i} + 2\mathbf{j} - \mathbf{k})$.
8. $\mathbf{i}t = \frac{1}{3}(\mathbf{i} - 2\mathbf{j} - 2\mathbf{k})$, $\mathbf{j}t = \frac{1}{3}(-2\mathbf{i} + \mathbf{j} - 2\mathbf{k})$, $\mathbf{k}t = \frac{1}{3}(2\mathbf{i} + 2\mathbf{j} - \mathbf{k})$.

6. SYMMETRIC LINEAR TRANSFORMATIONS

Besides the isometry, there is another important type of linear transformation as defined below.

7.19. DEFINITION OF A SYMMETRIC LINEAR TRANSFORMATION. A linear transformation t of a Euclidean space V is called symmetric iff

$$\mathbf{x}t \cdot \mathbf{y} = \mathbf{x} \cdot \mathbf{y}t \qquad \text{for all } \mathbf{x}, \mathbf{y} \in V.$$

Let $t \in L(V)$ be symmetric, $(\mathbf{u}_1, \mathbf{u}_2, \ldots, \mathbf{u}_n)$ be an orthonormal basis of V, and $A = (a_{ij})$ be the matrix representing t relative to this basis:

$$\mathbf{u}_i t = \sum_{k=1}^{n} a_{ik}\mathbf{u}_k, \qquad i = 1, 2, \ldots, n.$$

Clearly, $\mathbf{u}_i t \cdot \mathbf{u}_j = a_{ij}$, and

$$\mathbf{u}_i \cdot \mathbf{u}_j t = \mathbf{u}_i \cdot \sum_{k=1}^{n} a_{jk}\mathbf{u}_k = a_{ji}.$$

Thus, we have

$$a_{ij} = a_{ji}, \qquad i, j = 1, 2, \ldots, n,$$

and A is equal to its transpose A^T:

7.20 $$A = A^T.$$

A matrix having property 7.20 is called a *symmetric matrix*. For example,

$$\begin{pmatrix} 2 & -3 & 4 \\ -3 & 5 & 7 \\ 4 & 7 & 0 \end{pmatrix}$$

is a symmetric 3×3 matrix over $\mathbb{R}$. Symmetric matrices and symmetric linear transformations are related as follows.

7.21. THEOREM. A linear transformation t of a Euclidean space V is symmetric iff the matrix representing t relative to an orthonormal basis is symmetric.

Proof: We have already proved that if t is symmetric, then the matrix representing t is also symmetric. So let us assume that $t \in L(V)$ is represented by a symmetric matrix $A = (a_{ij})$ relative to an orthonormal basis $(\mathbf{u}_1, \mathbf{u}_2, \ldots, \mathbf{u}_n)$ of V. Then, as we showed above, $\mathbf{u}_i t \cdot \mathbf{u}_j = a_{ij} = a_{ji} = \mathbf{u}_i \cdot \mathbf{u}_j t$ for all i and j. Hence, for any $\mathbf{x} = \sum_{i=1}^{n} c_i\mathbf{u}_i$, $\mathbf{y} = \sum_{j=1}^{n} d_j\mathbf{y}_j$ in V, we have

$$\mathbf{x}t \cdot \mathbf{y} = \sum_{i=1}^{n} c_i(\mathbf{u}_i t) \cdot \sum_{j=1}^{n} d_j\mathbf{u}_j = \sum_{i=1}^{n}\sum_{j=1}^{n} c_i d_j(\mathbf{u}_i t) \cdot \mathbf{u}_j$$

$$= \sum_{i=1}^{n}\sum_{j=1}^{n} c_i d_j \mathbf{u}_i \cdot (\mathbf{u}_j t) = \mathbf{x} \cdot \mathbf{y}t.$$

Therefore, t is symmetric. This proves 7.21.

If W is a t-invariant subspace of V and $t \in L(V)$ is symmetric, then $W^\perp$ is also a t-invariant subspace of V. For, if $\mathbf{x} \in W$ and $\mathbf{y} \in W^\perp$, then $\mathbf{x}t$ is also in W and $\mathbf{x}t \cdot \mathbf{y} = 0$. Hence, $\mathbf{x} \cdot \mathbf{y}t = \mathbf{x}t \cdot \mathbf{y} = 0$, and $\mathbf{y}t \in W^\perp$. Thus, $W^\perp t \subset W^\perp$, and $W^\perp$ is t-invariant. This fact allows us to show that for each symmetric $t \in L(V)$, there exist irreducible t-invariant subspaces $W_1, W_2, \ldots, W_m$ of V, each of dimension 1 or 2, such that

$$V = W_1 \oplus W_2 \oplus \cdots \oplus W_m.$$

The proof of this result is the same as that for an isometry in 7.16.

Actually, there are no two-dimensional irreducible t-invariant subspaces of V if t is symmetric. To prove this, assume on the contrary that W is a two-dimensional irreducible t-invariant subspace of V. If $t' = t \mid W$, then, evidently, t' is a symmetric l.t. of W. The minimal polynomial $h(\lambda)$ of t' must be a prime polynomial of degree 2. We can get an idea of the form of $h(\lambda)$ by considering a matrix representation A of t relative to an orthonormal basis of W. By 7.21, A is symmetric; that is,

$$A = \begin{pmatrix} a & b \\ b & c \end{pmatrix}$$

for some $a, b, c \in \mathbb{R}$. Since the characteristic polynomial of A is of degree 2 and has $h(\lambda)$ as a factor (6.16), it must be $h(\lambda)$:

$$h(\lambda) = \det(\lambda I - A) = \lambda^2 - (a + c)\lambda + (ac - b^2).$$

However, this is not possible because the discriminant of $\det(\lambda I - A)$ is the nonnegative number $(a + c)^2 - 4(ac - b^2)$, or $(a - c)^2 + 4b^2$, and therefore $\det(\lambda I - A)$ is not a prime polynomial. Consequently, V has no two-dimensional irreducible t-invariant subspaces.

We conclude that the irreducible t-invariant subspaces of V are all one-dimensional. Hence, the following analogue of 7.18 holds.

7.22. THEOREM. If V is an n-dimensional Euclidean space and t is a symmetric linear transformation of V, then there exist one-dimensional t-invariant subspaces $W_1, W_2, \ldots, W_n$ of V, such that

$$V = W_1 \oplus W_2 \oplus \cdots \oplus W_n.$$

If we let

$$W_i = \mathbb{R}\mathbf{x}_i, \qquad |\mathbf{x}_i| = 1, i = 1, 2, \ldots, n,$$

in 7.22, then $\mathbf{x}_i t = d_i \mathbf{x}_i$ for some $d_i \in \mathbb{R}$, and t is represented by the matrix

$$D = (d_1) \oplus (d_2) \oplus \cdots \oplus (d_n)$$

relative to the orthonormal basis $(\mathbf{x}_1, \mathbf{x}_2, \ldots, \mathbf{x}_n)$ of V. Thus, the d_i are the characteristic values of t, and

$$\det(\lambda I - D) = (\lambda - d_1)(\lambda - d_2) \cdots (\lambda - d_n)$$

is the characteristic polynomial of t. Some of the d_i might be positive numbers, some negative, and some zero. The number r of nonzero d_i clearly is the *rank* of D, and hence also of t. The number k of positive d_i is often called the *index* of t.

Given any symmetric $A \in \mathbb{R}(n)$, we know by 7.21 that any $t \in L(\mathbb{R}^n)$ which is represented by A relative to an orthonormal basis $(\mathbf{u}_1, \mathbf{u}_2, \ldots, \mathbf{u}_n)$ of $\mathbb{R}^n$ is symmetric. In turn, t is represented by a diagonal matrix D relative to some orthonormal basis $(\mathbf{x}_1, \mathbf{x}_2, \ldots, \mathbf{x}_n)$ of $\mathbb{R}^n$ by 7.22. If $\mathbb{R}^n \xrightarrow{s} \mathbb{R}^n$ is the isometry defined by $\mathbf{x}_i s = \mathbf{u}_i$, $i = 1, 2, \ldots, n$, and if s is represented by the matrix P relative to the $\mathbf{x}$-basis, then P is an orthogonal matrix by 7.13. By the usual argument, $D = P^{-1}AP$, or, since $P^{-1} = P^T$, we have

$$D = P^T AP.$$

Two matrices A and B in $\mathbb{R}(n)$ are called *orthogonally similar* iff $B = P^T AP$ for some orthogonal matrix P. Our remarks above have proved the following result.

7.23. THEOREM. Every symmetric matrix A of $\mathbb{R}(n)$ is orthogonally similar to a diagonal matrix.

EXAMPLE 1: Let us find the diagonal matrix which is similar to the symmetric matrix

$$A = \begin{pmatrix} -1 & 3 \\ 3 & 7 \end{pmatrix}.$$

First, we see that the characteristic polynomial of A is

$$\det(\lambda I - A) = \lambda^2 - 6\lambda - 16 = (\lambda - 8)(\lambda + 2).$$

Hence, the characteristic values of A are 8 and -2, and A is similar to the diagonal matrix

$$D = \begin{pmatrix} -2 & 0 \\ 0 & 8 \end{pmatrix}.$$

Thus, the rank of A is 2 and the index of A is 1.

To find the orthogonal matrix P such that $D = P^T AP$, we let t be a l.t. of $\mathbb{R}^2$ which is represented by A relative to the usual orthonormal basis $\mathbf{u}_1 = (1, 0)$, $\mathbf{u}_2 = (0, 1)$ of $\mathbb{R}^2$. Now, $\mathbb{R}^2 = W_1 \oplus W_2$, where

$$W_1 = \mathbb{R}^2(t - 8) = \mathbb{R}(3\mathbf{u}_1 - \mathbf{u}_2), \quad W_2 = \mathbb{R}^2(t + 2) = \mathbb{R}(\mathbf{u}_1 + 3\mathbf{u}_2).$$

If we let

$$\mathbf{x}_1 = a(3\mathbf{u}_1 - \mathbf{u}_2), \qquad \mathbf{x}_2 = a(\mathbf{u}_1 + 3\mathbf{u}_2), \qquad \text{where } a = \frac{1}{\sqrt{10}},$$

then $W_1 = \mathbb{R}\mathbf{x}_1$, $W_2 = \mathbb{R}\mathbf{x}_2$, and $(\mathbf{x}_1, \mathbf{x}_2)$ is an orthonormal basis of $\mathbb{R}_2$. As in the proof of 7.23, we have

$$P = \begin{pmatrix} 3a & a \\ -a & 3a \end{pmatrix}, \qquad \text{where} \quad a = \frac{1}{\sqrt{10}}.$$

EXAMPLE 2: To find the diagonal matrix which is similar to the symmetric matrix

$$A = \begin{pmatrix} -2 & 1 & 0 \\ 1 & 0 & -1 \\ 0 & -1 & 2 \end{pmatrix},$$

we first find the characteristic polynomial of A:

$$\det(\lambda I - A) = \lambda^3 - 6\lambda = \lambda(\lambda - \sqrt{6})(\lambda + \sqrt{6}).$$

Hence, the characteristic values of A are 0, $\sqrt{6}$, and $-\sqrt{6}$, and A is similar to the diagonal matrix

$$D = \begin{pmatrix} 0 & 0 & 0 \\ 0 & \sqrt{6} & 0 \\ 0 & 0 & -\sqrt{6} \end{pmatrix}.$$

Evidently, the rank of A is 2 and the index of A is 1.

To find the orthogonal matrix P such that $P^TAP = D$, let $t \in L(\mathbb{R}^3)$ be represented by A relative to the usual orthonormal basis $(\mathbf{u}_1, \mathbf{u}_2, \mathbf{u}_3)$ of $\mathbb{R}^3$. Then $\mathbb{R}^3 = W_1 \oplus W_2 \oplus W_3$, where

$$W_1 = \mathbb{R}^3(t^2 - 6) = \mathbb{R}(\mathbf{u}_1 + 2\mathbf{u}_2 + \mathbf{u}_3),$$

$$W_2 = \mathbb{R}^3(t^2 + \sqrt{6}t) = \mathbb{R}[\mathbf{u}_1 + (2 + \sqrt{6})\mathbf{u}_2 - (5 + 2\sqrt{6})\mathbf{u}_3],$$

$$W_3 = \mathbb{R}^3(t^2 - \sqrt{6}t) = \mathbb{R}[(5 + 2\sqrt{6})\mathbf{u}_1 - (2 + \sqrt{6})\mathbf{u}_2 - \mathbf{u}_3].$$

By properly normalizing these vectors, we find that

$$P = \begin{pmatrix} a & b & c \\ 2a & d & -d \\ a & -c & -b \end{pmatrix},$$

where

$$A = \frac{1}{\sqrt{6}}, \quad b = \frac{1}{(2\sqrt{3}\sqrt{5 + 2\sqrt{6}})}, \quad c = (5 + 2\sqrt{6})b, \quad d = (2 + \sqrt{6})b.$$

EXERCISES

For each symmetric matrix A in Exercises 1 through 6, find the diagonal matrix D to which A is similar, and also find the orthogonal matrix P such that $D = P^TAP$.

1. $\begin{pmatrix} 3 & -1 \\ -1 & 3 \end{pmatrix}$.

2. $\begin{pmatrix} -1 & 8 \\ 8 & 11 \end{pmatrix}$.

3. $\begin{pmatrix} 1 & 1 \\ 1 & 1 \end{pmatrix}$.

4. $\frac{1}{9}\begin{pmatrix} -7 & 2 & 10 \\ 2 & 2 & -8 \\ 10 & -8 & -4 \end{pmatrix}$.

5. $\frac{1}{3}\begin{pmatrix} 1 & -2 & -4 \\ -2 & -2 & 2 \\ -4 & 2 & 1 \end{pmatrix}$.

6. $\begin{pmatrix} 0 & 1 & 0 \\ 1 & 0 & 1 \\ 0 & 1 & 0 \end{pmatrix}$.

7. Prove that for every $A \in \mathbb{R}(n)$, the matrix $B = A^T A$ is symmetric. Illustrate with some matrices from $\mathbb{R}(2)$ and $\mathbb{R}(3)$.
8. If $A \in \mathbb{R}(n)$ is nonsingular, prove that the symmetric matrix $B = A^T A$ has index n.
9. If B is a symmetric $n \times n$ matrix, such that $\mathrm{r}(B)$ equals the index of B, prove that $B = A^T A$ for some $A \in \mathbb{R}(n)$. [*Hint:* If the diagonal elements of a diagonal matrix D are nonnegative, then $D = C^2$ for some diagonal matrix C.]
10. Which isometries are symmetric? Give some examples. Describe all symmetric isometries of E_2 and E_3.
11. Prove that 0 is the only nilpotent symmetric l.t.

7. BILINEAR AND QUADRATIC FORMS

An expression such as

$$x_1^2 + 2x_1x_2 + x_1x_3 - 4x_2^2 - 6x_2x_3 + 7x_3^2$$

is called a quadratic form in the unknowns x_1, x_2, and x_3. This expression can be written in the symmetric form

$$x_1^2 + x_1x_2 + \tfrac{1}{2}x_1x_3 + x_2x_1 - 4x_2^2 - 3x_2x_3 + \tfrac{1}{2}x_3x_1 - 3x_3x_2 + 7x_3^2.$$

If we let A be the 3×3 symmetric matrix

$$A = \begin{pmatrix} 1 & 1 & \frac{1}{2} \\ 1 & -4 & -3 \\ \frac{1}{2} & -3 & 7 \end{pmatrix}$$

and X be the 1×3 matrix

$$X = \quad (x_1\ x_2\ x_3),$$

then the given quadratic form has the matrix form

$$XAX^T.$$

More generally, the expression

7.24 $$\sum_{i=1}^{n}\sum_{j=1}^{n} a_{ij}x_ix_j$$

is called a *quadratic form* in the unknowns $x_1, x_2, \ldots, x_n$, and $A = (a_{ij}) \in \mathbb{R}(n)$ is called the *matrix* of the form. Since every quadratic form can be written symmetrically, as illustrated above, we shall always assume that the matrix A of a quadratic form is symmetric. If we let

$$X = (x_1\, x_2 \cdots x_n),$$

an $n \times 1$ matrix, then X^T is a $1 \times n$ matrix, and 7.24 has the matrix form

7.25 $$XAX^T.$$

Instead of starting with n unknowns as above, we might start with the $2n$ unknowns $x_1, x_2, \ldots, x_n, y_1, y_2, \ldots, y_n$ and the $n \times n$ symmetric matrix $A = (a_{ij})$. Then, the expression

7.26 $$\sum_{i=1}^{n}\sum_{j=1}^{n} a_{ij}x_iy_j$$

is called a *symmetric bilinear form* in $2n$ unknowns. If we let

$$X = (x_1\, x_2 \cdots x_n), \qquad Y = (y_1\, y_2 \cdots y_n),$$

then 7.26 has the matrix form

7.27 $$XAY^T.$$

It is sometimes desirable to make a linear transformation of the unknowns in a bilinear or quadratic form, that is, to replace X by $X' = (x_1'\, x_2' \cdots x_n')$ and Y by $Y' = (y_1'\, y_2' \cdots y_n')$, where

$$X' = XC, \qquad Y' = YC$$

for a nonsingular matrix C. If we let $P = C^{-1}$, then $X = X'P$, $Y^T = Y'^T$, and

$$XAY^T = X'(PAP^T)Y'^T.$$

Since the matrix PAP^T is also symmetric, $X'(PAP^T)Y'^T$ is a bilinear form in the $2n$ unknowns $x_1', \ldots, x_n', y_1', \ldots, y_n'$. In a similar way, we can show that

$$XAX^T = X'(PAP^T)X'^T,$$

and $X'(PAP^T)X'^T$ is a quadratic form in the n unknowns $x_1', x_2', \ldots, x_n'$.

By 7.23, every symmetric matrix A is orthogonally similar to a diagonal matrix $D = (d_1) \oplus (d_2) \oplus \cdots \oplus (d_n)$: $D = PAP^T$ for some orthogonal matrix P. This proves the following result.

7.28. THEOREM. For every $n \times n$ symmetric matrix A, there exists a similar diagonal matrix $D = (d_1) \oplus (d_2) \oplus \cdots \oplus (d_n)$, and an orthogonal matrix $P = (p_{ij})$ such that $D = PAP^T$. If we let

$$x'_i = \sum_{j=1}^{n} p_{ij}x_j, \qquad y'_i = \sum_{j=1}^{n} p_{ij}y_j, \qquad i = 1, 2, \ldots, n,$$

then the symmetric bilinear form XAY^T is given by

$$XAY^T = \sum_{i=1}^{n} d_i x'_i y'_i,$$

and the quadratic form XAX^T by

$$XAX^T = \sum_{i=1}^{n} d_i x'^2_i.$$

We call $\sum d_i x'_i y'_i$ in 7.28 a *reduced form* of XAY^T and $\sum d_i x'^2_i$ a *reduced form* of XAX^T. Since the d_i's are unique, being the roots of the characteristic polynomial of A, a reduced form is unique except for the order in which the terms occur.

If $r(A) = m$ and index $A = k$ in 7.28, then we can assume that the unknowns are arranged so that $d_i > 0$ if $1 \leq i \leq k$, $d_i < 0$ if $k < i \leq m$, and $d_i = 0$ if $i > m$. Then, we have

7.29 $$XAX^T = \sum_{i=1}^{k} d_i x'^2_i - \sum_{i=k+1}^{m} d'_i x'^2_i,$$

where $d'_i = -d_i$ if $k < i \leq m$.

EXAMPLE 1: The quadratic form

$$x_1^2 - 2x_1x_2 - 4x_1x_3 + x_2^2 + 4x_2x_3 - 2x_3^2$$

has symmetric form

$$x_1^2 - x_1x_2 - 2x_1x_3 - x_2x_1 + x_2^2 + 2x_2x_3 - 2x_3x_1 + 2x_2x_3 - 2x_3^2.$$

Thus, if we let $X = (x_1\ x_2\ x_3)$ and A be the symmetric matrix

$$A = \begin{pmatrix} 1 & -1 & -2 \\ -1 & 1 & 2 \\ -2 & 2 & -2 \end{pmatrix},$$

then we can write the quadratic form as

$$XAX^T.$$

The characteristic polynomial of A is easily seen to be

$$\det(\lambda I - A) = \lambda^3 - 12\lambda = \lambda(\lambda - 2\sqrt{3})(\lambda + 2\sqrt{3}).$$

Hence, the characteristic values of A are $2\sqrt{3}$, $-2\sqrt{3}$, and 0, and XAX^T has reduced form (7.29)

$$XAX^T = 2\sqrt{3}(x_1'^2 - x_2'^2).$$

We won't actually find the orthogonal matrix P such that $X' = XP^T$. This process is amply illustrated in Example 2, p. 186. We observe that $r(A) = 2$ and index $A = 1$.

If we give values to the unknowns in a quadratic form XAX^T, say we let $x_1 = c_1, x_2 = c_2, \ldots, x_n = c_n$, then we obtain a value of the quadratic form, CAC^T, where $C = (c_1c_2 \ldots c_n) \in \mathbb{R}(1, n)$. The trivial value 0 is obtained for XAX^T if we let $x_1 = 0, x_2 = 0, \ldots, x_n = 0$.

A quadratic form XAX^T is called *positive definite* iff $CAC^T > 0$ for every nonzero $C \in \mathbb{R}(1, n)$. If XAX^T is not positive definite, but $CAC^T \geq 0$ for every $C \in \mathbb{R}(1, n)$, then XAX^T is called *positive semidefinite*. We can easily decide whether a quadratic form is positive definite or semidefinite by looking at its reduced form. If XAX^T is as given in 7.29, and if $k < m$, then by letting $x_1' = 0, \ldots, x_k' = 0, x_{k+1}' = 1, x_{k+2}' = 0, \ldots, x_n' = 0$, we see that the resulting value of XAX^T is negative. Also, if $m < n$, then by letting $x_1' = 0, \ldots, x_m' = 0, x_{m+1}' = 1, x_{m+2}' = 0, \ldots, x_n' = 0$, we see that the resulting value of XAX^T is zero. If $k = m = n$, then all $d_i > 0$, and XAX^T has only positive values. We summarize these remarks below.

7.30. THEOREM. The quadratic form XAX^T is positive definite iff A is nonsingular and index $A = r(A)$. It is positive semidefinite iff A is singular and index $A = r(A)$.

EXAMPLE 2: The quadratic form

$$5x_1^2 - 3x_1x_2 - 3x_2x_1 + 5x_2^2$$

has symmetric matrix

$$A = \begin{pmatrix} 5 & -3 \\ -3 & 5 \end{pmatrix}.$$

The characteristic polynomial of A is given by

$$\det(\lambda I - A) = (\lambda - 8)(\lambda - 2).$$

Hence, the quadratic form XAX^T has reduced form

$$8x_1'^2 + 2x_2'^2$$

for a proper change of unknowns. Clearly, index $A = r(A) = 2$, and XAX^T is positive definite by 7.30.

EXERCISES

In each of the following exercises, find a reduced form for the given bilinear or quadratic form. Tell which quadratic forms are positive definite and which are positive semidefinite.

1. $x_1y_1 + x_1y_2 + x_2y_1$.
2. $3x_1^2 + 4x_1x_2$.
3. $x_1^2 - 2x_1x_2 + x_2^2$.
4. $x_1y_1 - 2x_1y_2 - 2x_2y_1 + 4x_2y_2$.
5. $2x_1^2 - 6x_1x_2 + 10x_2^2$.
6. $\frac{1}{3}(7x_1^2 - 4x_1x_3 + 5x_2^2 + 4x_2x_3 + 6x_3^2)$.
7. $2(x_1x_2 + x_2x_3)$.
8. $2(x_1x_2 - x_1x_3 + x_2x_3)$.

8. QUADRATIC EQUATIONS

We are all familiar with quadratic equations in two unknowns, such as

$$x^2 + y^2 - 4x + 7y = 1,$$

and

$$x^2 - xy + 3y^2 + x - y = 3.$$

In general, an equation of the form

7.31 $$\sum_{i=1}^{n}\sum_{j=1}^{n} a_{ij}x_ix_j + \sum_{i=1}^{n} b_ix_i = d$$

is called a *quadratic equation* in n unknowns $x_1, x_2, \ldots, x_n$. As usual, we assume that $A = (a_{ij})$ is a nonzero symmetric matrix. If we let $X = (x_1\ x_2\ \cdots\ x_n)$ and $B = (b_1\ b_2\ \cdots\ b_n)$, then 7.31 has the matrix form

7.32 $$XAX^T + BX^T = d.$$

A quadratic equation in n unknowns, such as 7.31, can be graphed in an n-dimensional Euclidean space V. All we need do is to select a set of coordinate axes of V, that is, an orthonormal basis $(\mathbf{u}_1, \mathbf{u}_2, \ldots, \mathbf{u}_n)$ of V. Then the *graph* S of 7.31 relative to this basis is defined by

$$S = \left\{ \sum_{k=1}^{n} c_k\mathbf{u}_k \in V \;\middle|\; \sum_{i=1}^{n}\sum_{j=1}^{n} a_{ij}c_ic_j + \sum_{i=1}^{n} b_ic_i = d \right\}.$$

If $(\mathbf{u}_1, \mathbf{u}_2, \ldots, \mathbf{u}_n)$ and $(\mathbf{v}_1, \mathbf{v}_2, \ldots, \mathbf{v}_n)$ are two orthonormal bases of V and $P = (P_{ij})$ is the orthogonal matrix which transforms the $\mathbf{u}$-basis into the $\mathbf{v}$-basis,

$$\mathbf{v}_i = \sum_{j=1}^{n} p_{ij}\mathbf{u}_j, \qquad i = 1, 2, \ldots, n,$$

$$\mathbf{u}_j = \sum_{i=1}^{n} p_{ij}\mathbf{v}_i, \qquad j = 1, 2, \ldots, n,$$

then the graph S_1 of the quadratic equation

(1) $$XAX^T + BX^T = d$$

relative to the **u**-basis is the same as the graph S_2 of the equation

(2) $$X(PAP^T)X^T + (BP^T)X^T = d$$

relative to the **v**-basis. To see this, let $\sum c_k\mathbf{u}_k \in S_1$ and $C = (c_1\, c_2 \cdots c_n) \in \mathbb{R}(1, n)$. Hence, we have

$$CAC^T + BC^T = d.$$

Now, we see that

$$\sum_{k=1}^{n} c_k\mathbf{u}_k = \sum_{l=1}^{n}\left(\sum_{k=1}^{n} c_k p_{kl}\right)\mathbf{v}_l = \sum_{l=1}^{n} c_l'\mathbf{v}_l,$$

where $C' = (c_1'\, c_2' \cdots c_n') = CP^T$. Since

$$C'(PAP^T)C'^T + (BP^T)C'^T = CP^TPAP^TPC^T + BP^TPC^T = CAC^T + BC^T = d,$$

we see that $\sum c_l'\mathbf{v}_l \in S_2$. Hence, $S_1 \subset S_2$. Similarly, it may be shown that $S_2 \subset S_1$. Thus, we find that $S_1 = S_2$ as stated above.

We can select the orthogonal matrix P in such a way that $PAP^T = D = (d_1) \oplus (d_2) \oplus \cdots \oplus (d_n)$, a diagonal matrix. Then, $X(PAP^T)X^T = d_1x_1^2 + d_2x_2^2 + \cdots + d_nx_n^2$, and the quadratic equation is in reduced form. This proves the following basic theorem.

7.33. PRINCIPAL-AXIS THEOREM. Let V be an n-dimensional Euclidean space and S be the graph of a quadratic equation relative to some orthonormal basis of V. Then, there exists an orthonormal basis $(\mathbf{v}_1, \mathbf{v}_2, \ldots, \mathbf{v}_n)$ of V, such that S is the graph of a reduced quadratic equation

$$\sum_{i=1}^{n} d_ix_i^2 + \sum_{i=1}^{n} b_ix_i = d$$

relative to the **v**-basis.

The new coordinate axes $\mathbf{v}_1, \mathbf{v}_2, \ldots, \mathbf{v}_n$ are the "principal axes" referred to in the title of the theorem.

EXAMPLE 1: Let us describe the graph of the quadratic equation

$$2x^2 + 6xy + 10y^2 = 11$$

in $\mathbb{R}^2$. If we let $X = (x\ y)$ and

$$A = \begin{pmatrix} 2 & 3 \\ 3 & 10 \end{pmatrix},$$

then the equation has the form $XAX^T = 11$. The characteristic polynomial of A is

$$\det(\lambda I - A) = (\lambda - 11)(\lambda - 1).$$

Hence, A is orthogonally similar to the diagonal matrix

$$D = \begin{pmatrix} 11 & 0 \\ 0 & 1 \end{pmatrix},$$

and the graph of the given equation is the same as that of the reduced equation

$$11x^2 + y^2 = 11$$

relative to some orthonormal basis $(\mathbf{v}_1, \mathbf{v}_2)$ of V. We recognize the graph to be an ellipse, as sketched in Fig. 7.11.

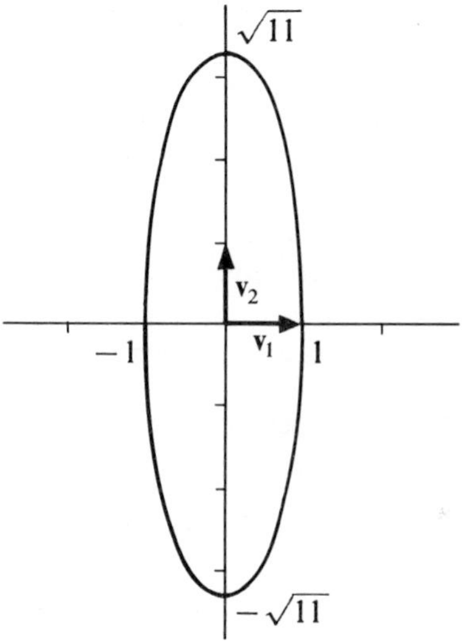

Figure 7.11 An ellipse.

EXAMPLE 2: Let S be the graph of the equation

$$9x^2 - 12xy + 4y^2 + 20x + 30y = 0$$

relative to the usual basis $(\mathbf{u}_1, \mathbf{u}_2)$ of $\mathbb{R}^2$. Thus, if we let

$$X = (x\ y), \qquad A = \begin{pmatrix} 9 & -6 \\ -6 & 4 \end{pmatrix}, \qquad B = (20\ 30),$$

the equation has the matrix form

$$XAX^T + BX^T = 0.$$

Now, we have

$$\det(\lambda I - A) = \lambda(\lambda - 13),$$

and therefore the characteristic values of A are 13 and 0. Hence, A is orthogonally similar to the diagonal matrix

$$D = \begin{pmatrix} 13 & 0 \\ 0 & 0 \end{pmatrix}.$$

To find the orthogonal matrix P such that $PAP^T = D$, let t be the l.t. of $\mathbb{R}^2$ represented by the matrix A relative to the basis $(\mathbf{u}_1, \mathbf{u}_2)$. We can easily show that $\mathbb{R}^2 t = \mathbb{R}(3\mathbf{u}_1 - 2\mathbf{u}_2)$ and $\mathbb{R}^2(t - 13) = \mathbb{R}(2\mathbf{u}_1 + 3\mathbf{u}_2)$. Thus, if

$$\mathbf{v}_1 = a(3\mathbf{u}_1 - 2\mathbf{u}_2), \qquad \mathbf{v}_2 = a(2\mathbf{u}_1 + 3\mathbf{u}_2), \qquad \text{where} \quad a = \frac{1}{\sqrt{13}},$$

then

$$\mathbb{R}^2 = \mathbb{R}\mathbf{v}_1 \oplus \mathbb{R}\mathbf{v}_2,$$

$\mathbf{v}_1$ has minimal polynomial $\lambda - 13$, $\mathbf{v}_2$ has minimal polynomial λ, and $\mathbf{v}_1$ and $\mathbf{v}_2$ are the principal axes of the graph. Hence, we have

$$P = \begin{pmatrix} 3a & -2a \\ 2a & 3a \end{pmatrix},$$

and S is the graph of the reduced equation $X(PAP^T)X^T + (BP^T)X^T = 0$, or

$$13x^2 + \frac{10}{\sqrt{13}}y = 0.$$

We recognize the graph to be a parabola.

EXAMPLE 3: Let S be the graph of the equation

$$x_1^2 + 4x_2x_3 + 3x_3^2 = 4$$

in $\mathbb{R}^3$. If we let $X = (x_1\ x_2\ x_3)$ and

$$A = \begin{pmatrix} 1 & 0 & 0 \\ 0 & 0 & 2 \\ 0 & 2 & 3 \end{pmatrix},$$

then the equation has matrix form

$$XAX^T = 4.$$

The symmetric matrix A has characteristic polynomial

$$\det(\lambda I - A) = (\lambda - 4)(\lambda - 1)(\lambda + 1).$$

Hence, the characteristic values of A are 4, 1, and -1, and A is orthogonally similar to

$$D = \begin{pmatrix} 4 & 0 & 0 \\ 0 & 1 & 0 \\ 0 & 0 & -1 \end{pmatrix}.$$

Therefore, S is also the graph of the reduced equation

$$4x_1^2 + x_2^2 - x_3^2 = 4$$

relative to some orthonormal basis of $\mathbb{R}^3$. Those who have studied quadric surfaces will recognize the graph of this equation to be a hyperboloid of one sheet.

EXERCISES

In each of Exercises 1 through 8, express the given equation in reduced form and identify its graph.

1. $xy = 1$.
2. $x^2 - 4xy + 4y^2 + 2\sqrt{5}x - \sqrt{5}y = 0$.
3. $3x^2 + 26\sqrt{3}xy - 23y^2 = 144$.
4. $29x^2 - 24xy + 36y^2 + 118x - 24y = 55$.
5. $x^2 - 4xy + y^2 = 4$.
6. $2x_1^2 + 4x_1x_3 + 4x_2^2 - 4x_2x_3 + 3x_3^2 = 3$.
7. $13x_1^2 + 8x_1x_2 + 4x_1x_3 + 13x_2^2 + 4x_2x_3 + 10x_3^2 = 36$.
8. $-x_1^2 + 4x_1x_3 + x_2^2 - 4x_2x_3 = 3$.
9. For $A, B \in \mathbb{R}(n)$, let us call A *congruent* to B iff there exists a nonsingular $P \in \mathbb{R}(n)$ such that $B = P^TAP$. Prove that congruence is an equivalence relation in $\mathbb{R}(n)$.
10. Prove that every symmetric matrix $A \in \mathbb{R}(n)$ is congruent to a diagonal matrix $B = (b_1) \oplus (b_2) \oplus \cdots \oplus (b_n)$, such that each b_i is either 0, 1, or -1. [*Hint:* A is orthogonally similar to a diagonal matrix $D = (d_1) \oplus (d_2) \oplus \cdots \oplus (d_n)$ by 7.23. Let C be the diagonal matrix $C = (c_1) \oplus (c_2) \oplus \cdots \oplus (c_n)$, such that $c_i = 1/\sqrt{d_i}$ if $d_i > 0$; $c_i = 1/\sqrt{-d_i}$ if $d_i < 0$; $c_i = 1$ if $d_i = 0$. What is the form of C^TDC?]
11. For every quadratic form XAX^T in n unknowns of rank m and index k, prove that there exists a change of variables $Y = XP$, P nonsingular, such that $XAX^T = y_1^2 + \cdots + y_k^2 - y_{k+1}^2 - \cdots - y_m^2$. (*Hint:* Use Exercise 10.)

Chapter 8

Elementary Divisors

1. IRREDUCIBLE SPACES

A vector space V over a field F is called *irreducible* relative to $t \in L(V)$ (or, t-irreducible) iff V cannot be expressed as a direct sum of two or more proper t-invariant subspaces. If the minimal polynomial $h(\lambda)$ of t has two or more distinct prime factors, then V is reducible by 6.12. Thus, before V can be irreducible, $h(\lambda)$ must be prime or a power of a prime. The following theorem characterizes irreducible spaces.

8.1. THEOREM. Let $t \in L(V)$ have minimal polynomial $p^m(\lambda)$, where $p(\lambda) \in F[\lambda]$ is a prime and $m \geq 1$. Then, V is irreducible relative to t iff $\deg p^m(\lambda) = \dim V$.

The proof of this theorem will occupy much of the present chapter. However, we can prove part of it immediately. Let $\dim V = n$. We know that $\deg p^m(\lambda) \leq n$ and also that $p^m(\lambda)$ is the minimal polynomial of some $\mathbf{x} \in V$ from our work in Chapter 5. Assume that

$$V = W_1 \oplus W_2$$

for some proper t-invariant subspaces W_1 and W_2. Then, $t = t_1 \oplus t_2$, where $t_i = t \mid W_i$. If $h_i(\lambda)$ is the minimal polynomial of t_i, then $h_i(\lambda)$ is a power of $p(\lambda)$, and $\deg h_i(\lambda) \leq \dim W_i$, $i = 1, 2$. Since $h_1(\lambda)$ and $h_2(\lambda)$ are powers of $p(\lambda)$, one is a factor of the other, say $h_1(\lambda)$ is a factor of $h_2(\lambda)$. To return to $\mathbf{x} \in V$, we can represent it in the form

$$\mathbf{x} = \mathbf{x}_1 + \mathbf{x}_2 \qquad \text{for some } \mathbf{x}_1 \in W_1,\ \mathbf{x}_2 \in W_2.$$

Evidently, $\mathbf{x}_1 h_1(t) = \mathbf{x}_2 h_2(t) = \mathbf{0}$, and therefore $\mathbf{x}_1 h_2(t) = \mathbf{x}_2 h_2(t) = \mathbf{0}$, since $h_1(\lambda)$ is a factor of $h_2(\lambda)$. Hence, we have

$$\mathbf{x} h_2(t) = \mathbf{x}_1 h_2(t) + \mathbf{x}_2 h_2(t) = \mathbf{0},$$

and the minimal polynomial of $\mathbf{x}$ is a factor of $h_2(\lambda)$. Therefore, $\deg p^m(\lambda) \leq \deg h_2(\lambda) \leq \dim W_2 < n$. Thus, we have proved that if V is reducible, then $\deg p^m(\lambda) < \dim V$, or, equivalently, that if $\deg p^m(\lambda) = \dim V$, then V is irreducible.

The proof that if V is irreducible then $\deg p^m(\lambda) = \dim V$ will be postponed until the next section. There we will prove that if $\deg p^m(\lambda) < \dim V$, then V is reducible.

If $t \in L(V)$ and W is a t-invariant subspace of V, then W is t-irreducible iff W is t'-irreducible, where $t' = t \mid W$. In view of 6.5 and 8.1, the irreducible t-invariant subspaces of V are the cyclic subspaces $W = \mathbf{x}F[t]$ for which the minimal polynomial of $\mathbf{x}$ is a power of a prime.

EXAMPLE: Let $t \in L(\mathbb{R}^3)$ be represented by the matrix

$$A = \begin{pmatrix} 1 & 0 & -1 \\ 1 & 1 & -1 \\ 0 & 0 & 1 \end{pmatrix}$$

relative to the usual basis $(\mathbf{u}_1, \mathbf{u}_2, \mathbf{u}_3)$ of $\mathbb{R}^3$. Then $\mathbf{u}_1$ has minimal polynomial $\lambda^2 - 2\lambda + 1$, and $\mathbf{u}_3$ has minimal polynomial $\lambda - 1$. Since $\mathbf{u}_2 t = \mathbf{u}_1 + \mathbf{u}_2 - \mathbf{u}_3$, $\mathbf{u}_2 t^2 = 2\mathbf{u}_1 + \mathbf{u}_2 - 3\mathbf{u}_3$, and $\mathbf{u}_2 t^3 = 3\mathbf{u}_1 + \mathbf{u}_2 - 6\mathbf{u}_3$, evidently $\mathbf{u}_2, \mathbf{u}_2 t, \mathbf{u}_2 t^2$ are l.i., whereas $\mathbf{u}_2, \mathbf{u}_2 t, \mathbf{u}_2 t^2, \mathbf{u}_2 t^3$ are l.d. Since $\mathbf{u}_2(t^3 - 3t^2 + 3t - 1) = \mathbf{0}$, $\mathbf{u}_2$ has minimal polynomial $\lambda^3 - 3\lambda^2 + 3\lambda - 1 = (\lambda - 1)^3$. Since $\deg (\lambda - 1)^3 = \dim \mathbb{R}^3 = 3$, $(\lambda - 1)^3$ must be the minimal polynomial of t also. Therefore, $\mathbb{R}^3$ is t-irreducible by 8.1. Thus, matrix A is similar to the Jordan matrix J of $(\lambda - 1)^3$:

$$J = \begin{pmatrix} 1 & 1 & 0 \\ 0 & 1 & 1 \\ 0 & 0 & 1 \end{pmatrix}.$$

EXERCISES

In each of Exercises 1 through 6, tell whether the given vector space V is irreducible relative to the given linear transformation t. If it is irreducible, find the Jordan matrix of t.

1. $V = \mathbb{R}^2$, $t \in L(V)$ defined by $\mathbf{u}_1 t = \mathbf{u}_2$, $\mathbf{u}_2 t = \mathbf{u}_1$.
2. $V = \mathbb{R}^2$, $t \in L(V)$ defined by $\mathbf{u}_1 t = \mathbf{u}_1 + 3\mathbf{u}_2$, $\mathbf{u}_2 t = -2\mathbf{u}_1 + 5\mathbf{u}_2$.
3. $V = \mathbb{R}^3$, $t \in L(V)$ defined by $\mathbf{u}_1 t = \mathbf{u}_2$, $\mathbf{u}_2 t = \mathbf{u}_3$, $\mathbf{u}_3 t = 0$.
4. $V = \mathbb{Q}^3$, $t \in L(V)$ defined by $\mathbf{u}_1 t = \mathbf{u}_1 - \mathbf{u}_3$, $\mathbf{u}_2 t = \mathbf{u}_2 + 2\mathbf{u}_3$, $\mathbf{u}_3 t = \mathbf{u}_3$.
5. $V = \mathbb{Q}^4$, $t \in L(V)$ defined by $\mathbf{u}_1 t = \mathbf{u}_2$, $\mathbf{u}_2 t = -\mathbf{u}_1 + \mathbf{u}_3$, $\mathbf{u}_3 t = \mathbf{u}_4$, $\mathbf{u}_4 t = -\mathbf{u}_3$.
6. $V = \mathbb{Q}^4$, $t \in L(V)$ defined by $\mathbf{u}_1 t = -2\mathbf{u}_1 + \mathbf{u}_2$, $\mathbf{u}_2 t = -2\mathbf{u}_2 + \mathbf{u}_3$, $\mathbf{u}_3 t = -2\mathbf{u}_3 + \mathbf{u}_4$, $\mathbf{u}_4 t = -2\mathbf{u}_4$.

7. If $t \in L(V)$ has minimal polynomial $p(\lambda)$, where $p(\lambda)$ is prime and $\deg p(\lambda) = \dim V$, then prove that V has no proper t-invariant subspaces.
8. Let $t \in L(V)$ have minimal polynomial $p^m(\lambda)$, where $p(\lambda)$ is prime and $\deg p^m(\lambda) = \dim V$, and define $W_i = Vp^i(t)$, $i = 0, 1, \ldots, m$. Prove that each W_i is a t-invariant subspace of V and that $V = W_0 \supset W_1 \supset \cdots \supset W_m = \{0\}$ are the only t-invariant subspaces of V. [*Hint:* We know that $V = \mathbf{x}F[t]$ for some $\mathbf{x} \in V$. If W is any proper t-invariant subspace of V and $f(\lambda)$ is the monic polynomial of least degree such that $\mathbf{x}f(t) \in W$, then show that $f(\lambda) = p^k(\lambda)$ for some integer k and that $W = Vp^k(t)$.]

2. REDUCIBLE SPACES

In this section, we shall complete the proof of Theorem 8.1. To be more specific, we shall prove the following result.

8.2. THEOREM. Let V be an n-dimensional vector space over a field F and $t \in L(V)$ have minimal polynomial $p^m(\lambda)$, where $p(\lambda)$ is a prime and $m \geq 1$. Then, there exist unique positive integers $m_1, m_2, \ldots, m_r$, and there exist vectors $\mathbf{x}_1, \mathbf{x}_2, \ldots, \mathbf{x}_r$, such that

(1) $$m = m_1 \geq m_2 \geq \cdots \geq m_r.$$

(2) $\mathbf{x}_i$ has minimal polynomial $p^{m_i}(\lambda)$ for each i.

(3) $V = W_1 \oplus W_2 \oplus \cdots \oplus W_r$, where $W_i = \mathbf{x}_i F[t]$ for each i.

The proof of 8.2 will be given after some preliminary remarks. We observe that if $\deg p^m(\lambda) = n$, then V is t-irreducible by 8.1. In this case, $r = 1$, $m = m_1$, and $\mathbf{x}_1$ is any vector such that $V = \mathbf{x}_1 F[t] = W_1$. Also, if $m = 1$, then 8.2 follows immediately from 6.13.

Let V be a vector space over a field F and $t \in L(V)$. For each t-invariant subspace W of V and each $\mathbf{x} \in V$, let us define

8.3 $$N(\mathbf{x}, W) = \{f(\lambda) \in F[\lambda] \mid \mathbf{x}f(t) \in W\}.$$

We call $N(\mathbf{x}, W)$ the *annihilator of* $\mathbf{x}$ *modulo* W. If $W = \{\mathbf{0}\}$, then $N(\mathbf{x}, W)$ is simply the ideal $N(\mathbf{x})$ defined in 5.5. We leave it to the reader to verify that $N(\mathbf{x}, W)$ is also an ideal of $F[\lambda]$. Since $N(\mathbf{x}, W)$ is an ideal, it has a unique monic generator $h(\lambda)$ by 5.3:

$$N(\mathbf{x}, W) = h(\lambda)F[\lambda].$$

We call $h(\lambda)$ the *minimal polynomial of* $\mathbf{x}$ *modulo* W. It is the monic polynomial $h(\lambda)$ of minimal degree, such that $\mathbf{x}h(t) \in W$. If $W = \{\mathbf{0}\}$, $h(\lambda)$ is simply the minimal polynomial of $\mathbf{x}$.

Continuing as in Chapter 5, let us define

8.4 $$N(W) = \{f(\lambda) \in F[\lambda] \mid Vf(t) \subset W\}.$$

Thus, $f(\lambda) \in N(W)$ iff $\mathbf{x}f(t) \in W$ for all $\mathbf{x} \in V$. If $W = \{\mathbf{0}\}$, then $N(W)$ is simply N of 5.9. We can easily show that $N(W)$ is an ideal of $F[\lambda]$, and

$$N(W) = \bigcap_{\mathbf{x} \in V} N(\mathbf{x}, W).$$

The unique monic generator $h(\lambda)$ of the ideal $N(W)$ is called the *minimal polynomial of t modulo W*. Thus, $h(\lambda)$ is the monic polynomial of minimal degree, such that $\mathbf{x}h(t) \in W$ for all $\mathbf{x} \in V$.

If W is a t-invariant subspace of V, $h(\lambda)$ is the minimal polynomial of t modulo W, and $k(\lambda)$ is the minimal polynomial of t, then $k(t) = 0$, and, therefore, $\mathbf{x}k(t) \in W$ for all $\mathbf{x} \in V$. Hence, $k(\lambda) \in N(W)$, and $k(\lambda)$ is a multiple of $h(\lambda)$, the generator of $N(W)$. This proves the following result.

8.5. THEOREM. If $t \in L(V)$ and W is a t-invariant subspace of V, then the minimal polynomial $h(\lambda)$ of t modulo W is a factor of the minimal polynomial $k(\lambda)$ of t, and

$$\deg h(\lambda) \leq \deg k(\lambda) \leq \dim V.$$

If $t \in L(V)$, W is a t-invariant subspace of V, and $h(\lambda)$ is the minimal polynomial of t modulo W, then it can be shown as in Chapter 5, in case $W = \{\mathbf{0}\}$, that there exists some $\mathbf{z} \in V$ such that $h(\lambda)$ is the minimal polynomial of $\mathbf{z}$ modulo W.

EXAMPLE 1: Let $t \in L(\mathbb{Q}^3)$ be represented by the matrix

$$A = \begin{pmatrix} 1 & 1 & -1 \\ 1 & 1 & 1 \\ 2 & 0 & 3 \end{pmatrix}$$

relative to the usual basis $(\mathbf{u}_1, \mathbf{u}_2, \mathbf{u}_3)$ of $\mathbb{Q}^3$. Since $(\mathbf{u}_1 + \mathbf{u}_2)t = 2(\mathbf{u}_1 + \mathbf{u}_2)$, we see that $W = \mathbb{Q}(\mathbf{u}_1 + \mathbf{u}_2)$ is a t-invariant subspace of $\mathbb{Q}^3$. To find the minimal polynomial of $\mathbf{u}_1$ modulo W, we first observe that $a\mathbf{u}_1 + b(\mathbf{u}_1 t) \notin W$ if $a \neq 0$ or $b \neq 0$. However, $a\mathbf{u}_1 + b(\mathbf{u}_1 t) + c(\mathbf{u}_1 t^2) \in W$ for some $a, b, c \in \mathbb{Q}$, not all zero. Now, we have

$$\mathbf{u}_1 t^2 = (\mathbf{u}_1 + \mathbf{u}_2 - \mathbf{u}_3)t = 2\mathbf{u}_2 - 3\mathbf{u}_3,$$

and, therefore, we find that

$$a\mathbf{u}_1 + b(\mathbf{u}_1 t) + c(\mathbf{u}_1 t^2) = d(\mathbf{u}_1 + \mathbf{u}_2),$$

or

$$a\mathbf{u}_1 + b(\mathbf{u}_1 + \mathbf{u}_2 - \mathbf{u}_3) + c(2\mathbf{u}_2 - 3\mathbf{u}_3) = d(\mathbf{u}_1 + \mathbf{u}_2)$$

iff

$$a + b = d, \qquad b + 2c = d, \qquad -b - 3c = 0.$$

A solution of this system of equations is seen to be

$$a = 2, \qquad b = -3, \qquad c = 1, \qquad d = -1.$$

Thus, we have

$$\mathbf{u}_1(2 - 3t + t^2) = -(\mathbf{u}_1 + \mathbf{u}_2) \in W,$$

and

$$h(\lambda) = \lambda^2 - 3\lambda + 2$$

is the minimal polynomial of $\mathbf{u}_1$ modulo W. In a similar way, we can show that $\lambda^2 - 3\lambda + 2$ is the minimal polynomial of both $\mathbf{u}_2$ and $\mathbf{u}_3$ modulo W. Since $\{\mathbf{u}_1, \mathbf{u}_2, \mathbf{u}_3\}$ is a basis of V, evidently $V(t^2 - 3t + 2) \subset W$ and $\lambda^2 - 3\lambda + 2$ is the minimal polynomial of t modulo W.

We observe, in this example, that $(\mathbf{u}_1 + \mathbf{u}_2)(t - 2) = \mathbf{0}$, and hence that

$$(\lambda^2 - 3\lambda + 2)(\lambda - 2)$$

is the minimal polynomial of $\mathbf{u}_1$ (and also $\mathbf{u}_2$ and $\mathbf{u}_3$). Since its degree is 3, the dimension of $\mathbb{Q}^3$, this polynomial is also the minimal polynomial of t.

We are now in a position to prove the theorem.

Proof of 8.2: As we remarked above, we need only consider the case in which $\deg p^m(\lambda) < n$. Since $p^m(\lambda)$ is the minimal polynomial of t, there exists some $\mathbf{x}_1 \in V$ such that $p^m(\lambda)$ is also the minimal polynomial of $\mathbf{x}_1$. If

$$W_1 = \mathbf{x}_1F[t],$$

then W_1 is a t-invariant subspace of V of dimension $\deg p^m(\lambda)$. For convenience, let

$$m_1 = m, \qquad h_1(\lambda) = p^{m_1}(\lambda), \qquad \dim W_1 = \deg h_1(\lambda) = k_1.$$

Next, let $h_2(\lambda)$ be the minimal polynomial of t modulo W_1. Then, we have

$$h_2(\lambda) = p^{m_2}(\lambda), \qquad m_2 \leq m_1,$$

and there exists some $\mathbf{y} \in V$ having $h_2(\lambda)$ as its minimal polynomial modulo W_1. If $\mathbf{y}h_2(t) \neq \mathbf{0}$, then, necessarily, $m_2 < m_1$, and we have

$$\mathbf{y}h_2(t) = \mathbf{x}_1 f(t) \qquad \text{for some } f(\lambda) \in F[\lambda].$$

Let $p^j(\lambda)$ be the minimal polynomial of y. Since $\mathbf{y}h_2(t) \neq \mathbf{0}$, we find that $m_2 < j \leq m_1$ and $\mathbf{y}h_2(t)p^{j-m_2}(t) = \mathbf{x}_1 f(t)p^{j-m_2}(t) = \mathbf{0}$. Hence, $h_1(\lambda)$ is a factor of $f(\lambda)p^{j-m_2}(\lambda)$, and $p^{m_1-(j-m_2)}(\lambda)$ is a factor of $f(\lambda)$. Since $m_1 - (j - m_2) \geq m_2$, $p^{m_2}(\lambda)$ is a factor of $f(\lambda)$, say $f(\lambda) = p^{m_2}(\lambda)g(\lambda)$. Now, let

$$\mathbf{x}_2 = \mathbf{y} - \mathbf{x}_1 g(t).$$

Then, $\mathbf{x}_2h_2(t) = \mathbf{0}$, whereas $\mathbf{x}_2p^i(t) \notin W_1$ if $i < m_2$. For otherwise, if $\mathbf{x}_2p^i(t) \in W_1$ for some $i < m_2$, then $\mathbf{y}p^i(t) = \mathbf{x}_2p^i(t) + \mathbf{x}_1g(t)p^i(t) \in W_1$, contrary to the choice of $\mathbf{y}$. If $\mathbf{y}h_2(t) = \mathbf{0}$, then let $\mathbf{x}_2 = y$. In either case, we have found an $\mathbf{x}_2 \in V$, such that $h_2(\lambda)$ is the minimal polynomial both of $\mathbf{x}_2$ and of $\mathbf{x}_2$ modulo W_1. Thus, $W_1 \cap W_2 = \{\mathbf{0}\}$, where $W_2 = \mathbf{x}_2F[t]$, and $W_1 + W_2 = W_1 \oplus W_2$.

To continue, let us assume that we have found an integer $l \geq 2$, integers $m_1, m_2, \ldots, m_l$, and vectors $\mathbf{x}_1, \mathbf{x}_2, \ldots, \mathbf{x}_l$, such that:

(1) $m = m_1 \geq m_2 \geq \cdots \geq m_l > 0$.
(2) The minimal polynomial of $\mathbf{x}_i$ is $h_i(\lambda) = p^{m_i}(\lambda)$, $i = 1, \ldots, l$.
(3) If $W_i = \mathbf{x}_iF[t]$, $i = 1, 2, \ldots, l$, and $U_i = W_1 + \cdots + W_i$, then $h_1(\lambda)$ is the minimal polynomial of t, $h_i(\lambda)$ is the minimal polynomial of t modulo U_{i-1}, $i = 2, \ldots, l$, and $U_l = W_1 \oplus W_2 \oplus \cdots \oplus W_l$.

If $U_l = V$, the theorem is proved (except for uniqueness). So, let us assume that $U_l \neq V$, and that $h(\lambda) = p^j(\lambda)$ is the minimal polynomial of t modulo U_l. Since $p^{m_l}(\lambda)$ is the minimal polynomial of t modulo U_{l-1}, necessarily $j \leq m_l$.

As above, we can select $\mathbf{y} \in V$, such that $h(\lambda)$ is the minimal polynomial of $\mathbf{y}$ modulo U_l. If $\mathbf{y}h(t) = \mathbf{0}$, let $\mathbf{x}_{l+1} = \mathbf{y}$. Otherwise, if $\mathbf{y}h(t) \neq \mathbf{0}$, we have

$$\mathbf{y}h(t) = \sum_{i=1}^{l} \mathbf{x}_i f_i(t) \qquad \text{for some } f_i(\lambda) \in F[\lambda].$$

We claim that $h(\lambda)$ is a factor of $f_i(\lambda)$ for each i. For if $h(\lambda)$ is a factor of $f_i(\lambda)$ for every $i > s$, then $f_i(\lambda) = h(\lambda)g_i(\lambda)$ for $i > s$, and we have

$$\mathbf{y}_1h(t) = \sum_{i=1}^{s} \mathbf{x}_i f_i(t), \qquad \text{where} \quad \mathbf{y}_1 = \mathbf{y} - \sum_{i=s+1}^{l} \mathbf{x}_i g_i(t).$$

Clearly, $h(\lambda)$ is the minimal polynomial of $\mathbf{y}_1$ modulo U_s; for otherwise, $h(\lambda)$ is not the minimal polynomial of $\mathbf{y}$ modulo U_l. Now, we see that $j \leq m_s$ and $\mathbf{y}_1p^{m_s}(t) = \sum_{i=1}^{s} \mathbf{x}_i f_i(t)p^{m_s-j}(t) \in U_{s-1}$. Hence, $\mathbf{x}_s f_s(t)p^{m_s-j}(t) = \mathbf{0}$, and $p^{m_s}(\lambda)$ is a factor of $f_s(\lambda)p^{m_s-j}(\lambda)$. Therefore, $p^j(\lambda)$ is a factor of $f_s(\lambda)$. We conclude that we can select $s = 1$. Thus, $f_i(\lambda) = h(\lambda)g_i(\lambda)$, $i = 1, 2, \ldots, l$, and if

$$\mathbf{x}_{l+1} = \mathbf{y} - \sum_{i=1}^{l} \mathbf{x}_i g_i(t),$$

then $h(\lambda)$ is the minimal polynomial of both $\mathbf{x}_{l+1}$ and $\mathbf{x}_{l+1}$ modulo U_l. If $W_{l+1} = \mathbf{x}_{l+1}F[t]$, then $W_{l+1} \cap U_l = \{\mathbf{0}\}$, and, therefore, $U_l + W_{l+1} = U_l \oplus W_{l+1}$.

We now have found integers $m_1, \ldots, m_l, m_{l+1}$ and vectors $\mathbf{x}_1, \ldots, \mathbf{x}_l, \mathbf{x}_{l+1}$, such that conditions (1) through (3) above are satisfied for l replaced by $l + 1$. The theorem, except for uniqueness, now follows in n such steps at the most.

The uniqueness is established by assuming that there is a positive integer s, positive integers $l_1, l_2, \ldots, l_s$ and vectors $\mathbf{y}_1, \mathbf{y}_2, \ldots, \mathbf{y}_s$ in V such that:

(1) $l_1 \geq l_2 \geq \cdots \geq l_s$.

(2) $p^{l_k}(\lambda)$ is the minimal polynomial of $\mathbf{y}_k$, $k = 1, 2, \ldots, s$.

(3) $V = U_1 \oplus U_2 \oplus \cdots \oplus U_s$, where $U_k = \mathbf{y}_k F[t]$, $k = 1, 2, \ldots, s$.

Clearly, $\mathbf{y}p^{l_1}(t) = \mathbf{0}$ for every $\mathbf{y} \in V$, so that $l_1 = m = m_1$. Assume that $l_1 = m_1$, $l_2 = m_2, \ldots, l_{j-1} = m_{j-1}$, and $l_j \leq m_j$. If we let $f = p^{l_j}(t) \in F[t]$, then we have

$$Vf = W_1 f \oplus W_2 f \oplus \cdots \oplus W_r f = U_1 f \oplus U_2 f \oplus \cdots \oplus U_s f.$$

Now, we see that

$$W_k f = (\mathbf{x}_k f)F[t], \qquad \mathbf{x}_k f \text{ has minimal polynomial } p^{m_k - l_j}(\lambda),$$

$$U_k f = (\mathbf{y}_k f)F[t], \qquad \mathbf{y}_k f \text{ has minimal polynomial } p^{l_k - l_j}(\lambda).$$

Hence, we have

$$\dim W_k f = \dim U_k f = \deg p^{l_k - l_j}(\lambda) \qquad \text{if} \quad k < j.$$

Clearly, $U_k f = 0$ if $k \geq j$. Thus, we have

$$\dim Vf = \sum_{i=1}^{j-1} \dim U_i f = \sum_{i=1}^{j-1} \dim W_i f.$$

Therefore, $W_k f$ must be zero if $k \geq j$, since $\dim Vf = \sum_{i=1}^{r} \dim W_i f$. Hence, $\mathbf{x}_j p^{l_j}(t) = \mathbf{0}$, and $m_j \leq l_j$. Thus, $m_j = l_j$. A similar argument, interchanging the roles of the l_k and m_k, would hold if we assumed that $m_j \leq l_j$ originally. If we continue this process, we get $m_k = l_k$ for every k, and therefore $r = s$. This proves the uniqueness of the integers $m_1, m_2, \ldots, m_r$, and concludes the proof of 8.2.

Each of the subspaces W_i in 8.2 is t-irreducible in the sense that it is t_i-irreducible, where $t_i = t \mid W_i$. This follows from 8.1, since $\dim W_i = \deg p^{m_i}(\lambda)$. Thus, V is expressed as a direct sum of irreducible subspaces in 8.2.

Example 2: Let $t \in L(\mathbb{Q}^4)$ be represented by the matrix

$$A = \begin{pmatrix} -2 & 0 & 0 & 0 \\ -1 & 0 & -1 & -3 \\ 1 & -2 & -1 & 3 \\ -1 & 2 & -1 & -5 \end{pmatrix}$$

relative to the usual $\mathbf{u}$-basis of $\mathbb{Q}^4$. Then $\mathbf{u}_1 t = -2\mathbf{u}_1$, and $\mathbf{u}_1$ has minimal polynomial $\lambda + 2$. Also, $\mathbf{u}_2 t = -\mathbf{u}_1 - \mathbf{u}_3 - 3\mathbf{u}_4$, $\mathbf{u}_2 t^2 = 4(\mathbf{u}_1 - \mathbf{u}_2 + \mathbf{u}_3 + 3\mathbf{u}_4)$, and hence $\mathbf{u}_2$ has minimal polynomial $\lambda^2 + 4\lambda + 4 = (\lambda + 2)^2$. Next, we see that $\mathbf{u}_3 t = \mathbf{u}_1 - 2\mathbf{u}_2 - \mathbf{u}_3 + 3\mathbf{u}_4$, $\mathbf{u}_3 t^2 = -4(\mathbf{u}_1 - 2\mathbf{u}_2 + 3\mathbf{u}_4)$, and hence $\mathbf{u}_3$ has minimal polynomial $\lambda^2 + 4\lambda + 4$. Finally, we have that $\mathbf{u}_4 t = -\mathbf{u}_1 + 2\mathbf{u}_2 - \mathbf{u}_3 - 5\mathbf{u}_4$, $\mathbf{u}_4 t^2 = 4(\mathbf{u}_1 - 2\mathbf{u}_2 + \mathbf{u}_3 + 4\mathbf{u}_4)$, and hence $\mathbf{u}_4$ has minimal polynomial $\lambda^2 + 4\lambda + 4$. The minimal polynomial of t is the l.c.m. of the minimal polynomials of $\mathbf{u}_1, \mathbf{u}_2, \mathbf{u}_3, \mathbf{u}_4$, namely $(\lambda + 2)^2$.

Since $\mathbf{u}_2$ has minimal polynomial $(\lambda + 2)^2$, we can let $\mathbf{x}_1 = \mathbf{u}_2$, $p(\lambda) = \lambda + 2$, $m = 2$, and $m_1 = 2$ in Theorem 8.2. Also, we have

$$W_1 = \mathbf{u}_2F[t] = \mathbb{Q}\mathbf{u}_2 + \mathbb{Q}(\mathbf{u}_2t).$$

Since $\mathbf{u}_1 \notin W_1$, $\lambda + 2$ is the minimal polynomial of $\mathbf{u}_1$ and also of $\mathbf{u}_1$ modulo W_1. Because $\mathbf{u}_3 \notin W_1$, whereas $\mathbf{u}_3(t + 2) = \mathbf{u}_1 - 2\mathbf{u}_2 + \mathbf{u}_3 + 3\mathbf{u}_4 \in W_1$, we find that $\mathbf{u}_3$ has minimal polynomial $\lambda + 2$ modulo W_1. Finally, $\mathbf{u}_4 \notin W_1$, whereas $\mathbf{u}_4(t + 2) = -\mathbf{u}_1 + 2\mathbf{u}_2 - \mathbf{u}_3 - 3\mathbf{u}_4 \in W_1$, and hence $\mathbf{u}_4$ has minimal polynomial $\lambda + 2$ modulo W_1. Therefore, $\lambda + 2$ is the minimal polynomial of t modulo W_1.

Because $\lambda + 2$ is the minimal polynomial of $\mathbf{u}_1$ and also of $\mathbf{u}_1$ modulo W_1, we can select $\mathbf{x}_2 = \mathbf{u}_1$, $m_2 = 1$, and

$$W_2 = \mathbf{u}_1F[t] = \mathbb{Q}\mathbf{u}_1$$

in Theorem 8.2. We still have not finished, however, since $W_1 + W_2 \neq \mathbb{Q}^4$.

Now, $\mathbf{u}_3 \notin W_1 + W_2$, whereas $\mathbf{u}_3(t + 2) = -\mathbf{u}_2(t + 2) \in W_1 + W_2$. Thus, $\lambda + 2$ is the minimal polynomial of $\mathbf{u}_2 + \mathbf{u}_3$ and also of $\mathbf{u}_2 + \mathbf{u}_3$ modulo $W_1 + W_2$. Hence, we can select $\mathbf{x}_3 = \mathbf{u}_2 + \mathbf{u}_3$, $m_3 = 1$, and

$$W_3 = (\mathbf{u}_2 + \mathbf{u}_3)F[t] = \mathbb{Q}(\mathbf{u}_2 + \mathbf{u}_3)$$

in Theorem 8.2. Since $W_1 + W_2 + W_3 = \mathbb{Q}^4$, we have finally represented $\mathbb{Q}^4$ as a direct sum of irreducible t-invariant subspaces,

$$\mathbb{Q}^4 = W_1 \oplus W_2 \oplus W_3,$$

as in Theorem 8.2.

EXAMPLE 3: Let $V = \mathbb{R}^6$ and $t \in L(V)$ be represented by the matrix

$$A = \begin{pmatrix} 0 & 0 & 0 & 0 & 1 & 0 \\ 0 & 0 & 1 & 0 & 0 & 0 \\ 1 & -1 & 0 & 0 & 0 & 0 \\ 0 & 0 & 0 & 0 & 0 & -1 \\ -1 & 0 & 0 & 0 & 0 & 0 \\ 0 & 0 & 0 & 1 & 0 & 0 \end{pmatrix}$$

relative to the usual basis of V. We can easily show that $\mathbf{u}_1$, $\mathbf{u}_4$, $\mathbf{u}_5$, and $\mathbf{u}_6$ have minimal polynomial $\lambda^2 + 1$, and that $\mathbf{u}_2$ and $\mathbf{u}_3$ have minimal polynomial $(\lambda^2 + 1)^2$. Hence, t has minimal polynomial $(\lambda^2 + 1)^2$. Since $\mathbf{u}_3$ has minimal polynomial $(\lambda^2 + 1)^2$, we can let

$$p(\lambda) = \lambda^2 + 1, \qquad m = m_1 = 2, \qquad \mathbf{x}_1 = \mathbf{u}_3,$$
$$W_1 = \mathbf{x}_1F[t] = \mathbb{R}\mathbf{u}_3 + \mathbb{R}(\mathbf{u}_3t) + \mathbb{R}(\mathbf{u}_3t^2) + \mathbb{R}(\mathbf{u}_3t^3)$$
$$= \mathbb{R}\mathbf{u}_1 + \mathbb{R}\mathbf{u}_2 + \mathbb{R}\mathbf{u}_3 + \mathbb{R}\mathbf{u}_5$$

in 8.2. The minimal polynomial of $\mathbf{u}_4$ modulo W_1 is the same as the minimal polynomial of $\mathbf{u}_4$, namely $\lambda^2 + 1$. Thus, we can let

$$m_2 = 1, \qquad \mathbf{x}_2 = \mathbf{u}_4, \qquad W_2 = \mathbf{x}_2F[t] = \mathbb{R}\mathbf{u}_4 + \mathbb{R}\mathbf{u}_6.$$

Clearly,

$$V = W_1 \oplus W_2$$

is a representation of V as a direct sum of irreducible t-invariant subspaces. The reader can verify that

$$V = U_1 \oplus U_2, \qquad \text{where} \quad U_1 = (\mathbf{u}_1 + \mathbf{u}_4)F[t], \quad U_2 = \mathbf{u}_5F[t]$$

is another representation of V as a direct sum of irreducible t-invariant subspaces. Do you see that this does not violate the uniqueness stated in 8.2?

EXERCISES

In each of the following exercises, show that the minimal polynomial of t is a power of a prime, and then represent V as a direct sum of irreducible t-invariant subspaces, as in 8.2.

1. $V = \mathbb{Q}^2$, $t \in L(V)$, defined by $\mathbf{u}_1t = -2\mathbf{u}_1$, $\mathbf{u}_2t = -2\mathbf{u}_2$.
2. $V = \mathbb{Q}^2$, $t \in L(V)$, defined by $\mathbf{u}_1t = 5\mathbf{u}_1$, $\mathbf{u}_2t = 5\mathbf{u}_2$.
3. $V = \mathbb{Q}^3$, $t \in L(V)$, defined by $\mathbf{u}_1t = \mathbf{u}_1$, $\mathbf{u}_2t = 2\mathbf{u}_1 - \mathbf{u}_2 + \mathbf{u}_3$, $\mathbf{u}_3t = 4\mathbf{u}_1 - 4\mathbf{u}_2 + 3\mathbf{u}_3$.
4. $V = \mathbb{Q}^3$, $t \in L(V)$, defined by $\mathbf{u}_1t = -4\mathbf{u}_1$, $\mathbf{u}_2t = -4\mathbf{u}_2$, $\mathbf{u}_3t = -4\mathbf{u}_3$.
5. $V = \mathbb{Q}^4$, $t \in L(V)$, defined by $\mathbf{u}_1t = -\mathbf{u}_2 + 2\mathbf{u}_3 + 2\mathbf{u}_4$, $\mathbf{u}_2t = -3\mathbf{u}_1 + 4\mathbf{u}_2 - 2\mathbf{u}_3 - 6\mathbf{u}_4$, $\mathbf{u}_3t = -2\mathbf{u}_2 + 2\mathbf{u}_3 + \mathbf{u}_4$, $\mathbf{u}_4t = -2\mathbf{u}_1 + 4\mathbf{u}_2 - 3\mathbf{u}_3 - 6\mathbf{u}_4$.
6. $V = \mathbb{Q}^4$, $t \in L(V)$ defined by $\mathbf{u}_1t = 2\mathbf{u}_2 + \mathbf{u}_3 - 2\mathbf{u}_4$, $\mathbf{u}_2t = 12\mathbf{u}_1 - 5\mathbf{u}_2 - 4\mathbf{u}_3 + 8\mathbf{u}_4$, $\mathbf{u}_3t = -9\mathbf{u}_1 + 6\mathbf{u}_2 + 6\mathbf{u}_3 - 6\mathbf{u}_4$, $\mathbf{u}_4t = 12\mathbf{u}_1 - 8\mathbf{u}_2 - 4\mathbf{u}_3 + 11\mathbf{u}_4$.
7. If $\dim V = n$ and $t \in L(V)$ has minimal polynomial $(\lambda - a)^{n-1}$, prove that V is a direct sum of two irreducible t-invariant subspaces, $V = W_1 \oplus W_2$, and give the dimensions of W_1 and W_2.
8. If $\dim V = n$ and $t \in L(V)$ is singular, then prove either that t has minimal polynomial λ^n or that V is reducible relative to t.

3. ELEMENTARY DIVISORS

Each linear transformation t of a vector space V over a field F has a minimal polynomial $h(\lambda)$ of the form

$$h(\lambda) = p_1^{s_1}(\lambda)p_2^{s_2}(\lambda)\cdots p_r^{s_r}(\lambda),$$

where the $p_i(\lambda)$ are distinct primes and each $s_i \geq 1$. By 6.12, there exist unique t-invariant subspaces $V_1, V_2, \ldots, V_r$ of V, such that

$$(1) \qquad V = V_1 \oplus V_2 \oplus \cdots \oplus V_r, \qquad t = t_1 \oplus t_2 \oplus \cdots \oplus t_r,$$

where each $t_i = t \mid V_i$ has minimal polynomial $h_i(\lambda) = p_i^{s_i}(\lambda)$. For each i such that $\deg h_i(\lambda) = \dim V_i$, the subspace V_i is t-irreducible by 8.1. Otherwise, if $\deg h_i(\lambda) < \dim V_i$, then, by 8.2, we have

$$V_i = W_{i1} \oplus W_{i2} \oplus \cdots \oplus W_{ir_i}, \tag{2}$$

where $W_{ij} = \mathbf{x}_{ij}F[t]$ for some $\mathbf{x}_{ij} \in V$. While the $\mathbf{x}_{ij}$ in (2) are not unique, the number r_i of them is unique, and the minimal polynomials of the $\mathbf{x}_{ij}$ are also unique. Of course, each W_{ij} is t-irreducible. On combining (1) and (2), we obtain the following basic result.

8.6. FUNDAMENTAL THEOREM ON DIRECT SUMS. Let V be a vector space over a field F. Then, for each $t \in L(V)$, there exist unique polynomials $q_1(\lambda), q_2(\lambda), \ldots, q_m(\lambda)$, each a power of a monic prime, and irreducible t-invariant subspaces $W_1, W_2, \ldots, W_m$ of V, such that $t_i = t \mid W_i$ has minimal polynomial $q_i(\lambda)$ for each i, and

$$V = W_1 \oplus W_2 \oplus \cdots \oplus W_m.$$

Since each W_i is irreducible, it is cyclic; that is, $W_i = \mathbf{z}_iF[t]$ for some $\mathbf{z}_i \in V$, and the minimal polynomial of $\mathbf{z}_i$ is $q_i(\lambda)$. Thus, $\deg q_i(\lambda) = \dim W_i$ for each i, and, by 6.9, we have

$$\dim V = \sum_{i=1}^{m} \deg q_i(\lambda).$$

We are now in a position to make the following definition.

8.7. DEFINITION OF ELEMENTARY DIVISORS. For each $t \in L(V)$, the polynomials $q_1(\lambda), q_2(\lambda), \ldots, q_m(\lambda)$ of 8.6 are called the elementary divisors of t.

Thus, the elementary divisors of each $t \in L(V)$ are primes or powers of primes, and the sum of the degrees of the elementary divisors equals the dimension of V.

All the elementary divisors need not be different. For example, the elementary divisors of $1 \in L(V)$ are $\lambda - 1, \lambda - 1, \ldots, \lambda - 1$ (n elements), because $\lambda - 1$ is the minimal polynomial of 1, and $V = F\mathbf{x}_1 \oplus F\mathbf{x}_2 \oplus \cdots \oplus F\mathbf{x}_n$ is a representation of V as a direct sum of 1-irreducible subspaces, where $\{\mathbf{x}_1, \mathbf{x}_2, \ldots, \mathbf{x}_n\}$ is any basis of V. Similarly, the l.t. 0 has minimal polynomial λ and elementary divisors $\lambda, \lambda, \ldots, \lambda$ (n elements).

Let $t \in L(V)$ have elementary divisors $q_1(\lambda), q_2(\lambda), \ldots, q_m(\lambda)$. Hence, there exist t-irreducible subspaces $W_1, W_2, \ldots, W_m$ of V, such that

$$V = W_1 \oplus W_2 \oplus \cdots \oplus W_m, \qquad t = t_1 \oplus t_2 \oplus \cdots \oplus t_m,$$

and $t_i = t \mid W_i$ has minimal polynomial $q_i(\lambda)$. If A_i is a matrix representation of t_i, then

$$A = A_1 \oplus A_2 \oplus \cdots \oplus A_m$$

is a matrix representation of t by 6.11. The minimal polynomial $h(\lambda)$ of t is simply $[q_1(\lambda), q_2(\lambda), \cdots, q_m(\lambda)]$, the l.c.m. of the $q_i(\lambda)$. On the other hand, $q_i(\lambda) = \det(\lambda I_i - A_i)$ by 5.17, where I_i is the $r_i \times r_i$ identity matrix, and $r_i = \dim W_i$, $i = 1, 2, \cdots, m$. Hence, we have

$$\det(\lambda I - A) = \det(\lambda I_1 - A) \det(\lambda I_2 - A_2) \cdots \det(\lambda I_m - A_m)$$
$$= q_1(\lambda)q_2(\lambda) \cdots q_m(\lambda).$$

Thus, the product of the elementary divisors is the characteristic polynomial of A, and also of t. We state these results below.

8.8. THEOREM. If $t \in L(V)$ has elementary divisors $q_1(\lambda)$, $q_2(\lambda)$, . . . , $q_m(\lambda)$, minimal polynomial $h(\lambda)$, and characteristic polynomial $f(\lambda)$, then we have

$$h(\lambda) = [q_1(\lambda), q_2(\lambda), \ldots, q_m(\lambda)],$$
$$f(\lambda) = q_1(\lambda)q_2(\lambda) \cdots q_m(\lambda).$$

Since $h(\lambda)$ is obviously a factor of $f(\lambda)$, we have finally completed the proof of the Hamilton–Cayley theorem (6.16).

If the minimal polynomial $h(\lambda)$ of $t \in L(V)$ has the form

$$h(\lambda) = p_1^{k_1}(\lambda)p_2^{k_2}(\lambda) \cdots p_m^{k_m}(\lambda)$$

for distinct monic primes $p_1(\lambda)$, $p_2(\lambda)$, . . . , $p_m(\lambda)$, then necessarily $p_1^{k_1}(\lambda)$, $p_2^{k_2}(\lambda)$, . . . , $p_m^{k_m}(\lambda)$ are elementary divisors of t. These are the only elementary divisors iff $\deg h(\lambda) = \dim V$. If $\deg h(\lambda) < \dim V$, then the other elementary divisors are of the form $p_i^j(\lambda)$ for some i and some $j \le k_i$. If we also know the characteristic polynomial $f(\lambda)$ of t, then we know the product of all the elementary divisors, but we do not necessarily know the individual elementary divisors.

In Example 1, p. 199, we showed that $t \in L(\mathbb{Q}^3)$ had minimal polynomial

$$h(\lambda) = (\lambda - 2)^2(\lambda - 1).$$

Since $\deg h(\lambda) = \dim \mathbb{Q}^3 = 3$, the prime power factors of $h(\lambda)$,

$$(\lambda - 2)^2, \qquad \text{and} \qquad \lambda - 1,$$

are all the elementary divisors of t.

An inspection of Example 2, p. 202, shows that $t \in L(\mathbb{Q}^4)$ has minimal polynomial

$$h(\lambda) = (\lambda + 2)^2.$$

Hence, $(\lambda + 2)^2$ is one of the elementary divisors, and the others are also powers of the prime $\lambda + 2$. Since $\mathbb{Q}^4$ is a direct sum of three irreducible subspaces, there are three elementary divisors,

$$(\lambda + 2)^2, \qquad \lambda + 2, \qquad \text{and} \qquad \lambda + 2.$$

For Example 3, p. 203, the elementary divisors are

$$(\lambda^2 + 1)^2, \qquad \text{and} \qquad \lambda^2 + 1.$$

Hence, the minimal polynomial is $(\lambda^2 + 1)^2$.

EXAMPLE: Let $V = \mathbb{Q}^6$ and $t \in L(V)$ be represented by the matrix

$$A = \begin{pmatrix} 0 & 1 & 0 & 1 & 0 & 0 \\ 1 & 0 & 0 & 0 & 1 & 0 \\ 1 & 0 & -1 & 0 & 0 & 1 \\ 1 & -1 & 0 & 0 & 0 & 0 \\ 2 & -2 & 0 & -1 & 2 & 0 \\ -1 & 1 & -2 & 1 & -4 & 1 \end{pmatrix}$$

relative to the usual $\mathbf{u}$-basis of $\mathbb{Q}^6$. Then, $\mathbf{u}_1 t = \mathbf{u}_2 + \mathbf{u}_4$, $\mathbf{u}_1 t^2 = 2\mathbf{u}_1 - \mathbf{u}_2 + \mathbf{u}_5$, $\mathbf{u}_1 t^3 = \mathbf{u}_1 + \mathbf{u}_4 + \mathbf{u}_5$. We verify that $\mathbf{u}_1$, $\mathbf{u}_1 t$, $\mathbf{u}_1 t^2$ are l.i., whereas $\mathbf{u}_1 - \mathbf{u}_1 t - \mathbf{u}_1 t^2 + \mathbf{u}_1 t^3 = \mathbf{0}$. Therefore, the minimal polynomial of $\mathbf{u}_1$ is

$$\lambda^3 - \lambda^2 - \lambda + 1 = (\lambda - 1)^2(\lambda + 1).$$

In turn, we find that

$\mathbf{u}_1$ has minimal polynomial $(\lambda - 1)^2(\lambda + 1)$,

$\mathbf{u}_2$ has minimal polynomial $(\lambda - 1)^2$,

$\mathbf{u}_3$ has minimal polynomial $(\lambda - 1)^2(\lambda^2 + 1)$,

$\mathbf{u}_4$ has minimal polynomial $(\lambda - 1)^2(\lambda + 1)$,

$\mathbf{u}_5$ has minimal polynomial $(\lambda - 1)^2(\lambda + 1)$,

$\mathbf{u}_6$ has minimal polynomial $(\lambda - 1)^2(\lambda + 1)(\lambda^2 + 1)$.

Since the l.c.m. of the minimal polynomials of the $\mathbf{u}_i$ is

$$h(\lambda) = (\lambda - 1)^2(\lambda + 1)(\lambda^2 + 1),$$

$h(\lambda)$ is the minimal polynomial of t.

There are three distinct prime factors of $h(\lambda)$, namely $\lambda - 1$, $\lambda + 1$, and $\lambda^2 + 1$. Thus, by 6.12, we have

$$V = V_1 \oplus V_2 \oplus V_3,$$

where

$V_1 = V(t + 1)(t^2 + 1)$ has basis $\{\mathbf{u}_1 + \mathbf{u}_4, \mathbf{u}_2, \mathbf{u}_1 - \mathbf{u}_2 + \mathbf{u}_5\}$,

$V_2 = V(t - 1)^2(t^2 + 1)$ has basis $\{3\mathbf{u}_1 - 3\mathbf{u}_2 - 2\mathbf{u}_4 + \mathbf{u}_5\}$,

$V_3 = V(t - 1)^2(t + 1)$ has basis $\{\mathbf{u}_3 - \mathbf{u}_4 + \mathbf{u}_5, 2\mathbf{u}_1 - \mathbf{u}_2 - \mathbf{u}_3 - \mathbf{u}_4 + 2\mathbf{u}_5 + \mathbf{u}_6\}$.

We can easily check that

$\mathbf{u}_1 + \mathbf{u}_4$ has minimal polynomial $\lambda - 1$,

$\mathbf{u}_2$ has minimal polynomial $(\lambda - 1)^2$,

$$3\mathbf{u}_1 - 3\mathbf{u}_2 - 2\mathbf{u}_4 + \mathbf{u}_5 \text{ has minimal polynomial } \lambda + 1,$$
$$\mathbf{u}_3 - \mathbf{u}_4 + \mathbf{u}_5 \qquad \text{has minimal polynomial } \lambda^2 + 1.$$

If we have

$$W_1 = (\mathbf{u}_1 + \mathbf{u}_4)F[t], \qquad W_2 = \mathbf{u}_2F[t],$$
$$W_3 = (3\mathbf{u}_1 - 3\mathbf{u}_2 - 2\mathbf{u}_4 + \mathbf{u}_5)F[t], \qquad W_4 = (\mathbf{u}_3 - \mathbf{u}_4 + \mathbf{u}_5)F[t],$$

then $V_1 = W_1 \oplus W_2$, $V_2 = W_3$, $V_3 = W_4$, and

$$V = W_1 \oplus W_2 \oplus W_3 \oplus W_4.$$

Each of the W_i is irreducible by 8.1. Thus,

$$\lambda - 1, \qquad (\lambda - 1)^2, \qquad \lambda + 1, \qquad \lambda^2 + 1$$

are the elementary divisors of t by 8.7. Note that the sum of their degrees is 6, the dimension of $\mathbb{Q}^6$, although the degree of the minimal polynomial $h(\lambda)$ of t is 5.

EXERCISES

Find the elementary divisors of each of the following linear transformations, and express the vector space V as a direct sum of irreducible invariant subspaces.

1. $V = \mathbb{Q}^2$, $t \in L(V)$, defined by $\mathbf{u}_1t = 3\mathbf{u}_1$, $\mathbf{u}_2t = -\mathbf{u}_2$.
2. $V = \mathbb{Q}^2$, $t \in L(V)$, defined by $\mathbf{u}_1t = \mathbf{u}_2$, $\mathbf{u}_2t = 6\mathbf{u}_1 + \mathbf{u}_2$.
3. $V = \mathbb{Q}^3$, $t \in L(V)$, defined by $\mathbf{u}_1t = -2\mathbf{u}_1$, $\mathbf{u}_2t = \mathbf{u}_3$, $\mathbf{u}_3t = 6\mathbf{u}_2 + \mathbf{u}_3$.
4. $V = \mathbb{Q}^3$, $t \in L(V)$, defined by $\mathbf{u}_1t = \mathbf{u}_1 + \mathbf{u}_2 + \mathbf{u}_3$, $\mathbf{u}_2t = -\mathbf{u}_3$, $\mathbf{u}_3t = 2\mathbf{u}_2 + 3\mathbf{u}_3$.
5. $V = \mathbb{Q}^3$, $t \in L(V)$, defined by $\mathbf{u}_1t = 2\mathbf{u}_1 - \mathbf{u}_2 - 2\mathbf{u}_3$, $\mathbf{u}_2t = -6\mathbf{u}_1 - 3\mathbf{u}_2 + 2\mathbf{u}_3$, $\mathbf{u}_3t = 8\mathbf{u}_1 + 3\mathbf{u}_2 - 3\mathbf{u}_3$.
6. $V\ \mathbb{Q}^4$, $t \in L(V)$, defined by $\mathbf{u}_1t = -\mathbf{u}_1 - \mathbf{u}_2 + \mathbf{u}_3 + \mathbf{u}_4$, $\mathbf{u}_2t = -\mathbf{u}_3 - \mathbf{u}_4$, $\mathbf{u}_3t = -\mathbf{u}_3$, $\mathbf{u}_4t = \mathbf{u}_2 - \mathbf{u}_3 - 2\mathbf{u}_4$.
7. $V = \mathbb{Q}^4$, $t \in L(V)$, defined by $\mathbf{u}_1t = \mathbf{u}_2$, $\mathbf{u}_2t = \mathbf{u}_1 + \mathbf{u}_2 + \mathbf{u}_3$, $\mathbf{u}_3t = \mathbf{u}_4$, $\mathbf{u}_4t = \mathbf{u}_3 + \mathbf{u}_4$.
8. $V = \mathbb{Q}^4$, $t \in L(V)$, defined by $\mathbf{u}_1t = -2\mathbf{u}_1 + 4\mathbf{u}_2 - 3\mathbf{u}_3 - 6\mathbf{u}_4$, $\mathbf{u}_2t = -2\mathbf{u}_1 + 3\mathbf{u}_2 - 3\mathbf{u}_4$, $\mathbf{u}_3t = -\mathbf{u}_1 + 2\mathbf{u}_2 - \mathbf{u}_3 - 2\mathbf{u}_4$, $\mathbf{u}_4t = -\mathbf{u}_2 + 2\mathbf{u}_3 + 2\mathbf{u}_4$.
9. Describe the possible elementary divisors of a nilpotent $t \in L(V)$ (that is, $t^k = 0$ for some $k > 0$).
10. Let $N \in F(n)$ have 1's down the diagonal just above the main diagonal and 0's elsewhere. Show that N is nilpotent. Prove that every nilpotent matrix is similar to a direct sum of nilpotent matrices of the form of N.
11. If the characteristic polynomial of $t \in L(V)$ is a power of a prime polynomial, describe the possible elementary divisors of t.
12. A linear transformation t of V is called *idempotent* iff $t^2 = t$. Describe

the possible elementary divisors and characteristic polynomials of an idempotent l.t. Give examples.

13. Let A and B be $n \times n$ matrices over a field F such that $A^2 = 0$ and $B^2 = 0$. Prove that A and B are similar iff $r(A) = r(B)$.

4. JORDAN NORMAL FORM

For each $n \times n$ matrix A over a field F, we can find an n-dimensional vector space V over F and a $t \in L(V)$ such that t is represented by A relative to some basis of V. Let

$$q_1(\lambda), q_2(\lambda), \ldots, q_m(\lambda)$$

be the elementary divisors of t. Thus, we have

$$V = W_1 \oplus W_2 \oplus \cdots \oplus W_m, \qquad t = t_1 \oplus t_2 \oplus \cdots \oplus t_m$$

for some irreducible t-invariant subspaces W_i of V and some $t_i = t \mid W_i$. Each $q_i(\lambda)$ is both the minimal polynomial and the characteristic polynomial of t_i. Since $q_i(\lambda)$ is a power of a prime, it has a Jordan matrix J_i relative to this prime. Clearly, J_i represents t_i relative to some basis of W_i. Hence, we see that

$$J = J_1 \oplus J_2 \oplus \cdots \oplus J_m$$

represents t relative to a basis of V which is a composite of bases of the individual W_i. Since A and J represent the same l.t., they are similar. We call J a *Jordan normal form* of matrix A. It is unique except for the order of the J_i.

Starting with any collection $q_1(\lambda), q_2(\lambda), \ldots, q_m(\lambda)$ of powers of prime polynomials in $F[\lambda]$, let $J_1, J_2, \ldots, J_m$ be the corresponding Jordan matrices over F and $J = J_1 \oplus J_2 \oplus \cdots \oplus J_m$. If $n = \deg q_1(\lambda) + \cdots + \deg q_m(\lambda)$ and V is an n-dimensional vector space over F, and if t is any l.t. of V represented by J relative to some basis of V, then $V = W_1 \oplus W_2 \oplus \cdots \oplus W_m$, and $t = t_1 \oplus t_2 \oplus \cdots \oplus t_m$ relative to this basis, where each W_i is an irreducible t-invariant subspace, $t_i = t \mid W_i$, and t_i has minimal polynomial $q_i(\lambda)$. Thus, it is evident that $q_1(\lambda), q_2(\lambda), \ldots, q_m(\lambda)$ are the elementary divisors of t and that J is a Jordan normal form of a matrix representing t.

EXAMPLE 1: Let us find some $t \in L(\mathbb{Q}^9)$ having elementary divisors

$$\lambda + 1, \qquad (\lambda + 1)^3, \qquad \lambda - 5, \qquad (\lambda - 5)^2, \qquad \lambda^2 + \lambda + 1.$$

The Jordan matrices of these polynomials are, respectively,

$$A_1 = (-1), \qquad A_2 = \begin{pmatrix} -1 & 1 & 0 \\ 0 & -1 & 1 \\ 0 & 0 & -1 \end{pmatrix}, \qquad A_3 = (5),$$

$$A_4 = \begin{pmatrix} 5 & 1 \\ 0 & 5 \end{pmatrix}, \qquad A_5 = \begin{pmatrix} 0 & 1 \\ -1 & -1 \end{pmatrix}.$$

Hence, $J = J_1 \oplus J_2 \oplus J_3 \oplus J_4 \oplus J_5$ is a Jordan normal form of a matrix representing t. Thus, we have

$$J = \begin{pmatrix} -1 & 0 & 0 & 0 & 0 & 0 & 0 & 0 & 0 \\ 0 & -1 & 1 & 0 & 0 & 0 & 0 & 0 & 0 \\ 0 & 0 & -1 & 1 & 0 & 0 & 0 & 0 & 0 \\ 0 & 0 & 0 & -1 & 0 & 0 & 0 & 0 & 0 \\ 0 & 0 & 0 & 0 & 5 & 0 & 0 & 0 & 0 \\ 0 & 0 & 0 & 0 & 0 & 5 & 1 & 0 & 0 \\ 0 & 0 & 0 & 0 & 0 & 0 & 5 & 0 & 0 \\ 0 & 0 & 0 & 0 & 0 & 0 & 0 & 0 & 1 \\ 0 & 0 & 0 & 0 & 0 & 0 & 0 & -1 & -1 \end{pmatrix}.$$

Now, let $t \in L(\mathbb{Q}^9)$ be represented by J relative to the usual **u**-basis of $\mathbb{Q}^9$. Then, the minimal polynomial of $\mathbf{u}_1$ is $\lambda + 1$, of $\mathbf{u}_2$ is $(\lambda + 1)^3$, of $\mathbf{u}_5$ is $\lambda - 5$, of $\mathbf{u}_6$ is $(\lambda - 5)^2$, and of $\mathbf{u}_8$ is $\lambda^2 + \lambda + 1$. Evidently,

$$\mathbb{Q}^9 = \mathbf{u}_1\mathbb{Q}[t] \oplus \mathbf{u}_2\mathbb{Q}[t] \oplus \mathbf{u}_5\mathbb{Q}[t] \oplus \mathbf{u}_6\mathbb{Q}[t] \oplus \mathbf{u}_8\mathbb{Q}[t]$$

is a representation of $\mathbb{Q}^9$ as a direct sum of irreducible t-invariant subspaces. Therefore, the elementary divisors of t are as given.

Linear transformations of vector spaces over the complex field $\mathbb{C}$ have simple representing Jordan normal forms due to the fact that the prime polynomials in $\mathbb{C}[\lambda]$ are all of the first degree. Thus, if V is an n-dimensional vector space over $\mathbb{C}$ and $t \in L(V)$, the elementary divisors of t have the form

$$(\lambda - a_1)^{k_1}, (\lambda - a_2)^{k_2}, \ldots, (\lambda - a_m)^{k_m}$$

for some m distinct $a_i \in \mathbb{C}$ and some integers $k_i > 0$. Since the Jordan matrix of $(\lambda - a)^k$ has the form

$$\begin{pmatrix} a & 1 & 0 & \ldots & 0 & 0 \\ 0 & a & 1 & \ldots & 0 & 0 \\ & & \cdots\cdots & & & \\ & & \cdots\cdots & & & \\ 0 & 0 & 0 & \ldots & a & 1 \\ 0 & 0 & 0 & \ldots & 0 & a \end{pmatrix},$$

the Jordan normal form of t is a direct sum of m such matrices.

EXAMPLE 2: Let $t \in L(\mathbb{C}^6)$ have elementary divisors

$$(\lambda - 1), \qquad (\lambda - 1)^2, \qquad \lambda + 3, \qquad (\lambda + i)^2.$$

Then, the Jordan matrices of these polynomials are

$$J_1 = (1), \qquad J_2 = \begin{pmatrix} 1 & 1 \\ 0 & 1 \end{pmatrix}, \qquad J_3 = (-3), \qquad J_4 = \begin{pmatrix} -i & 1 \\ 0 & -i \end{pmatrix},$$

and a Jordan normal form of t is $J = J_1 \oplus J_2 \oplus J_3 \oplus J_4$:

$$J = \begin{pmatrix} 1 & 0 & 0 & 0 & 0 & 0 \\ 0 & 1 & 1 & 0 & 0 & 0 \\ 0 & 0 & 1 & 0 & 0 & 0 \\ 0 & 0 & 0 & -3 & 0 & 0 \\ 0 & 0 & 0 & 0 & -i & 1 \\ 0 & 0 & 0 & 0 & 0 & -i \end{pmatrix}.$$

EXERCISES

Find a Jordan normal form of the matrix representing t in each of the following exercises.

1. $t \in L(\mathbb{R}^3)$ has elementary divisors $\lambda - 1, \lambda + 1, \lambda + 2$.
2. $t \in L(\mathbb{R}^3)$ has minimal polynomial $\lambda^3 + 1$.
3. $t \in L(\mathbb{C}^3)$ has minimal polynomial $\lambda^3 + 1$.
4. $t \in L(\mathbb{R}^5)$ has elementary divisors $(\lambda + 3), (\lambda + 3), (\lambda + 3)^3$.
5. $t \in L(\mathbb{C}^5)$ has elementary divisors $(\lambda + 1 + i)^2, (\lambda + 1 - i)^2, \lambda + 1 - i$.
6. $t \in L(\mathbb{C}^4)$ has minimal polynomial $\lambda^4 - 2$.
7. $t \in L(\mathbb{R}^4)$ has minimal polynomial $\lambda^4 - 2$.
8. $t \in L(\mathbb{C}^6)$ has minimal polynomial $\lambda^6 - 1$.

Find a Jordan normal form of each of the following matrices over $\mathbb{C}$.

9. $\begin{pmatrix} -1 & 1 \\ 0 & 1 \end{pmatrix}$.

10. $\begin{pmatrix} 0 & 1 \\ -1 & 0 \end{pmatrix}$.

11. $\begin{pmatrix} 2 & -1 & -1 \\ -4 & -1 & 1 \\ 4 & 3 & 1 \end{pmatrix}$.

12. $\begin{pmatrix} 2 & 0 & 0 \\ -4 & -2 & 0 \\ 4 & 4 & 2 \end{pmatrix}$.

13. $\begin{pmatrix} 0 & 1 & 0 \\ 0 & 0 & 1 \\ 1 & 0 & 0 \end{pmatrix}$.

14. $\begin{pmatrix} 0 & 1 & 4 & -2 \\ -1 & 0 & -2 & 0 \\ 0 & 0 & -2 & 1 \\ 0 & 0 & -5 & 2 \end{pmatrix}$.

15. $\begin{pmatrix} 1 & 0 & 0 & 0 & 0 \\ 0 & 1 & 0 & 0 & 0 \\ 0 & 0 & 1 & 0 & 0 \\ 1 & 0 & 0 & 1 & 0 \\ 0 & 0 & 1 & 0 & 1 \end{pmatrix}$.

16. $\begin{pmatrix} 1 & 0 & 0 & 0 & 0 \\ 0 & 1 & 0 & 0 & 0 \\ 0 & 0 & 1 & 0 & 0 \\ 1 & 0 & 0 & 1 & 0 \\ 0 & 0 & 0 & 0 & 1 \end{pmatrix}$.

5. UNITARY SPACES

When dealing with a vector space V over the complex number field $\mathbb{C}$, it is convenient to consider a somewhat different inner-product operation than that defined in 1.39. Thus, we make the following definition.

8.9. DEFINITION OF A UNITARY SPACE. A vector space V over $\mathbb{C}$ is called a unitary space iff it has an inner product operation $V \times V \dot{\to} \mathbb{C}$ satisfying the following four properties.

(1) $(\mathbf{x} + \mathbf{y})\cdot\mathbf{z} = \mathbf{x}\cdot\mathbf{z} + \mathbf{y}\cdot\mathbf{z}, \qquad \mathbf{z}\cdot(\mathbf{x} + \mathbf{y}) = \mathbf{z}\cdot\mathbf{x} + \mathbf{z}\cdot\mathbf{y}$ for all $\mathbf{x}, \mathbf{y}, \mathbf{z} \in V$.

(2) $(a\mathbf{x})\cdot\mathbf{y} = a(\mathbf{x}\cdot\mathbf{y})$ for all $a \in \mathbb{C}$, $\mathbf{x}, \mathbf{y} \in V$.

(3) $\mathbf{x}\cdot\mathbf{y} = \overline{\mathbf{y}\cdot\mathbf{x}}$ for all $\mathbf{x}, \mathbf{y} \in V$.

(4) $\mathbf{x}\cdot\mathbf{x} \geq 0$ for all $\mathbf{x} \in V$; $\mathbf{x}\cdot\mathbf{x} > 0$ whenever $\mathbf{x} \neq \mathbf{0}$.

In property (3), $\overline{\mathbf{y}\cdot\mathbf{x}}$ indicates the complex conjugate of $\mathbf{y}\cdot\mathbf{x}$. Thus, if $c = a + bi \in \mathbb{C}$, where $a, b \in \mathbb{R}$, then $\bar{c} = a - bi$. If in (3) we let $\mathbf{x} = \mathbf{y}$, then we get $\mathbf{x}\cdot\mathbf{x} = \overline{\mathbf{x}\cdot\mathbf{x}}$, that is, $\mathbf{x}\cdot\mathbf{x} \in \mathbb{R}$. Hence, it makes sense in (4) to state that $\mathbf{x}\cdot\mathbf{x} \geq 0$, since $\mathbf{x}\cdot\mathbf{x}$ is a real number.

The n-dimensional vector space $\mathbb{C}^n$ over $\mathbb{C}$ is not a unitary space if we define an inner product by 1.41. Thus, for example, $(i, 0)\cdot(1, 0) = i$, whereas the conjugate of $(1, 0)\cdot(i, 0)$ is $-i$. That is, 8.9(3) is not satisfied. However, $\mathbb{C}^n$ is a unitary space if we define an inner product as follows.

8.10 $\quad (c_1, c_2, \ldots, c_n)\cdot(d_1, d_2, \ldots, d_n) = c_1\bar{d}_1 + c_2\bar{d}_2 + \cdots + c_n\bar{d}_n.$

We leave the verification that $\mathbb{C}^n$ is unitary to the reader. Henceforth, the inner product in $\mathbb{C}^n$ is assumed to be given by 8.10.

We are all familiar with the absolute value $|c|$ of a complex number $c = a + bi$, where $a, b \in \mathbb{R}$: $|c| = \sqrt{c\bar{c}} = \sqrt{a^2 + b^2}$. Similarly, each $\mathbf{z}$ in a unitary space V has length $|\mathbf{z}|$ defined by

$$|\mathbf{z}| = \sqrt{\mathbf{z}\cdot\mathbf{z}}.$$

We easily verify that

$$|c\mathbf{z}| = |c|\,|\mathbf{z}| \qquad \text{for all } c \in \mathbb{C},\ \mathbf{z} \in V.$$

In a unitary space V, the analogue of 1.40 is as follows:

8.11 $$\left(\sum_{i=1}^{n} a_i\mathbf{x}_i\right)\cdot\left(\sum_{j=1}^{m} b_j\mathbf{y}_j\right) = \sum_{i=1}^{n}\sum_{j=1}^{m} a_i\bar{b}_j(\mathbf{x}_i\cdot\mathbf{y}_j).$$

We leave the proof to the reader.

Just as in a Euclidean space, vectors $\mathbf{x}$ and $\mathbf{y}$ in a unitary space V are called *orthogonal* iff $\mathbf{x}\cdot\mathbf{y} = 0$. Also, a set $\{\mathbf{v}_1, \mathbf{v}_2, \ldots, \mathbf{v}_k\}$ of vectors of V is called orthogonal iff all $\mathbf{v}_i \neq \mathbf{0}$ and $\mathbf{v}_i\cdot\mathbf{v}_j = 0$, whenever $i \neq j$. Theorem 7.2 holds for V as well as for a Euclidean space. If $|\mathbf{v}_i| = 1$ for each i, then an orthogonal set $\{\mathbf{v}_1, \mathbf{v}_2, \ldots, \mathbf{v}_k\}$ is called an *orthonormal* set. Each finite-dimensional unitary space V has an orthonormal basis by a proof similar to that of 7.4. Finally, for each subspace S of V, $S^\perp$ is a subspace defined as in 7.5, and $V = S \oplus S^\perp$ as in 7.6.

Corresponding to an isometry of a Euclidean space is the unitary transformation of a unitary space defined as follows.

8.12. DEFINITION OF A UNITARY TRANSFORMATION. A linear transformation t of a unitary space V is called a unitary transformation iff

$$|\mathbf{x}t| = |\mathbf{x}| \qquad \text{for all } \mathbf{x} \in V.$$

We leave it for the reader to prove that $t \in L(V)$ is unitary iff (see 7.10)

8.13 $$\mathbf{x}t\cdot\mathbf{y}t = \mathbf{x}\cdot\mathbf{y} \qquad \text{for all } \mathbf{x}, \mathbf{y} \in V.$$

Henceforth, let V denote a finite-dimensional unitary space and $U(V)$ denote the set of all unitary transformations of V. Just as in 7.9, we can show that $U(V)$ is a multiplicative group.

If $(\mathbf{u}_1, \mathbf{u}_2, \ldots, \mathbf{u}_n)$ is an orthonormal basis of V and $t \in U(V)$, then $\mathbf{u}_it\cdot\mathbf{u}_jt = \mathbf{u}_i\cdot\mathbf{u}_j = \delta_{ij}$, and therefore $(\mathbf{u}_1t, \mathbf{u}_2t, \ldots, \mathbf{u}_nt)$ is also an orthonormal basis of V. Conversely, if $t \in L(V)$ maps an orthonormal basis onto an orthonormal basis, then $t \in U(V)$.

Let $t \in U(V)$ be represented by the matrix $A = (a_{ij})$ relative to the orthonormal basis $(\mathbf{u}_1, \mathbf{u}_2, \ldots, \mathbf{u}_n)$ of V. Then, we have

$$\begin{aligned}\delta_{ij} = \mathbf{u}_it\cdot\mathbf{u}_jt &= \left(\sum_{k=1}^{n} a_{ik}\mathbf{u}_k\right)\cdot\left(\sum_{l=1}^{n} a_{jl}\mathbf{u}_l\right)\\ &= \sum_{k=1}^{n}\sum_{l=1}^{n} a_{ik}\bar{a}_{jl}\delta_{kl}\\ &= \sum_{k=1}^{n} a_{ik}\bar{a}_{jk}.\end{aligned}$$

That is, we have

8.14 $$A\bar{A}^T = I,$$

where $\bar{A} = (\bar{a}_{ij})$. Of course, $\bar{A}^TA = I$ also. A matrix $A \in \mathbb{C}(n)$ satisfying 8.14 is called a *unitary matrix*. We state this result below.

8.15. THEOREM. Every unitary transformation is represented by a unitary matrix relative to an orthonormal basis.

It is evident that if $c = \det A$, then $\bar{c} = \det \bar{A}$ for every $A \in \mathbb{C}(n)$. Hence, for each unitary matrix A,

$$\det A \det \bar{A}^T = \det A \det \bar{A} = 1, \qquad \text{and} \qquad |\det A| = 1.$$

8.16. THEOREM. For each unitary matrix A, $|\det A| = 1$.

If $t \in U(V)$ and S is a t-invariant subspace of V, then $S^\perp$ is also a t-invariant subspace. The proof is the same as that for 7.15. We also have the following analogue of 7.16.

8.17. THEOREM. For each $t \in U(V)$, there exist one-dimensional t-invariant subspaces $W_1, W_2, \ldots, W_n$ of V, such that

$$V = W_1 \oplus W_2 \oplus \cdots \oplus W_n.$$

The proof is the same as that for 7.16, once we realize that there are no primes in $\mathbb{C}[\lambda]$ of degree 2 or higher.

If in 8.17 we select $\mathbf{v}_i \in W_i$ so that $|\mathbf{v}_i| = 1$, then $\{\mathbf{v}_1, \mathbf{v}_2, \ldots, \mathbf{v}_n\}$ is an orthonormal basis of V. Now, we have

$$\mathbf{v}_i t = a_i \mathbf{v}_i, \qquad i = 1, 2, \ldots, n$$

for some $a_i \in \mathbb{C}$, and $|\mathbf{v}_i t| = |\mathbf{v}_i| = |a_i \mathbf{v}_i| = |a_i| = 1$. Each a_i is a characteristic value of t, and the polynomials

$$\lambda - a_1, \lambda - a_2, \ldots, \lambda - a_n$$

are the elementary divisors of t by 8.7. Thus, each $t \in U(V)$ is represented by a diagonal matrix

$$(a_1) \oplus (a_2) \oplus \cdots \oplus (a_n), \qquad \text{with} \quad |a_i| = 1 \quad \text{for each } i,$$

relative to the basis $(\mathbf{v}_1, \mathbf{v}_2, \ldots, \mathbf{v}_n)$.

Corresponding to a symmetric l.t. of a Euclidean space is the following l.t. of a unitary space.

8.18. DEFINITION OF A HERMITIAN LINEAR TRANSFORMATION. A linear transformation t of a unitary space V is called Hermitian iff $\mathbf{x}t \cdot \mathbf{y} = \mathbf{x} \cdot \mathbf{y}t$ for all $\mathbf{x}, \mathbf{y} \in V$.

Let $t \in L(V)$ be Hermitian, $(\mathbf{v}_1, \mathbf{v}_2, \ldots, \mathbf{v}_n)$ be an orthonormal basis of V, and $A = (a_{ij})$ be the matrix representation of t relative to the $\mathbf{v}$-basis. Then, we have

$$\mathbf{v}_i t = \sum_{k=1}^{n} a_{ik} \mathbf{v}_k, \qquad i = 1, 2, \ldots, n,$$

and

$$\mathbf{v}_i t \cdot \mathbf{v}_j = \left(\sum_{k=1}^{n} a_{ik} \mathbf{v}_k \right) \cdot \mathbf{v}_j = a_{ij},$$

$$\mathbf{v}_i \cdot \mathbf{v}_j t = \mathbf{v}_i \cdot \left(\sum_{k=1}^{n} a_{jk} \mathbf{v}_k \right) = \bar{a}_{ji}$$

by 8.11. Since $\mathbf{v}_i t \cdot \mathbf{v}_j = \mathbf{v}_i \cdot \mathbf{v}_j t$, we have $a_{ij} = \bar{a}_{ji}$ for all i and j. Hence, we have

8.19 $$A = \bar{A}^T.$$

A matrix $A \in \mathbb{C}(n)$ satisfying 8.19 is called a *Hermitian matrix.* Our remarks above have proved part of the following result.

8.20. THEOREM. A linear transformation t of a unitary space V is Hermitian iff the matrix representing t relative to an orthonormal basis is Hermitian.

We leave the rest of the proof of 8.20 to the reader.

For each Hermitian $t \in L(V)$ and each t-invariant subspace S of V, it can be shown that $S^\perp$ is also a t-invariant subspace. The proof follows in a manner similar to that for a symmetric l.t. in Chapter 7. Then, the proof of 7.22 carries over directly to V. We state this result below.

8.21. THEOREM. For each Hermitian $t \in L(V)$, there exist one-dimensional t-invariant subspaces $W_1, W_2, \ldots, W_n$ of V, such that

$$V = W_1 \oplus W_2 \oplus \cdots \oplus W_n.$$

If we choose $\mathbf{v}_i \in W_i$ so that $|\mathbf{v}_i| = 1$, then $(\mathbf{v}_1, \mathbf{v}_2, \ldots, \mathbf{v}_n)$ is an orthonormal basis of V. If $\mathbf{v}_i t = d_i \mathbf{v}_i$, then t is represented by the diagonal matrix

$$D = (d_1) \oplus (d_2) \oplus \cdots \oplus (d_n)$$

relative to the $\mathbf{v}$-basis. Hence, D is Hermitian by 8.20, and $D = \bar{D}^T$. Therefore, $d_i = \bar{d}_i$ for each i, and the d_i's are all real numbers. Thus, the characteristic values of a Hermitian l.t. are all real. Of course, the elementary divisors of t are also real polynomials, being $\lambda - d_1, \lambda - d_2, \ldots, \lambda - d_n$.

Let A be any matrix representation of the Hermitian $t \in L(V)$ relative to an orthonormal basis $(\mathbf{u}_1, \mathbf{u}_2, \ldots, \mathbf{u}_n)$ of V, and D be the diagonal matrix representation of t above. Then, A is similar to D: $D = P^{-1}AP$, where the matrix $P = (p_{ij})$ is defined by (3.28)

$$\mathbf{u}_i = \sum_{j=1}^{n} p_{ij} \mathbf{v}_j, \qquad i = 1, 2, \ldots, n.$$

Since P maps an orthonormal basis of V into an orthonormal basis, P is unitary by 8.15. Hence, $P^{-1} = \bar{P}^T$, and we have proved the following result.

8.22. THEOREM. Every Hermitian matrix A is unitarily similar to a real diagonal matrix D, that is,

$$D = \bar{P}^T A P$$

for some unitary matrix P.

EXAMPLE 1: The Hermitian matrix

$$A = \begin{pmatrix} 3 & -i \\ i & 3 \end{pmatrix}$$

has characteristic polynomial

$$\det(\lambda I - A) = (\lambda - 4)(\lambda - 2).$$

Hence, A is unitarily similar to the real diagonal matrix

$$D = \begin{pmatrix} 4 & 0 \\ 0 & 2 \end{pmatrix}.$$

To find the unitary matrix P such that $\bar{P}^T A P = D$, we can show that if $V = \mathbb{C}^2$ and $t \in L(V)$ is represented by A relative to the usual $\mathbf{u}$-basis of V, then we have

$$W_1 = V(t-2) = \mathbb{C}\mathbf{v}_1, \qquad \text{where} \quad \mathbf{v}_1 = \frac{1}{\sqrt{2}}(\mathbf{u}_1 - i\mathbf{u}_2),$$

$$W_2 = V(t-4) = \mathbb{C}\mathbf{v}_2, \qquad \text{where} \quad \mathbf{v}_2 = \frac{1}{\sqrt{2}}(\mathbf{u}_1 + i\mathbf{u}_2).$$

Now, W_1 and W_2 are t-invariant subspaces of V and

$$V = W_1 \oplus W_2.$$

Also, $(\mathbf{v}_1, \mathbf{v}_2)$ is an orthonormal basis of V. Since $\bar{P}^T$ maps the $\mathbf{u}$-basis into the $\mathbf{v}$-basis, we find that

$$\bar{P}^T = \frac{1}{\sqrt{2}}\begin{pmatrix} 1 & -i \\ 1 & i \end{pmatrix}, \qquad \text{and} \qquad P = \frac{1}{\sqrt{2}}\begin{pmatrix} 1 & 1 \\ i & -i \end{pmatrix}.$$

We can easily check that $\bar{P}^T A P = D$.

EXAMPLE 2: The Hermitian matrix

$$A = \begin{pmatrix} 1 & 1 & 1+i \\ 1 & 1 & -1-i \\ 1-i & -1+i & 0 \end{pmatrix}$$

has characteristic polynomial

$$\det(\lambda I - A) = \lambda^3 - 2\lambda^2 - 4\lambda + 8 = (\lambda - 2)^2(\lambda + 2).$$

Hence, A has characteristic values 2 and -2, and elementary divisors $\lambda + 2$, $\lambda - 2$, $\lambda - 2$. That is, A is unitarily similar to the real diagonal matrix

$$D = \begin{pmatrix} -2 & 0 & 0 \\ 0 & 2 & 0 \\ 0 & 0 & 2 \end{pmatrix}.$$

We leave it to the reader to verify that $D = \overline{P}^T AP$, where P is the unitary matrix

$$P = \frac{1}{2}\begin{pmatrix} -i & 1 & \sqrt{2} \\ i & -1 & \sqrt{2} \\ 1+i & 1-i & 0 \end{pmatrix}.$$

We could continue in the same vein as in Chapter 8, studying Hermitian quadratic forms, and so on. However, such study fits more properly in an advanced treatise on linear algebra. Several excellent texts in this area are listed in the bibliography.

EXERCISES

In each of Exercises 1 through 6, find the real diagonal matrix which is unitarily similar to the given Hermitian matrix.

1. $\begin{pmatrix} 1 & 1+i \\ 1-i & 0 \end{pmatrix}.$

2. $\begin{pmatrix} -2 & i \\ -i & 1 \end{pmatrix}.$

3. $\begin{pmatrix} 0 & 1-i & 0 \\ 1+i & 0 & i \\ 0 & -i & 0 \end{pmatrix}.$

4. $\begin{pmatrix} 1 & i & 0 \\ -i & -1 & 1 \\ 0 & 1 & 1 \end{pmatrix}.$

5. $\begin{pmatrix} 0 & 0 & i \\ 0 & 0 & 0 \\ -i & 0 & 0 \end{pmatrix}.$

6. $\begin{pmatrix} 0 & 1+i & 0 & 0 \\ 1-i & 0 & 1-i & 0 \\ 0 & 1+i & 0 & i \\ 0 & 0 & -i & 0 \end{pmatrix}.$

BIBLIOGRAPHY

1. E. Artin, *Geometric Algebra*, New York: Interscience, 1957.
2. I. M. Gel'fand, *Lectures in Linear Algebra*, New York: Interscience, 1961.
3. W. H. Greub, *Linear Algebra*, New York: Academic Press, 1963.

4. N. Jacobson, *Lectures in Abstract Algebra*, vol. II, New York: Van Nostrand, 1953.
5. A. I. Mal'cev, *Foundations of Linear Algebra*, San Francisco: W. H. Freeman, 1963.

Index